Steel Works Analysis

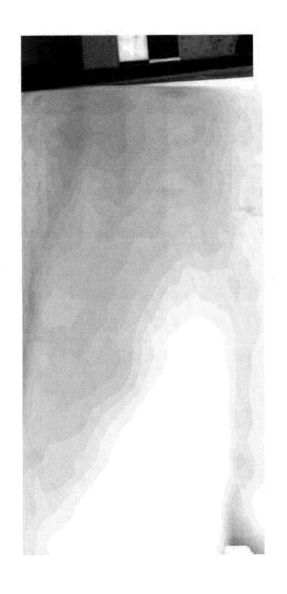

STEEL WORKS ANALYSIS

STEEL WORKS ANALYSIS

BY

JOHN OLIVER ARNOLD

AND

F. IBBOTSON

RESPECTIVELY PROFESSOR AND LECTURER IN METALLURGY
AT THE UNIVERSITY OF SHEFFIELD

THIRD EDITION, THOROUGHLY REVISED AND ENLARGED

WHITTAKER AND CO.

2, WHITE HART STREET, PATERNOSTER SQUARE, LONDON
AND 64 AND 66, FIFTH AVENUE, NEW YORK

1907

CHISWICK PRESS: CHARLES WHITTINGHAM AND CO.
TOOKS COURT, CHANCERY LANE, LONDON.

PREFACE TO FIRST EDITION

This little work has been written specially for assistants in steel works laboratories and students taking up the analytical chemistry of iron and steel with a view to becoming steel works chemists. The great object kept in view by the author has been to produce a *practical* book: he has therefore avoided compilation, and written from personal experience. The first essential in any analytical process is accuracy: when this can be combined with rapidity, well and good; but where speed is obtained at the expense of accuracy, the result is worse than useless, it is misleading. On the other hand, the appalling elaboration with which the authors of some text-books proceed to separate possible or impossible traces of rarely occurring elements from those invariably present, often defeats its own object, and together with a great loss of time, introduces errors far greater than those it is intended to avoid. It is to be regretted that the writers of books on iron and steel analysis usually deem it necessary to describe without comment every method—good, bad, and indifferent—which has ever been published, thus leaving the student in doubt as to which is really the best process to employ. The author has

v

described only methods which he has proved to be reliable, or in a few difficult cases approximate.

The scheme of the book will be found to be somewhat new, and, it is trusted, convenient. The practical operations are fully described in their proper order in distinct paragaphs. Then following each method is an article setting forth the theory of the reactions involved. It should always be borne in mind, that even when using the most accurate method, a conscientious attention to details and *cleanliness* are absolutely necessary to ensure an accurate result, whilst dirty, slovenly analysis is sure to go wrong and be detected sooner or later. As a guide to students, typical analyses of the materials herein dealt with are tabulated at the end of the book. The author cannot too strongly urge students to remember the fact that a steel chemist and an analytical machine who turns out so many estimations per day are two very different personalities. Analysts deficient in a thorough knowledge of elementary chemistry, physics, and mathematics, and the principles of qualitative analysis, can claim to rank only with skilled artisans: in chemical analysis the head and the hands should always work together. For this reason the theoretical side of the question has been somewhat fully dealt with; this many may regard as unnecessary, because students before taking up quantitative work are expected, as the result of a previous course of pure chemistry, to know all about the ordinary reactions of the metals. In this matter the author's experience of a large number of such students has led him to expect

nothing, and he has seldom been disappointed. Even
with students really well grounded in pure chemistry, the
possession of knowledge and the ability to apply it are
two widely different things; also it should be remembered,
that many of the separations of the metals described in
text-books on qualitative analysis are exceedingly crude,
and quite unfitted for accurate quantitative work. The
author, it will be noticed, has mixed English and metric
weights and measures, thus sacrificing scientific consist-
ency on the altar of convenience. It is to be hoped, however, that before long the first-named system will be
relegated to its proper place amongst the curiosities in
the British Museum. It will be found that the author
has sometimes criticized the errors of others, but he is
nevertheless aware that a scientific book without mistakes
would constitute something new under the sun, and he
will regard as a favour the correction of any inaccurate
statements contained herein. The author is indebted to
his demonstrators, Mr. J. Jefferson and Mr. F. K. Knowles,
for checking the accuracy of the calculations exemplified,
and the strengths of the various volumetric solutions
specified.

J. O. A.

THE TECHNICAL SCHOOL,
    SHEFFIELD, 1894.

PREFACE TO SECOND EDITION

THE second edition of this book does not differ from the first, except that mistakes or misprints in formulæ, etc., have been rectified. The author has to acknowledge in this matter the assistance of Mr. F. Ibbotson, B.Sc.

J. O. A.

SHEFFIELD UNIVERSITY COLLEGE,
October, 1899.

PREFACE TO THIRD EDITION

THE twelve years which have elapsed since the issue of the first edition of this book, have been marked by phenomenal advances in the metallurgy of steel. The addition to the list of steel-making elements of molybdenum, titanium, vanadium, and even tantalum, has for the steel analyst complicated an already complex problem. Although the general scheme of the work remains unaltered, nevertheless in the Third Edition it has been naturally necessary to delete obsolete operations, to include new and rapid methods, and to describe improvements in processes formerly of only moderate accuracy. The section on gas analysis has been revised and brought up to date, and in this connection the authors have to tender their thanks to their colleague Mr. J. H. Wrenks.

The latest and most accurate method for the calorimetry of fuels is fully described, and in this matter the authors have to thank their colleague Mr. F. K. Knowles.

A new feature of the book will be found in the inclusion of methods for the analysis of bearing metals, viz., brasses, bronzes, and white metals.

For crucible steel chemists the authors have written a brief but, it is hoped, lucid special chapter on the analysis

xi

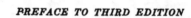

of high-speed steels. The authors will welcome corre-
spondence calling attention to misprints in formulæ or to
points of dubious accuracy in the text.

J. O. A.

F. I.

THE UNIVERSITY, SHEFFIELD,
   1907.

CONTENTS

xiii

STEEL WORKS ANALYSIS

THE STEEL WORKS LABORATORY AND ITS APPLIANCES

As the authors have upon several occasions been requested to advise on the installation of a works laboratory, they have deemed it advisable to devote a brief article to the consideration of this subject. It will be assumed that the services of one analyst and a laboratory boy will be employed.

The Laboratory.

This should include two rooms, divided by a passage 5 ft. wide, namely, a small room, say 10 ft. sq. for the balance, and a larger room, say 20 ft. by 10 ft. for the laboratory itself. These rooms should be lofty, say 15 ft. high, and as far away as possible from steam-hammers, so as to avoid the effect of vibration on the balance. A ceiling sheathed with wood is desirable in the larger room; the possible falling of pieces of whitewash or plaster loosened by the action of acids is thus prevented. The benches should be of thoroughly seasoned non-resinous wood and stoutly built. That on which the balance is placed must be very rigid. The supply-tube for

B

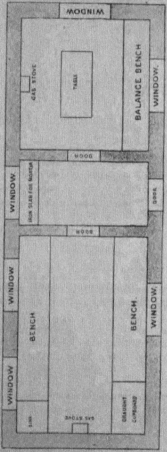

FIG. 1.

gas should be 2 in. in diameter, and the earthenware sink should be supplied with a tap connected with a good head of water if a filter-pump is to be used. To the main gas-pipe should be attached at least six Bunsen branches for $\frac{1}{2}$ in. rubber tubing; the taps for these branches are most convenient when placed under the bench, within easy reach of the hand. A draught cupboard of glass or white tiles is very desirable to carry off the more irritating fumes. In this must be at least two branches and taps for Bunsens; also a large, ordinary jet at the top of the cupboard to create a draught at the exit,— the latter should be of earthenware piping. The lower halves of the cupboard front should slide in grooves, and be fastened in any desired position by means of strong wooden pegs placed in holes in the framework. Hinges or cords should not be used, as they are soon corroded by the action of acids. Both rooms will require numerous convenient shelves, drawers, and cupboards. A suggestive sketch of a plan of the laboratory thus briefly described will be seen in Fig. 1. The ventilation may be effected preferably through louvres on the ridge of the roof, or by means of swinging upper windows. Hot-water pipes or gas fires are best for heating the rooms, because they create no dust. In the passage, which much assists in isolating the balance from the fumes of the laboratory, should be a thick iron plate well supported by brick-work, and recessed for the reception of the steel mortar used for crushing hard alloys incapable of being drilled.

Analytical Appliances.

The balance.—Of these the balance is the most important item. In purchasing this it is true economy to buy a somewhat expensive instrument, that is to say, one provided throughout with agate or rock-crystal planes and knife edges. When the latter are in steel, they are sure sooner or later to corrode, and seriously impair the sensitiveness of the instrument. A *sine qua non* for steel works where analyses must be turned out quickly, is a rapid, short-beam balance; the length of beam should not exceed 8 inches. The supporting wires to which the pans are attached should be parallel, and sufficiently far apart to readily admit of the weighing of potash *bulbs*, etc. The pointer should be sensitive to $\frac{1}{10000}$ of a gramme. For steel works use the authors have found the 8-in. beam balance, with round pans, made by Oertling, a sound and reliable instrument at a moderate price. For use with this a set of weights from 50 grammes downwards will be found convenient. The interior of the balance-case should always be kept dry by the presence of several little pots of strong commercial sulphuric acid. These, however, should be only half full, and require watching, otherwise the absorbed moisture will fill up the pot and run over. In fact, it is advisable to wash out and dry the jars and replenish them with strong acid about once a month.

Weighings should never be made directly on the balance-pan, but on a sufficiently large and conveniently bent slip of aluminium foil; the latter is carefully counterpoised on the other pan by means of a little piece of lead.

The analytical balance should never be employed for weighing out large quantities of re-agents: a comparatively coarse pair of scales should be used for such purposes.

The gas-muffle furnace.—One of these is almost indispensable to accurate working. It should be fitted with a "salamander" muffle, which, though somewhat expensive so far as first cost is concerned, is really an economy, as it lasts out two or three ordinary clay muffles. When lighting the furnace, withdraw the muffle, throw a burning wax-match on the iron burners, turn on the gas, and replace the muffle.

Heating plates.—These are of cast-iron $\frac{1}{4}$ in. in thickness; four of them will be found convenient, namely, two $12'' \times 12''$, one $12'' \times 24''$ (for the draught cupboard), and one $9'' \times 9''$ (for the carbon bath). The plates are supported on quadrupods, and heated by Bunsen burners placed underneath them.

Bunsen burners.—The small tubes at the bottom of these lamps require removing in order to get a flame of large volume, which spreads over a considerable area in the middle of the heating-plate. In order to obtain the maximum heat, the plates usually require lowering well into the Bunsen flame by cutting shorter the legs of the quadrupod.

Water bath.—This consists of a somewhat deep cast-iron vessel enamelled inside, and provided with a series of copper rings, which support evaporating dishes of various sizes over the boiling water.

Air bath.—This is of copper, and the supply of gas to the small Bunsen burner by which it is heated is adjusted by means of a Reichardt's mercury regulator, so that the temperature of the shelf is always about 100° C. By a little preliminary attention to the screw and thermometer till the right position is obtained, a steady temperature ranging not more than one degree on either side of 100 is readily ensured.

Foot blow-pipe.—This is useful for fusions requiring a high temperature, such as are necessary in the analysis of fire-bricks, etc.

Filter pump.—Where a good head of water is available, one of the very cheap but effective glass pumps now obtainable is often useful. It requires fitting over the sink into which the waste-pipe runs. The exhausting tube may be led round to the bench, where it is attached to the side tube of a strong, conical filter vessel. The india-rubber stopper of the latter carries a plain $2\frac{1}{4}$ in. funnel, in the apex of which must be placed a perforated platinum cone.

The foregoing apparatus requires to be used with judgment; many precipitates filter so rapidly as to render its employment unnecessary. For finely-divided precipitates such as $BaSO_4$ and WO_3 it should never be used. But in the case of slimy, slow-filtering precipitates, such as that obtained from ammonium acetate in the combined molybdate and magnesia process for estimating phosphorus, the pump is of great value in saving time.

Flasks.—For most purposes, the ordinary, nearly globular flask serves very well, but for precipitation purposes a vessel designed by Mr. J. Taylor, and known as the registered flask, is most suitable. In form it is a cone with a radiused bottom, so that every part of the vessel can be reached by the "policeman" used for detaching adhering precipitate from the sides. Watch-glasses serve well for flask covers.

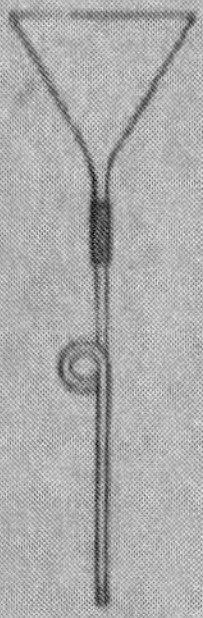

Beakers.—These are convenient in two designs, namely, the lipped conical beaker (used chiefly for the reception of useless filtrates), and the wide form with spout. (*In the following pages, when the term beaker is used, unless otherwise specified, the latter form is referred to.*) Concave clock-glasses, rather larger in diameter than the vessel itself, form the handiest covers for beakers.

Funnels.—These are, as a rule, best ribbed, but for finely-divided precipitates, such as $BaSO_4$, a plain funnel is safest. It is also sometimes advisable in such cases to cut off the stem of the funnel about half an inch from the apex; this of course renders the filtration slower, whilst a looped glass tube attached to the stem by india-rubber tubing (Fig. 2) considerably increases the rate of flow.

FIG. 2.

It is important that all funnels should have the correct angle, namely 60°, so that the circular filter-papers will fit perfectly.

Funnel hangers.—These useful little articles may be bent out of thin glass rods; they are made as follows: six inches of $\frac{1}{8}''$ diameter glass rod is heated in the middle, and bent with a radius of $\frac{3}{8}''$ to an angle of 180°. Each limb of the hanger is then heated two inches from the end, and bent sharply to an angle of 105°: the hanger is placed on the edge of the beaker with the radius inside, and in this the funnel is supported (Fig. 3).

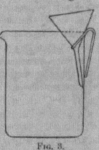

Fig. 3.

Filter-driers.—These consist of glazed earthenware cylinders $\frac{1}{4}''$ thick, 2″ high, by $1\frac{1}{2}''$ inside diameter. Filters containing the washed precipitate are removed from the funnel, and placed in the drier on the hot plate to dry before ignition. The cylinders also serve to support the covers, placed concave side downward, of beakers, the contents of which are evaporating on the plate.

Desiccators.—These should have the ground surfaces slightly greased to render them air-tight. In the bottoms layers of pumice stone in rough pieces about $\frac{1}{2}$ in. square are half-covered with strong sulphuric acid. Crucibles placed in the vessels to cool are best supported in a well-fitted pipe-stem triangle.

Wash-bottles.—For general use a 40-oz. flask with a jet of medium fineness will be found most convenient. In addition to two such large flasks (one for hot and the other for cold water) it is also advisable to fit up two or three 12-oz. flasks for special washing liquids, *e.g.* 2% nitric acid. One or two straight-shooting jets of fine bore should be made and treasured like old gold; they are invaluable for washing precipitates, such as the yellow phosphorus compound, off the filter-paper, and also for washing small and possibly slightly soluble precipitates, for which only such a volume of washing liquid as is absolutely necessary should be used.

Filter-papers.—For collecting precipitates to be weighed ashless papers (which have been washed free from iron with HCl, and from silica with HF) should be used. They may be purchased in packets of three convenient sizes, namely, 90 mm., 110 mm., and 125 mm. diameter, corresponding respectively to 2″, $2\frac{1}{4}$″, and 3″ funnels. The smaller size should also be obtained in two degrees of rapidity; the slow, close-grained filter being used for finely-divided precipitates like $BaSO_4$. For ordinary purposes the cheaper thick white German paper sold in sheets should be employed, and cut to size as required. For use in estimating manganese, circles $9\frac{1}{4}$″ diameter are requisite, which may be cut out by folding pieces of paper about 10″ sq. into four, and then cutting out the circle round a brass quadrant of $4\frac{5}{8}$″ radius and $\frac{1}{16}$″ thick. For collecting precipitates which have to be washed off the paper, 90 mm. diameter circles of hardened parchment-like surface will be found very convenient. Quick-filtering papers of this description can now be purchased in packets.

Filtration through ashless paper pulp.—The clippings left after the circular discs of ashless filter paper have been cut out can now be purchased at a comparatively small cost, and provide, when reduced to pulp, an admirable filtering medium. They are torn into shreds, placed in a wide-mouthed glass bottle, and reduced to a fine pulp by shaking vigorously with distilled water for five minutes. The filtration is conducted as follows:

A smooth funnel is fitted with a perforated porcelain filter plate, the holes in which are not too fine, and after closing the end of the funnel stem (cut off straight) with the thumb, sufficient water is poured into the funnel to fill the stem and just cover the filter plate, care being taken that no air bubble is trapped beneath the plate. Pulp is then poured on to yield a filtering medium about one-eighth of an inch in thickness, the plate adjusted to horizontality, if necessary, by means of a glass rod, and after allowing to drain, the circumference of the upper surface of the pulp is tucked in by means of a pointed glass rod or a pair of forceps. The filtration and washing of a precipitate are then carried out as usual. The funnel is then inserted in the cork of any ordinary suction flask or bottle, and the column of liquid which remains in the stem removed from it by mouth suction, the precipitate being thereby partially dried.

In transferring the precipitate to the crucible for ignition the edge of the filter is lifted at any point by means of the forceps, the filter then removed by grasping its under surface, and placed, upper surface downwards, in the ignition crucible. The plate is then removed and is invariably found to be free from adhering precipitate, and it only remains to detach the particles adhering to the sides of the funnel and place them with the main bulk on the pulp. To this end, the funnel is grasped in the left hand with the stem horizontal and its end directed towards the palm; a small piece of wetted ashless paper, roughly triangular in shape, is inserted with an apex of the triangle in the throat of the funnel, and whilst pressing it tightly against the sides, a slow rotary movement is imparted to the funnel by pressing the rim with the thumb of the left hand. At the same time the paper is gradually brought outwards towards the rim of the funnel, and thus completely brings away with it all adhering particles. If necessary, a second small piece of paper can be used for removing any traces left behind by unskilful manipulation of the first, and for detaching any tiny particles adhering to the ends of the forceps. After drying the whole on the hot plate, or at the mouth of the muffle, the precipitate is ignited as usual.

When it is desirable to weigh a precipitate directly on the balance pan, thereby dispensing with the necessity of weighing the crucible, a piece of dry ashless paper is placed in the bottom of the latter, and upon this the filter is placed when it is removed from the funnel. After ignition the precipitate can almost invariably be brushed completely out of the crucible.

For all precipitates of the granular or crystalline type, this form of filtration is very rapid, and it is obvious that the washing is thorough. Precipitates like tungstic oxide and barium sulphate demand a greater thickness of pulp, and pulp filtration is altogether unsuitable, except under powerful suction, for slimy precipitates like aluminium hydrate or zinc sulphide.

It would appear from the above description that considerably more paper is used than in ordinary filtrations. As a matter of fact, when the operator has attained sufficient skill in removing the adhering particles from the sides of the funnel, he will find that the total consumption of paper is no greater and that no allowance is necessary for ash.

COST OF APPARATUS.

The cost of equipping a laboratory with the necessary apparatus is estimated by the authors at about seventy pounds.

CLASSIFICATION OF STEEL WORKS ANALYSIS.

A STEEL works analyst may be called upon to report upon the following materials:

SECTION I.

METALS.

1. Wrought iron.
2. Steel.
3. Pig-iron.
4. Spiegel and ferro-manganese.
5. Ferro-chrome.
6. Ferro-silicon.
7. Ferro-aluminium and aluminium metal.
8. Ferro-tungsten and tungsten metal.
9. Ferro-nickel and metallic nickel.
10. Ferro-molybdenum and molybdenum metal.
11. Ferro-vanadium.
12. Ferro-titanium.
13. Ferro-tantalum.

SECTION II.

ORES.

14. Iron ores.
15. Manganese ores.
16. Chrome iron ore (Chromite).
17. Tungsten ores (Wolfram and Scheelite).

SECTION III.

REFRACTORY MATERIALS.

18. Acid furnace linings—
    (*a*) Ganister, silica bricks and sand.
    (*b*) Ordinary fire-bricks and clays.
19. Basic furnace linings—
    (*a*) Bauxite and Chromite.
    (*b*) Lime and magnesia bricks.
    (*c*) Dolomitic limestones.

SECTION IV.

FUELS.

20. Coal and coke.
21. Producer gases.

SECTION V.

SUNDRIES.

22. Slags.
23. Boiler water.
24. Brass, bronze and white metals.

SECTION I. METALS.

As far as chemical constitution is concerned, these two products are not separated by any well-defined line of division, so that the same series of analytical operations serve as a rule for both; but it must be remembered that a distinction exists between the two in the fact that steel (except puddled, shear, and blister steels) has always been submitted to complete fusion and is thus practically free from involved slag. Wrought iron, puddled, blister, and shear steels have, however, never got beyond a pasty state of semi-fusion, and have in consequence more or less slag mechanically mixed with their structure.[1]

Steel always contains more or less of the following elements in addition to iron: carbon, silicon, manganese, sulphur, and phosphorus; the determination of these elements constitutes an ordinary complete analysis. Besides these constituents, there may be present by design or accident the following: tungsten, chromium, aluminium, nickel, copper, arsenic, molybdenum, vanadium, tantalum, and titanium.

In addition to these elements, steel contains the gaseous

[1] No satisfactory method has at present been found to accurately separate the constituents of the slag from those actually alloyed with the iron.

13

bodies hydrogen [1] and nitrogen, and sometimes oxygen: the last probably exists as dissolved ferrous oxide; it is not definitely known whether the two first-named gases are combined with or merely occluded in the iron.

For the determination of hydrogen and oxygen reliable and satisfactory methods have yet to be found.[2] Professor Ledebur has made some determinations of oxygen as water by heating steel drillings to redness for several hours in a current of pure dry hydrogen, and one of the authors has attempted to estimate the hydrogen as water by combusting the steel in drillings in pure oxygen; but owing to the elaborate precautions necessary, both methods are tedious, and the results at best of dubious value.

Mr. A. H. Allen has devised a method for the determination of the nitrogen present in steel as ammonia by means of the Nessler test,[3] but unfortunately, as far as is known, the determination of the minute percentage of this gas present is of small importance from a practical

---

[1] See important research by Mr. J. Parry, "Journal of Iron and Steel Inst.," 1881, Part I, p. 189; and experiment by Arnold, "Proceedings of Inst. Mechanical Engineers," April, 1893, p. 158.

[2] Mr. J. Parry has proposed a method for the estimation of the oxygen which he alleges to exist in steel as Fe_3O_4. The process consists in dissolving the steel at a gentle heat in a saturated solution of bichromate of potash, containing one-sixth its volume of strong sulphuric acid. The residue is filtered off, washed with water, then with potash solution to remove silica, and finally with water. It is dried, ignited, and weighed, the result being calculated to Fe_3O_4.

By this method it is possible in annealed high carbon steel to find 1% of oxide of iron *when that compound is not present*. The residue consists not of Fe_3O_4 but of some undecomposed carbide of iron (of which in tool steel about 15% exists), from which on ignition the carbon burns off, leaving the iron as Fe_3O_4.

[3] "Chemical News," vol. xli, p. 231.

point of view.[1] The steel chemist should not, however, ignore the smallest fact connected with the study of the marvellously complex material he is called upon to examine. Of all the elements connected with steel, carbon is by far the most important: as the blood is the life, so is the carbon the steel. This element may exist in iron in at least three forms—(a) graphite, or scales of free carbon mechanically mixed up with the structure of the metal. This form separates in steel high in carbon under certain abnormal conditions of rolling or annealing. (b) Combined carbon exists as a carbide of iron, which the researches of Abel[2] and Müller[3] indicate to possess the formula Fe_3C, or approximately it contains 93.3% of iron and 6.7% of carbon. Generally speaking, the carbon in normal steels exists almost entirely as this modification, chiefly in the form of metallic scales. Sometimes, however, it is more or less diffused in a fine state of division. (c) Hardening carbon. This is found in hardened steel. When such steel is polished, and treated with very dilute nitric acid, it is seen as a dark velvety powder upon the surface of the metal. It is probably more loosely associated with the iron than the combined (or cement) carbon, and is possibly merely a solution of carbon in iron. (Since writing the above a systematic research by J. O. Arnold and A. A. Read, published in the "Journal of the Chemical Society" for August 1894, has amplified and somewhat modified the above statements.)

[1] See Appendix for determination of nitrogen.
[2] "Proceedings of the Institute of Mechanical Engineers," 1885.
[3] "Stahl und Eisen," No. 5.

THE DETERMINATION OF TOTAL CARBON BY COMBUSTION.

This process gives the total carbon present irrespective of its form of existence.

The determination of carbon by combustion is the most important operation the steel chemist has to undertake, because upon its accuracy depends the value of the indispensable and rapidly made colour tests to be described later on. It may be carried out either with or without the separation of the carbon from the iron.

SEPARATION OF THE CARBON.

The liberation of the carbon from the steel may be effected in three ways: (a) by the action of weak hydrochloric acid and a galvanic current on a small bar of the steel (Binks and Weyl); (b) by the action of gaseous chlorine on steel drillings at a low red heat (Wohler); (c) by the action on steel drillings of a solution of cupric chloride or sulphate. The combustion of the impure residue, consisting chiefly of carbon, may be effected, first, by dry combustion at a red heat with oxygen; secondly, by moist combustion at a comparatively low temperature with sulphuric and chromic acids (Ulgren).

These three methods were made the subject of a long research by one of the authors on a specially prepared standard steel, and the results yielded by all three, together with a detailed account of (c), are appended.

Preparation of the Standard Steel.

In order to obtain for the experiments an ample supply of homogeneous material, an acid Bessemer ingot 14 in. square was selected, and hammered down to blooms 6 in. square; the centre bloom was then taken and rolled into a billet 3 in. square. From the centre of this billet a bar 2 ft. long by 2 in. square was planed. From this bar, in the different parts of which no variation of carbon could be detected by the colour test, all the bars and drillings used in the research were taken.

It may here be remarked, once and for all, that all samples of steel or iron used for analysis should consist of drillings or turnings obtained with a dry tool, the use of oil or water being strictly prohibited, also that analyses made on filings are of very little value, because the sample is certain to be more or less contaminated with fragments of the file teeth.

Liberation of the Carbon by Electrolysis.

The steel, in the form of a bar ¼ in. square and 2 in. long, was made the anode of an electrolytic cell, about one-third of it being immersed in highly diluted hydrochloric acid. A porous cell contained the cathode, which consisted of a sheet of platinum foil. A current from a single Bunsen element was passed for eighteen hours, at the end of which the bar was removed, carefully washed and dried. The loss of weight represented the amount of steel used. The carbonaceous residue was carefully collected, dried and burnt in a current of pure oxygen. The results are appended:

c

Experi-ment No.	Weight of Steel taken.	Weight of CO_2 obtained.	Carbon per cent.
1	4·5652	0·0778	0·465
2	3·3522	0·0588	0·478
3	3·6999	0·0628	0·463
4	5·7453	0·0919	0·436
5	6·9287	0·1151	0·453
Mean	4·8583	0·0813	0·459

Greatest difference 0·042°/₀ carbon.

Liberation of the Carbon by Chlorine Gas.

A dried and carefully purified current of chlorine gas was passed over a small weight (2 to 2½ grammes) of the fine drillings contained in a porcelain boat heated to redness in a glass tube. The ferric chloride sublimed beyond the heated boat leaving the carbonaceous residue in the latter in the form of a velvety-black powder which was afterwards burnt in oxygen. The results are appended in the following table :

No. of Ex-periment.	Weight of Steel taken for analysis.	Weight of CO_2 obtained.	°/₀ Carbon.
1	2·25	0·0371	0·450
2	2·00	0·0321	0·438
3	2·25	0·0407	0·493
4	2·50	0·0418	0·456
5	2·00	0·0375	0·511
Mean	2·20	0,0378	0·470

Greatest difference, 0·073°/₀ C.

Moist Combustion Process.

The carbonaceous residues treated in the following experiments were obtained exactly as described in the cupric chloride method hereinafter recommended by the authors as most convenient and accurate for the estimation of carbon by combustion (p. 24).

Fig. 4.

The washed moist asbestos plug on which the carbon had been collected was transferred to a wide 8-oz. flask F (Fig. 4), fitted with a rubber stopper carrying an exit bend A and a stoppered funnel B, the latter also fitted with a small rubber stopper and glass bend. To the plug was then added $7\frac{1}{2}$ grammes of chromic acid dissolved in 15 cc. of water, the stopper was inserted, and 50 cc. of strong H_2SO_4 were introduced into the funnel, which was then closed with its stopper. The flask was next placed on the sand-bath C, the ends A and D were then respectively connected by means of thick-walled tubing to the bulb E and the tube C, Fig. 7, the flask and sand-bath, in fact, taking the place of the combustion-tube and furnace in the dry combustion apparatus. After weighing and replacing the absorption-tubes, G and H, the tap of the funnel was opened till the 50 cc. of H_2SO_4 had run into the flask, this process, if necessary, being assisted by the aspirator J. After closing the top of the funnel gentle heat was applied to the mixture of carbon and chromic and sulphuric acids, the heating was continued until the mass turned green and semi-solid from the formation of chromic sulphate, and white fumes began to appear in the flask. It was found necessary to go to this stage to ensure the complete oxidation of the carbon. The Bunsen was turned out, and two litres of air were aspirated through the flask from the gas-holder. The absorption tubes were then re-weighed to determine the weight of the CO_2 evolved. The reactions in this process may be formulated as follows:

$$6 \; H_2SO_4 + 4 \; CrO_3 + 3 \; C = 3 \; CO_2 + 2 \; Cr_2(SO_4)_3 + H_2O$$

The authors have observed in carrying out this process, that sometimes the fumes of SO_2 assume a peculiar physical condition in which they are not condensed in the sulphuric acid drying bulbs, and even to some extent pass the potash tubes. The results obtained by moist combustion are usually somewhat low, as will presently be seen, unless, as is often the case, no blank determination is made on the re-agents used. In the present set of experiments a washed plug 15 cc. of the chromic acid solution and 50 cc. of strong H_2SO_4 were dealt with as though a carbon determination were being made. The increase in the absorption-bulbs was 5·5 milligrammes, equivalent on the experiments to a mean + error of 0·044% C. As to whether this error was really due to carbonaceous matter in the re-agents, or to the faintly visible vapour of difficulty condensed SO_3, or to both, the authors are not sure; however, the corrected results of the estimations made by this process are set forth in the subjoined table:

No. of Experiment.	Weight of Steel taken.	Weight of CO_2 obtained.	% Carbon.
1	3·00	0·0544	0·495
2	3·25	0·0536	0·446
3	3·50	0·0610	0·475
4	3·75	0·0637	0·463
5	4·00	0·0668	0·455
Mean	3·50	0·0598	0·469

Greatest difference, 0·049%.

One more process now remains to be dealt with, namely, the dry combustion of the residue obtained by treating the steel with cupric chloride; this after some modifications was the method finally adopted by the authors, and they have no hesitation in stating, that if conscientiously carried out, it will be found to be the most accurate and convenient process.

Before describing the manipulative details of the method, it will be well to complete the tabular comparisons of the various processes. Five estimations by that last named gave the following results:

No. of Experiment.	Weight of Steel taken.	Weight of CO_2 obtained.	% Carbon.
1	4·00	0·0735	0·501
2	3·50	0·0626	0·488
3	3·00	0·0560	0·509
4	4·00	0·0715	0·487
5	4·00	0·0725	0·494
Mean	3·70	0·0672	0·496

Greatest difference, 0·022%.

The following table gives comparatively the mean results obtained from the five estimations made by each method. It should be understood, that before these results were recorded many preliminary experiments were made in each process to find out the most favourable conditions for the analysis.

Method of Liberation.	Method of Combustion.	Mean % Carbon.	Greatest difference between results Carbon %.
Galvanic . .	Dry	0·459	0·042
Chlorine. . .	Dry	0·470	0·073
Cupric chloride	Wet	0·469	0·049
Cupric chloride	Dry	0·496	0·022

If the mean result of the last method, namely, 0·496 %, be taken to represent the true carbon, the greatest difference 0·022 % indicates a ± error of 0·011 %, and if the process be carried out with every care by a practised manipulator, this amount may be regarded as the experimental error to which the process is liable, being constant within reasonable limits almost independently of the mass of carbon present. This is proved by the following tables of results obtained on two steels, one considerably higher and the other much lower in carbon than the standard steel. By colour comparison with the latter, two more 14-in. ingots were selected, and bars were obtained from them in the same manner as already described for the 0·496 % steel.

The steel on which the experiments detailed in the first table (p. 23) were made registered by the colour test 0·27 % C. The second steel, the combustions upon which are recorded in the second table (p. 23), showed by colour 0·80 % C.

Mr. A. A. Blair, in his work on the "Chemical Analysis of Iron," referring to the ammonio-cupric chloride and dry combustion process, states that " duplicate results

TABLE I.

No.	Weight of Steel.	Weight of CO_2.	℅ Carbon.
1	4·75	0·0430	0·247
2	4·50	0·0387	0·235
3	4·50	0·0402	0·244
4	4·25	0·0389	0·250
5	4·00	0·0372	0·253
Mean	4·40	0·0396	0·246
Greatest difference, 0·018℅.			

TABLE II.

No.	Weight of Steel.	Weight of CO_2.	℅ Carbon.
1	3·00	0·0852	0·775
2	3·50	0·1010	0·788
3	3·25	0·0946	0·793
4	3·75	0·1088	0·791
5 [1]	4·00	0·1126	0·768
Mean	3·50	0·1004	0·783
Greatest difference, 0·025℅.			

[1] A little carbon was lost during filtration.

should rarely vary more than 0·005 of a ℅ of carbon." In other words, working on 3 grammes of steel, a ± error of 0·000075 gramme of carbon. Odd pairs of results may by chance agree thus closely, but a series of combustions from which alone the true experimental

error can be determined, shows, as already indicated, an
unavoidable difference equal to four times the percentage
given by Mr. Blair.

Liberation of Total Carbon by Cupric Chloride and Dry Combustion of the Residue.

(Time occupied, about $1\frac{1}{2}$ working days.[1])

Preparation of Re-agents.

No. 1 Solution.—Weigh out into a 60-oz. beaker,
marked for 1 litre, 250 grammes of pure cupric chloride,
dissolve in hot water, and make up to 1,000 cc.; bring the
solution to boiling, and add, drop by drop, a strong solution of caustic potash till the liquid is milky with a permanent pale-blue precipitate of cupric hydrate. Boil up
well, say for 15 minutes, then allow to stand for a day or
two, till the hydrate and often a yellow basic precipitate
have settled. (The object of thus neutralizing with potash
is to remove from the copper salt any free acid present
which might liberate a small portion of the carbon in the
steel in the form of gaseous hydrocarbons.[2]) Filter off the
clear solution into a perfectly clean stoppered Winchester
quart, rub the filter-paper well before using to detach any

[1] The "time occupied" given with each process means the time
over which the operation extends, and not that the analyst is wholly
engaged for that period upon the estimation. As a matter of fact, an
expert chemist with ample appliances can, in the case of certain
steels, make two complete ordinary analyses in a working day of
seven hours.

[2] The B. A. Committee regard such evolution as apocryphal when
using ammonio-cupric chloride, but the authors have observed a
distinct evolution of gas bubbles with acid $CuCl_2$ solution.

loose fibres and so avoid getting them into the solution. Now, as all through the analysis, rigorous precautions must be taken to prevent the accidental introduction of extraneous carbon into the estimation.

No. 2 Solution.—Dissolve 600 grammes of pure cupric chloride and 300 grammes of clean common salt (*NaCl*) in boiling water. Make up the solution to 1800 cc., and then add 200 cc. of fuming *HCl* solution, mix thoroughly and filter, etc., as described for No. 1 solution.

Asbestos.—Fine, silky Italian asbestos must be carefully picked out into thin fibres: these are then worked up into a woolly mass, are strongly ignited in a muffle furnace, allowed to cool under cover, and are then preserved in a well-stoppered, wide-mouthed bottle.

Cupric oxide.—The purest form of this re-agent is made by cutting up into pieces about $\frac{1}{4}$ in. square, electrotype copper foil. The fragments of copper are then placed in an old porcelain dish, and are heated for several hours in the muffle till converted into oxide. Copper gauze, rolled into a cylinder thick enough to just slide into the combustion tube, and similarly ignited to oxide, also answers very well. These preparations the authors prefer to the granulated copper oxide of the shops, which sometimes gives off even after prolonged ignition gases capable of absorption by caustic potash.

Potash pumice.—For the preparation of this re-agent a considerable quantity of pumice stone is coarsely powdered. The fine powder is then removed through a copper sieve about 7 in. in diameter, with a rim 1 in. deep, and perforated with holes $\frac{1}{32}$ of an inch in diameter. The coarser residue is treated in a similar sieve with holes $\frac{1}{8}$ in. in diameter, the fragments passing through being used for the preparation of the re-agent. The grains are placed

in a porcelain dish, and potash solution is added till the
pumice is saturated with it. The mass is then gently
heated and stirred with a glass rod until quite dry. Any
clotted masses are then carefully broken up into their
constituent grains by means of the rod, and whilst still
warm the re-agent is placed for preservation in a well-
stoppered bottle.

Calcium chloride.—Ordinary chloride of calcium is
heated, at first cautiously, in a porcelain dish till it ceases
to give off water, and is converted into a dry, spongy
mass. The original salt has lost two-thirds of its combined
water, thus :

$$(CaCl_2, 6\ H_2O) = (CaCl_2,\ 2\ H_2O) + 4\ H_2O$$

The mass is broken up and sieved exactly as described
for the pumice, only this exceedingly hydroscopic substance must be kept as hot as possible during the sieving
operation, and the granules when obtained should receive
a good final heating before being bottled. They must
also be hot when introduced into the absorption-tube
described later on.[1]

Caustic potash solution.—Make when required by dissolving 25 grammes of stick potash in 50 cc. of distilled
water.

Mixture of chromic and sulphuric acids.—To 100 cc. of
water contained in a thin beaker add 100 cc. of strong
sulphuric acid. When cold, dissolve in the mixture as
much chromic acid as it will take up. Preserve for use in
a stoppered bottle.

Oxygen.—This is taken, as wanted, from a cylinder of
the compressed gas and passed into the glass gas holder

---

[1] Granulated calcium chloride, ready for use in combustion work,
can now be purchased. It is advisable, however, to pass a dry current
of CO_2 over it, followed by a current of dried air.

(A Fig. 7) after bubbling through a strong solution of caustic potash.

The Process.

Liberation of the carbon.—Weigh out from 3 to 5 grammes of the steel drillings into a 20-oz. beaker, provided with a glass rod crusher and a concave cover. Add 25 cc. of No. 1 solution for each gramme of steel taken; allow to stand for at least four hours, occasionally well stirring and crushing the precipitated copper until no gritty feeling is any longer perceptible. Now add 50 cc. of No. 2 solution for each gramme of steel present, when the dirty-looking yellow scum of basic iron and copper salts will be dissolved. The beaker and its contents are now heated to about 60° C., and the liquid is frequently stirred till all the precipitated copper is dissolved, and nothing but carbonaceous flocks remain. The beaker is then put aside for at least an hour to allow the residue to settle. Time is thus saved, as the almost black, supernatant liquid then passes rapidly through the filter before the latter becomes clogged with carbon.

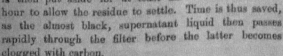

FIG. 5.

Collection of the residue.—This is effected in the filter apparatus sketched in Fig. 5. A perfectly cleaned and dried tube A about 500 mm. long by 15 mm. *inside diameter*, is supported in a wooden clamp stand; in it is packed a plug about 20 mm. long of the carefully-shredded recently-ignited silky asbestos fibres B. *This plug must be very carefully fitted.* It should be loose enough to allow the filtrate to pass through at a fairly rapid rate, but sufficiently compact to retain every particle of carbon. It is shaped and placed in position by means of a long, flat-headed glass rod and the tube C, which is 250 mm. long and 12 mm. *outside* diameter, and supports the plug in position in the larger tube. The latter is filled up (using the stirring-rod as a guide) with the dark liquid, and as much as possible should be got through before throwing any carbon on the plug. Every particle of carbon is then carefully washed into the tube, which during the intervals of filtration should be kept covered with a little porcelain crucible lid. The beaker also should never be left uncovered. The residue is well washed with hot dilute *HCl* solution, and then thoroughly with distilled water till quite free from acid. This may be tested by means of dilute solution of nitrate of silver. The washings from the tube should produce no opalescence in the silver solution.

In the foregoing operation, when the dark cuprous solution has all passed through, it will be readily seen whether the packing of the asbestos has been efficient. If dark channels of carbon reach the bottom of the plug, start the estimation afresh; if, however, all is satisfactory, proceed as follows:

Drying the residue.—Into a 3-in. porcelain dish place a roughly-made pad of ignited asbestos, about 40 mm. in diameter and 2 mm. thick. Then on to this, by means of the long, flat-headed glass rod, carefully slide the plug out of the filtration-tube, carbon side down: if this is skilfully done, not a particle of carbon will adhere to the edge of the tube. Should, however, any remain, it is removed with a small piece of ignited asbestos, the latter being placed, of course, on the pad. The dish and its contents are put into an air-bath, and maintained at a temperature of about 100° C. till the plug is quite dry.

Packing the combustion-tube.—The tube in which the combustion is made may be of porcelain or carefully selected refractory but not brittle glass; if of the latter, it will only serve safely for one estimation. Its length should be about 700 mm.,[1] and its inside diameter *must be* 20 mm., in order to allow the carbon plug to be easily inserted. The sharp edges of the tube should be removed with a file, so that they do not cut the corks. The arrangement inside the tube is shown in Fig. 6: B is a closely packed column of fragments of recently-ignited cupric oxide (*CuO*). It is secured in position by the ignited asbestos plugs A and C. In these channels are made for the passage of the gases in the position shown in the sketch by means of a clean, stout, pointed copper wire. D is the carbon-plug, E the pad, packed and channeled as shown.

Combustion of the residue.—The tube is placed in a sufficiently long (20 tap) Hofmann or other combustion furnace, so that the pad E is at least three burners within the furnace.

FIG. 6.

[1] A shorter tube involves the risk of scorched corks.

Into the tube are now firmly inserted the india-rubber corks, by means of which it is attached to the apparatus sketched in Fig. 7: A is a glass gas-holder containing pure oxygen (the stoppers and taps of this vessel should all be well greased); B is a bulb charged with strong caustic potash solution; C is a tube filled with potash pumice; D is the furnace and tube (the end of the latter at which the carbon plug is placed is connected with the tube C); E is a bulb charged with the mixture of chromic and sulphuric acids and water; F is a bulb containing concentrated sulphuric acid; G is a bulb charged with strong potash solution; H is a tube packed one-third (next the furnace) with potash pumice and two-thirds with dry chloride of calcium; I is a valve, the bend containing a little strong sulphuric acid to prevent the possible absorption of moisture by the tube H from the aspirator J. The parts of this apparatus must be tightly coupled up with *sound* thick-walled rubber tubing. The tightness of the apparatus should be tested by coupling everything up, closing the gas-holder, and opening the aspirator tap, when the passage of the air through the bulbs soon ceases if the whole arrangement is air-tight. Nip the tube attaching I to the aspirator, and remove and replace the bung of the latter to restore the equilibrium. All being ready, the gas-holder is detached from C, and a litre of air is gently aspirated through the system to remove all CO_2. The aspirator tap is shut and the gas-holder is re-attached to C, the tap opened, and a steady stream of gas is passed through the apparatus till the pressure is equalized. The absorption-tubes G and H are now detached, their open ends as well as those of F and I being stoppered for the time being with little pieces of india-rubber tubing,

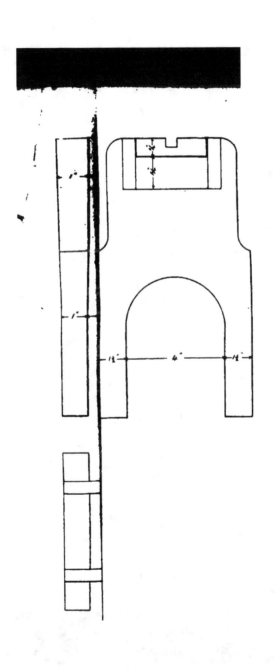

closed at one end with glass rod. The absorption-tube H
is provided with a horse-hair loop, which serves to
suspend it on the hook of the balance-pan. The tubes
are placed for five minutes in the balance-case, and
are then very carefully weighed without their stoppers,
having been previously wiped with a clean old linen
handkerchief. Having been re-attached to the apparatus,
the combustion is proceeded with as follows: slightly
open the aspirator tap and that of the gas-holder, so as
to pass through the bulbs a gentle bubble by bubble current of oxygen, which must be maintained throughout
the operation. The first burner under the copper oxide
(next E) is very cautiously lighted by means of a taper,
the gas being quickly and repeatedly turned in and out
till the tube is warm enough to have evaporated the
condensed moisture first formed from the vicinity of the
burner. *If this precaution is not faithfully carried out,
the tube, if of glass, will probably crack.* Next, one by
one, with the same precaution, light alternate burners
under the copper-oxide till the whole column is being
heated; then place the fire-clay covers over this portion
of the tube. As soon as the oxide is red-hot, quietly one
by one light the jets to the end of the furnace next C.
The carbon flashes off and burns readily, but the heat
should be continued after having placed on the remainder
of the fire-clay covers till the asbestos plug is thoroughly
red-hot. The portion of the tube containing the copper
oxide must be watched, if glass is used, and if it shows
any signs of sagging out, the temperature at that point
must be moderated by turning out a tap or two. As
soon as the combustion is finished the gas-holder tap is
shut, the tube nipped and detached, and the air is very
gradually admitted till the pull of the aspirator is

normal. At least a litre of air is then aspirated, the absorption-tubes are detached with the precaution already given, are stoppered, and after remaining five minutes in the balance-case are again wiped and re-weighed. The increase registers the weight of CO_2, which contains

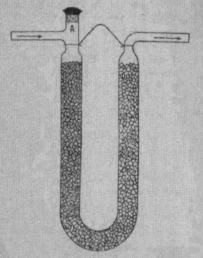

Fig. 9.

27·27% of carbon. (If the precautions advised during the various detachments of the parts of the apparatus are not observed, the violent passage of gas through the liquid re-agents may splash them from one tube to the other, a disaster necessitating a long delay for re-filling.)

Details of apparatus.—A dimensioned sketch (Fig. 8) of one of the wooden stands used to support the above apparatus may be useful. It will be noted, that the only movable corks employed are those in the combustion-tube. The dry absorption-tubes are of special design (Fig. 9): they are filled through a little funnel at the neck A, through which the pumice or chloride of calcium granules are shaken. When filled, the neck is firmly corked and her-metically closed by seal-ing-wax, the latter being carefully heated over a small Bunsen flame till smooth and rounded. Every chemist who has been engaged in organic analysis will have had painful experience of the fragile nature of Geiss-ler's bulbs. Arnold has therefore designed a pot-ash bulb combining effi-ciency, strength, and sim-plicity. It is sketched in Fig 10. The space

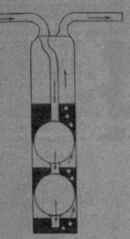

FIG. 10.

between the cylinder and the two inner bulbs should not exceed 0·20 mm. When this dimension is correct, pressure through the inlet tube splits up the liquid into three layers, so that gas passing through these bulbs first comes into contact with the film of the re-agent on the inside of the bulbs; it then passes through the lower layer of absorbent, is next placed between the lower and middle layers of the liquid, then passes between the moist surfaces of the first bulb and the

D

cylinder in a layer only 0·2 mm. thick; again bubbles through the absorbent, and passes into the space between the second and third layers of liquid; once more passes between the bulb and cylinder, and finally bubbles through the upper layer of absorbent. The bulbs present comparatively little outer surface to the condensation of moisture, and every part of them is readily wiped before weighing.

Theory of the Combustion Process.

The action of No. 1 solution removes the iron from the carbon with which it is combined or mixed as the case may be, and leaves the latter in flocks, mixed with metallic copper, thus respectively:

$$Fe_3C + 3 CuCl_2 = 3 FeCl_2 + 3 Cu + C$$
$$Fe + CuCl_2 = FeCl_2 + Cu$$

In the first reaction carbide of iron and cupric chloride yield ferrous chloride, copper, and carbon. In the second reaction the iron is merely removed as ferrous chloride, leaving admixed graphite and copper.

The ferrous chloride in solution oxidizes from the air, and basic ferric chloride is precipitated in yellowish flakes. From the action of the excess of cupric chloride formed upon the precipitated copper, dirty-white cuprous chloride is precipitated, this salt being insoluble in a neutral solution. These precipitates, however, are readily dissolved by the free HCl in the No. 2 solution, the latter also acting upon the copper thus:

$$CuCl_2 + Cu = 2 CuCl$$

Cupric chloride and copper yield cuprous chloride

soluble in *HCl*. The presence of the sodium chloride
assists the solution of the copper by forming a double
chloride, $CuNaCl_2$. The carbonaceous residue contains
combined water, often some silica and phosphide of iron,
and particularly sulphide of copper. The latter in steel
high in sulphur and low in carbon may, by the production of SO_2 during the combustion, give rise to
serious error, hence the mixed chromic and sulphuric
acids bulb E, which oxidizes the gaseous SO_2 to sulphuric acid,[1] in addition to condensing the bulk of the
water given off by the residue. The latter may also
contain tungsten and chromium, so that the student
need not be alarmed at a pink (Fe_2O_3), yellow (WO_3),
greenish (Cr_2O_3), or dark (CuO) residue remaining on
the plug after the strong ignition in oxygen.

The tubes B and C serve to thoroughly purify the
oxygen from any gases capable of being absorbed by
potash.

The column of oxide of copper ensures the conversion

---

[1] One of the authors made the following experiments on a basic
steel or rather iron ingot, containing under 0·1°/₀ of carbon and 0·09°/₀
of sulphur, in consequence of the carbon by combustion being considerably higher than that obtained by the colour test. A residue
from 3 grammes of steel was collected upon a paper filter, and after
thorough washing, was dried at 100°. The dried mass was removed
from the paper, transferred to a beaker, and boiled with strong nitric
acid. The solution was evaporated to dryness, and the dried mass
was extracted with water containing a few drops of *HCl*. The liquid
was filtered off, and a few drops of a 10°/₀ $BaCl_2$ solution was added;
a precipitate of $BaSO_4$ was at once obtained.

Another residue was prepared and burnt off exactly as for a combustion, the gases, however, being passed after leaving the combustion-
tube into a Geissler apparatus containing an acidified solution of
potassium permanganate. The first bulb was totally and the second
partially decolorized by the evolved SO_2.

of any small quantity of CO (which is insoluble in potash) that might be produced during the burning of the carbon, thus:

$$CO + CuO = Cu + CO_2$$

Carbonic oxide and cupric oxide yield copper and carbonic anhydride. It also seems to prevent any traces of chlorine present in the residue getting forward to the potash bulbs by converting it into $CuCl$; the latter may be occasionally seen as a faint brown sublimate on the portion of the tube just in front of the oxide. The sulphuric acid bulb F serves to remove the last traces of moisture from the gases before passing to the potash bulb G; the latter absorbs the CO_2 thus:

$$CO_2 + 2\ KHO = K_2CO_3 + H_2O$$

Carbonic anhydride and potassic hydrate yield potassic carbonate and water. The formation of the crystals of carbonate of potash may often be watched inside the bulbs. The potash pumice in the first limb of the tube H absorbs most of the moisture taken up by the gases when passing through the potash solution: if the tube were totally filled with calcic chloride the latter would soon liquefy, cake in the upper part of the limb, and thus prevent the passage of the gases. The chloride of calcium filling the remainder of the tube effectually prevents any moisture being carried away.

With reference to the number of combustions capable of being carried out with the foregoing arrangement, the tubes B C F and H should serve, with care, for fifty estimations, but the bulbs E G and the valve I should be recharged for every ten estimations. When not in use every portion of the apparatus should be tightly stoppered, and the absorption-tubes are perhaps best preserved in the balance-case.[1] The following model of the record of a carbon by combustion may be useful to the student:

July 13, 1888.

Carbon by combustion on drillings marked sp.
Weight of steel taken 3 grammes.

Weights of absorption-tubes before combustion:

KHO bulb, 34·4410
$CaCl_2$ tube, 59·1505

93·5915

Weights of absorption-tubes after combustion:

KHO bulb, 34·4670
$CaCl_2$ tube, 59·1844

93·6514
93·5915

·0599 gramme CO_2
27·27

4193
1198
4193
1198

3)1·633473

0·544°/₀ Carbon.

As the authors' experience has taught them that students who have been through a course of chemical

[1] The student should grasp the fact, that the weight of invisible condensed vapour, always under ordinary circumstances present upon the surfaces of glass, porcelain, and platinum apparatus, varies palpably with comparatively small differences in the temperature of the vessels, so that the absorption-tubes in each set of weighings should have as nearly as possible coincident temperatures. Hence the advisability of leaving them in the balance-case for some minutes before each weighing.

arithmetic, and are supposed to know all about it, are often, as a matter of fact, all at sea when a practical application of their knowledge is required, here, once and for all, the principle involved in the calculation of the percentage of the element in any weighed precipitate, etc. from a known weight of the original substance, will be fully set out. The foregoing is a short method for practical calculations, based upon and giving exactly the same result as the long method, which is as follows:

If 100 grammes of CO_2 contain 27·27 grammes of carbon

0·0599   ,,   ,,   ,, x ,,   ,,

As $100 : 0·0599 :: 27·27 : x$

$$x = \frac{0·0599 \times 27·27}{100} = 0·0163 \text{ gramme C.}$$

If 3 grammes of steel contain 0·0163 gramme of C.

100   ,,   ,,   ,, x ,,   ,,

As $3 : 100 :: 0·0163 : x$

$$x = \frac{0·0163 \times 100}{3} = 0·544\% \text{ C. as before.}$$

Calculation of Percentage Composition of CO_2

$$C = 12 \times 1 = 12$$
$$O_2 = 16 \times 2 = 32$$
$$\overline{44}$$

44 parts by weight of CO_2 contain 12 parts by weight of Carbon.

100   ,,   ,,   ,, x ,,   ,,   ,,

As $44 : 100 :: 12 : x$

$$x = \frac{100 \times 12}{44} = 27·27\%$$

Direct Combustion of Steel in a current of Oxygen.

The complete decarbonization of steel of any composition by passing a current of oxygen over the drillings can always be effected if a sufficiently high temperature is maintained. Porcelain tubes protected from direct contact with the flames by a wrapping of asbestos cloth, or in other ways, will stand heating to bright redness again and again before cracking. Any type of furnace capable of heating at the most 10 inches length of the tube to bright redness may be used. Furnaces of the ordinary muffle type are now largely used carrying several tubes at once.

A layer of ignited copper oxide, 4 to 5 inches long, occupies one-half of the heated portion of the tube, the remaining half accommodates the boat with its drillings.

The drillings should obviously be as thin as possible. It is often possible from a packet of drillings submitted for analysis to pass several grammes through a sieve of 30 meshes to the linear inch, and these provide a most admirable sample. Many substances have been used for mixing with the drillings, some of which furnish oxygen whilst others are not decomposed at a red heat. The latter, *e.g.* ignited magnesite, ignited alumina, etc., serve the purpose of mechanically separating the drillings as much as possible. Of this type, trimanganic tetroxide is as satisfactory and as generally reliable as any.

Special re-agent required.

Pure precipitated anhydrous manganese dioxide is passed through a sieve of 60 meshes to the inch in order to break up all lumps. The sieved oxide is strongly ignited in a platinum dish till, on cooling, it is found to have assumed throughout the mass the characteristic reddish brown colour of trimanganic tetroxide. The reagent is preserved in a well-stoppered bottle.

The Process.

(Time occupied, ¾ hour.)

Transfer 2·727 grammes of the drillings to a cylindrical weighing bottle 2 in. high, 1 in. in diameter, and then add 2 grammes of the prepared oxide. Before mixing, carefully shake more than half of the oxide into the previously ignited boat now standing on a white tile, and press the oxide down with a clean spatula so as to form a covering for the sides and bottom of the boat. The stopper is then placed in the weighing bottle and the drillings mixed with the remainder of the oxide by shaking, after which the mixture is emptied into and along the length of the boat. Any adherent particles are removed by gently tapping the bottle open end downwards on the tile and brushing from the latter into the boat. The boat and contents are then placed just inside the combustion tube to be warmed.

The weighed absorption bulbs having been placed in position, the tap of the aspirator is opened slightly, the warm boat is pushed into the fully heated tube and the bung quickly replaced. The top of the aspirator is then fully opened, and when bubbling has nearly ceased, oxygen is carefully admitted until the steel begins to burn. This is evidenced by a falling off in the rate of bubbling through the absorption train. The supply of oxygen is then increased and maintained at as high a rate as is consistent with safety. When the steel is nearly burned the rate of bubbling rapidly increases, and the oxygen supply must again be carefully controlled. Complete decarbonization of the steel has taken place when the oxygen enters and leaves the combustion tube at equal rates. From one to two litres of air are then aspirated through the apparatus to sweep all the carbon dioxide completely into the bulbs and ensure air filling all space in them not occupied by re-agents. The pressure is then carefully equalized, the bulbs removed, stoppered and placed in the balance case to cool before being finally weighed.

The oxide of manganese when prepared as directed should be free from blank, *i.e.*, when ignited in a stream of purified air or oxygen it should yield no carbon dioxide. All fresh batches should be tested, after ignition, by conducting a blank determination on 2 grammes exactly as described, the steel being of course omitted.

DETERMINATION OF COMBINED CARBON BY THE COLOUR TEST (Eggertz).

(Time occupied, about ¾ hour.)

The most used and abused process in the whole range of iron and steel analysis.[1]

---

[1] It is usual in text-books to state that the process consists in estimating the depth of colour produced in a dilute nitric acid solution of the steel, the intensity of the brown colour being proportional to the combined carbon present. This preamble is followed by directions to prepare by combustion a standard steel containing about 1% carbon to be used for the comparisons. It cannot be too strongly

To avoid errors in making the colour test, the student should bear in mind the following facts:

1. That the colour varies with the form (excluding graphite) in which the carbon exists in the steel: annealed steel gives a somewhat different tint from that obtained from the same steel in a normal state, although in both cases the carbon exists in combination with the iron. Hardened steel, in which comparatively little carbide of iron is present, yields a much lighter colour than that obtained from the normal steel.

2. With, as far as we know, coincident forms of carbon, the colour of the solution obtained from a hard steel is found to be deeper than that obtained from a mild steel, when volumes of the liquids containing the colouring matter have been adjusted in accordance with the percentages of carbon obtained by combustion, that is to say, a 1% steel when compared with a 0·25% standard would register, after a fashion, considerably

stated, that the colour is *not* proportional to the carbon present, except under certain special conditions, and even then within a limited range. No competent steel analyst would ever think of using a 1% standard to estimate the carbon in a mild steel. The authors of almost every work on iron and steel analysis which has been published during the last fifteen or twenty years have been so imbued with the proportional colour fallacy, that they figure with monotonous regularity a stand containing a long vista of hermetically sealed "proportional colour" tubes, charged with either very weak coffee or with so-called permanent colour solutions of inorganic metallic salts. The articles describing this delusion usually end up with the complacent assurance, that by its means combined carbon "may be readily determined within 0·01%." A friend has for some time been watching with interest the molecular changes taking place in the tubes of a rack of "permanent colour standards" in which, in a moment of weakness, he invested two guineas. At present the 0·1% standard is darker than the 0·3%.

over 1%. Coincident tints, however, would never be obtained. (See paragraph 4.)

3. Normal, crucible, open-hearth, and Bessemer steels of like carbon do not give exactly the same shade of colour.

4. Colours may be obtained of equal depths but varying tints.

5. The colouring matter is sensitive to daylight, being distinctly paler when exposed for a few hours.

6. The colour is not due to dissolved carbon in the elementary condition, but to an organic compound consisting of carbon, hydrogen, nitrogen, and oxygen. Variations in the composition, and consequently colour, of this compound are probable.

7. Over-heated steel sometimes gives to nitric acid a peculiar deep, blood-red tint. The cause of this phenomenon is obscure, but well worth investigation. For instance, an over-heated open-hearth ingot, containing 0.2% of carbon, gave a colour which as nearly as could be estimated recorded the carbon as over 2%. In another case a small steel shot, accidentally somewhat over-heated in "letting down" to drill for analysis, contained in the centre 0·85% of carbon, whilst the outside registered about 1·15%. These cases are remarkable, because with a burnt steel a low carbon result is usually expected.

8. Colour tests on mild steels are more reliable than those registered by hard steels.

From the foregoing paragraphs may be deduced the ideal conditions under which this process should be employed.

(a) The standard and the steel to be tested should have been made by the same process.

(*b*) The standard and steel should be in the same physical condition as far as this can be secured by mechanical means.

(*c*) The standard should not differ greatly in its percentage of carbon from that present in the steel under analysis.

(*d*) The solutions of the steels and standards should be made at the same time and under identical conditions, and the comparisons should be made without delay.

(*e*) Above all, the standard should be above suspicion, its carbon contents having been settled as the mean of several concordant combustions made on different weights of steel from a homogeneous bar.[1]

When all these conditions are observed, a more accurate analytical process than the colour test cannot be desired, but the authors are too well aware that very often an observance of all the precautions quoted in the ideal case is not possible; however, most of the conditions can always be secured, and if even these are followed, the colour test, though not accurate in every instance, is nevertheless of the greatest practical value, on account of the rapidity with which the results can be obtained.

The Process.

Sampling the steel.—This is a matter requiring a little consideration, or misleading reports may be handed in.

[1] J. O. Arnold and A. A. Read have shown ("Journal Chemical Society," August, 1894) the possible existence of a subcarbide of iron, and the certain existence of double carbides of iron and manganese. The last-named seem to give a lighter colour than carbide of iron *per se*. (See memoir above quoted.)

In steel bars, and particularly billets, surface drillings should be avoided, as they are lower in carbon than the main portion of the steel. In one case known to us, several tons of 3-in. billets of specified carbon "seventy" = 0·7% were rejected on the ground that several independent analysts had returned results showing them to vary in carbon from 0·25 to 0·35%. On investigating the matter, it was found that the drillings sent for analysis had been skimmed with a very wide angle drill from the surface of the billets. Deeper drillings from the same places sent to one of the analysts were reported by him to contain by colour test 0·69% carbon.

When the heat is considered to which it is necessary to raise a 16-in. ingot before rolling into billets, it is not surprising that some of the surface carbon should be oxidized.

In the case of cemented steel bar (blister steel) the colour test is of dubious accuracy, firstly, because the colour yielded by this material is difficult to match with an ordinary standard; and secondly, because it is not easy to get an average sample even from a single bar.

During the process of cementation the carbonization proceeds from the outside of the bar. This, therefore, is much richer in carbon than the middle, at all events, in the case of mild shearing bars showing "sap," and containing about $\frac{3}{4}$% of carbon. The best plan (after cleaning both sides from rust and scale) is to drill right through the bar, and thoroughly mix the whole of the drillings; even then it is advisable to do several estimations, and take the mean of the results.

Steel which has been hardened and tempered should always be thoroughly "let down" by cautiously heating the material to a fair red, and then allowing it to cool in

air before sampling. All drillings should be taken with
dry tools, quite free from oil, etc. *Filings are worthless,*
and particles of scale, sand, etc., should be carefully
avoided. In the case of very thin sections of steel, incapable of being drilled, the sample should be filed bright
on both sides, and be then sheared into small pieces
suitable for weighing out for analysis.

Weighing out.—In open hearth and Bessemer steel
works the analyst is usually aware of the approximate
carbon in the steels to be tested, from the fact that the
heats or blows have been made for special purposes, such
as dead-mild, carbon 0·1%, Bessemer rails, 0·45%,
open-hearth wagon springs, 0·65%, etc., so that each
day's dead-mild heats are dissolved up with and tested
by the dead-mild standard, spring heats with the spring
standard, and so on. In crucible steel works the fractures
of the ingots convey to an experienced eye a fairly
accurate idea of the percentage of carbon present. In
cases where the carbon is absolutely unknown a preliminary trial must be made, in order to find out roughly
what carbon is present, so as to compare it with the
nearest standard. The following table shows the weights
required of various percentages of carbon, the volume of
dilute nitric acid required in each case, and the approximate percentage of carbon in suitable standards.

% C. in Steel.	% C. in Standard (approximately).	Weight of Steel, grammes.	Size of test tube, inches.	Vol. of Acid, cc.
1·3 to 1·7	1·50	0·05	$6 \times \frac{1}{2}$	3
1·1 „ 1·3	1·20	0·05	,,	3
0·8 „ 1·1	0·90	0·10	,,	4
0·4 „ 0·8	0·60	0·10	,,	3
0·2 „ 0·4	0·30	0·10	,,	2
0·1 „ 0·2	0·15	0·30	6×1	6

The test tubes used should be of thin glass, and preferably of equal bore; they must be *scrupulously clean*, and *quite dry* inside. A slip of gummed paper should be attached to each, and upon this should be legibly written the carbon contents of the standard, or the distinguishing mark of the steel to be tested, as the case may be. The tubes are then conveyed to the balance in a rack. Having carefully weighed out the steels, transfer the drillings by tapping and, if necessary, by brushing without loss to their proper tube.

Dissolving the sample.—To each tube the requisite volume of chemically pure (chlorine free) nitric acid of specific gravity 1·20[1] is added from a 50 cc. burette. The tubes are then left in the rack for a few minutes till the first violent evolution of nitrous fumes has ceased. The brown organic flocks containing the carbon will then be noted floating about in the already coloured acid. The tubes are next placed on the hot plate in a bath of just boiling water, and are occasionally shaken till bubbles of gas are no longer given off, and the solutions are clear. This will be in from 15 to 30 minutes— the time varying with the quantity of brown flocks to be dissolved. It will be found that when the tubes are placed in a slanting position, some of the solution of ferric nitrate is liable to dry on the sides; also, that when they touch the bottom of the bath, bumping sometimes occurs. To remedy this, J. O. Arnold designed the carbon bath sketched in Fig. 11. The specially made glass beaker has no radiused sides; it measures 5 in. in diameter by 5 in. deep. The glazed china cover is per-

[1] Best made by the hydrometer. It may, however, be approximately obtained by mixing 250 cc. distilled water with 175 cc. of nitric acid of specific gravity 1·43.

forated with holes, either $1\frac{1}{8}$ in. or $\frac{5}{8}$ in. in diameter, to admit the two sizes of test tubes employed. The tubes

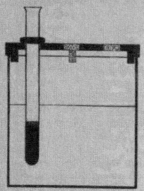

are supported on the cover by means of nicely-fitting india-rubber gauge glass rings, slipped on to the tubes to such a height that their bottoms are about one inch from the beaker. When the solution is complete, the tubes and their contents must be well cooled in a vessel of cold water before testing, because the liquids are much darker whilst hot than when cold.

Comparing the colours.— The pairs of graduated tubes used for this purpose are conveniently of two sizes. Each pair must be of equal bore and thickness of glass, and the latter should be untinged with colour. The tubes must always be thoroughly washed out before using. The first pair should be 12 cc. graduated in tenths, and have an inside diameter of about 10 mm. They are used for

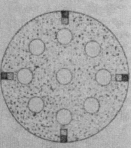

Fig. 11.

all steels containing 0·2% and upwards of carbon. The second pair, used only for steels containing between 0·1 and 0·2% of carbon, should be of 20 cc. capacity, graduated in half cc. One of each pair of tubes should be

marked S with a diamond: into this cautiously pour the
solution of the standard steel, rinse out the dissolving-
tube with a small quantity of distilled water, of course
pouring the washings into the comparison-tube. The
liquid in the latter is now very carefully diluted to the
mark by means of a fine jet of distilled water: be careful
not to overshoot the point, remembering that the drain-
ings from the side of the tube will usually measure nearly
$\frac{1}{16}$ of a cc. Close the mouth of the tube with the finger
—*which should be clean*—and invert the liquid two or
three times till of even colour throughout. Treat the
steel to be tested in a similar manner, not of course filling to the mark, but gradually diluting and mixing the
solution till the tints in the two tubes as nearly as possible match. The percentage is then read off. Probably
the best and certainly the simplest background against
which to compare the colours is a piece of clean filter-
paper saturated with water, and stuck upon a pane of
glass in a window having a north light; in any case,
sunlight must be avoided. In determining the final
point change sides with the tubes, because it will usually
be found that an apparent match of tints is disturbed
by this alteration in relative position. When a point is
reached at which the steel being tested looks a shade
light on one side and a shade dark on the other side
of the standard, the true reading has been obtained.
The following table will indicate to the student the
manner in which the standards are diluted, and the
volumes of liquid registered by the unknown steels are
read off as percentages. The carbons in the table are
given in round numbers. In actual practice figures in
the second decimal place will probably be involved, when
of course the dilution of the standard is made to cor-

respond thus, a 0·78% standard must be diluted to 7·8 cc.

C. %, in Standard.	Dilute Standard to cc.	To convert cc. regis- tered by Steel into Carbon %.		
1·50	7·50	Divide them by 5		
1·20	6·00	,,	,,	5
0·90	9·00	,,	,,	10
0·60	6·00	,,	,,	10
0·30	3·00	,,	,,	10
0·15	15·00	,,	,,	100

Steels leaving a Residue insoluble in Nitric Acid.

High carbon steels occasionally leave a black residue of graphite, high tungsten steels deposit yellow tungstic acid, and wrought iron, puddled, and blister steels sometimes leave a small dark powdery precipitate of slag, etc.[1] All these solids require filtering off before making the comparisons. A plain funnel one inch in diameter, containing a minute circular filter-paper,[2] is supported over the graduated tube in such a manner that the stem of the funnel reaches about half an inch down the tube. The solution is then passed through the filter, the latter, the dissolving tube and the residue, being of course washed colour-free with a fine jet of distilled water. The clear liquid is then compared as already described.

[1] This fact may serve to distinguish wrought iron from dead-mild steel.

[2] A penny serves very well to cut this out to.

Steels for which the Colour Test is not available.

These comprise steels containing large percentages of elements yielding coloured solutions with nitric acid: such are chromium, copper, and nickel, particularly the first-named metal. When only moderate percentages of nickel or copper are present, fairly accurate colour results may be obtained, and the same remark applies to very small percentages of chromium. In certain special steels, where the percentage of the colouring element is practically constant, a standard containing the same amount of that element may be prepared. In some instances the authors have found a modified application of the alkaline colour test devised by Mr. Stead [1] for the determination of carbon in ingot iron to be useful, inasmuch as chromium, nickel, and copper are precipitated as hydrates along with the iron by the caustic soda employed in this process, but as a rule the safest way out of the difficulty is to estimate the carbon by the combustion method.

DETERMINATION OF GRAPHITE IN STEEL.

Graphite occurs in steel when the latter has contained a high percentage of combined carbon, and has been under the influence of certain abnormal physical conditions. For instance, the authors have found that by prolonged annealing it is possible to convert most of the carbon in a steel containing say 1.5% of that element from the combined to the graphitic condition. Again, in rolling hard file steel, the unwelcome phenomenon of a

[1] "Journal of the Iron and Steel Institute," 1883, No. 1, page 213.

partial separation of graphite sometimes occurs, resulting
in the production of what is technically known as " black
steel."

The determination of graphite is often made by dissolving the steel in hydrochloric acid, diluting the solution,
collecting the insoluble residue on a paper filter, washing
it with hydrochloric acid and water, and afterwards with
caustic potash solution and water, to dissolve out the
silica. The residue, or as much of it as is possible, is
then washed from the paper into a platinum dish—the
contents of the latter are evaporated to dryness—the
dish and its contents are weighed, strongly ignited and
again weighed, and the difference between the two
weighings is taken as graphite. This method is a slovenly
process, open to several objections, and the authors
strongly advise the student not to use it. When a determination of graphite is worth doing at all, it is worth
doing accurately, especially as this occupies very little
more time than the crude method just briefly described.

Determination of Graphite by Combustion.

Weigh out 5 grammes of the steel into a 20-oz. beaker,
put on the cover, and add cautiously in several portions
100 cc. of dilute nitric acid, spec. gravity 1·2. Digest the
solution at about 100° C. until all the iron, and the flocks
containing the combined carbon, have passed into solution; collect the residue on asbestos exactly as described
on page 27, washing, however, first thoroughly with cold
water, then with very dilute ammonia (1 cc. of liquid
ammonia, spec. gravity 880, mixed with 99 cc. of distilled
water), and finally with hot water. Dry and burn the

residue, collecting and weighing the evolved CO_2 exactly as described on page 28 *et seq.*, igniting, however, *as strongly as possible*, graphite being much less combustible than the residue containing combined carbon.

Theoretical Considerations.

The authors prefer to dissolve the steel in dilute nitric instead of hydrochloric acid, in order to sharply separate the combined from the free carbon. The latter acid, it is true, evolves most of the carbide carbon in the form of gaseous hydrocarbons, but in high carbon steels, in which only the determination of graphite is likely to be required, more or less combined carbon, which has escaped from or evaded combination with the hydrogen, remains with the graphite in the solid form. With the strength of acid specified, and at the temperature given, the authors are of opinion that no graphite is converted into CO_2 or passes into solution. Another advantage of nitric acid is, that it retains the silicon (sometimes in the case of steel castings present in considerable quantity) in solution, whereas *HCl* liberates it as gelatinous silicic acid, which seriously impedes the rapidity of the filtration. The reason for using cold water in washing away neutral or faintly acid solutions of iron salts may be here stated once and for all. *Hot water is very liable to throw down precipitates of insoluble basic iron salts into the pores of filter-paper or asbestos.* The dilute ammonia converts any free nitric acid in the residue or asbestos into nitrate of ammonia, thus—

$$HNO_3 + NH_3 = (NH_4)NO_3$$

Any traces of the latter salt present on burning the

residue are converted into water and nitrous oxide
thus—

$$(NH_4)NO_3 = 2H_2O + N_2O$$

If any nitric acid remains in combination with the graphite, it will during the combustion be converted into water
and brown peroxide of nitrogen gas thus—

$$2\,HNO_3 = H_2O + 2\,NO_2 + O$$

The latter will be absorbed in the sulphuric acid drying
bulb, forming nitro-sulphonic acid.

THE ACTION OF ACIDS ON STEEL.

Before going on to describe the estimation of elements
other than carbon, it will be well to tabulate for the
student the reactions of acids upon steel. It is, however,
only necessary to consider those obtained with

Hydrochloric acid $\}$ Weak
Sulphuric acid $\quad\}$ oxidants.
Nitric acid $\}$ Powerful
Aqua regia $\}$ oxidants.

Hydrochloric Acid.

The liquid usually known in the laboratory by this
name is really a saturated solution of gaseous *HCl* in
water: it has a spec. gravity of about 1·2, and contains
approximately about 40% of true *HCl*. The reactions
of this strong solution on the elements of steel may be
formulated thus—

Iron is converted into pale-green ferrous chloride, which

remains in solution whilst the co-produced hydrogen gas escapes thus—

$$Fe + 2\,HCl = FeCl_2 + 2\,H$$

Carbon existing as carbide of iron is almost totally converted into gaseous hydrocarbons, which escape. This is due to the action on the carbon of the nascent hydrogen liberated from the acid.

Graphite remains suspended in the solution; it may, however, to some extent absorb or form weak compounds with the acid or gases present.

Silicon existing as silicide of iron is probably, at the moment of its liberation (in the nascent condition) from the iron, oxidized by the water present to gelatinous silicic acid with an evolution of hydrogen, thus—$Si + 4\,H_2O = H_4SiO_4 + 4\,H$. The silicic acid remains partly suspended and partly dissolved in the acid.

Manganese existing alloyed with the iron and carbon, liberates hydrogen from the acid, and remains in solution as manganous chloride, thus—

$$Mn + 2\,HCl = MnCl_2 + 2\,H$$

Sulphur existing as sulphide of iron is totally converted into invisible sulphuretted hydrogen gas, which escapes, thus—

$$FeS + 2\,HCl = FeCl_2 + H_2S$$

Phosphorus existing as phosphide of iron remains to a slight extent in solution as phosphoric acid; most of it, however, escapes as phosphoretted hydrogen, PH_3.

Arsenic existing as arsenide of iron is converted by the strong acid into volatile liquid arsenious chloride $AsCl_3$, very liable to escape as vapour.

Tungsten existing alloyed with the iron and carbon remains chiefly as a dark, insoluble residue, consisting of a mixture of the metal and its lower oxides, the latter being to some extent soluble in the acid.

Chromium existing alloyed with the iron and carbon is probably in the first instance converted into blue chromous chloride, with evolution of hydrogen, thus— $Cr + 2\ HCl = CrCl_2 + 2\ H$; the chromous salt, however, is very rapidly converted into green chromic chloride by atmospheric oxygen, thus—

$$2\ CrCl_2 + 2\ HCl + O = 2\ CrCl_3 + H_2O\ [1]$$

Nickel existing alloyed with the iron and carbon evolves hydrogen from the acid, and remains in solution as pale-green nickelous chloride, thus—

$$Ni + 2\ HCl = NiCl_2 + 2\ H$$

Aluminium existing alloyed with the iron remains in solution as chloride, hydrogen being given off, thus—

$$Al + 3\ HCl = AlCl_3 + 3\ H$$

Copper existing alloyed with the iron is sometimes present in small quantities, and remains in solution as green cupric chloride, $CuCl_2$.

Titanium.—It is very dubious whether this element is ever present in commercial steel; if so, it will be converted into soluble titanic acid, thus—

$$Ti + 4\ H_2O = H_4TiO_4 + 4\ H$$

Molybdenum existing alloyed with the iron and carbon is converted chiefly into molybdic acid which remains in solution unless present in large quantities, when some of it separates out. The green colour of the solution obtained by dissolving molybdenum steels in hydrochloric acid is due to the formation of one of the many chlorides

---

[1] In very rich chrome steels a small insoluble residue of carbide of chromium may remain.

of this metal, but the chlorides are unstable in presence of water, yielding the acid by atmospheric oxidation.

$$2\ MoCl_2 + 5\ H_2O + 3(O) = 2\ H_2MoO_4 + 6\ HCl$$

Vanadium existing alloyed with the iron and carbon is partly carried into solution probably as an oxychloride and partly left as a black insoluble residue containing carbon and iron also.

Tantalum existing alloyed with the iron and carbon is partly carried into solution as a chloride and partly left as a black insoluble residue containing carbon and iron also.

Sulphuric Acid.

The concentrated acid, sp. gravity 1·843, practically corresponds to the formula H_2SO_4. Steel is little soluble in the strong liquid, the sulphates formed, being insoluble in the acid, coat the metal and protect it from further action. The dilute acid used as a solvent for steel is made up of one volume of the strong acid and six volumes distilled water. The action of the dilute acid on steels is almost perfectly analogous to that of HCl, only, of course, the corresponding metallic sulphates, $FeSO_4$, $Al_2(SO_4)_3$, etc., are produced. As a rule, HCl is the most convenient to use, but when it is desired to retain the solution of iron in the ferrous condition, sulphuric acid is distinctly superior, because ferrous sulphate $(FeSO_4)$ is not nearly so readily oxidized by the air to ferric sulphate $(Fe_2(SO^4)^3)$ as is ferrous chloride $(FeCl_2)$ to ferric chloride $(FeCl_3)$.

Arsenic, however, remains as dark arsenide of iron, liable to be converted into arsenious acid $As(HO)_3$, and some of the latter may be reduced by the action of the nascent hydrogen AsH_3 being evolved.

Nitric Acid.

The strong acid, sp. gravity 1·43, contains about 68% of true HNO_3; it has no action on steel in the cold (the metal assuming what is known as the passive condition), and even on boiling the dissolution is very slow. The acid used for a steel solvent has a specific gravity of 1·2, and contains about 34% of true HNO_3. The attack of this dilute acid on steel is violent. The reactions taking place are as follows:

Iron is converted into pale-green ferric nitrate. Fe $(NO_3)_3$, which remains in solution, and the brown oxides of nitrogen N_2O_3 and NO_2 are thrown off.

Carbon has already been dealt with in the article on the colour test (see p. 41).

Graphite.—The dilute acid does not seem to form any volatile or soluble carbon compounds with this substance. It is possible, however, that the graphite absorbs or forms weak compounds with the acids and gases present.

Silicon remains in solution as silicic acid, which appears to form with the nitric acid and nitrate of iron some compound which does not decompose when heated at 250° C., and is soluble in HCl. The silica, however, separates on evaporating down the last-named solution.

Manganese remains in solution as manganous nitrate $Mn(NO_3)_2$.

Sulphur is oxidized to sulphuric acid, and remains in solution as ferric sulphate $Fe_2(SO_4)_3$.

Phosphorus is oxidized to phosphoric acid, and remains in solution as phosphoric acid.

Arsenic is oxidized to arsenic acid, and remains in solution as arsenic acid.

Tungsten is oxidized to tungstic acid, H_2WO_4, which passes into solution. In self-hardening steels, however, in which the percentage of tungsten is very high (10%), a portion of the metal is precipitated as insoluble yellow WO_3.

Chromium, when present in small quantities, passes into solution as chromic nitrate $Cr(NO_3)_3$. When, however, it is present to any great extent, it remains in the form of insoluble metallic scales of impure chromium.

Nickel passes into solution as nickelous nitrate $Ni(NO_3)_2$.

Aluminium remains in solution as aluminic nitrate $Al(NO_3)_3$.

Copper passes into solution as cupric nitrate $Cu(NO_3)_2$.

Titanium is oxidized, and remains dissolved as titanic acid H_4TiO_4.

Molybdenum is oxidized to molybdic acid.

Vanadium is oxidized to metavanadic acid and remains in solution.

Tantalum is oxidized to hydrated tantalic oxide (Ta_2O_5 x H_2O) and remains partly in solution and partly in suspension.

Nitro-hydrochloric Acid or Aqua Regia.

On mixing together strong nitric and hydrochloric acids, the two combine and form a yellowish-red fluid of great use as a powerful oxidizing agent. The liquid contains in solution two gases, namely, deep yellow nitrosyl chloride and free chlorine. The reaction may be expressed thus—

$$3\ HCl + HNO_3 = NOCl + Cl_2 + 2\ H_2O$$

For the purposes of steel analysis this re-agent should

be made by mixing four volumes of concentrated hydrochloric acid solution and one volume of strong nitric acid
(sp. gr. 1·43). These proportions are important in connection with a point bearing upon the estimation of
silicon, which will be referred to later on (*vide infra*).
When the liquid has acquired its full colour, which will
be in the course of a few hours, it is ready for use. Its
reactions upon the elements of steel are in some instances
similar to those of nitric acid, whilst in certain cases they
are the same as those obtained with HCl.

Iron is violently attacked, and passes into solution as
deep yellow *ferric* chloride $FeCl_3$ (HCl alone yields *ferrous*
chloride $FeCl_2$).

Combined carbon is no doubt to some extent oxidized
to CO_2, but the greater portion passes into solution, and
on evaporating the liquid separates out in the form of a
finely-divided brownish precipitate.

Graphite is possibly to a small extent oxidized to CO_2,
but the bulk of it remains as an insoluble residue. It
is probable, however, that it forms a weak compound
with the acids and gases present.[1]

Silicon is oxidized to silicic acid, most of which passes
into solution: it, however, entirely deposits on evaporation to dryness as insoluble SiO_2, *providing the volume of
strong hydrochloric acid before specified is used for the
preparation of the re-agent*. If too much nitric acid is
present the whole of the silica is not rendered insoluble,
some of it passing into solution again when the dry mass
is taken up in HCl.

[1] Brodie has shown that nitro-sulphuric acid acts appreciably upon
graphite, forming a compound which, when ignited, gives off oxygen,
hydrogen, and sulphuric anhydride SO_3, leaving a finely-divided
residue of pure graphite.

Manganese remains in solution as manganous chloride $MnCl_2$.

Sulphur is oxidized, and passes into solution as yellow ferric sulphate $Fe_2(SO_4)_3$.

Phosphorus is oxidized, and remains dissolved as phosphoric acid.

Arsenic is converted into arsenic acid, and on evaporation to dryness some liquid chloride $AsCl_3$ is formed, which vaporizes and escapes.

Tungsten is oxidized, being partly converted into insoluble yellow WO_3, and partly into the hydrated acid H_2WO_4, which passes into solution.

Chromium is dissolved to green chromic chloride $CrCl_3$. If, however, a considerable percentage of the element is present an insoluble metallic residue, rich in chromium, remains unacted upon by the acids.[1]

Nickel passes into solution as $NiCl_2$.

Aluminium is dissolved, forming colourless aluminic chloride $AlCl_3$.

Copper passes into solution as green cupric chloride $CuCl_2$.

Titanium passes into solution as colourless titanic acid H_4TiO_4.

Molybdenum, *Vanadium*, and *Tantalum* are oxidized to the acids corresponding to the oxides MoO_3, V_2O_5 and Ta_2O_5 respectively.

A careful study of the foregoing reactions will give to the student a good idea why a certain acid should be used in the first stage in the estimation of a certain element, and yet must be carefully avoided in the preliminary solution having for its object the determination of some other element.

[1] This metallic residue is usually free from sulphur and phosphorus.

The Determination of Silicon.

In the literature of iron and steel analysis it may be often noticed, that the authors insist very strongly on the necessity in making an estimation of silicon of determining how much exists as Si combined with the iron, and how much as SiO_2 in the involved slag. In modern well-fused steels, except locally, and as the result of some accidental and abnormal circumstance, there is practically no slag. In high-class wrought irons, such as Lancashire hearth Swedish rolled bars, there are found under the microscope formidable-looking streaks of dark cinder; yet, when the iron is analyzed, the total silicon will be found to be about 0·02%. In low grade English bars, however, the slag is present in much larger quantities: certain sections under the microscope appear indeed to contain more slag than iron. It may be that occasionally, for research purposes, an estimation of the slag (and its composition) in wrought iron is required, but from an everyday, practical point of view the subject may be at once dismissed. There is an analytical tradition to the effect that when iron containing silicon in combination is dissolved in strong hydrochloric acid, some silicuretted hydrogen gas SiH_4 is evolved, and that consequently the results are liable to be low. It is therefore usually deemed necessary for the determination of silicon to employ either aqua regia or nitro-sulphuric acid as a preliminary solvent, in order to prevent the formation of SiH_4. These precautions knock down a man of straw, as the evolution of SiH_4 is a myth. The results given by the aqua regia process and by Drown's nitro-sulphuric method [1] are

---

[1] This method is described under the analysis of pig-iron on p. 255.

quite accurate, but the evaporation takes longer, and the fumes are more irritating than when HCl is used. The authors some years ago, by means of triplicate estimations on many samples of steel occurring in ordinary laboratory practice proved the results obtained by the three methods to be identical, and the following figures, obtained in the laboratory of the metallurgical department of the Sheffield University by Messrs. McWilliam and Brunton, establish it conclusively:

TABLE II.—HIGH SILICON STEEL.

No.	Grammes of Steel.	Solvent.	Weight of SiO_2.	Si %.
1	3	HCl	0·2768	4·306
2	3	,,	0·2788	4·337
3	3	aqua regia	0·2749	4·276
4	3	,, ,,	0·2784	4·331

A final attempt was made to evolve SiH_4 from the high silicon steel under specially favourable conditions. The hydrochloric acid was allowed to act upon the drillings in the cold for eighteen hours in an atmosphere of hydrogen: the evolved gases were passed through aqua regia to oxidize any SiH_4 given off to silicic acid. The silicon in the flask in which the steel had been treated, and that present in the aqua regia, were then estimated in the usual manner with the following results:—

Weight in grammes of		Si %
SiO_2 in flask	0·2713	4·223
SiO_2 in aqua regia	0·0010	0·016
Total	0·2723	4·239

TABLE I.—STEEL FOR CASTINGS.

No.	Grams taken.	Solvent.	Weight of SiO$_2$.	% Silicon.	Remarks.
1	3	35 cc. Hydrochloric acid, sp. gr. 1·16.	0·0202	0·314	Evaporated to dryness, re-dissolved in 25 cc. HCl, sp. gr. 1·16, and 50 cc. of water.
2	3		0·0203	0·316	
3	3	35 cc. Aqua Regia.	0·0201	0·313	Same treatment as Nos. 1 and 2.
4	3		0·0200	0·311	
5	3	30 cc. HNO$_3$, sp. gr. 1·20. 20 cc. H$_2$SO$_4$, sp. gr. 1·80. 20 cc. of water.	0·0204	0·317	Evaporated until copious white fumes were evolved, and then diluted and boiled with water.
6	3		0·0205	0·319	
7	3	20 cc. H$_2$SO$_4$, sp. gr. 1·80. 66 cc. of water.	0·0203	0·316	Same treatment as Nos. 5 and 6.
8	3		0·0206	0·320	
9	3	35 cc. HNO$_3$, sp. gr. 1·20.	0·0010	0·016	Same treatment as Nos. 1 and 2.
10	3		0·0011	0·017	

The foregoing series of experiments conclusively prove that no silicon is evolved as SiH_4 when steel is dissolved in hydrochloric acid solution.

The Process.

(Time occupied, about 3 hours.)

Weight taken.—Weigh out 4·67 grammes of drillings into a 20-oz. beaker.

Dissolving.—Put on the cover, and add down the lip 50 cc. of strong hydrochloric acid solution. Place the beaker on the hot plate, and heat quietly until the steel is dissolved; then, still keeping on the cover, boil briskly till the acid becomes quite thick with precipitated ferrous chloride. To hasten the analysis the boiling should be kept up as long as no spitting occurs, and the drops of condensed acid from the underside of the cover do not endanger the safety of the beaker by falling upon the hot bottom and cracking it.

Evaporating to dryness.—Next, remove the beaker to a cooler part of the plate, take off the cover and place it, concave side downwards, on an earthenware filter-drier. Gradually increase the heat under the beaker, carefully avoiding spitting, till the mass is quite dry. Remove the hot vessel from the plate, and *hold it in the hand till fairly cool:* if the heated beaker is at once placed in contact with the comparatively cold bench it will probably crack.

Re-dissolving.—When cool, replace the cover (nothing having been lost from its under surface), and add to the dry chlorides enough strong hydrochloric acid solution to

F

thoroughly saturate them (an excess does no harm).
Heat for a few minutes with the strong acid till the
chlorides have lost any red appearance; then add about
75 cc. of water, and boil well till every particle of chloride
of iron is dissolved.

Filtering.—Next collect the precipitate of silica on an
ashless filter-paper, contained in a 2¼-in. ribbed funnel
supported on a conical beaker. First of all, rinse the
underside of the cover into the filter, if necessary using a
policeman to detach any adhering splashed-up particles
of silica; then pour through the solution, thoroughly
wash out the beaker, after going over the whole of the
inside with the policeman of course, finally, carefully
washing any silica adhering to the latter on to the filter-
paper. All the washing must be done with cold water.

Washing. — Now comes the point at which most
students at first go wrong in estimating silicon. *Every
trace of iron salt must be washed from the filter-paper.* It
is not sufficient that no yellow tinge is noticeable, the
paper must be washed repeatedly and alternately with
hot dilute *HCl*, and cold water. The former may be
heated in a beaker, and should be poured round the
edges of the filter by means of a glass rod; also direct
the wash-bottle jet upon the edges of the paper: if these
are well washed the rest of the filter and the silica will
take care of themselves. Finally, thoroughly wash with
cold water.

Drying.—As soon as the last washings have passed
through, carefully transfer the paper from the funnel to
a filter-drier, and heat on the plate till quite dry.

Igniting.—Then fold it up and place in a clean, care-
fully-weighed platinum crucible which has been recently
ignited and allowed to cool in the desiccator. The tared

cover of the crucible may be left in the balance-case. Ignite the crucible and its contents in the muffle till the silica is *snow white*.

Weighing.—Allow the crucible to cool in the desiccator, put on the cover, and carefully re-weigh. The increase over the original weighing is SiO_2, containing 46.7% Si. The weight of the silica multiplied by 10 gives the percentage of silicon in the steel.

Methods for Special Steels.

The foregoing process is not applicable to tungsten steels, a method for which is given on p. 161.

In the case of chrome steels, it often happens that after carrying out the above method the silica is not white, owing to the presence of a little oxide of chromium. This should be separated by adding to the crucible containing the impure SiO_2 about 2 grammes of pure acid potassium sulphate $KHSO_4$;[1] the latter is cautiously heated till fused, then more strongly, till white fumes of sulphuric acid are given off; when cold, the mass of potassium sulphate is dissolved out with dilute hydrochloric acid, and the purified silica is filtered off, washed, dried, ignited, and weighed exactly as before described.

Theory of the Process.

The hydrochloric acid, as already shown (p. 55), converts the silicon into silicic acid. In steels containing much over 0.1% of silicon, some of the silica will be

[1] For the preparation of this salt see p. 325.

noticed on the surface of the liquid and sides of the
beaker as a yellowish scum. The yellow coloration is
due to the air in the beaker bringing about a conversion
of a little of the pale-green solution of ferrous chloride
with which the particles are saturated into yellow ferric
chloride, thus—

$$2\ FeCl_2 + 2\ HCl + O = 2\ FeCl_3 + H_2O$$

On evaporating to dryness, more ferric chloride is
formed, whilst the silica is dehydrated and rendered
quite insoluble in acids and water, thus—

$$H_4SiO_4 = SiO_2 + 2\ H_2O$$

On re-dissolving the chlorides of iron and manganese,
and also the phosphorus salts present, the silica, together
with a small quantity of combined carbon which has not
been evolved as hydrocarbon, and any graphite present,
remains suspended in the liquid. The carbon communi-
cates to the silica a dirty appearance, but, on being burnt
off, leaves it a snow-white powder. If the residue has a
reddish tinge or a deep, red-brown ring of Fe_2O_3 round
it, the filter-paper has not been properly washed. If the
ignition has not been strong enough, the precipitate
may be gray with carbon, especially in steel containing
graphite which requires a prolonged burning. In weighing the precipitate, it should be always remembered that
SiO_2 is very hygroscopic, and unless proper precaution is
taken, absorbed aqueous vapour may cause the result to
be recorded higher than is actually the case.

The reason for taking 4·67 grammes of steel is to do
away with any calculation. This weight is $\frac{1}{10}$ the amount
of Si contained in 100 parts of SiO_2, hence the weight
of $SiO_2 \times 10 = {}^{28}/_{60}\ Si$.

As a rule, the ashless filters of the size used in a $2\frac{1}{4}$-in.

funnel leave a negligible residue: if not, $\frac{1}{5}$ the weight of the residue left by igniting five papers in the same packet as the filter used, must be deducted from the weight obtained.

Model of Record.

22 Jan. '84.   Axle Steel.   Blow No. 124.

Weight taken 4·67 grammes.

Weight of crucible and cover + SiO_2 + ash   31·6327
Weight of crucible and cover   31·6263

0·0064 = SiO_2 + ash.

·0064
− ·0006 weight of filter ash.

Grammes SiO_2 ·0058 × 10 = 0·058°/ₒ Si.

Or

·0058
46·7

3736
2335

4·67)·27086(0·058°/ₒ Si as above.
2335

3736
3736

. . . .

The reactions taking place during the purification of the silicon contaminated with Cr_2O_3 are as follow: the acid sulphate on heating strongly forms the normal sulphate, and gives off sulphuric acid thus—2 $HKSO_4$ =

$K_2SO_4 + H_2SO_4$; the latter in contact with the oxide of chromium at a comparatively high temperature converts it into soluble chromic sulphate, thus —

$$Cr_2O_3 + 3 H_2SO_4 = Cr_2(SO_4)_3 + 3 H_2O$$

The silica is left mechanically mixed with the mass of sulphates, and the latter, being quite soluble in dilute hydrochloric acid, are dissolved whilst the insoluble SiO_2 remains as a white residue.

GRAVIMETRIC DETERMINATION OF MANGANESE.

(Re-agent required $(C_2H_3O_2) NH_4$.)

Preparation.—A strong solution of ammonium acetate is best made in the following manner:—Place in a 40-oz. beaker 100 cc. of pure liquid ammonia 880, and add to it the British Pharmacopeia solution of acetic acid containing about 33% of true $C_2H_4O_2$ till the liquid, after thoroughly stirring, turns blue litmus paper red: a volume of acid several times greater than that of the ammonia will be required. Preserve the solution in a well-stoppered bottle. It should be colourless, and form no dark deposit: if the latter precipitates the re-agent is not fit to use, the acid having been impure with tarry matter, which may seriously interfere with the sharp separation of the manganese from the iron. The reaction taking place between the ammonia and the acetic acid is as follows:

$$AmHO + C_2H_4O_2 = Am(C_2H_3O_2) + H_2O$$

Ammonium hydrate and acetic acid yield ammonium acetate and water.

The Ammonium Acetate Process.

Mr. A. A. Blair, in his admirable compilation of the various methods proposed for iron and steel analysis, remarks that the acetate method for the determination of manganese is tedious, and for low manganese steels, objectionable on account of the fact that only one gramme of the steel can be conveniently operated upon.

There is no doubt that if it were necessary to go through the series of chemical gymnastics advocated by Mr. Blair, the acetate method would be found to be extremely tedious, but fortunately for steel analysts, such necessity does not exist. As a matter of fact, an accurate determination of the manganese in 2 or 3 grammes of steel can be readily made by the acetate process in about four hours.

The Method.

Weight taken.—For ordinary steels weigh out into a 40-oz. beaker, marked on the side at 450 cc., exactly 2·4 grammes of steel.

Dissolving—Cover the beaker, and add down the lip 50 cc. of fuming hydrochloric acid. Very quietly boil the liquid on a hot plate till the steel has dissolved, then add 3 cc. of strong nitric acid (sp. gr. 1·43); boil for two minutes, and dilute with hot water to the 450 cc. mark.

Neutralizing.—Heat the liquid to incipient boiling, remove the cover, rinsing the liquid upon the underside into the beaker, next add to the solution dilute liquid ammonia[1] little by little, and finally drop by drop, with constant stirring till the solution has become much darker in colour, and a faint, permanent precipitate has produced a slight turbidity. Carefully avoid over-shooting this point by a too rash addition of ammonia. The above neutralization must be carried out with great care, the liquid being well stirred at a nearly boiling heat with a glass rod after each addition of ammonia till the precipitate at first formed is re-dissolved, being also careful to work down into the solution any precipitate which may adhere to the sides of the beaker.

Precipitating the iron.—Next add 50 cc. of *cold* ammonium acetate solution little by little, with constant stirring, then wash and remove the glass rod, replace the cover, and gradually bring the contents of the beaker to a full boil, which should be maintained for two minutes but not more, then remove from the plate.

Filtering.—Take off the cover, let it drain into the beaker, and place it concave side downwards on an earthenware filter-drier. Pour the solution and bulky, dark red-brown precipitate into a clean flask, graduated at the lower part of the neck for 605 cc.; well wash the cover and beaker with hot water, of course adding the washings to the liquid in the graduated flask; next by means of the wash-bottle jet dilute the liquid with hot water to about 605·5 cc., and render the whole mass thoroughly homogeneous by stirring with a thermometer. As the liquid cools, withdraw the thermometer just clear of it from time to time, till, after the thermometer has drained, the meniscus of the fluid is coincident with the 605 cc. mark. *Note the temperature,* and remove the thermometer with-

[1] Made by adding 25 cc. of cold distilled water to the same volume of 880 ammonia solution.

out washing. Now support over a dry flask, graduated low down in the neck at 500 cc., a 5-in. ribbed funnel containing a *dry* filter of thick German paper, the edges of which are $\frac{1}{2}$ in. below those of the funnel: the latter should also be provided with a 6-in. diameter cover. Pour the liquid and precipitate very gently at first upon the filter, and allow rather less than 500 cc. to pass through. The glass cover should, as far as possible, be kept on the funnel during the filtration to prevent undue evaporation. The precipitate and the unfiltered fluid may now be thrown away. Place the 500 cc. flask on the heating plate and put in it a clean dry thermometer, and raise the temperature to that previously noted; throw out the slight excess of liquid with the thermometer, till, on withdrawing the latter the meniscus of the liquid registers exactly 500 cc. at the original temperature.

Evaporating the filtrate.—Pour the clear or very faintly yellow liquid into a 40-oz. beaker, carefully washing out the flask with hot water, and adding the washings to the main quantity. Next boil down the contents of the beaker either briskly with the cover on, or quietly with the cover off, to about 250 cc.

Removal of traces of iron.—Filter the evaporated liquid, in which may be suspended a small brown precipitate, through a 2-in. ribbed funnel into a 30-oz. registered flask; carefully rinse out the beaker with hot water, and well wash the filter paper with the same; remove the funnel, and thoroughly cool the *crystal clear* liquid by immersing the flask in a trough of cold water, or allowing a stream from the tap to play upon the flask whilst the liquid is shaken around.

Precipitating the manganese.—When cold, add 4 cc. of pure bromine, and give to the liquid a circular motion till only 2 or 3 small drops of bromine remain undissolved, and the solution has a somewhat deep, reddish-brown colour. Next add quietly 30 cc. of 880 liquid ammonia, shake the liquid cautiously round, and place the flask on the hot plate, keeping its contents just short of boiling till the liquid is crystal clear, and the dark-brown precipitate has gathered into rapidly settling flocks.

Filtering off the precipitate.—Collect the precipitate on an ashless filter contained in a 2-in. ribbed funnel; see that every particle is washed out of the flask, if necessary calling in the aid of a long policeman to detach any adhering film or flocks. Wash the paper and its contents thoroughly with hot water, allow to drain, and dry it in the manner already described for the estimation of silicon (see page 66).

Igniting and weighing.—When quite dry fold the filter and place it in a platinum crucible, previously carefully ignited, cooled and tared, and strongly ignite in a gas muffle for 15 minutes. Allow the crucible to go quite cold in the desiccator and re-weigh. The increase is due to Mn_3O_4 containing 72% of metallic manganese. The calculation must be made on the basis that the steel containing the manganese weighed 2 grammes. The colour of the precipitate should be a not very deep red-brown: it should be powdery, and free from any lumpy appearance, otherwise oxide of iron is probably present. As Mn_3O_4 is not hygroscopic, it may, without sensible error, be carefully brushed out of the crucible on to the foil of the balance-pan and weighed direct.

Colorimetric Determination of Ferric Oxide in the Manganese Precipitate.

If any doubt exists as to the purity of the precipitate from Fe_2O_3 (or if it has not been deemed necessary to evaporate the filtrate containing the manganese to half bulk), the latter should be tested for, and if present, estimated colorimetrically, the weight found being of course deducted from that of the Mn_3O_4.

Standard iron solution.—Make a standard solution of ferric chloride by dissolving in a small covered beaker 0·0701 gramme of clean drillings of pure Swedish bar iron (containing 99·8% Fe) in 15 cc. strong *HCl*. When the metal is in solution add to the ferrous chloride 3 *drops* of nitric acid, sp. gr. 1·43. Briskly boil the ferric chloride for a few minutes, and then gently evaporate it to very low bulk, dilute and transfer every trace of the iron solution from the beaker and cover into a 1000 cc. flask, and fill to the mark with distilled water. Next pour the litre of liquid into a large beaker, which must be clean and quite dry; stir thoroughly with a glass rod, and pour back into the flask: by this treatment a homogeneous liquid is obtained corresponding to 0·0001 gramme of Fe_2O_3 in each cc. It should be transferred to a well-stoppered bottle, and its strength legibly labelled.

Estimation of the iron.—Brush the manganese precipitate into a small beaker, put on the cover, add a few cc. of strong *HCl* to dissolve the precipitate, and boil briskly. If any appreciable quantity of iron is present, the solution will have a yellow colour: quietly evaporate off most of the acid, and dissolve up the semi-dry chlorides in 2 cc. of water. Drain the solution into a

20 cc. graduated tube, rinse out of the beaker and add
to the main liquid every trace of chloride solution, using
altogether about 6 cc. of water at three times. Now add
to the tube 1 cc. of a *colourless* solution of sulphocyanide
of ammonium containing about 5% of the salt;[1] add
distilled water to 10 cc., and thoroughly mix the contents of the tube. If much iron is present the liquid will
be blood-red in colour, and even if mere traces of iron
are contained in the manganese precipitate, a pinkish
tinge will be developed. The student with a little experience will be able to judge at once, roughly, the
weight of oxide of iron present. If, as is generally the
case, only a moderate colour is produced, deliver from a
20 cc. burette graduated in tenths into another graduated
20 cc. tube exactly 1 cc. of the standard iron solution;
add 8 cc. of water and 1 cc. of the sulpho-cyanide solution, mix well, and compare the tints of the liquids in
the two tubes in the manner already described on p. 49
for the estimation of carbon by colour. If the standard
is the darker, the oxide of iron present may be ignored,
being under $\frac{1}{10000}$ of a gramme; if the tints are equal
the oxide weighs that amount; if, however, the standard
is lighter than the solution of the precipitate, make up a
fresh standard, taking 2 cc. of the iron solution, 7 cc. of
water, and 1 cc. of sulphocyanide solution. If the standard is still too light, make up fresh standards, advanc-
ing by $\frac{1}{10000}$ of a gramme of oxide till the required
coincident tint is obtained. The last standard will be
made up of 9 cc. of iron and 1 cc. of sulphocyanide
solution, giving a colour corresponding to 0·0009 gramme
of ferric oxide, or a + error of 0·032$\%$ manganese on

[1] An excess must be avoided, as it destroys the colour; on the
other hand, too little fails to develop the full tint.

2 grammes of steel. When such an error is approached it is indicative of some violation by the student of the instructions previously given. It may, however, be due to the use of impure re-agents, introducing during the analysis organic substances other than acetates which have prevented the complete separation of the iron. With pure re-agents and skilful manipulation the amount of Fe_2O_3 seldom exceeds 0·0002 gramme, or a + error of 0·007°/$_0$ Mn.

The reaction taking place between the ferric chloride and the ammonium sulphocyanide (or thiocyanate) is as follows:

$$FeCl_3 + 3 \; AmSCy = Fe(SCy)_3 + 3 \; AmCl$$

Yellow   Colourless   Blood-red   Colourless

Ferric chloride and ammonium thiocyanate yield ferric thiocyanate and ammonium chloride.

Model of Record and Calculation of Result.

Feb. 2, 1884.

Estimation of manganese in open-hearth steel drillings marked *SH.* Weight of steel taken 2·4 grammes.

$$
\begin{array}{rr}
\text{Crucible} + Mn_3O_4 = & 29{\cdot}6467 \\
\text{Weight of crucible} = & 29{\cdot}6283 \\
\hline
 & {\cdot}0184 \\
-\text{ash} & {\cdot}0003 \\
\hline
 & {\cdot}0181 \\
-Fe_2O_3 \text{ by colour} & {\cdot}0002 \\
\hline
Mn_3O_4 = & {\cdot}0179 \\
 & 72 \\
\hline
 & 358 \\
 & 1253 \\
\hline
2) & \overline{1{\cdot}2888} \\
\hline
 & 0{\cdot}644°/_0 \; Mn.
\end{array}
$$

Theory of the foregoing Modification of the Acetate Process.

The authors long ago discarded the use of nitric acid for the preliminary solution of the steel. This acid, which possesses the advantage of at once yielding the iron in the ferric condition, also brings into solution the brown organic matter containing the carbon. This, when present in some quantity, as in the case of tool steel, has a decided tendency to prevent the complete precipitation of the iron, retaining a small quantity in solution till the final precipitation of the hydrate of manganese with bromine and ammonia; it will then of course be found with the ignited Mn_3O_4 as Fe_2O_3.

The nitric acid added to the solution of *ferrous* chloride oxidizes (chlorinizes) it to *ferric* chloride, thus:

$$FeCl_2 + HNO_3 + HCl = FeCl_3 + H_2O + NO_2$$

Pale-green ferrous chloride, nitric and hydrochloric acids yield yellow ferric chloride, water, and the deep brown gas, peroxide of nitrogen. The manganese remains as *manganous* chloride $MnCl_2$, and an indispensable condition for the process is, that no ferrous chloride must be present, *because ferrous acetate is soluble in water acidulated with acetic acid.* During the neutralization with ammonium hydrate, the free hydrochloric and nitric acids are converted respectively into neutral ammonium chloride and nitrate, thus:

$$HCl + AmHO = AmCl + H_2O$$
$$HNO_3 + AmHO = AmNO_3 + H_2O$$

The further addition of ammonia beyond the point of neutralization of the free acids results in the formation of highly basic ferric salts before the formation of a permanent precipitate. (See theory of estimation of nickel, p. 194.)

On the addition of ammonium acetate, the iron is precipitated as an indefinitely constituted mixture of ferric acetate and hydrate $[x\ Fe_2(C_2H_3O_2)_6 + y\ Fe_2(HO)_6]$, generally known as basic ferric acetate, and some free acetic acid is liberated. The complex reactions bringing about this result are not clearly known, but the precipitate with variations in composition varies in appearance; three different types must be mentioned:

1. A rather dark red-brown precipitate, which settles fairly rapidly and filters moderately quickly, the filtrate being clear and colourless.

2. A slimy precipitate of a yellowish red-brown colour, which filters very slowly, the filtrate being often coloured.

3. A rapidly subsiding brick-dust coloured precipitate, the finely-divided portions of which usually pass through the pores of the paper with the filtrate.

The first-mentioned precipitate is the one the student should always endeavour to obtain. Its formation indicates a sharp separation of the iron and manganese, and proves that the neutralization has been successfully performed. If the practical instructions already given are carefully carried out, the second and third highly objectionable forms of precipitate will not be obtained. When, however, some accidental departure from the conditions under which the analysis should be made results in the production of either of these modifications of basic ferric acetate, it is always advisable to start the analysis again, and obtain the proper precipitate.

The object of evaporating the solution containing the manganous acetate to half its original bulk, is to ensure the precipitation of any iron present in the filtrate. A small quantity sometimes remains dissolved with the manganese, but is thrown down during the second boiling. The bromine is added as an *oxidizing agent* to convert the manganous into manganic hydrate at the moment of its precipitation with ammonia. Manganous hydrate $Mn(HO)_2$ *is soluble in ammonium salts*; manganic hydrate $Mn_2O_2(HO)_2$, however, is *quite insoluble* in their presence, and is therefore completely precipitated thus:

1. $(C_2H_3O_2)_2Mn + 2\ AmHO = Mn(HO)_2 + 2\ (C_2H_3O_2)Am$. Manganous acetate and ammonium hydrate yield manganous hydrate and ammonium acetate.

2. $2\ Mn(HO)_2 + Br_2 = Mn_2O_2(HO)_2 + 2\ HBr$

Manganous hydrate, bromine, and water yield manganic hydrate and hydrobromic acid.

The last-named is of course neutralized by the excess of ammonia present, thus:

3. $HBr + AmHO = AmBr + H_2O$. Hydrobromic acid and ammonium hydrate yield ammonium bromide and water.

Of course these three reactions take place practically simultaneously, and it will be observed that the bromine acts as an oxidant by decomposing water, combining with the hydrogen, and liberating the (nascent) oxygen.

The use of a fixed alkali, namely, sodium carbonate for neutralizing and sodium acetate for precipitating, has been insisted upon as being absolutely necessary to ensure success, because the manganic hydrate is alleged not to be completely precipitated in the presence of large quantities of ammonium salts. As a matter of fact, the employment of ammonium compounds is attended by several advantages over the use of sodium salts, which, in the authors' opinion, produce instead of prevent error. Where possible, precipitations from solutions of the fixed alkalies should always be avoided; there is little doubt that the belief in the partial solubility of manganic hydrate in ammonium chloride and bromide arose through chemists accepting, without personal investigation, the statement of Fresenius to that effect.

The ignition should be made with the lid off the crucible, in a *hot* muffle furnace, and be continued for ten minutes after the filter-paper has all been burned off, otherwise the residue may not strictly conform to the formula Mn_3O_4, which, under the above conditions, it will possess.

Only one other point remains to be explained. The student, having made even one estimation of manganese, will readily appreciate the difficulty of washing the large iron precipitate till free from manganese, and also the time that will be thus lost. In the instructions given, this difficulty has been entirely done away with by taking only $\frac{5}{6}$ of the filtrate; the manganese in the $2\cdot4$ grammes of steel taken for analysis was obtained in a solution of known temperature occupying at that temperature 600 cc. (The extra 5 cc. form a correction for two small sources of error, first, the volume of the precipitate itself; second, the slight concentration of the hot liquid from evaporation during filtration.) Therefore, in 500 cc. of the liquid at a like temperature, equalling $\frac{5}{6}$ of the total volume, there will be contained the manganese present in $\frac{5}{6}$ of the weight of steel originally taken, and $\frac{5}{6}$ of $2\cdot4$ grammes $= 2$ grammes.

There is no necessity in estimating manganese in ordinary steel to precipitate the iron twice, or indeed, as one author recommends, three times. The method just dealt with gives, with a little practice, remarkably sharp separations, as will be seen from the following table, embodying results obtained on various steels by single and double precipitations of the iron:

Blow No. or mark.	% Manganese by single precipitation.	% Manganese by double precipitation.	
418	0·684	0·684	=
419	0·745	0·763	+ ·019
420	0·710	0·710	=
SCX	0·634	0·634	=
SH	0·644	0·655	+ ·011
124	1·364	1·357	− ·007

Determination of Manganese in Special Steels.

Nickel and copper.—If the steel in which the manganese is being determined contains nickel or copper, a portion of the last-named metals will pass into the filtrate containing the manganese, and although the hydrates of nickel and copper are both soluble in ammonia, small percentages are nevertheless very liable to be carried down with the manganese precipitate: to prevent the possibility of this, pass through the boiling manganese filtrate (at that stage when it has been concentrated to 250 cc. to throw down the last traces of iron) a brisk current of washed sulphuretted hydrogen from a Kipp's apparatus for five minutes. The nickel and copper are completely precipitated as black sulphides NiS and CuS. These are filtered off along with the previously precipitated residue of iron, and are well washed with water containing a little H_2S in solution. The manganese in the filtrate is then precipitated in the usual manner with bromine and ammonia.

High silicon, tungsten, and graphite.—When these substances are present, they remain suspended in the solution, and may interfere with the accurate determination of the exact point at which the liquid is neutralized: it is therefore advisable to commence the analysis on 2·88 grammes of drillings, and after the oxidation of the hydrochloric acid solution of the steel with nitric acid, to evaporate the liquid to about 10 cc., and then to transfer it without loss to a 60 cc. flask; dilute to the mark when cold, mix the liquid thoroughly, and filter off through dry paper contained in a 2-in. funnel 50 cc. of the liquid into a dry marked flask. This 50 cc. of solution will contain ⅚ of 2·88 or 2·4 grammes of steel. It is transferred without loss to the marked 40-oz. beaker, diluted to 450 cc., and the analysis proceeded with as usual.

Chromium and aluminium.—These elements, although their hydrates and acetates are under ordinary circumstances soluble in free acetic acid, are, under the conditions present during the estimation of manganese, completely carried down with the iron precipitate, as the authors have never found them present in the residue of Mn_3O_4.[1]

VOLUMETRIC DETERMINATION OF MANGANESE.

Method I. (Ford and Williams, modified.)

(Time occupied, about 1 hour.)

Re-agents required.

Pure iron.—This must be obtained in the form of clean drillings from Swedish Lancashire hearth bar, preferably

[1] See, however, determination of manganese in high-speed steels on p. 248.

of the brand known as "little S" ⑤, which is manufactured from the middle bed Dannemora ore, and usually contains 99·8% of iron.

Dilute solution of $K_6(C_3N_3)_4Fe_2$.—Dissolve one *small* fragment of this salt (usually known as red prussiate of potash, or potassium ferricyanide) in 10 cc. of distilled water. This solution should be freshly made for each set of indications.

Standard solution of $K_2Cr_2O_7$. — Dissolve 1·7813 grammes of pure dry, selected crystals of potassium bichromate in about 250 cc. of hot water contained in a 20-oz beaker. When cold, carefully transfer the solution without the smallest loss into a clean litre flask; dilute exactly to the mark with cold distilled water, and mix the contents of the flask till perfectly homogeneous. Store this solution in a well-stoppered bottle, and label it "100 cc. $= 0·2036$ gramme *Fe*, or 2% *Mn* on 5 grammes of steel."

The Process.

Dissolving.—Dissolve 5 grammes of drillings weighed out into a 20-oz. covered beaker in 60 cc. of nitric acid, sp. gr. 1·2, and quietly boil down to about 30 cc.

Precipitation of MnO_2.—Next add 10 cc. of nitric acid, sp. gr. 1·43, and then very cautiously 5 grammes of pure, dry, powdered chlorate of potash ($KClO_3$), boil for a few minutes (of course with the cover on), and twice more repeat the treatment with strong nitric acid and potassic chlorate, thus using altogether 30 cc. of HNO_3 and 15 grammes of $KClO_3$. After the last addition boil well, remove from the plate, dilute with 75 cc. of hot water, and shake round the contents of the beaker.

Filtering.—Allow the precipitate to settle somewhat, and then collect it upon a 110 mm. pure filter contained in a 2¼-in. funnel, detaching as far as possible every particle of adhering precipitate from the sides of the beaker by means of a policeman. It sometimes happens that a ring composed of a thin film of precipitate defies removal; the weight of this, however, is so minute that it may be ignored without sensible error. The precipitate and filter paper must now be thoroughly washed with hot water till quite free from nitric acid, and the drops from the stem of the funnel will no longer turn blue litmus paper red.

Titrating.—When weighing out the steel for analysis, there should also be weighed out into a perfectly clean, dry 10-oz. flask 0·204 gramme of the Swedish iron drillings, and about the time the washing of the precipitate is commenced, add to the flask 70 cc. of dilute sulphuric acid (1 in 7), place a watch-glass on the flask, and boil on the hot plate till the last particle of iron is dissolved. Then remove the flask and rinse the drop from the underside of the watch-glass. Next fold the filter containing the brown precipitate, and cautiously drop it bodily down the neck of the flask into the iron solution. Shake the liquid round once or twice till the whole of the precipitate has dissolved and only white filter paper remains.

Fill up a 50 cc. burette, graduated in tenths, and carefully set the meniscus of the liquid at zero. The standard solution is then run into the flask till the whole of the ferrous sulphate is oxidized. The exact point at which this occurs is determined by the indicator solution of ferricyanide. Two or three rows of small drops of the latter are placed upon a glazed white porcelain slab by means of a glass rod. As long as any unoxidized iron remains in the flask, a drop of the liquid withdrawn on a glass rod and placed on a slab close to a drop of ferricyanide solution will, on the two drops being allowed to mingle, produce a blue coloration, which fades in intensity as the final point is approached. As soon as this happens, not more than half a cc. of bichromate solution should be added between each trial. In deciding when the iron solution has ceased to re-act with the indicator, it must be recollected that the chromic sulphate produced in the reaction has itself a greenish tint, so that a drop of the liquid *per se* should be compared on the slab alongside the drop mixed with ferricyanide. It should also be remembered, that when the proportion of ferrous salt becomes very small, the colour is not developed for perhaps half a minute. With a little practice, it will be found much easier to carry out the foregoing titration than to describe it.

If under 1% of manganese is present in the steel under examination, the burette after the meniscus of its contents has been run down exactly to the 50 cc. mark, will require refilling, and the amount of iron prescribed is only capable of registering a maximum of 2% of manganese, which of course more than meets the case of ordinary steels. *The student should be very careful after each addition of bichromate to shake the flask round so as to thoroughly mix the liquids.*

Reading off the percentage.—Subtract the number of cc.s used for 100: each cc. of the remainder equals $\cdot02\%$ of manganese, therefore, remainder $\times \cdot 02 = \% \ Mn$.

Examples.

1. 34 cc. of bichromate solution were required.
   Then $100 - 34 = 66$, and $66 \times \cdot 02 = 1\cdot 32\%$ *Mn.*

2. 87·5 cc. of bichromate solution were required.
   Then $100 - 87\cdot 5 = 12\cdot 5$, and $12\cdot 5 \times \cdot 02 = 0\cdot 25\%$ *Mn.*

Theory of the Foregoing Method.

The fact that in a strong nitric acid solution manganous nitrate is, by a complex reaction, oxidized to insoluble manganese dioxide on the addition of $KClO_3$ was first noticed by Hannay. The peroxide of manganese precipitate is, however, contaminated with basic iron and potash salts, and hence cannot be weighed direct. On dissolving the precipitate in a solution of ferrous sulphate containing an excess of free sulphuric acid, the following reaction takes place :

$$MnO_2 + 2\ FeSO_4 + 2\ H_2SO_4 = MnSO_4 + Fe_2(SO_4)_3 + 2\ H_2O$$
$$\underset{(55)}{} \quad \underset{(56)}{}$$

Peroxide of manganese, ferrous sulphate, and sulphuric acid yield manganous sulphate, ferric sulphate, and water. It is therefore evident that 55 (55×1) parts by weight of manganese in the form of dioxide, oxidize 112 (56×2) parts by weight of ferrous iron into ferric iron. If a known weight and an excess of ferrous iron is present, it is evident that if the unoxidized excess can be accurately determined the amount of iron oxidized by the manganese will then be known, and consequently the weight of the manganese itself. The excess of ferrous iron is estimated by observing how much $K_2Cr_2O_7$ is required to oxidize it according to the following reaction (Penny's process):

$$K_2Cr_2O_7 + 6FeSO_4 + 7H_2SO_4 = 3Fe_2(SO_4)_3 + Cr_2(SO_4)_3 + K_2SO_4 + 7H_2O$$
$$\text{(39)(52)(16)} \quad \text{(56)}$$

Potassium bichromate, ferrous sulphate, and sulphuric acid yield ferric, chromic, and potassic sulphates and water. 294 (78 + 104 + 112) parts by weight of $K_2Cr_2O_7$ oxidize 336 (56 × 6) parts of iron from the ferrous to the ferric condition; the weight of iron used is found thus:

Required the weight of iron which 2% of manganese in 5 grammes of steel will oxidize.

2% of 5 grammes $= \dfrac{5 \times 2}{100} = 0\cdot1$ gramme of Mn.

Then if 55 parts of Mn oxidize 112 parts of Fe } $\dfrac{112 \times \cdot1}{55} = 0\cdot2036$ gr. Fe.
      $0\cdot1$,,   ,,   ,, x ,,   ,, }

But the iron employed contains $99\cdot8\%$ Fe.

Hence if $99\cdot8 = \cdot2036$ } $\dfrac{\cdot2036 \times 100}{99\cdot8} = 0\cdot204$ gramme Fe.
     $100\cdot0 = x$ }

That is to say, $0\cdot204$ gramme of the slightly impure iron is equivalent to $0\cdot2036$ gramme of chemically pure metal.

Then if 336 parts of Fe require 294 parts of $K_2Cr_2O_7$
     $0\cdot2036$,,   ,,   ,, x ,,   ,,
     $\dfrac{294 \times \cdot2036}{336} = 0\cdot178125$ gramme of $K_2Cr_2O_7$

This weight (dissolved in 100 cc.) is equal in oxidizing power to $0\cdot1$ gramme of manganese in the form of MnO_2; for 1000 cc. ten times the weight would be required, or $1\cdot7813$ grammes. The accuracy of the solution should be proved by titrating $0\cdot204$ gramme of Swedish iron dissolved in excess of H_2SO_4 in the manner already described; exactly 100 cc. should be required to complete the oxidation. If however, the solution is too strong, the required quantity of water to adjust it is calculated; if too weak, the necessary $K_2Cr_2O_7$ to bring it up to strength is weighed out and dissolved in the 900 cc. of remaining solution. Examples:

1. It was found that only 99·6 cc. were required, hence each 99·6 cc. require diluting with 0·4 cc. of water, therefore the 900 cc. left require:

$$\frac{900 \times \cdot 4}{99 \cdot 6} = 3 \cdot 7 \text{ cc. of water adding to them to}$$

make the standard solution correct.

2. On titrating 100·5 cc. of the standard solution were required.

Hence in 900 cc. the error is equivalent to 4·5 cc. of water devoid of bichromate.

Then if 1000 cc. require 1·7813 grammes $K_2Cr_2O_7$

    4·5   ,, x ,,   ,,

$$\frac{1 \cdot 7813 \times 4 \cdot 5}{1000} = 0 \cdot 008 \text{ gramme } K_2Cr_2O_7$$

Thus 8 milligrammes of bichromate are required to bring the solution to its proper strength, which should, however, be checked by a second titration. In works laboratories it is best to make up and standardize a large Winchester quart (holding several litres) of solution.

The blue colour produced by *ferrous* salts with potassium ferricyanide is due to a precipitate, or, in dilute solutions, to an emulsion of ferrous ferricyanide or Turnbull's blue, which has the empirical formula $Fe_3(CN)_{12}$. *Ferric* salts give only a very faint brown coloration with dilute solutions of red prussiate of potash. It will be seen that the principle underlying the reactions occurring in the volumetric estimation of manganese is:

1. The measurement of the oxygen taken by the residual ferrous iron from the bichromate.

2. From the above datum the determination of the oxygen originally yielded to the ferrous iron by the manganese dioxide.

In the first-named reaction chromic anhydride CrO_3 is reduced to chromic oxide Cr_2O_3, and the ferrous oxide FeO is oxidized to ferric oxide Fe_2O_3.

In the second reaction, manganese peroxide MnO_2 is reduced to manganous oxide MnO, and the liberated atom of oxygen converts its atomic equivalent of FeO to Fe_2O_3.

The student should thoroughly master these reactions, because they will be again used for several analyses to be described later on. Their mastery necessitates a thorough knowledge of elementary inorganic chemistry, particularly with reference to the displaceable hydrogen of acids, the existence of higher and lower basic oxides, and the formation of both acid-forming and basic oxides by the same metal.

Method II. (Reddrop and Ramage, modified.)

(Time occupied, 20 minutes.)

Re-agents required.

Decinormal potassium permanganate.—This is made by dissolving 3·16 grammes of the pure re-crystallized salt in distilled water and making up to 1000 cc. The solution should be stored in a dark blue Winchester, and when not in use kept in the dark. It retains its strength under these circumstances very well, but it is advisable to check it from time to time, and either adjust it in the manner already described for bichromate solutions, or introduce the necessary correction in the subsequent calculation of the result obtained in the process. The determination of the strength is rapidly accomplished by titration against a known weight of ferrous iron. Pure bar iron is not to be recommended in this case because the carbon it contains, small in amount though it is, exerts an appreciable influence, being readily oxidized by the permanganate. Pure, dry, re-crystallized ferrous ammonium sulphate, 1·96 grammes, is weighed out and transferred to a small flask, dissolved in distilled water, 1 or 2 cc. of strong sulphuric acid added, and the permanganate run in from a burette, freely at first and slowly towards the end of the titration, until a permanent pale pink colour is obtained, the flask being all the time kept in motion. Exactly 50 cc. of the permanganate solution should be required.

Ferrous ammonium sulphate solution.—A decinormal solution of this salt is obtained by dissolving exactly 39·2 grammes of the pure crystals in water acidulated with sulphuric acid and making up to 1000 cc. As the solution, however, slowly loses its reducing power by the oxidation of the iron, it is advisable to prepare it by weighing off approximately 40 grammes of the crystals, dissolving, and making up to the litre mark. The solution should contain from 20 to 30 cc. of strong sulphuric acid in each litre.

Sodium bismuthate.—This re-agent is a brown amorphous powder and is an article of commerce. It may be prepared in the laboratory as follows:—20 parts of caustic soda are heated nearly to redness in an iron crucible, and 10 parts of dried basic nitrate of bismuth added in

small quantities at a time; 2 parts of sodium peroxide
are then added and the whole fusion then poured out on
an iron plate. The melt is powdered, treated five or six
times with water to dissolve out the excess of soluble
sodium compounds which are removed by decantation,
and the residue dried, powdered and finely sieved.

The Process.

Dissolving, etc.—Weigh off exactly 1·1 grammes of the
drillings into a small flask and add 30 cc. nitric acid
s.g. 1·20. When the violent action has subsided, bring
to boiling on the hot plate and add from time to time a
pinch of sodium bismuthate in order to oxidize the carbonaceous matter. On the introduction of this re-agent
the colour of permanganic acid momentarily flashes up,
but equally quickly disappears again, being used up in
the oxidation of the carbon, and by decomposition at the
temperature of the solution. The amount of bismuthate
to be added depends upon the amount of carbon in the
sample. Mild steels require only a few milligrams added
all at once, and no serious error is introduced in such
cases by its entire omission, but hard steels, white irons,
spiegels, etc., demand considerably more, and very grave
errors would result from the incomplete oxidation of the
carbon by the bismuthate in the hot solution. The
student will find no difficulty after a little experience
in deciding the point of complete oxidation, and a further guide is furnished in most cases by the steel itself.
Most steels contain a sufficient amount of manganese
to yield, when the oxidation of the carbonaceous matter

is complete, a permanent brown precipitate of hydrated peroxide of manganese. This precipitate is then just taken into solution by the addition of a few drops of sulphurous acid or ferrous sulphate solution and the contents of the flask at once cooled under the tap.

Oxidizing.—To the thoroughly-cooled liquid add from $1\frac{1}{2}$ to 2 grammes of sodium bismuthate, and shake the flask several times during a period of about three minutes. Allow to settle.

Filtration.—Prepare a filter of asbestos, recently ignited, and pour on the richly-coloured supernatant liquid without disturbing the solid residue consisting of excess of bismuthate more than necessary. Shake up the latter several times with small quantities of dilute nitric acid of 2% strength, allowing to settle each time and pouring the liquid through the filter. The washing is complete when the liquid comes through the filter perfectly colourless.

The titration.—Two burettes are filled to the mark, one with the standard solution of decinormal permanganate and the other with the ferrous ammonium sulphate solution. The flask containing the assay is then placed under the latter and the ferrous solution run in with shaking until the colour is more than completely discharged, being replaced by a pale green one. The flask is then placed under the permanganate burette and the solution run in a drop at a time until a pale but pronounced pink colouration is produced.

Standardizing the ferrous solution.—After taking the readings of both burettes, about 20 cc. of the ferrous solution are run into the same flask without washing out the finished assay and the titration with permanganate again performed, the exact end point being accurately

The actual metallic manganese in 316 parts of $KMnO_4$ is $2 \times 55 = 110$, and in each cc. of $\dfrac{N}{10}$ permanganate the actual metallic manganese is therefore 0·0011 gramme, and represents 0·1% of Mn when working on 1·1 gramme of steel.

The student may be inclined to view with suspicion any process in which ferrous sulphate is used for titrating purposes in the presence of such a powerful oxidant as nitric acid, but it should be remembered that although the steel is dissolved originally in acid of s.g. 1·20, the subsequent washing with 2% acid considerably reduces the acid strength of the filtrate and provides a solution which as a matter of fact is without action in the cold on acidified ferrous solutions except on unnecessarily prolonged standing.

When a steel contains chromium, the addition of bismuthate to the hot solution for the purpose of destroying the organic colouring matter converts some of this element to chromic acid. This, of course, would react in the final titration with ferrous sulphate, and make the manganese result too high. It is necessary in such cases to add rather more sulphurous acid than is just required to clear the precipitated manganese peroxide, thus reducing the chromic acid again. After cooling, the assay should be proceeded with as quickly as possible to completion, and experience will show that, operating in cold solutions, the amount of chromium oxidized in the time occupied is negligible.

When a determination is finished, the asbestos filter is transferred to a wide-mouthed bottle containing hydrochloric acid which immediately decomposes and dissolves the sodium bismuthate, generating chlorine gas.

When a new determination is to be made, the same asbestos can be used for preparing a filter, but particular care must be taken to wash away from it every trace of free chlorine or of hydrochloric acid before commencing the filtration. The presence of the latter is, as already stated, altogether inadmissible, as it decomposes permanganate solutions, thus:

$$2\ KMnO_4 + 16\ HCl = 2\ KCl + 2\ MnCl_2 + 8\ H_2O + 5\ Cl_2$$

Method III. (Walters, modified.)

(Time occupied, 15 minutes.)

Re-agents required.

Ammonium persulphate.—This is a white crystalline solid, slightly deliquescent, and is an article of commerce.

Solution of silver nitrate.—Dissolve approximately 1·7 gramme of the pure salt in distilled water, and dilute to 1000 cc.

Solution of sodium arsenite.—Dissolve about 5 grammes of pure arsenious oxide, As_4O_6, in 5 or 6 times its weight of sodium bicarbonate by boiling the two solids together with 200 cc. of water. The solution is diluted when cold to 1 litre. This, the stock solution, is approximately 10 times stronger than necessary; for use, therefore, 10 cc. of it are diluted with 90 cc. of water.

H

The Process.

Dissolving.—Weigh 0·25 gramme of the sample, and the same weight of a steel, the manganese contents of which are known, and transfer them separately to small boiling tubes about an inch in diameter. Add to each 10 cc. of nitric acid s.g. 1·20, and when the effervescence has subsided, boil by holding the naked tubes in the bunsen flame until nitrous fumes are all expelled.

Oxidation.—Now add 10 cc. of the silver nitrate solution to each tube, and then approximately 1 gramme of the ammonium persulphate re-agent. Wash down any clinging particles of the latter, and slowly raise the whole mixture to the boiling point again. The permanganate colour soon develops and reaches its maximum intensity at the boiling point, to the accompaniment of a copious evolution of oxygen. Cool off rapidly under the tap, so as to stop the effervescence and retain a certain amount of unchanged persulphate to the decomposition of which the generation of oxygen is due.

Titration.—The richly-coloured solutions are transferred to small flasks, the latter in turn placed on a white tile under a burette charged with the sodium arsenite solution and the solution run in in a stream of rapid drops whilst the contents of the flask are kept in motion. The end point is reached when the permanganate colour is just replaced by a characteristic pale green one. If any uncertainty exists as to the termination of the reaction, another gramme of ammonium persulphate may be added, the liquid heated to boiling, cooled off, and the solution titrated again.

Calculation of Result.—This is done at once, for the

number of cc. of the arsenite solution required for a definite percentage of manganese is furnished by the standard steel and a simple proportion yields the required figure for the unknown sample.

Remarks.—The sodium arsenite, made as directed, obviously need have no fixed strength. It is run in each assay against the standard steel; approximately 1 cc. of it represents 0·1% of Mn. Different operators will use different amounts of the same arsenite solution in titrating the same amount of permanganate. The cause of this consists primarily in the fact that the latter contains a certain amount of undecomposed ammonium persulphate capable of re-oxidizing the manganese. When, for instance, a titration is adjudged to be finished, the purple colour will again develop even in the cold after a few minutes' standing, and as the oxidizing power is at work during the titration, different results will be secured because different operators will take different amounts of time in reaching the end. The results are in all cases reliable, nevertheless, provided the standard steel is treated in all respects like the unknown sample.

Theory of the Process.

The oxidizing power of persulphates depends upon their decomposition in hot solution with generation of oxygen.

$$(NH_4)_2S_2O_8 + H_2O = (NH_4)_2SO_4 + H_2SO_4 + O$$

The decomposition is much more rapid in the presence of silver nitrate, which acts essentially as a catalytic agent. Probably silver persulphate is momentarily formed, and is at once decomposed again, silver nitrate being again formed and ready to transform more of the ammonium salt, thus:

$$Ag_2S_2O_8 + 2\ HNO_3 + H_2O = 2\ AgNO_3 + 2\ H_2SO_4 + O$$

The nascent oxygen effects the change to permanganate according to the skeleton equation:

$$2\ MnO + 5\ (O) = Mn_2O_7$$

and we have, using ammonium persulphate, the enlarged equation:

$$2\ Mn(NO_3)_2 + 5\ Am_2S_2O_8 + 8\ H_2O = 2\ HMnO_4 +$$
$$5\ Am_2SO_4 + 5\ H_2SO_4 + 4\ HNO_3$$

expressing the oxidation of a manganous salt (nitrate) to the condition of permanganic acid.

The oxidation of sodium arsenite to sodium arsenate at the expense of the permanganic acid may be formulated thus:

$$2\ HMnO_4 + 5\ Na_3AsO_3 + 4\ HNO_3 = 5\ Na_3AsO_4 +$$
$$2\ Mn(NO_3)_2 + 3\ H_2O.$$

COLORIMETRIC DETERMINATION OF MANGANESE.

The Red Lead Process.

(Time occupied, about 2 hours.)

This method bears a general resemblance to that by means of which combined carbon is estimated by colour, and several of the precautions given as absolutely necessary to obtain accurate results for the latter process apply with equal force to the present method. In the first place, a set of standard steels the manganese present in which has been settled as the mean of several concordant estimations, is required. The following table shows a useful set of standards, the percentage of manganese in the steels with which the respective standards should be employed, and the most convenient weight of steel to be taken for analysis.

Approximate Manganese % in the standard steel.	per cent. of Manganese in the steel under examination.	Convenient weight in grammes to use for analysis.
0·15	0·1 to 0·2	0·15
0·30	0·2 ,, 0·4	0·10
0·60	0·4 ,, 0·8	0·07
1·00	0·8 ,, 1·2	0·05
1·40	1·2 ,, 1·6	0·03

In the authors' opinion, it is not advisable to attempt to estimate manganese by the colour test much above the limit indicated in the above table.

The Process.

Re-agent required: pure, clean red lead, $Pb_3O_4 = (PbO)_2PbO_2$.

Weighing out.—Weigh out into clean, dry test tubes, 6 in. long by $\frac{1}{2}$-in. diameter, and marked at 10 cc., equal weights of the steels and their requisite standards, the percentage of the latter and the distinguishing number of the former being attached by means of a little square of gummed paper.

Dissolving.—Add to each tube from a burette 3 cc. of nitric acid, sp. gr. 1·2, and dissolve the steels exactly as for carbons on p. 47.

Diluting.—Next dilute each solution with 3 cc. of water.

Addition to Pb_3O_4.—After well boiling the bath for five minutes, add to each tube about 1 gramme of red-lead, which is conveniently delivered into the solutions from a glass tube. The latter may be made to measure out the proper weight of re-agent in the following manner. Take a glass tube 6 mm. in diameter and about 200 mm. long, and grind its ends level on stretched emery cloth. Then fit into it a glass rod ground quite flat at one end, and having a knob at the other, so that when the bulged-out portion rests on one end of the tube, the flat face of the rod is 9 mm. from the other end. The rod should very closely fit the bore of the tube. Completely and compactly fill the vacant portion with Pb_3O_4 by dipping it into the wide-mouthed bottle holding the re-agent. Withdraw the glass rod (which during the filling requires holding tightly in position), and with another made in exactly the same way, and of the same diameter, but 230 mm. long, cautiously project the moulded and adherent piece of red-lead into the acid.

Boiling.—Next briskly boil the bath for five minutes.

Diluting.—Take out the tubes, and with the wash-bottle jet dilute each solution till the meniscus of the liquid is on the 10 cc. mark.

Mixing.—Well mix the contents of each tube by means of a flat-headed glass rod plunger. The latter, after shaking free from adherent liquid, may be used from solution to solution without perceptible error.

Settling in the dark.—Next place the rack containing the tubes in a dark cupboard, and allow the deep brown PbO_2 to settle for at least an hour, till the liquid is quite clear from suspended oxide.

Comparing the colours.—The purple liquids are then conveyed to 20 cc. stoppered and graduated tubes by

means of a 5 cc. ball pipette of such a size that the ball
lodges on top of the test tube, whilst the pointed end of
the stem is at least one inch from the bottom; the mark
of the pipette should be just above the ball. Withdraw
and deliver exactly 5 cc. of each solution into the comparing tubes: the pipette need not be washed, but should
be shaken free from visible liquid at each withdrawal. The
standard is made up to the mark, the stopper of the tube
inserted, and the liquid thoroughly mixed, just as in the
carbon test. The solution of the unknown steel is diluted
and mixed (always using the stopper and not the finger to
close the mouth of the tube), till the colours match when
compared against the wet filter-paper, after using the
precaution referred to on p. 49, of reversing the relative
positions of the tubes before deciding on the final reading.
The following table indicates the volume to which the
various standards should be diluted, and the conversion
of the cc.s registered by the steels under analysis into
percentages.

Mn % in standard, say,	Dilute to cc.	To convert cc. registered by Steel into % Mn.
0·14	7·0	Multiply by 0·02
0·31	6·2	,, ,, 0·05
0·58	11·6	,, ,, 0·05
1·03	10·3	,, ,, 0·10
1·42	14·2	,, ,, 0·10

Examples.

1. With the 0·14 standard the unknown steel matched
at 6·2 cc. $6\cdot2 \times \cdot02 = 0\cdot124$, say $0\cdot12\%$ Mn.

2. With the 0·58 standard the steel registered 10·4 cc. 10·4 × ·05 = 0·52% *Mn*.

3. With the 1·42 standard steel required diluting to 13·7 cc. 13·7 × ·1 = 1·37% *Mn*.

Theory of the Colour Process.

When the red-lead is added it forms nitrate of lead, and precipitates dark PbO_2, thus:

$$(2\,PbO + PbO_2) + 4\,HNO_3 = 2\,Pb(NO_3)_2 + 2\,H_2O + PbO_2$$

The PbO_2 by a complex reaction oxidizes the manganous nitrate into purple red permanganic acid $HMnO_4$, the colour being within reasonable limits proportional to the manganese present. The solution is gradually bleached by light, hence the advisability of allowing the excess of peroxide of lead to settle in the dark. Permanganic acid is readily reduced (of course losing its colour) by contact with organic matter;[1] for this reason it is safer to make the comparisons in stoppered tubes. The success of this colour process seems to a great extent to depend upon having the manganese present in exceedingly small quantities, together with a fairly large excess of PbO_2. The method is not available for chrome steels.[2] Some chemists prefer to carry out the oxidation in a bath of chloride of calcium solution, which boils at about 110° C. Such a liquid may be obtained by dissolving 500 grammes of

[1] The carbon colouring matter seems to be destroyed during the process.

[2] These are not completely soluble in nitric acid, and, moreover, the dissolved chromium is converted by the PbO_2 into yellow chromic acid H_2CrO_4.

the fully hydrated salt $(CaCl_2 + 6\ HO)$ in 500 cc. of water, but the authors have never found its employment attended by any noticeable advantage.

The red-lead used should be ascertained by a blank experiment (made on 3 cc. of 1·20 acid, 3 cc. of water, and 1 gramme of Pb_3O_4) to be quite free from every trace of manganese, otherwise the amount added to each tube must be exactly weighed so as to give a constant error: this procedure, however, should if possible be avoided, as samples of manganese-free red-lead are obtainable.

Other Methods.

The colorimetric estimation of manganese can be much more quickly accomplished by using either sodium bismuthate or ammonium persulphate, since these re-agents so rapidly transform manganese salts into permanganic acid.

It is often convenient to effect the determination on the solutions left in the comparing tubes when the "colour carbon" test has been done. About one-quarter of a gramme of sodium bismuthate is added, and after mixing the liquid allowed to stand. A measured amount of the clear supernatant liquid is decanted and its colour compared with that yielded by a standard steel of known manganese contents.

In the case of ammonium persulphate, several cc. of a very dilute solution of silver nitrate (about 1 gramme of the solid in a litre of water) are added before the addition of the re-agent (0·25 gramme). After heating to the boiling point, cool off rapidly and compare measured fractional volumes as before.

As a guide to the student, the figures of an actual estimation by the persulphate method are appended. The colour carbon determination not being required, ·05 g. of the sample and the same weight of a standard steel ($Mn = 0·82\%$) were weighed into dry test tubes, dissolved in 3 cc. HNO_3, 1·20, 3 cc. of silver nitrate solution added after boiling out nitrous fumes over naked flame, ·25 gramme (approximately) of ammonium persulphate added, the liquids heated to boiling and at once cooled off. They were then transferred to 100 cc. flasks, diluted to the mark, and after mixing, 10 cc. of the standard steel solution transferred to a comparing tube. Its colour was matched by 10 cc. of the sample after diluting the latter to 12·5 cc. The Mn was therefore:

$$(0·82 \times 12·5) \div 10 = 1·025\%.$$

Comparative values of the methods given for estimating Manganese.

Gravimetric.—There is no doubt that when time permits the gravimetric process is the best to use, being the most uniformly reliable method, and in disputed cases it should always be appealed to.

Volumetric.—The volumetric processes are valuable for rapidly obtaining practically accurate results within a long range of percentage when time presses.

Colorimetric.—The colour tests are useful for deciding roughly in about fifteen minutes the quantity of manganese present in any given steel, and are of great service in works making each day a considerable number of steel heats of practically constant composition, in all of which the chemist is required to rapidly check the percentage of manganese present. In such cases, a set of standards is not necessary: for instance, in an open-hearth works the manganese is usually kept pretty constant at about 0·5%. Then, with a standard approximating this percentage, although in a heat abnormally high or low in manganese the metal might not be accurately estimated, the colour test would nevertheless indicate the composition to be seriously wrong, and the working up or delivery of the steel could be delayed till a gravimetric or volumetric estimation had been made.

The authors' experience of the comparative results obtained by skilled operators when working these processes is that the bismuthate method yields results coincident with the gravimetric, whilst the Ford and Williams method gives 0·02% less manganese. The persulphate method, *per se*, only gives accurate results when the titration is performed very rapidly. The colour tests may be as much as 0·03% above or below the actual figure.

GRAVIMETRIC DETERMINATION OF SULPHUR.

Re-agent required.

Barium chloride.—A 10% solution of barium chloride ($BaCl_2$) is made by dissolving about 60 grammes of the pure hydrated salt in half a litre of water. Filter if necessary, and store in a stoppered bottle for use.

The Process.

(Time occupied, about $1\frac{1}{2}$ days.)

Weight taken.—Weigh out 6 grammes of the steel into a 20-oz. beaker.

Dissolving.—Put on the cover, and pour down the lip 10 cc. at a time 60 cc. of aqua regia, allowing the violent reaction to subside after each addition. Add a crystal or two of pure potassium nitrate and quietly boil on the plate till the steel is dissolved, and then more briskly, till the solution gives indications of spitting.

Evaporation to dryness.—Move the beaker to a less hot part of the plate, take off the cover, allowing the drop of liquid on it to drain down the inside of the beaker, and place it convex side up on a filter-drier. Cautiously evaporate the liquid to complete dryness, and bake the dry mass of ferric chloride on the hottest part of the plate for at least half an hour.

Re-dissolving.—Remove the beaker, holding it in the hand or placing it on a pad of warm asbestos till moderately cool. Replace the cover, and dissolve up the dry mass by boiling it with 40 cc. of strong *HCl* solution.

Evaporation to low bulk.—Very gently evaporate down till the dark-brown mirror-like liquid measures not more than 10 cc.

Fractional filtration.—Add 10 cc. of water, and wash the solution without loss into a 60 cc. graduated flask: place the flask in cold water, and when its contents have cooled, dilute to the mark and thoroughly mix. Filter

off 50 cc. through a dry 110 mm. pure filter into a
graduated flask. Transfer the liquid from the latter
into a clean, dry 20-oz. beaker, and well wash out the
flask with a little water, of course adding the washings
to the main solution.

Precipitation.—Next add 20 cc. of the 10% solution
of $BaCl_2$, when the bulk of the liquid should measure
about 100 cc. Well mix the liquid in the beaker by
shaking it round, put on the cover, and allow the solution to stand for a night.

Filtration.—In the morning filter off the precipitate
on to a 90 mm. close-grained paper contained in a 2-in.
plain funnel with a short stem supported in a 100 cc.
measuring-glass. Pass through as much as possible of
the clear supernatant liquid without much disturbing the
precipitate, and throw away the iron solution after ascertaining it to be free from suspended, finely-divided
precipitate. It is probable that when the main quantity
of the latter is thrown upon the filter some will pass
through into the filtrate,[1] and as long as this happens,
the latter must be re-passed through the paper till the
pores of the filter are filled up and the liquid passes
through quite clear. Every particle of the barium precipitate must of course be washed out of the beaker into
the filter.

Washing.—Very carefully wash the edges of the paper
alternately with very dilute hot HCl (5 cc. of strong HCl
solution of 45 cc. water) and cold water till quite free
from iron salts, when a few drops of the washings added
to a dilute solution of ammonium sulphocyanide will
develop no pink tinge.

Drying.—Dry the precipitate as usual on the hot plate

[1] This difficulty is obviated by the use of a compact pulp filter.

by removing it from the funnel and supporting it in an earthenware cylinder.

Igniting and weighing.—Fold the paper and ignite in the muffle in a clean, tared 2-in. porcelain crucible till quite white. When thoroughly cold, remove the crucible from the desiccator and re-weigh. The increase is sulphate of barium $BaSO_4$, containing 13·7% of sulphur. The result is of course calculated on 5 grammes of steel.

Blank estimation of sulphur in re-agents.—It is frequently necessary, in order to ensure accurate results, that a blank estimation of the sulphur existing in the re-agents used be made, and the weight of $BaSO_4$ thus obtained be deducted from the apparent weight of $BaSO_4$ derived from the steel. In order to save time, the best plan is to set aside a Winchester quart each of aqua regia and hydrochloric acid, and in these determine, once and for all, as the mean of a duplicate estimation, the weight of $BaSO_4$ resulting from the exact volume of these acids employed in an estimation of the sulphur in the steel. This is best done by going through the analysis exactly as in an actual determination, except that a crystal or two of potassium nitrate is used to fix the sulphur which exists in the re-agents as free H_2SO_4 as non-volatile sulphate of potassium.

Without this precaution the sulphuric acid would be driven off on evaporating the original solution to dryness, and the result might indicate really impure acids to be sulphur-free. Perfectly sulphur-free acids are somewhat rare, and the manufacturer's assurance on this point must never be taken for granted.

Model of Record and Calculation.

June 30, 1889.   Drillings from steel rail.   Blow 740.
Weight taken 6 grammes.

Crucible + ppt. + ash = 25·6192
Weight of crucible = 25·5727

·0465
− (Blank + ash) =   ·0072

$BaSO_4$ =   ·0393
13·7

2751
1179
393

5)·53841

0·108°/₀ *S*

Theory of the Aqua Regia Process.

On dissolving the steel, the nitro-hydrochloric acid oxidizes the sulphide of iron present to sulphuric acid, which at low bulk becomes potassium sulphate; the silica is rendered insoluble by the evaporation to dryness, and is separated by the fractional filtration, which dispenses with the necessity of washing the filter-paper. On adding the solution of barium chloride to the slightly hydrochloric acid solution of the potassium sulphate, insoluble barium sulphate is precipitated thus—

$$K_2SO_4 + BaCl_2 = 2\,KCl + BaSO_4$$

It was formerly deemed necessary, in order to ensure

accurate results, to evaporate the solution of ferric
chloride till a scum began to form upon its surface, thus
getting a liquid containing practically no free hydrochloric acid. It was also the rule to precipitate the
$BaSO_4$ from a largely diluted solution. The necessity
for these precautions, like many other chemical tradi-
tions, had no foundation in fact. Mr. L. Archbutt, in a
very useful investigation on this point, proved that
better results are obtained in a fairly concentrated solution containing a moderate excess of free acid, than under
the old conditions. Subsequent trials by the authors
fully confirmed the accuracy of Mr. Archbutt's main conclusion, but his plan of precipitating the $BaSO_4$ from a
rather concentrated solution of ferric chloride at a boiling
heat is, in the authors' opinion, inadvisable, the ignited
precipitate under these conditions being frequently red
with a small quantity of oxide of iron, due to the precipitation with the barium sulphate of obstinately retained
basic iron salt, insoluble in very dilute hydrochloric
acid.

Gravimetric Determination of Sulphur by the Evolution Method (Fresenius, modified).

On referring to the reactions of hydrochloric acid upon
steel (page 55), it will be seen that the sulphide of iron
existing diffused throughout the mass of the steel, is
totally decomposed by the acid with evolution of H_2S gas.
Many methods have from time to time been proposed,
having for their object the oxidation of the evolved
sulphuretted hydrogen to sulphuric acid, so that the
latter on precipitation as $BaSO_4$ should become the

measure of the sulphur in the steel. The best method of this type is that in which the H_2S is oxidised by bromine; for this purpose, one of the authors has devised the modification about to be described.

Apparatus required.

Fill up the arrangement sketched in Fig. 13: A is a glass gas-holder filled with hydrogen, previously washed through strong caustic soda solution;[1] B is a full-necked 12-oz. flask, carrying in its india-rubber stopper an inlet tube for the hydrogen, a 50 cc. stoppered separator, and an outlet bend for the gases evolved from the steel; the rack c is, however, replaced by the absorption cylinder × of about 150 cc. capacity, 30 mm. internal diameter, marked at 20 and 120 cc., and having below the first-named mark a glass tap (Fig. 12). The top of the parallel cylinder is ground inside, and provided with a well-fitting glass stopper. During the absorption, however, it is closed with an india-rubber stopper carrying a curved inlet tube (on which has been blown a bulb 0·2 mm., smaller than the inside diameter of the cylinder), and an outlet bend. Y (Fig. 12) is a washing cylinder containing strong caustic soda solution, and it is attached between × (Fig. 12) and aspirator D (Fig. 13). The parts of the apparatus are connected together with good thick-

[1] Prepare the hydrogen from dilute hydrochloric acid and granulated zinc placed in a filter pump vessel, with a side leading tube. The flask is fitted with an india-rubber bung carrying a 50 cc. stoppered separator from which to deliver the acid. The strong $NaHO$ solution is contained in a washing cylinder fitted with an india-rubber bung with two holes carrying the usual bent tubes.

I

walled india-rubber tubing, and the india-rubber stopper
in the absorption cylinder must have been freed from

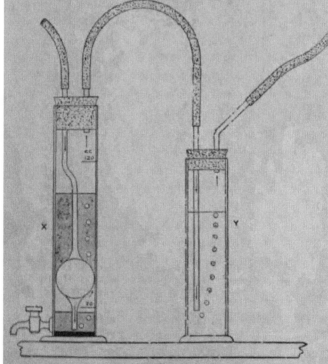

Fig. 12.

surface sulphur by boiling with dilute caustic soda, and
afterwards in several changes of water.

The Process.

(Time occupied, about 4 hours.)

Weight taken.—Weigh out into the 10-oz. flask 6 grammes of the steel in drillings.

Removing the air.—Cover the drillings with about 30 cc. of recently-boiled water (under which the hydrogen inlet tube must dip), and set up the apparatus, having previously charged the absorption cylinder with 3 cc. of pure bromine and 90 cc. of a saturated solution of bromine water. Having seen that the system is airtight by opening the aspirator tap (when the passage of air through the cylinders should soon cease), gently open the hydrogen tap, and pass about half a litre of the gas through the apparatus.

Dissolving.—Shut off the hydrogen, and run in from a separator about 50 cc. of strong HCl, and close the tap without quite emptying the bulb. The steel may at first be left to dissolve in the cold, being afterwards assisted to complete dissolution by gently heating the sand-bath, and finally bringing the clear acid solution just to boiling. Then remove the lamp, quietly aspirate about half a litre of hydrogen through the apparatus to carry forward every trace of H_2S into the bromine tube; then close the aspirator tap, and force through the hydrogen till the equilibrium inside the apparatus is restored.

Precipitation of the SO_3.—Detach the bromine tube from the flask and the washing cylinder. Remove and rinse the bulb tube inside and out, and dilute the contents of the cylinder with distilled water to the 120 cc. mark. Put in the glass stopper, and well mix the liquid by inverting two or three times. Take out the stopper,

and tap off into a clean 20-oz. beaker 100 cc. of the brown
solution containing the sulphur in 5 grammes of steel.
Cover the beaker, and bring its contents to boiling on a
plate in the draught cupboard till the bromine is driven
off; then add down the lip 5 cc. of pure strong HCl
solution and 20 cc. of the 10% solution of barium
chloride. Boil for 15 minutes, to render the precipitated
$BaSO_4$ crystalline, in which condition it is less liable to
pass through the pores of the filter-paper.

Treatment of the precipitate.—The barium sulphate may
be at once filtered off: it is washed, dried, ignited, and
weighed exactly in the manner already described for the
estimation of sulphur by the aqua regia method on page
110, only, as the liquid from which the $BaSO_4$ was precipitated was free from iron salts, the filter will not
require washing with dilute hydrochloric acid, but with
hot water only.

Theoretical Considerations.

The reason for using recently-boiled water for covering the drillings is, that during the preliminary hydrogen
aspiration, they are liable to become somewhat rusted by
the action of the dissolved oxygen in ordinary water, from
which the oxygen is expelled on boiling. The rust or
Fe_2O_3 would form $FeCl_3$ on the addition of HCl, and the
ferric chloride might possibly decompose, and thus prevent the evolution of a small volume of H_2S by the
reaction given on p. 220. A similar reason exists for
sweeping out the air, the oxygen of which converts a
little of the H_2S into sulphuric acid, which remains in
the flask.

The action of the bromine on the evolved H_2S gas is formulated in the following equation—

$$H_2S + 8\ Br + 4\ H_2O = 8\ HBr + H_2SO_4$$

Sulphuretted hydrogen, bromine, and water yield a mixture of hydrobromic and sulphuric acids: the bromine used must of course be sulphur-free, and in setting up any modification of the foregoing installation, it must always be borne in mind that india-rubber stoppers and tubing contain sulphur oxidizable by bromine, and if carelessly arranged may lead to mysteriously high results. The cylinder of sodic hydrate solution serves to absorb the bromine vapour carried away with the gases, which, if allowed to escape into the air of the laboratory, would prove exceedingly irritating to the eyes and lungs. The reaction of the absorption is—

$$2\ NaHO + 2\ Br = NaBr + NaBrO + H_2O$$

Sodic hydrate and bromine yield sodium bromide, sodium hypobromite, and water. It will be noticed that the bromine absorption tube is constructed on the principle already described on p. 33 for potash bulbs.

Volumetric Determination of Sulphur.

Method I. (Arnold and Hardy.)[1]

Re-agent required.

Standard solution of lead acetate.—Pick out from the centre of larger crystals of pure acetate of lead $[Pb(C_2H_3O_2)_2,\ 3\ H_2O]$ small bright fragments of the

[1] "Chemical News," 1888, No. 1496.

fully hydrated salt, and weigh out into a litre flask
1·182 grammes, dissolve in 100 cc. of distilled water
and 10 cc. of P.B. acetic acid, then with distilled water
make up the liquid to exactly 1000 cc., and thoroughly
mix the solution to ensure equal diffusion of the lead
salt. Preserve the standard fluid in a well-stoppered
bottle, labelled, "$Pb(C_2H_3O_2)_2$.   2 cc. = 0·01% S in two
grammes of steel."

The Process.

(Time occupied, about $1\frac{1}{4}$ hours.)

Weight taken.—Weigh out into an 8-oz. full-necked
dry flask 2 grammes of drillings, and cover them with
30 cc. of recently-boiled distilled water.

The apparatus.—Attach the flask to the apparatus
sketched in Fig. 13. A is a glass gas-holder containing
hydrogen washed through a strong solution of caustic
soda ; B is the flask carrying an india-rubber stopper in
which is an inlet tube (dipping under the surface of the
water), a 50 cc. stoppered separator, and an exit bend
for the gases ; C is a rack containing from three to thir-
teen tubes (according to the nature of the material under
analysis), each previously charged with 2 cc. of the
standard lead solution accurately delivered from a burette.
A full-sized sketch of a pair of the bulb tubes is given
in Fig. 14. They work upon the principle of the potash
bulb described on p. 36. The first tube in the rack is
not charged with standard solution, but with 1 cc. of
distilled water ; it acts as a condenser for fumes of HCl.
D is a glass aspirator, graduated in half litres. Throughout, the apparatus should be provided with well-fitting

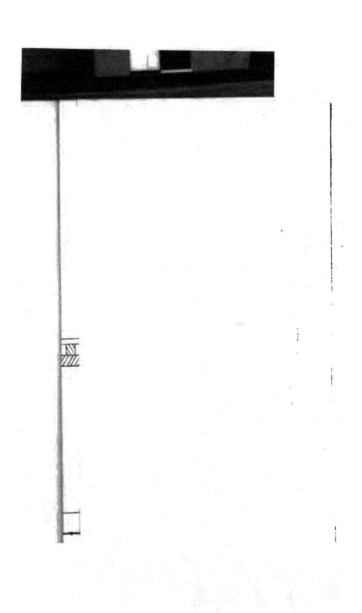

first in an emulsified condition, but afterwards precipitates in flocks in the first one or two tubes. As the solution reaches boiling-point, open the hydrogen tap, and
carry forward the last traces of H_2S into the registering
tubes by aspirating about half a litre of the gas. Then
read off the percentage. Each tube blackened equals
0.01% S. There is no difficulty in reading to 0.005%
represented by the last tube, being evidently only
partially saturated with sulphur at the end of the process.

Cleaning the tubes and bulbs.—These are readily cleared
from adhering PbS by respectively filling and dipping
them with and into warm dilute nitric acid, after which
they must be very thoroughly washed with water before
being again used, otherwise the next estimation will be
worthless, owing to the oxidation of the dark PbS to
colourless $PbSO_4$ by any traces of nitric acid present.

Theoretical Considerations.

The principle of the evolution method has been already
described in the article on the bromine process. The
reaction between the lead acetate and the evolved H_2S
is—

$$Pb(C_2H_3O_2)_2 + H_2S = PbS + 2\ C_2H_4O_2$$

Lead acetate and hydrogen sulphide yield dark-brown
sulphide of lead and free acetic acid. By the above
equation it will be seen (remembering that the original
lead salt contained three molecules of water) that 378
parts by weight of the acetate combine with 31.98
parts of sulphur. The standard solution was made by

dissolving 1·182 grammes of acetate in 1000 cc. of water.

Therefore $\frac{1\cdot182}{1000} = 0\cdot001182$ parts of acetate combine with—

$$\frac{31\cdot98 \times 0\cdot001182}{378} = 0\cdot0001 \text{ parts of } S.$$

or 1 cc. $= 0\cdot005^\circ/_\circ$ S in 2 grammes of steel.

$\therefore$ 2 cc. $= 0\cdot010^\circ/_\circ$ S ,, ,, ,,

The remarkable absorptive power of the bulbs enables them to sharply separate each increment of one-hundredth $^\circ/_\circ$, no H_2S reaching a bulb till the lead in its fellow next the evolution flask has fixed its equivalent of sulphur; but the proportions of the bulbs and cylinders must be accurate, so that the liquid is always divided into two layers during the passage of gas, one above and the other below the bulb. If the latter is too small the liquid will remain unbroken, if it is too large, nearly the whole of the solution will be driven to the top of the bulb, leaving a small layer of liquid through which the gases do not bubble at the bottom of the inlet tube: the dimensions should be strictly in accordance with the full-sized sketch. The phosphoretted hydrogen evolved from the steel has no action upon the lead salt, and the current of hydrogen aspirated at the end of the dissolution carries forward from the saturated tubes the H_2S present merely in aqueous solution till it is fixed by its equivalent of lead in the next unsaturated tube. It is an interesting fact, that the evolution of sulphur during the process is not proportional to the steel dissolved, because when only about half the steel has passed into solution, about two-thirds of the total sulphur has been evolved.

It is of great importance that the acid used be devoid

of *free* chlorine, which would oxidize the H_2S to H_2SO_4, in which form it would remain in the flask, and its registration in the lead tubes would be missed. The acid should be tested with starch and pure KI in the manner described on p. 211, the hydrochloric being substituted for the acetic acid.

After many years' experience of the working of this process in carrying out many hundreds of estimations (occasionally checked by precipitating the sulphur as $BaSO_4$), the authors have no hesitation, as far as the cases of completely soluble steels and bar-irons are concerned, in pronouncing it to be a most accurate and rapid method. The process, however, in the case of gray hematite pig-irons containing about 0.05% of sulphur has not worked so satisfactorily, results as much as 0.02% low having been occasionally registered; but with spiegel and Swedish white iron good results have been obtained.

METHOD II

Re-agents required.

Pure sodium hydrate solution.—One pound of the pure solid (from sodium metal) is dissolved in water, and the solution transferred to a Winchester quart, which is then filled by the addition of water. This is a stock solution capable of lasting for a great number of determinations, as only 10 cc. are required for each.

$\frac{N}{50}$ *Iodine solution.*—Weigh off accurately 2·54 grammes of pure re-sublimed iodine, transfer to litre-flask, and dissolve by adding water and about 5 grammes of potassium iodide. Dilute to the mark.

$\frac{N}{50}$ *Sodium thiosulphate solution.*—Dissolve 4·96 grammes of the pure crystals in water and dilute to 1000 cc. This solution is made purposely for checking the strength of the iodine. This is done by measuring off, say, 50 cc. of the iodine solution and adding the thiosulphate from a burette until the colour of the liquid is almost discharged. A few drops of starch solution are then added, and the addition of thiosulphate continued until the blue colour is just discharged.

Apparatus required.

The steel is dissolved in a flask of about 20 oz. capacity, standing on a sand dish over a Bunsen burner. The flask is closed with a two-holed bung, one hole carrying a thistle or tap funnel for the introduction of the acid, and the other a delivery tube in the form of a 50 cc. pipette. The stem of the pipette is bent in two places, one on either side of the bulb, and in such a way that when one open end is passed through the bung of the evolution flask, the main length of the pipette with the bulb is inclined at 45 degrees to the horizontal. The other bend is made to the same angle, and the open end passes through the bung of a 3-bulbed U-tube, the other branch of which need not be closed.

The Process.

(Time occupied, about 45 minutes.)

Weigh off 5 grammes of the steel into the flask, and join up with the U-tube charged with 10 cc. of the sodium hydrate solution. Introduce a hot mixture of 25 cc. of hydrochloric acid and an equal volume of water by means of the funnel and allow the steel to dissolve. The solution is promoted by putting a small flame under the flask, and towards the finish the heat is increased. When all the steel is dissolved, the liquid is boiled for about five minutes. During the action, condensed steam and acid collect in the bulb of the pipette and run back into the evolution flask. (This primitive arrangement of air condenser answers all requirements, but as a further precaution it is permissible to introduce an empty bottle between the pipette and the U-tube.) The liquid in the U-tube is rinsed into a small beaker, diluted to about 30 cc., and a mixture of 6 or 7 cc. of strong hydrochloric acid with 20 cc. of water added. The solution should now be acid, and the liberated sulphuretted hydrogen is determined by adding a few drops of starch solution and then running in the standard iodine until the blue colour is developed.

Each cc. of $\frac{N}{50}$ iodine = 0·00032 gramme sulphur.

Example: A steel, the sulphur in which was known to be 0·044% was treated as described above; and 7·5 cc. of iodine were used.

$$7·5 \times ·00032 = ·0024 \text{ gramme sulphur.}$$

$$\text{Percentage} = ·0024 \times \frac{100}{5} = ·048.$$

The authors are of opinion that this method, whilst yielding results sufficiently accurate for practical purposes and in a comparatively short time, is not so reliable as the one previously described. Its indications are much more reliable if, instead of calculating the sulphur percentage directly from the amount of iodine used in the titration, a steel of known sulphur contents is assayed in the same way with each batch of samples, and the amount of iodine used up on the standard be taken to represent the known percentage of sulphur irrespective altogether of the actual strength of the iodine.

Theoretical Considerations.

The sulphuretted hydrogen evolved when the steel is dissolved in hydrochloric acid is absorbed by the caustic soda with formation of sodium sulphide.

$$2\ NaHO + H_2S = Na_2S + 2\ H_2O$$

The dilute acid neutralizes the excess of sodium hydrate, and also decomposes the sodium sulphide liberating a small amount of sulphuretted hydrogen in the solution.

$$NaHO + HCl = NaCl + H_2O$$
$$Na_2S + 2\ HCl = 2\ NaCl + H_2S$$

The liberated H_2S reacts with the iodine, forming hydriodic acid and free sulphur.

$$H_2S + I_2 = 2\ HI + S$$

The slightest excess of free iodine added beyond what is demanded by this equation reacts with the starch indicator, producing blue iodide of starch. From the preceding equation, one atom of sulphur (32 parts) demands 2 atoms of iodine (254 parts), and since each cc.

of the standard iodine solution contains 0·00254 gramme
iodine, it is equivalent to 0·00032 gramme of sulphur.

The Gravimetric Determination of Phosphorus in Steel.

There are several accurate gravimetric methods by
means of which phosphorus may be determined in steel.

The Rapid Process (Stead and Cook).

(Time occupied, about 2 hours.)

Re-agent required.

A 10% *solution of ammonium molybdate.*—This is
prepared by dissolving 50 grammes of the pure, absolutely phosphorus-free salt in about 400 cc. of hot water.
The solution when cold is diluted to 500 cc., is filtered,
and preserved for use in a stoppered bottle.

The Method.

Weight taken.—Weigh out two grammes of the *perfectly clean* steel drillings into a 20-oz. beaker.

Dissolving.—Pour down the lip of the covered beaker
30 cc. of nitric acid, sp. gr. 1·2. When the first violent
reaction has subsided, heat the liquid on the plate till
the steel has dissolved, then add 7 cc. of strong *HCl*
solution, and boil the liquid for a few minutes.

Precipitation with ammonia.—Remove the beaker from
the plate, rinse the cover and sides of the beaker, and
replace the former. Allow the liquid to stand until

moderately cool. Pour down the lip of the beaker, little by little, dilute ammonia (half 880, half water), well shaking round the beaker after each addition of alkali till the acids are neutralized, the iron completely precipitated as hydrate, and an excess of 4 or 5 cc. of the ammoniacal liquid has been added. The beaker must be well shaken round, till the mass forms a fluid paste smelling strongly of ammonia.

Re-dissolving the iron.—Pour down the lip of the beaker from a 10 cc. measuring-glass strong nitric acid, 1 cc. at a time (well shaking round after each addition), till the iron precipitate has completely dissolved. Then add 3 cc. more of the strong nitric acid. Boil down the liquid till it measures about 40 cc., and any splashings of hydrate of iron formed during the treatment with ammonia have dissolved off the cover and sides of the beaker.

Precipitating the phosphorus.—Remove the beaker from the plate, take off and rinse the cover, and by means of a pipette deliver into the centre of the hot liquid 15 cc. of the 10% solution of ammonium molybdate. Gently shake the liquid round, till any pale yellow flocks of precipitated hydrate of molybdenum have dissolved. Next digest the contents of the beaker on a comparatively cool corner of the plate or on the top of the air-bath (occasionally well shaking it round) for fifteen or twenty minutes, till the yellow precipitate readily settles to the bottom of the beaker on standing a little after the last shaking.

Filtering.—Collect the precipitate on a 90 mm. hardened filter-paper, contained in a 2-in. funnel. Rinse out the beaker (the aid of a policeman should not be required) with a fine jet of water containing about

2% of strong nitric acid. Wash the paper, and pre-cipitate three or four times till free from any visible traces of iron solution, and allow the filter to drain.

Drying the precipitate—Cautiously spread out the filter paper on the convex side of a 5-in. clock-glass, so that the edge of the paper nearest the precipitate projects over the edge of the glass. Then, by means of a very fine jet of cold water, wash the precipitate into a clean, tared platinum or porcelain dish about $2\frac{1}{2}$ in diameter. With a sufficiently fine wash-bottle jet 20 cc. of water should suffice for this purpose. Place the dish on the hot plate over a little beaker of boiling water, and evaporate its contents to dryness. Remove the dish, and dry it outside with a clean duster, and place for five minutes in the air-bath at 100° C.

Weighing.—Allow to cool in a desiccator, and, as quickly as possible, the yellow precipitate being hygro-scopic, re-weigh the dish; the increase is ammonio-phospho-molybdate, containing 1·65% of phosphorus.

Example of Calculation.

May 6, 1880.   Bessemer Rail.   Blow 932.
Weight taken 2 grammes.
Dish + precipitate = 32·6394
Weight of dish = 32·5482

$$·0912$$
$$1·65$$

$$4560$$
$$5472$$
$$912$$

$$2)·150480$$

$$0·075°/_o \ P.$$

Theoretical Considerations.

The foregoing modification of the molybdate process is essentially that devised by Messrs. Stead and Cook for the determination of phosphorus in basic steels practically free from silicon, it being a canon of analytical faith, that silicic acid was carried down from its nitric acid solution with the molybdic precipitate. This, however, as far as ordinary steels are concerned, was a groundless fear, as one of the authors has proved that even with steels containing 0·2% of silicon, practically the whole of the silica is found in the filtrate on evaporating the latter twice to dryness with strong hydrochloric acid. This fact extends the applicability of the process, which, however, should only be employed within the following limits:

(*a*) For steels containing 0·04% and upwards of phosphorus.

(*b*) For steels absolutely free from any insoluble residue, such as tungsten, scale, etc.

(*c*) For steels containing under 1% of combined carbon, because an excessive amount of organic colouring matter has a tendency to prevent the complete precipitation of the phosphorus.

The authors, to ensure the complete original solution of the silicon, have slightly modified the directions given by Messrs. Stead and Cook for dissolving the steel. Irrespective of this point, they have never been able to follow the published instructions, namely, to " dissolve two grammes of the steel in 12 cc. of nitric acid, sp. gr. 1·42, and 5 cc. of water," simply because two grammes of steel will not completely dissolve in such a mixture.

The foregoing method is rapid, and when carried out with care, gives concordant and accurate results; but slight violations of the empirical conditions necessary for success may cause the process to register percentages in some cases seriously below, in others considerably higher, than the true phosphorus. The conditions under which the yellow precipitate is formed are not well understood.[1] It was formerly supposed that chlorides should be absent, but it is now generally admitted that, excepting hydrogen chloride, they even favour the precipitation, if coincident with the other absolutely necessary conditions, which are specified below.

1. The iron must be in nitric acid solution, with free acid in some excess. If, however, the excess is too great the result is low, or in extreme cases no precipitate is obtained. If insufficient free nitric acid is in the liquid, the latter is dark in colour, and the precipitate thrown down has a reddish tinge, due to the presence of basic nitrate of iron carried down with it.

2. The presence of a large amount of ammonium nitrate is necessary.

3. The presence of a large excess of ammonium molybdate, say 500 times the weight of the phosphorus present, is very important.

4. The temperature of the precipitation must be kept well under 100° C., or free molybdic acid may be precipitated, causing a high result. A prolonged digestion may also produce the same effect.

5. The total bulk of liquid in which the phosphorus is precipitated should measure from 50 to 60 cc.

It will be seen on comparing the above with the

[1] See, however, Handeshagen's paper, "Chem. News," vol. 60, pp. 169 *et seq.*

practical directions that the necessary conditions are
there secured; but the student should carefully make
some experiments on a series of weighings from one
steel, trying to get accurate results, high results, or low
results by respectively adhering to or suitably violating
the conditions given. He will thus learn how to estimate
"phosphorus by molybdate" with a far more enduring
knowledge than written instructions can convey.

The reactions taking place during the determination
of phosphorus by the rapid molybdate process are as
follow:

1. The phosphide of iron present in the steel is
oxidized by the nitric acid to phosphoric acid (see
p. 58), and the silicon forms a stable solution of silicic
acid (see p. 58).

2. The neutralization of the free nitric and hydrochloric acids by ammonia with formation respectively of
ammonium nitrate and chloride, takes place thus:

$$HNO_3 + AmHO = AmNO_3 + H_2O$$

$$HCl + AmHO = AmCl + H_2O$$

3. The complete precipitation of the iron as hydrate
(and to the extent of the phosphoric acid present as
phosphate) by the excess of ammonia, occurs thus:

$$Fe(NO_3)_3 + 3\ AmHO = Fe(HO)_3 + 3\ AmNO_3$$

4. The neutralization of the excess of ammonia and
the re-solution of the precipitated hydrate (and phosphate) of iron by excess of nitric acid, takes place thus:

$$Fe(HO)_3 + 3\ HNO_3 = Fe(NO_3)_3 + 3\ H_2O$$

5. The precipitation of ammonio-phospho molybdate

by the addition of excess of ammonium molybdate, is effected thus:

$$H_3PO_4 + 12\ Am_2MoO_4 + 23\ HNO_3 =$$

$$Am_3PO_4 \cdot 12\ MoO_3 \cdot 2\ HNO_3 \cdot H_2O + 21\ AmNO_3 + 11\ H_2O$$
(The yellow precipitate.)

The yellow compound containing the phosphorus cannot be ignited in the ordinary way, because when strongly heated it decomposes, leaving a fixed residue of dubious composition.

On drying at 100° C. it loses water and nitric acid leaving a residue with the composition $(Am_3PO_4 \cdot 12\ MoO_3)$, which coincides with the 1·65% of phosphorus which universal practice has indicated to be present.

Other Methods for Determination of Phosphorus.

Re-agent required.

Standard solution of ferric iron.—This is prepared by dissolving in a 20-oz. beaker 2·505 grammes of pure Swedish Lancashire hearth bar-iron in 35 cc. of strong HCl solution, and then adding 3 cc. of strong nitric acid to peroxidize the iron. The solution is boiled down, and finally very gently evaporated, till crystals of ferric chloride begin to separate. These are re-dissolved in cold water, the iron solution is transferred without loss to a 250 cc. graduated flask, diluted to the mark, thoroughly mixed, and is stored for use in a stoppered bottle labelled " Standard $FeCl_3$ Solution, 1 cc. = 0·01 gramme Fe."

The next three processes to be described have in common up to a certain point a series of identical operations which will be next dealt with. They may all be employed in cases for which the rapid molybdate method is not suitable, namely, for high carbon steels, and for bar-iron, blister, and cast steels of Swedish origin, which usually do not contain more than 0·02% of phosphorus. The combined method is perhaps the most strictly accurate, and in the authors' experience has yielded slightly higher results than any of the others.

The Preliminary Process.

Weight taken.—Weigh out into a 20-oz. covered beaker 5 grammes of the steel.[1]

Dissolving.—Add down the lip of the beaker 50 cc. of nitric acid, sp. gr. 1·2. This should be added 10 cc. at a time, allowing the violent reaction to subside between each addition. Then quietly boil the contents of the beaker till the drillings have dissolved.

Evaporating to dryness.—The solution is then evaporated to complete dryness. The rapidity with which this is accomplished depends to a considerable extent upon the skill of the operator. Any attempt to boil or even to evaporate quickly to dryness without careful attention will entail the loss of the estimation, as the result of a violent spitting of the iron solution. The best plan is to boil down briskly in the centre of the plate till symptoms of spitting develop, and then to alter the

---

[1] Or decide on the weight to be taken for analysis after reference to the table on p. 258.

position of the beaker so as to bring one side on the portion of the plate just over the edge of the Bunsen flame. The solution on the warmer side of the beaker will then gradually become dry, and the gentle boiling may be continued till there is danger of the drops falling from the cover breaking the hot beaker. At this stage it must be placed on a pipe-stem triangle, and after removing the cover the liquid is carefully evaporated to complete dryness, the dry mass being exposed to a strong final heating in the centre of the plate.

Re-dissolving.—The hot beaker having been allowed to cool in the hand or on a warm asbestos pad, the cover is replaced, and the oxide of iron is dissolved by boiling it with 50 cc. of strong hydrochloric acid.

Reducing the iron.—Transfer the ferric chloride solution without loss to a 30-oz. registered flask, and dilute with hot water to 200 cc. Next add, little by little, constantly shaking round the flask, dilute ammonia (half 880, half water), till the acid is neutralized and a slight permanent precipitate is obtained; then add, so as to rinse down the sides of the flask, about 100 cc. of strong sulphurous acid solution.[1] The liquid is then well boiled, again neutralized as before with dilute ammonia, 20 cc. of sulphurous acid are added, and the liquid is again briskly boiled till the solution is pale-green in colour, and the smell of SO_2 has disappeared.

Precipitating the $FePO_4$.—Add to the ferrous solution from a pipette 5 cc. of the standard iron solution; shake the liquid well round and bring it to boiling, and gradually add 25 cc. of hot ammonium acetate solution, after which continue the boiling for a few minutes.

[1] Made by saturating distilled water with SO_2 evolved from a syphon of the liquefied gas.

Filtering.—Remove the flask from the plate, and allow the precipitate to settle somewhat. It is then collected on a 110 mm. paper, using either the filter-pump or attaching to a $2\frac{1}{4}$-in. ribbed funnel the filtering loop sketched in Fig. 2. The hot flask should be held in a thick duster, and as much as possible of the clear liquid should be got through before disturbing the precipitate. The at first clear, greenish filtrate soon becomes yellow and turbid, and an apparently large amount of a flaky scum of basic ferric acetate is formed on the surface of the liquid and the sides of the flask. Allow the flask to drain thoroughly into the filter, but do not attempt any washing beyond removing the drop of liquid from the lip of the flask; the filter also is allowed to drain well, and the loop is removed.

Dissolving up the precipitate.—Hang the funnel inside a clean 20-oz. beaker, and boil 30 cc. of strong hydrochloric acid in the flask in which the precipitation took place, till the precipitated scum has passed into solution. Then cautiously drop the hot yellow liquid round the edges of the filter-paper till the precipitate is dissolved up; well rinse the flask out into the filter, and wash the latter with hot dilute hydrochloric acid and cold water till free from any yellow tinge, using, however, as little wash liquid as possible.

Evaporating to low bulk.—Remove the funnel and hanger, cover the beaker, and briskly boil down the solution to low bulk, finally gently evaporating with the cover off to about 5 cc.

The yellow liquid thus obtained is next further dealt with in a manner dependent upon which process is to be employed for the final precipitation of the phosphorus. The case of each method will be presently considered.

Theoretical Considerations.

The preliminary solution in nitric acid converts the iron into ferric nitrate, and oxidizes the phosphide of iron to phosphoric acid (see p. 58). On strongly baking the dry mass of ferric nitrate, it is to a great extent denitrated, leaving ferric oxide Fe_2O_3 mixed with highly basic nitrate; the carbonaceous colouring matter is also decomposed. The highly acid ferric chloride solution requires neutralizing before reduction, because the presence of a large amount of free acid prevents the perfect de-chlorinization of the ferric to ferrous chloride. The result would be a bulky precipitate difficult to deal with during the filtration, which, however, could only be obtained by the addition of a very large volume of ammonium acetate. The action of the sulphurous acid on the nearly neutral solution of ferric chloride is as follows :

$$2\ FeCl_3 + H_2SO_3 + H_2O = 2\ FeCl_2 + H_2SO_4 + 2\ HCl\ [1]$$

Ferric chloride, sulphurous acid, and water yield ferrous chloride, sulphuric and hydrochloric acids. The addition of 0·05 gramme of ferric iron is to ensure the presence of sufficient ferric salt to precipitate the whole of the phosphorus present as ferric phosphate which is insoluble in an acetic acid solution of ammonium acetate. The 5 cc. added are amply sufficient to precipitate 0·15% P in 5 grammes of steel.

The traces of free mineral acids liberated by the

[1] The second neutralization is necessary to remove the free hydrochloric and sulphuric acids liberated on the first addition of SO_2.

second addition of sulphurous acid [1] are neutralized, and acetic acid is substituted in their place by the decomposition of the ammonium acetate with the formation respectively of ammonium sulphate and chloride, thus:

$$H_2SO_4 + 2\ Am(C_2H_3O_2) = Am_2SO_4 + 2\ C_2H_4O_2$$
$$HCl + Am(C_2H_3O_2) = AmCl + C_2H_4O_2$$

The phosphate of iron mixed with some basic acetate is then precipitated. On dissolving up the unwholesome-looking mixture, the whole of the phosphorus which was contained in the 5 grammes of steel is concentrated into a solution, in which is associated with it only a comparatively small portion of the iron in which it was originally distributed, and the removal of the bulk of the iron in the form of soluble ferrous acetate much facilitates and renders more accurate the subsequent precipitation of the minute percentage of phosphorus present.

Magnesia Process.

Re-agent required.

Magnesia mixture.—Dissolve 25 grammes of pure magnesium chloride and 25 grammes of pure ammonium chloride in hot water; cool the solution, make up the volume to 200 cc., and add 50 cc. of 880 ammonia solu-

---

[1] The amount of free sulphuric and hydrochloric acids liberated on the first addition of H_2SO_4 amounts to many grammes, thus preventing a complete reduction. Hence the necessity for a second neutralization.

tion. Allow the mixture to stand for a day or two, and filter off the clear liquid into a green glass-stoppered bottle provided with an india-rubber stopper.

The Method.

(Time occupied, about 2 days.[1])

Converting the iron into citrate.—Rinse the sides and cover of the beaker containing the 5 cc. of yellow liquid (obtained at the end of the common preliminary operations), and add 15 grammes of pure citric acid, together with a little water to bring the crystals into complete solution.

Precipitating.—Next add dilute ammonia till the liquid is strongly alkaline, and finally 2 cc. of magnesia mixture. Shake the contents of the beaker well round, cover the latter, and allow it to stand for about twenty-four hours. The total volume of liquid should not exceed 50 cc.

Filtering.—Collect the crystalline precipitate on a 90 mm. filter, carefully detaching every particle adhering to the sides of the beaker with a policeman, and very thoroughly wash the paper with water strongly alkaline with ammonia (1 volume of 880 to 3 volumes of water).

Weighing.—The precipitate is dried, ignited in the muffle in a tared platinum crucible, and weighed with the usual precaution. Its formula is $Mg_2P_2O_7$ (magnesium pyrophosphate), containing 27·93% of phosphorus. It should be quite white.

[1] Including the preliminary operations.

Theoretical Considerations.

The citric acid prevents the precipitation of the iron on the subsequent addition of ammonia by forming a soluble double citrate of iron and ammonium:

$$[FeAm_3 \ (C_6H_5O_7)_2]$$

The phosphorus is precipitated as a double phosphate of ammonium and magnesium $(AmMgPO_4) + $ Aqua. This compound on ignition loses water and ammonia, thus:

$$2 \ NH_4MgPO_4 = Mg_2P_2O_7 + H_2O + 2 \ NH_3$$

The foregoing process has been included on account of its chemical interest, but its employment in steel works laboratories has been abandoned by general consent because of the long period necessary for the complete precipitation of the phosphorus.

The Long Molybdate Method (Riley).

Re-agent required.

Nitric acid solution of ammonium molybdate and nitrate.—Dissolve in a 60-oz. beaker 50 grammes of pure molybdic acid (MoO_3) in 200 cc. of dilute ammonia (80 cc. of 880 and 120 cc. of water). Then add without hesitation in one quick pouring 750 cc. of nitric acid, sp. gr. 1·2. Heat the liquid at about 70° C. for an hour or two, allow it to stand for a day, and filter off the clear liquid for use. In the bottle in which it is preserved, yellow molybdic acid separates after a time, and care must then be taken that none of this precipitate is suspended in the solution when the latter is poured out for precipitating phosphorus; the liquid must, if necessary, be re-filtered before using.

The Process.

(Time occupied, about 1 day.[1])

Obtaining the iron in nitric acid solution.—To the 5 cc. of liquid in hydrochloric acid solution obtained at the end of the common operation, add dilute ammonia till the hydrochloric acid is neutralized, the iron precipitated, and a distinct excess of ammonia is present after thoroughly shaking round the contents of the beaker. Then add, drop by drop, strong nitric acid, till the precipitate is just re-dissolved, being careful to bring into solution any particles adhering to the sides of the beaker as the result of shaking. Bring the liquid to boiling and remove from the plate.

Precipitating the phosphorus.—Add to the hot solution down the lip of the beaker 30 cc. of the clear nitric acid solution of ammonium molybdate; well shake round the liquid, the volume of which should be about 50 cc.

Estimating the phosphorus.—The contents of the beaker are digested, the precipitate filtered off, washed, dried, and weighed, precisely in the manner described for the rapid molybdate process on page 128, in which article also the theoretical considerations have been fully dealt with.

[1] Including the preliminary operations.

The Combined Method.[1]

(Time occupied, about $1\frac{1}{4}$ days.[2])

In this process the yellow phosphorus precipitate obtained in the last method is well digested at a temperature of about 100°, which ensures the precipitation of every trace of phosphorus, and is admissible because the co-precipitation of some free molybdic acid is a matter of comparative indifference. The precipitate is filtered off, and it and the filter-paper are washed till free from iron with the 2% solution of nitric acid.

Dissolving the molybdate precipitate.—The funnel is hung inside a small beaker, and the precipitate is dissolved in the smallest possible quantity of hot dilute ammonia, after which the paper is well washed with a fine jet of hot water.

Precipitating the phosphorus.—To the strongly ammoniacal fluid add 2 cc. of strong hydrochloric acid (to form $AmCl$), and shake the liquid round to redissolve any precipitated molybdic acid in the excess of ammonia. At this point the volume of the liquid should be made up with strong ammonia to 48 cc. registered by a diamond scratch or slip of paper previously placed upon the beaker. Next, holding the beaker in the right hand, and continuously rotating its contents, slowly deliver, drop by drop, from a pipette held in the left hand, 2 cc. of magnesia mixture. With occasional shaking the authors have found the precipitation of the phosphorus to be practically complete in two

[1] J. O. Arnold, "Chemical News," No. 1114, p. 147.
[2] Including the preliminary operations.

hours, but it is perhaps safest to allow the beaker to
stand over-night.

Estimating the phosphorus.—The precipitate is filtered
off, washed, dried, ignited, and weighed exactly in the
manner described in the article on the magnesia process,
but to the weight obtained on the balance one milligramme is added as a correction for the slight solubility
of ammonium magnesium phosphate in dilute ammonia
solution.

Theoretical Considerations.

Most of the points calling for explanation have been
already dealt with in the magnesia process. The reason
for slowly adding the precipitant whilst the liquid containing the phosphorus is in rapid motion is, that experience has shown that under these conditions the
theoretical composition of the precipitate is best secured.
The correction for the solubility of the precipitate—
namely, one milligramme of pyrophosphate for each
50 cc. of solution—is usually also applied to the volume
of washing liquid used. This procedure, however, the
authors' practice indicates to be inaccurate, inasmuch as
the ammonium magnesium phosphate when once precipitated is practically insoluble in dilute ammonia solution. In precipitating phosphoric acid with magnesia,
the presence of a large excess of ammonium chloride is
advisable to prevent the possibility of a co-precipitation
with the double phosphate of any $Mg(HO)_2$. The latter
is soluble in $AmCl$.

SUPPLEMENTARY METHODS FOR DETERMINATION
OF PHOSPHORUS.

Gravimetric (Ibbotson and Brearley.[1])

(Time accupied, about 40 minutes.)

Re-agents required.

Molybdate re-agent.—This is prepared by dissolving
10 grammes of pure molybdic oxide in a mixture of 17 cc.
·880 ammonia with 25 cc. of water, and then pouring
the clear solution into 125 cc. of nitric acid s.g. 1·20.
The amount used in each assay is filtered off when wanted
from this stock solution.

4% solution of lead acetate.—Dissolve approximately
4 grammes of lead acetate crystals in 100 cc. of water.
The turbid solution is cleared by the addition of a few
cc. of acetic acid.

The Process.

Weighing, dissolving, etc.—For ordinary steels 2
grammes of drillings are weighed out and brushed into
a registered conical flask of about 10-oz. capacity, and
45 cc. of nitric acid s.g. 1·20 then added. When the
brisk effervescence has subsided, heat the solution to
boiling, and add, a few drops at a time, a strong solution
of potassium permanganate made by shaking a few of
the solid crystals in a test-tube with water. When a
brown precipitate of hydrated manganese peroxide or a

[1] "Chemical News," No. 83, p. 122.

pink colour of undecomposed permanganate persists for
one minute's boiling after the last addition, add in small
quantities at a time a solution of ferrous sulphate, prepared similarly, until the precipitate (or pink colour) has
disappeared, leaving a clear yellow solution.

Formation of the yellow precipitate.—Cautiously add
4 cc. of ·880 ammonium hydrate and shake the flask to
dissolve up the precipitate of ferric hydrate momentarily
formed in the excess of nitric acid present. When all
splashings have been dissolved, 30 cc. of clear, filtered
solution of the ammonium molybdate re-agent are added.
The flask may then either be closed with an india-rubber
bung and shaken vigorously for not more than five
minutes, or else set aside for about fifteen minutes in a
warm place in order to effect complete precipitation of
the yellow compound without contamination with molybdic acid.

Conversion to lead molybdate.—It is permissible to
filter off the ammonium phosphomolybdate, dry it and
finish the assay as usual, but less time is consumed by
converting the molybdenum contents of the precipitate
into lead molybdate by the following operations. The
yellow precipitate is filtered off through a small pulp
filter and well washed with cold 2% nitric acid. The
funnel is then placed in the neck of the flask in which
the precipitation was made, and 4 cc. of concentrated
ammonium hydrate poured in drops over the precipitate.
The latter quickly dissolves. Wash the funnel and pulp
twice with hot water, and then pour the whole filtrate
once more through the same filter, catching the liquid
in a similar flask. The original flask is washed out
several times with hot water, the washings being of
course passed through the filter; the latter is finally

washed twice with hot water. The flask containing the
ammoniacal solution is set on the plate, and the empty
flask by its side after putting in it 50 cc. of ammonium
acetate with about 10 grammes of ammonium chloride
previously dissolved in water and filtered if necessary.
When both solutions boil, 10 cc. of hydrochloric acid
are added to the ammoniacal solution, and then 10 cc.
of the 4% lead acetate solution. This mixture is then
at once poured into the boiling mixture of acetate and
chloride of ammonium, washing in every trace of the
acid lead solution. Pure lead molybdate, $PbMoO_4$ is precipitated as a nearly white granular precipitate. It is
filtered off through pulp, washed with hot water and
ignited. Its weight, multiplied by 0·007, represents the
phosphorus in the 2 grammes of steel weighed out.

Example of Calculation.

Lead molybdate, brushed on pan, weighed 0·1124 gramme.

$$
\begin{array}{r}
0\cdot1124 \\
\cdot007 \\
\hline
2)\,\overline{\cdot0007868} \\
\hline
\cdot0003934 \times 100 = 0\cdot039\%\ \text{Phosphorus.}
\end{array}
$$

Theoretical Considerations.

The addition of potassium permanganate to the nitric
acid solution of the steel completely oxidizes the carbonaceous colouring matter. This is made evident by
the progressive falling off in depth of colour up to the
point of complete oxidation when a further addition of
permanganate reacts with the manganous nitrate formed

L

by its decomposition in the earlier stages to yield a precipitate of peroxide (hydrated).

$$2 \ KMnO_4 + 3 \ Mn(NO_3)_2 + 2H_2O = 5 \ MnO_2 + 2 \ KNO_3$$
$$+ 4 \ HNO_3$$

The permanganate also serves another useful purpose
in that it hastens the conversion of phosphorus existing
as metaphosphoric acid into orthophosphoric, the latter
alone yielding precipitates with ammonium molybdate.

$$\underset{\text{metaphosphoric acid.}}{HPO_3} + H_2O = \underset{\text{orthophosphoric acid.}}{H_3PO_4}$$

The precipitate of manganese dioxide is carried into
solution by ferrous sulphate. This reaction is the basis
of the Ford and Williams manganese estimation, and has
been dealt with on p. 87.

The 4 cc. of concentrated ammonia are added for the
purpose of generating ammonium nitrate in the solution.

$$AmHO + HNO_3 = AmNO_3 + H_2O$$

The yellow precipitate when dissolved in ammonia
yields a mixture of ammonium phosphate and molybdate.

$$Am_3PO_4 \cdot 12 \ MoO_3 + 24 \ AmHO = Am_3PO_4$$
$$+ 12 \ Am_2MoO_4 + 12 \ H_2O$$

Acidification of the mixture produces molybdic acid,
but there is no precipitation either of lead chloride,
phosphate or molybdate when lead acetate is added, the
first of these being soluble in hot solutions, and the other
two in the excess of acid used.

$$Am_2MoO_4 + 2 \ HCl = 2 \ AmCl + H_2MoO_4$$

When this solution is poured into the mixture of
ammonium acetate and chloride, the free hydrochloric

acid is changed to acetic acid, in which lead molybdate is insoluble. This compound precipitates whilst lead phosphate remains unprecipitated on account of its solubility in the ammonium chloride.

$$H_2MoO_4 + Pb(C_2H_3O_2)_2 = PbMoO_4 + 2\ HC_2H_3O_2$$

The carrying out of the precipitation in the manner and order specified ensures the formation of lead molybdate in the form of a rapidly-settling and easily-filtering precipitate.

The factor 0·007 which converts lead molybdate to phosphorus is calculated as follows:

Am_3PO_4 ·12 MoO_3, the yellow precipitate, contains one atom of phosphorus, weight 31. Each of the 12 atoms of Mo in the yellow precipitate yields one molecule of $PbMoO_4$, hence

P yields 12 $PbMoO_4$

31 „ 12 $(207 + 96 + 64) = 4404$

4404 parts of $PbMoO_4$ represent 31 parts of phosphorus

$$1 \quad „ \quad „ \quad „ \quad \frac{31}{4404} = ·007 \quad „$$

VOLUMETRIC (Handy).[1]

(Time occupied, 30 minutes.)

Re-agents required.

Molybdate re-agent.—Same as in preceding method.

Standard solution of nitric acid.—To 1,800 cc. of distilled water add 20 cc. of strong nitric acid.

[1] "Chemical News," vol. 76, p. 324.

Standard solution of sodium hydrate.—Dissolve about 15 grammes of the pure solid, and make up to 2000 cc.

Phenol-phthalein indicator.—Half a gramme of the solid is dissolved in a mixture of 50 cc. of water with 50 cc. of absolute alcohol.

The Process.

Dissolving and precipitating.—2 grammes of the drillings are dissolved in 45 cc. of nitric acid of s.g. 1·20, and the solution treated exactly as in the preceding method up to the precipitation of the phosphorus as ammonium phosphomolybdate. (If the flask be closed and the contents shaken for five minutes, the total time consumed in the determination may be reduced from thirty to twenty minutes.)

Filtering, etc.—The precipitate is collected on a small filter, and after washing several times with cold 2% nitric acid, is washed several times further with a solution of potassium nitrate of the same strength until the washings are free from acid. The thorough removal of free acid by the nitrate washing is very important; pure water alone would dissolve traces of the precipitate.

Dissolving and titrating.—The filter is placed bodily in a clean flask and from 10 to 20 cc. of the standard sodium hydrate solution run in from a burette. The reading is noted. After shaking round to dissolve the yellow precipitate completely, the liquid is diluted to about 50 cc., and two drops of the phenol-phthalein indicator are added. The intensely red solution is then brought under a burette charged to the zero mark with the standard nitric acid solution, and the latter is delivered in drops until the red colour is just discharged.

Standardising.—A measured volume, 20 to 30 cc., of the standard soda solution are now run into the same flask and the solution again titrated with the nitric acid, the amount of which should be almost equal to the soda added. The data thus obtained are sufficient for calculating the result, provided the exact strength of the alkali has been determined in terms of a known weight of pure dry "yellow precipitate." The authors prefer, however, to obtain this information indirectly by carrying out an assay on a steel whose phosphorus contents are exactly known.

Example of Calculation.

In an actual determination, 16·7 cc. of $NaHO$ were used, and then 10·5 cc. of HNO_3 for the neutralization. The standardizing of the solutions in the same flask gave 25 cc. $HNO_3 = 22·5$ cc. $NaHO$, and the figures for a standard steel containing 0·058% of phosphorus were 16·4 cc. $NaHO$ and 12·1 cc. HNO_3.

From the standardization of the acid and alkali we have

$$25 \text{ cc. } HNO_3 = 22·5 \text{ cc. } NaHO$$
$$1 \text{ cc. } \,\, = \frac{22·5}{25} = 0·90 \text{ cc. } NaHO$$

From the standard steel figures we get for ·058% of phosphorus, a consumption of sodium hydrate amounting to

$$16·4 \text{ less } 12·1 \times 0·90 = 5·5 \text{ cc.}$$

The actual determination gives for the sodium hydrate used up

$$16\cdot7 \text{ less } 10\cdot5 \times 0\cdot90 = 7\cdot25 \text{ cc.}$$

The percentage of phosphorus is therefore

$$\frac{\cdot058 \times 7\cdot25}{5\cdot5} = \cdot076$$

Examples of Comparative results.

Analysis of Basic Bessemer rail steel.

A.   By Magnesia.   Weight taken 5 grammes.

Crucible + precipitate = 28·0621
Weight of crucible = 28·0465

$$\cdot0156 \quad \text{gramme } Mg_2P_2O_7$$
$$27\cdot93$$

16758
13965
2793

5)·435708

0·087°/₀ Phosphorus.

B.   By Rapid Molybdate.   Weight taken 2 grammes.

Dish + precipitate = 32·6394
Weight of dish = 32·5357

$$\cdot1037 \quad \text{gramme yellow precipitate.}$$
$$1\cdot65$$

5185
6222
1037

2)·172105

0·086°/₀ Phosphorus.

C. By Slow Molybdate. Weight taken 5 grammes.

Dish + precipitate = 32·8056

Weight of dish = 32·5375

$$\overline{\quad 0·2681 \quad}$$

$$\frac{·2681 \times 165}{5} = 0·088°/_o \text{ P.}$$

D. By the Combined Method. Weight taken 5 grammes.

Crucible + precipitate = 28·0619

Weight of crucible = 28·0462

$$\overline{\quad ·0157 \quad}$$

$$\frac{·0167 \times 27·93}{5} = 0·093°/_o \text{ P.}$$

E. By the Lead Molybdate method. Weight taken 2 grammes.

Weight of $PbMoO_4 = 0·2601$ gramme.

$$·2601 \times ·007 \times 50 = 0·091°/_o \text{ P.}$$

Greatest difference in the five determinations = 0·007°/_o.

Determination of Phosphorus in Special Steels.

In the cases of tungsten, high silicon, graphite, or high chrome steels, a modification must be introduced, the nature of which is determined by the method to be adopted for the determination of the phosphorus.

The procedure described under the estimation of phosphorus in high-speed steels on p. 249 up to the formation of the yellow precipitate can be applied here if the lead molybdate or the volumetric method are to be subsequently employed.

For all the other methods proceed as follows: Dissolve 6 grammes in nitric acid (1·20), evaporate and bake, take up in hydrochloric acid, evaporate and bake again. Dissolve up in 40 cc. of strong hydrochloric acid and transfer without loss to a 60 cc. flask. Cool, dilute to the mark, and pass through a dry filter, collecting 50 cc. in a graduated flask. Transfer to a 30-oz. registered flask, dilute, reduce, etc., in the manner already described for the preliminary operations.

Presence of arsenic.—In steels containing much arsenic, the yellow precipitate may contain traces of this element as ammonium-arsenio-molybdate, thus making the phosphorus determination too high. The arsenic is eliminated by the following treatment: Dissolve as before, evaporate, take up with hydrochloric acid, evaporate, bake and take up again with the same acid. (A portion of the arsenic by this treatment will have been expelled as the volatile trichloride.) Filter if necessary, and place the solution in a 30-oz. registered flask, diluting to about 200 cc. Now add about 5 grammes of pure zinc filings and allow to stand until the iron is completely reduced, as indicated by a spot test with potassium thiocyanate. Cool, add about half a gramme of pure precipitated zinc sulphide and cork up for a short time. Filter off the precipitated arsenic sulphide and any undissolved zinc. The filtrate is boiled to expel sulphuretted hydrogen, a few cc. of standard ferric iron solution or several small crystals of potash alum added, and the phosphorus precipitated by adding an excess of ammonium acetate. The precipitated phosphate of iron (with basic acetate) or of aluminium is then filtered off, washed, and dissolved in the acid demanded by the subsequent method selected.

Time-Table Summary.

As previously stated, the determination of the carbon, silicon, manganese, sulphur, and phosphorus constitutes

an ordinary complete analysis of a steel. Before dealing
with special steels, therefore, a consideration of the time
occupied on the complete analysis of an ordinary steel
may suitably be undertaken here. In connection with
each determination described, the approximate time required for the execution of the various operations has
been indicated, and from these the two following tables
are compiled. It will be noticed that with the exception
of the carbon determination, which is the same in both,
the second table contains the most rapid methods; but
it is obvious that a number of suitable combinations
could be made by the student to meet his own requirements.

TIME-TABLE I.

Method.	Hours.	Minutes.
Carbon by direct combustion . .	0	45
Silicon by *HCl* method	3	0
Manganese by bismuthate . .	0	20
Sulphur by Arnold's method . .	1	15
Phosphorus as $PbMoO_4$	0	40

Total time = 6 hours.

TIME-TABLE II.

Method.	Hours.	Minutes.
Carbon by direct combustion . .	0	45
Silicon by nitrosulphuric acid . .	1	30
Manganese by persulphate . . .	0	15
Sulphur by evolution (Method II)	0	45
Phosphorus by Handy's method .	0	30

Total time = 3¾ hours.

A comparison of the two tables shows that the large difference in the total times is accounted for chiefly by the difference between the times of the silicon methods. Both these are essentially processes which, after having been started, require no attention during the subsequent evaporation, so that not only does the difference in total time amount to very little, but it becomes by no means a difficult matter to turn out an ordinary complete in the course of a morning of three to three and a half hours. Taking for example the first table, which contains on the whole the most reliable processes, an arrangement of the work on the lines indicated below brings the total time within the limits specified.

(1) Light the burners under the furnace and weigh drillings and Mn_3O_4 for direct combustion. (2) Weigh off for phosphorus, manganese, and silicon determinations. (3) Dissolve for silicon determination and set the solution to evaporate. (4) Dissolve for phosphorus and manganese determinations and bring the former up to the addition of the molybdate re-agent and the latter up to the addition of the bismuthate to the cold solution. Set the phosphorus determination in a warm place not exceeding 80° C. (5) Weigh off for sulphur determination, and set going. (6) Introduce boat in the by now fully heated tube for carbon determination, and set going. (7) Finish determination of manganese. (8) Transform yellow precipitate in phosphorus determination to lead molybdate and allow to stand. The order of the remaining operations will depend entirely on circumstances. The silicon determination may require attention, having reached the "spitting" stage, and the sulphur and carbon determination may require some superintendence. The filtration of the lead molyb-

date, disconnection of the parts of the sulphur apparatus, of the parts of the combustion apparatus, the extraction of the baked silicon residue, etc., together with the necessary ignitions and weighing, are all matters which circumstances will decide.

Assuming that the chemist has the help of a laboratory assistant, it is evident that an orderly arrangement of work will enable him to turn out two complete analyses per working day.

DETERMINATION OF ARSENIC (Stead, modified).

(Time occupied, 1 day.)

Re-agents required.

Standard arsenic solution.—Weigh off accurately 0·66 gramme of pure arsenious oxide, transfer to a litre flask, add about 4 grammes of sodium bicarbonate and 100 cc. of water, heat with occasional shaking until the oxide dissolves completely, cool and dilute to the mark with water. Each cc. of this solution contains 0·0005 gramme arsenic.

Standard iodine solution.—Weigh off exactly 1·70 gramme of pure resublimed iodine, transfer to a litre flask and dissolve in water containing several grammes of potassium iodide. After making up to the mark transfer to a dark blue bottle, and when not in use keep in the dark.

These solutions should be titrated against each other. 25 cc. of the standard arsenic solution are run into a small flask from a burette, two or three cc. of a saturated solution of sodium bicarbonate in water added, then two drops of freshly prepared starch solution, and the iodine solution run in from another burette until a blue colour is developed. The solutions should be equivalent to one another.

The Process.

Dissolving, etc.—In the case of all ordinary steels 10 grammes of drillings are weighed out and transferred to a small conical flask. The latter is provided with a plug pierced with one hole and carrying a short glass delivery tube bent once at right angles. The end of the latter is joined up by india-rubber connecting tubing to an Arnold's potash bulb, and the connecting tubing is provided with a good screw clip. The potash bulb is supported at such a height that when coupled up with the conical flask the latter rests near the edge of and on the hot plate. Finally the potash bulb is charged with about 2 cc. of bromine and then filled with bromine water so as to cover the upper inner bulb.

Everything being ready, the drillings are covered with a mixture of 80 cc. strong hydrochloric acid with an equal bulk of water, the bung is quickly inserted and the flask set near the edge of the plate. The escaping hydrogen bubbles vigorously through the bromine bulb, causing considerable loss of bromine vapour, the irritating effect of which is counteracted by exposing a small beaker containing a few drops of strong ammonia near the outlet of the absorption bulb. As the action proceeds the heat under the evolution flask may be increased, and the liquid finally brought to boiling to effect solution of the last particles and to vapourize more or less completely the bromine still remaining in the absorption bulb. Before removing the burner, close the screw clip tightly and then remove the bung; by so doing the bromine water is not sucked back into the evolution flask.

Precipitating the arsenic.—The flask is placed under the water tap so as to be thoroughly cooled. In the meantime the bromine water in the absorption bulb is emptied and well washed into a beaker, and the liquid boiled to complete expulsion of the last traces of bromine. The now colourless solution, after cooling, is rinsed into the evolution flask, and about one gramme of pure precipitated zinc sulphide added together with 10 cc. of strong hydrochloric acid. The flask is at once closed with a tightly fitting plug so as to retain the generated sulphuretted hydrogen under pressure, and the contents of the flask are shaken from time to time during a period of ten minutes.

Filtration.—The mixture of arsenic sulphide, carbonaceous residue, etc., is filtered off through a small but compact pulp filter, well washed with 10% hydrochloric acid and finally once with water. The whole filter and its contents are transferred to a clean 40-oz. beaker and distilled water added up to about 750 cc. The liquid is then vigorously boiled during a period of at least three hours until the bulk is reduced to about 20 cc.

Titration of the arsenic.—The liquid with the pulp and unchanged carbonaceous matter is filtered through another pulp filter and thoroughly washed with hot water. The filtrate is cooled, 10 cc. of a saturated solution of sodium bicarbonate added along with two drops

of starch liquor, and then titrated with the standard
iodine solution. Each cc. of the iodine solution, if
exactly equivalent in strength to the standard arsenic
solution, represents $0·005\%$ of arsenic when working
on 10 grammes of steel.

Theory of the Process.

The small amount of arsenic usually present in steel
and pig-iron is partly evolved as arsenuretted hydrogen
and partly passes into solution when the material is
decomposed with dilute hydrochloric acid. The evolved
portion is oxidized to arsenic acid by the bromine and
is retained in the absorption bulb.

$$AsH_3 + 4 \ Br_2 + 4 \ H_2O = H_3AsO_4 + 8 \ HBr$$

After expelling the excess of bromine the solution is
returned to the evolution flask and the arsenic precipitated as sulphide by the sulphuretted hydrogen
generated from the zinc sulphide and free acid.

$$ZnS + 2 \ HCl = ZnCl_2 + H_2S$$
$$2 \ H_3AsO_4 + 4 \ H_2S = As_2S_3 + 4 \ H_2O + S$$

That portion of the arsenic remaining in the evolution
flask exists either as the trichloride or as arsenious acid,
and the zinc sulphide precipitates it from both these
compounds.

$$2 \ AsCl_3 + 3 \ H_2S = As_2S_3 + 6 \ HCl$$
$$2 \ H_3AsO_3 + 3 \ H_2S = As_2S_3 + 6 \ H_2O$$

The arsenic sulphide, filtered off with carbonaceous
matter, etc., is boiled for a long time with water in

order to effect its complete hydrolysis according to the equation

$$As_2S_3 + 6\ H_2O = 2\ H_3AsO_3 + 3\ H_2S$$

The sulphuretted hydrogen is expelled by the boiling and the arsenious acid carried into solution. After making alkaline with sodium bicarbonate the arsenic is titrated with free iodine, the least excess of which strikes with the starch indicator a blue colour.

$$H_3AsO_3 + I_2 + H_2O = H_3AsO_4 + 2\ HI$$

Normal sodium carbonate as well as the hydrate interfere with the development of the blue colour marking the end of the reaction, hence the necessity for using sodium bicarbonate, which must be present in quantity sufficient to neutralize the liberated hydriodic acid.

SPECIAL STEELS.

Arsenic is never purposely introduced into steels except for purely research purposes. For steels that contain comparatively large amounts of arsenic the preceding process requires some modification.

After dissolving the sample, it will be noticed that a black scum of arsenide of iron remains on the surface of the liquid in the evolution flask. After cooling, the zinc sulphide is added as usual and the mixed precipitate collected, after some little time, on the pulp filter and well washed as described. The filter and contents are then transferred to the evolution flask and the bromine water from the absorption bulb added to the mixture. If necessary a further small quantity of bromine is added so as to give a rich colour to the solution, and the liquid is then boiled after adding 5 to 10 cc. of hydrochloric acid. A few small crystals of potassium iodide are then added, the mixture well shaken, and a slight but pronounced excess of sulphurous acid added to remove the liberated iodine. The liquid is boiled to expel the excess of sulphur dioxide and then well cooled. If, after cooling, any colour develops, remove by adding one drop of sulphurous acid and then add the zinc sulphide as before. After allowing to stand under slight pressure for some time, filter, wash thoroughly with a hot mixture of equal parts of strong hydrochloric acid and water, then once with water only. Transfer to the large beaker and boil with water as before.

Theory of the Process.

The precipitated scum of arsenide of iron is readily oxidized to arsenic acid by the bromine water added from the absorption bulb and is thereby carried into solution. The object of adding potassium iodide is to effect a reduction to arsenious acid so as to get a complete precipitation as sulphide in as little time as possible :

$$H_3AsO_4 + 2\ KI + H_2O = H_3AsO_3 + 2\ KHO + I_2$$

The liberated iodine is converted to hydriodic acid by the sulphurous acid :

$$I_2 + H_2SO_3 + H_2O = H_2SO_4 + 2\ HI$$

Determination of Tungsten (and Silicon).

This element is introduced into water-hardening steels in the proportion of about $2\frac{1}{2}\%$, whilst self-hardening steels contain about 10%. Of the first-named class of steel, 2 grammes should be taken for analysis, but for the richer alloy 1 gramme is sufficient. The estimation is a tedious process, sometimes occupying a day and a half: water steels can always be drilled, but the self-hardening material has sometimes to be sampled for analysis in the form of crushed, or semi-crushed, fragments obtained from a small-sized bar.

Method I.

Dissolving.—Weigh out the steel into a 20-oz. covered beaker, dissolve by heating with 50 cc. of nitric acid, sp. gr. 1·2; boil down to low bulk, remove the cover, and place the beaker on a pipe-stem triangle.

First evaporation to dryness.—Next carefully evaporate to dryness, remove from the triangle, and bake well in the middle of the plate. Now allow the beaker to cool with the usual precaution, and dissolve up the dry mass of oxide of iron by boiling with 30 cc. of strong *HCl*, and again carefully evaporate to complete dryness.

Third evaporation.—Take up as before in 30 cc. of *HCl*, and gently vaporise the bulk of the acid, going down to about 5 cc.

Filtering.—Dilute with 50 cc. of water, and filter off the precipitate through a close-grained filter, contained in a $2\frac{1}{4}$-in. funnel, the latter being supported in a 100 cc. measuring-glass. Get through and throw away as much

M

as possible of the clear iron solution before disturbing
the precipitate with wash water, because some of the
finely-divided WO_3 will probably pass through the pores
of the paper, and the filtrate must be re-passed through
the filter till the interstices of the latter are filled up and
the liquid comes through quite clear. This is readily
ascertained by holding up the measuring-glass to the
light, and carefully examining the fluid contents for suspended matter. The paper and precipitate must now be
washed *quite free from ferric chloride*[1] with cold, very
dilute (5%) hydrochloric acid and cold water. After
drying in the usual manner, the filter is ignited in a clean,
tared platinum crucible, and the latter, when cold, is re-
weighed. The increase is (x $WO_3 + y$ SiO_2).

Treatment with HF.—To the ignited mass in the crucible add 2 cc. of *pure*[2] aqueous hydrofluoric acid. The
latter is quietly evaporated off in the draught cupboard,
and the crucible is re-ignited, cooled, and re-weighed.
The loss from the second weighing = SiO_2, containing
46·7% Si; the increase over the first weighing of the
crucible = WO_3, containing 79·3% of tungsten.

Theoretical Considerations.

On dissolving the steel in nitric acid when only about
3% tungsten is present, it passes into solution as tungstic

---

[1] In rich alloys the final residue may be examined for Fe_2O_3 by
fusing it with $HKSO_4$. If present, the weight must be estimated
colorimetrically and deducted. The aqueous extract from the fusion
is made up to a known volume, and the iron in a portion of the
filtered liquid is determined as described on p. 75.

[2] The aqueous acid should leave no residue on evaporation.

acid, probably forming a compound somewhat analogous
to that produced under the same conditions by silicic
acid (see p. 59). If, however, 10% tungsten is present,
some of the WO_3 separates as an insoluble yellow precipitate. The conversion by baking of the ferric nitrate
into oxide also determines the decomposition of the organic carbon compound, which, had the preliminary
solution, as often advocated, been made in aqua regia,
would have separated in a slimy condition, and thus have
rendered still slower an already tedious filtration. The
second evaporation to dryness and the third to low bulk
with HCl ensure the complete separation of the tungstic
acid, some of which, with only one or two evaporations,
is liable to remain dissolved in the hydrochloric acid solution. The treatment with hydrofluoric acid of the mixed
residue of tungstic anhydride and silica brings about a
volatilization of the latter, thus—

$$SiO_2 + 4\ HF = SiF_4 + 2\ H_2O$$

Silica and hydrogen fluoride yield gaseous fluoride of
silicon and water. The alleged liability of some of the
WO_3 to volatilize with the silicon unless sulphuric acid
is present has no foundation in fact.

The method found in most text-books for separating
tungstic and silicic anhydrides is based upon the solubility of WO_3 and the insolubility of SiO_2 in hot ammonia
solution. This process is absolutely worthless—

(a) Because strongly baked WO_3 is not always completely soluble in ammonia.

(b) Because SiO_2 obtained from H_4SiO_4 by evaporation of a hydrochloric acid solution is almost completely
soluble in hot ammonia solution, as L. Dufty has conclusively shown.

Method II. (Brearley.)

(Time occupied 1½ hours.)

Dissolving, etc.—To 2 grammes of the drillings in a 20-oz. beaker add a large excess (50 cc.) of strong hydrochloric acid, heat the mixture up to boiling, and then remove the beaker to the corner of the plate so as to keep the liquid hot without much expulsion of the acid. Now add from time to time a few drops only of strong nitric acid, allowing several minutes between each addition. In this way the steel is decomposed without any separation of tungstic oxide. When complete decomposition has been brought about, sufficient nitric acid should have been added to oxidize the iron, and the liquid will be clear except for a floating scum of carbonaceous matter.

Evaporation.—The beaker is then pushed to the hottest part of the plate and the solution evaporated to low bulk but not to dryness. During the evaporation tungstic oxide separates out and increases in amount as the bulk of the liquid is reduced. To the evaporated solution, now measuring say 10 cc., hot water is added up to about 50 or 60 cc., and after boiling for two minutes the beaker is set aside to allow the tungstic oxide to settle.

Filtration, etc.—Filter through pulp and wash with 5% hot hydrochloric acid. Ignite in a weighed platinum crucible or shallow dish. The residue consists of tungstic oxide, nearly all of the silica from the silicon of the steel, and traces of ferric oxide. It will also contain chromic oxide if the steel is a chromiferous one. These

impurities are removed and allowed for by the treatment
described fully under the analysis of high speed steels
for tungsten on p. 247.

It generally happens that a film of tungstic oxide
sticks obstinately to the sides of the beaker, and cannot
be removed by the policeman. A small piece of ashless
filter paper moistened with a drop or two of ammonia
will usually remove it, or the film may be dissolved off
with several drops of ammonia and the solution evaporated to dryness in the weighed ignition dish before adding the filter with the precipitate.

The results obtained by the above method are not
more than $0·02\%$ below the truth.

Theory of the Process.

The chief point in connection with the foregoing
method is that of effecting complete decomposition of
tungsten steels (or even rich alloys) before any separation of tungstic oxide occurs. To this end a large excess
of hydrochloric acid is used in the first instance, and the
strength of the hot acid is maintained throughout the
subsequent treatment, thus holding the tungstic oxide
in solution.

The time of the operation may be lessened by adding
hot water immediately after WO_3 begins to precipitate,
instead of continuing the evaporation to low bulk. If
sufficient water is added to yield a mixture containing
not more than one part of strong acid to four parts of
water, the amount of tungstic oxide left in solution
corresponds to not more than $0·06\%$ working on 2
grammes of steel.

GRAVIMETRIC DETERMINATION OF CHROMIUM AS OXIDE.
(J. O. Arnold.[1])

Re-agent required.

Fusion mixture.—Intimately mix 100 grammes each of pure dry powdered potassium nitrate, potassium carbonate, and sodium carbonate; preserve the mixture in a well-stoppered bottle.

The Process.

(Time occupied, about 1 day.)

Weight taken.—Weigh out into a covered 20-oz. beaker 2·4, 1·2, or ·6 grammes of the steel according to its richness in chromium. The weight last mentioned is suitable for a steel containing say 6% of the metal.

Dissolving.—Add in the case of 2·4 grammes of steel 30 cc. of strong hydrochloric acid; gently heat on the plate till the drillings have dissolved, and then boil the liquid down to low bulk. The evaporation is then slowly continued with the cover off so as to obtain the chlorides in a compact, dry cake at the bottom of the beaker. The residue must not be baked, but is merely taken quietly to dryness in such a manner that the cover and sides of the beaker are free from splashing.

Pulverizing the chlorides.—Allow the mass to go cold, and then, with the aid of a steel spatula the brittle cake may be cut up into several easily detached pieces, which are carefully transferred to a 3-in. porcelain dish. Any strongly adhering particles of chloride which cannot be brushed out are dissolved in a very few cc. of strong

[1] "Chemical News," 1880, No. 1098.

hydrochloric acid, the covered beaker being heated on
the plate till all soluble matter is taken up. The solution,
together with any insoluble residue, is transferred with
the aid of a fine jet of water into a deep 3-in. platinum
dish, into which any chlorides adhering to the spatula
are also washed. The dish is then placed over a little
beaker of boiling water, and its contents, which should
never exceed 15 cc., are evaporated to dryness. Whilst
the evaporation is proceeding the main portion of the
chlorides in the porcelain dish (which should be placed
on a sheet of glazed white paper) is reduced to a fine
powder by means of a little round-headed pestle made
out of $\frac{1}{2}$-in. diameter glass rod, after which the pestle is
cleaned from adhering chlorides by means of a pen blade
and camel's hair brush. When the contents of the
platinum dish are dry it is taken off the beaker, and is
well wiped outside.

Fusion.—Carefully transfer the powdered chlorides
from the porcelain to the platinum dish, well rinsing the
latter by means of the pestle with several fractions of
30 grammes of fusion mixture, after which the remainder
of the latter is added to the chlorides, and the whole is
intimately mixed with the pestle into a uniformly tinted
powder. After brushing the pestle gently tap down the
mixture, cover the dish, and place it on a pipe-stem
triangle supported on a tripod, and, cautiously at first,
heat the mass over a good Bunsen burner for about
fifteen minutes till the excess of alkalies is quite liquid;
then remove the lamp.

Extracting the fusion.—When moderately cool place
the dish and cover in a 20-oz. beaker containing 200 cc.
of nearly boiling water: in two or three minutes, by
means of a glass rod, tilt the cover so that a portion can

be washed, take hold of the cover by the washed edge, lift it out of the solution, well rinse it all over, and remove. By means of the glass rod occasionally rotate the dish till the alkaline salts have all dissolved, and the oxide of iron is completely detached in the form of a red powder. The crucible is then washed and removed by means similar to those employed in the case of the cover. Thoroughly stir the liquid with a glass rod, and wash and remove the latter.

Filtering off the iron and manganese.—Transfer the hot liquid and precipitate in the beaker without loss to a 301 cc. graduated flask marked low down in the neck, and dilute to about 301·5 cc. By means of a long chemical thermometer thoroughly stir the yellow liquid till uniform in colour; withdraw the thermometer just clear of the meniscus, till the latter by the contraction of the liquid reaches the mark. Note the temperature of the solution, allow the oxide of iron to settle for a few minutes, and then through a dry double paper contained in a 2¼-in. ribbed funnel filter off into a 250 cc. dry graduated flask about 249·5 cc. of the perfectly clear yellow liquid; remove the funnel, and heat the flask on the plate till its contents approach the previously noted temperature. Then, by means of the thermometer, throw out drops of the fluid till 250 cc. at the original temperature are obtained.

Reducing.—Pour and wash out every trace of the solution from the flask into a 20-oz. covered beaker, and add down the lip 25 to 35 cc. of strong hydrochloric acid till no more CO_2 is evolved, and the colour of the liquid has changed from yellow to clear green. Bring the liquid to boiling, and keep it in ebullition till the brown fumes in the upper part of the beaker have disappeared.

First precipitation.—Next, very cautiously, a little at a time, add to the gently boiling liquid down the lip of the beaker dilute ammonia solution till the hydrochloric acid is neutralized, a permanent pale-green precipitate is obtained, and a very faint excess of ammonia is present. Then remove the beaker to a cooler part of the plate, and digest it just short of boiling till the precipitate has collected into flocks and the liquid is crystal clear.

Filtering.—Allow the precipitate to settle, and do not disturb it more than necessary till most of the clear filtrate has been poured through a 110 mm. paper. Then throw the precipitate on the filter, rinse out the beaker with hot water, wash the edges of the filter-paper once, and allow it to drain.

Re-dissolving the precipitate.—Hang the funnel inside the beaker in which the precipitation took place, and by means of hot, slightly diluted hydrochloric acid, dissolve the precipitate, using the smallest possible quantity of solvent, and well wash the paper with a fine jet of cold water. The filter is then put under cover till required for re-filtering the solution if necessary.

Separating SiO_2 and WO_3.—Cover the beaker containing the green chloride solution, briskly boil down to low bulk, and then, without the cover, quietly evaporate the liquid till green crystals are deposited. (These, if further heated, turn red, and are re-dissolved with difficulty.) Add 5 cc. of strong hydrochloric acid, and heat till the crystals are re-dissolved, if necessary adding a little water. The liquid is then carefully examined to ascertain if any silica or yellow tungstic acid has precipitated. If so, the liquid, after diluting with 20 cc. of water, is passed through the paper previously used into a clean 20-oz. beaker, and the paper is then exhaustively washed. If, however, the liquid is clear, which is often the case, it is diluted to 200 cc., and heated to boiling in the covered beaker.

Re-precipitating the chromium.—The chromium is next precipitated with well-diluted ammonia (1 of 880 to 3 of water) exactly as described for the first precipitation.

Final filtration and washing.—Filter off on a 110 mm. pure paper contained in a 2½-in. funnel as before, but in the present case every particle of precipitate is carefully detached by means of a policeman, and the beaker is thoroughly rinsed out with hot water. The paper is thrice washed round the edges with nearly boiling water without disturbing the precipitate, which, if stirred up by a too vigorous application of the jet, is liable to a small extent to pass through the pores of the paper. After the last washing, allow the filter to drain: the filtrate should be crystal clear.

Weighing.—The paper is detached from the funnel and dried in the usual manner. It is strongly ignited in a tared platinum crucible, and when quite cold the latter is removed from the dessicator and re-weighed. The increase is Cr_2O_3, containing 68·5% of metal.

Example of a trial Determination.

To 2·4 grammes of a steel free from chromium 0·0678 gramme of pure dry $K_2Cr_2O_7$ was added, corresponding to 1°/₀ of chromium.

Result.

Crucible + ppt. = 28·6320
Weight of crucible = 28·6034
               ·0286
               68·5
            ────────
              1430
              2288
              1716
            ────────
         2)1·95910
         ────────
         0·97955 say 0·98°/₀ Chromium.

Theoretical Considerations.

The preliminary solution and evaporation to dryness with hydrochloric acid yields the mixed chlorides of the metals iron, chromium, and manganese, together with silica, traces of phosphate and sulphate of iron, and a little carbonaceous matter. The action of the fusion mixture converts the iron to Fe_2O_3 absolutely insoluble in water, the chromium to a mixture of the yellow chromates of potassium and sodium K_2CrO_4 and Na_2CrO_4, the manganese to green alkaline manganates K_2MnO_4 and Na_2MnO_4.

The silica is converted into alkaline silicates (see p. 369), whilst any sulphates or phosphates present form respectively the sulphates and pyrophosphates of potassium and sodium, *e.g.* Na_2SO_4 and $Na_4P_2O_7$. The potassium nitrate is converted into nitrite KNO_2. On extracting the fusion in hot water the alkaline manganates decompose, and the manganese is totally precipitated as hydrated dioxide. The alkaline chromates, silicates, sulphates, and pyrophosphates pass into solution together with the excess of carbonates and the potassium nitrite. On acidifying the yellow filtrate with hydrochloric acid, the liquid for a moment assumes a much deeper yellow colour, owing to the formation of bichromates, thus—

$$2\ K_2CrO_4 + 2\ HCl = K_2Cr_2O_7 + 2\ KCl + H_2O$$

The hydrochloric acid then liberates nitrous acid from the potassium nitrite, when the bichromate is reduced to green chromic chloride with evolution of nitrous fumes, whilst the pyrophosphates are converted into orthophosphates. On the addition of ammonia, green chromic hydrate is precipated thus—

$$CrCl_3 + 3\ AmHO = Cr(HO)_3 + 3\ AmCl$$

The above hydrate is soluble in a large excess of ammonia, hence the necessity for using only a faint excess. With the precipitate will be found any traces of phosphoric acid P_2O_5 combined with a portion of the hydrate, but in steels containing only about 0·05% P, the residue of phosphorus not evolved as PH_3 (amounting to about 20% of the total P present) causes only a trifling + error,[1] which, in fact, seems to compensate for the small loss of chromium occurring during the analysis. It is hardly necessary to state after the above remarks, that the fusion mixture employed should be absolutely free from phosphates. In steels in which the phosphorus is somewhat high and the percentage of chromium present is small, the hydrate method should not be used, but the process described in the next article should be employed. The reason for re-precipitating the chromic hydrate is, that it may be contaminated with a little silica, and is invariably impure with small quantities of alkaline salts, from which, on the second precipitation, it is free. The extra 1 cc. over the 300 cc. of liquid containing the chromium in 2·4 grammes of steel is a correction for the volume of the ferric oxide, and for a slight concentration of the solution by evaporation during filtration.

[1] In a steel containing about 0·1% of P, the error from the phosphorus oxidized to phosphoric acid (P_2O_5) during the dissolution of the steel in HCl will equal on 2 grammes of steel 0·03 to 0·04% Cr, equivalent to about 1 milligramme of P_2O_5.

Influence of Special Elements on the Analysis.

Copper and nickel both remain with the oxide of iron in the respective forms of CuO and NiO. When tungsten is present, it totally passes into solution with the yellow chromates as alkaline tungstate, but by reason of its partial solubility in hydrochloric acid and its complete solubility in ammonia, the tungstic acid is completely got rid of during the analysis, and the final precipitate is free from it. The case of aluminium requires special treatment, which will be described at the end of the next article.

Gravimetric Estimation of Chromium as Phosphate.
(Arnold and Hardy.[1])

(Time occupied, about $1\frac{1}{4}$ days.)

This process should always be employed for the gravimetric estimation of small quantities of chromium in steels containing say $0.1\%\ P$. It is also useful in cases of dispute as an alternative method of determination.

Re-agent required.

10% *solution of sodium phosphate.* — Dissolve 25 grammes of ordinary phosphate of soda $(Na_2HPO_4, 12\ Aq)$ in 250 cc. of water. The filtered liquid is best kept for use in a green glass bottle with an india-rubber stopper.

[1] "Chemical News," 1888, No. 1482.

The Process.

The method is carried out exactly in the manner described for the hydrate process, except that before the first precipitation 10 cc. of the 10% solution of phosphate of soda are added. Also the precipitate is weighed as $Cr_6P_4O_{19}$ containing $42\cdot48\%$ Cr. The weighing should be made in a covered crucible (in the manner described on p. 67 for the determination of silicon), because the basic phosphate is somewhat hygroscopic.

Theory of the Process.

When phosphoric acid, P_2O_5, and salts of chromic oxide, Cr_2O_3, are in solution together, if the former be largely in excess the precipitate obtained on digesting the liquid with a slight excess of ammonia is uncertain in composition. It may be the normal salt $Cr_2P_2O_8 = (Cr_2O_3, P_2O_5)$, but is sometimes a mixture of normal and basic salt, and sometimes a mixture of normal and acid phosphate, but in the presence of the theoretical amount or of a moderate excess of P_2O_5 chromic oxide is completely precipitated as a definite basic phosphate $Cr_6P_4O_{19}$.

The data upon which the foregoing statements are founded are set forth in the following table extracted from the original memoir published in the "Chemical News." Various weights of pure dry $K_2Cr_2O_7$ in dilute hydrochloric acid solution were reduced by means of sulphurous acid. The chromium was then precipitated by a faint excess of ammonia in the presence of varying amounts of phosphoric acid introduced by means of a solution of sodium phosphate carefully standardized by magnesia. Results :

Ratio of Molecules.		Grammes.				
Cr_2O_3.	P_2O_5.	Cr_2O_3.	P_2O_5.	Precipitate obtained.	Theory.	
					$Cr_6P_4O_{19}$.	$Cr_3P_2O_8$.
—	—	0·0265	0·0221	0·0430	0·0430	—
—	—	0·0258	0·0221	0·0415	0·0418	—
—	—	0·0516	0·0387	0·0830	0·0837	—
—	—	0·0258	0·0600	0·0500	—	0·0500
—	—	0·0546	0·0800	[1]0·0990	0·0885	0·1056
3	2	0·0389	0·0240	0·0625	0·0629	—
1	1	0·0258	0·0240	0·0420	0·0417	—
1	16	0·0258	0·3840	[2]0·0560	0·0417	0·0500
1	32	0·0258	0·7680	0·0496	—	0·0500

[1] Indefinite basic phosphate.　　　　[2] Indefinite acid phosphate.

Therefore, in the first precipitation, when a large excess of sodium phosphate is present, the constitution of the phosphate is uncertain, except that it will certainly contain P_2O_5 somewhat in excess of that necessary to form $Cr_6P_4O_{19} = (3\ Cr_2O_3,\ 2\ P_2O_5)$; but on the second precipitation conditions are secured under which the results obtained in the above table prove that the definite basic phosphate is thrown down, whilst the small excess of P_2O_5 combines with the free ammonia present to form Am_3PO_4, which may be proved by well washing a first precipitate, and adding a nitric acid solution of ammonium molybdate to the filtrate from the second precipitate.

Determination of minute quantities of Chromium.

In estimating percentages of chromium falling below 0·1% weigh out 12 grammes of steel, and obtain the chromium associated with a comparatively small quantity of iron exactly in the manner described for obtaining the second precipitate in the estimation of aluminium on page 201, of course adding enough phosphate of soda to precipitate chromium equivalent to ·1% of 12 grammes, using rather more sulphurous acid and ammonium acetate, and precipitating from a more dilute solution. The paper containing the precipitate is, after drying, ignited in a small platinum dish, the residue is mixed with 2 or 3 grammes of fusion mixture, and fused in the usual manner. The extract is made up to 120 cc., 100 cc. are filtered off, and on this volume the analysis is proceeded with as already described; the chromium is weighed as basic phosphate, and the result calculated on 10 grammes of steel. Mr. J. E. Stead has published results[1] which seem to indicate that chromium is almost universally present in small quantities in British iron and steel products. Mr. Stead tabulates percentages as low as 0·006, but as the results were obtained by an indirect volumetric process, involving the use of re-agents so readily reduced as potassium permanganate, and so easily oxidized as ferrous sulphate, the authors are of opinion that the unavoidable errors of analysis in the method employed are *per se* capable of indicating an apparent % of chromium so minute as that quoted. Deservedly high as is the reputation of Mr. Stead as a steel analyst, chemists

[1] "Journal of the Iron and Steel Institute," 1893, No. 1, p. 168.

should not absolutely accept his volumetric results till they have been confirmed by the above process, in which a precipitate of pure phosphate of chromium is actually seen and directly weighed.

Comparative Advantages of the Hydrate and Phosphate Methods.

In all Swedish steels and in high-class English Bessemer and open-hearth products, the hydrate process is undoubtedly the best to use; the precipitate is less bulky, more soluble in hydrochloric acid, less liable to pass through the paper on washing, and, if the hydrochloric acid solution of the first precipitate is inadvertently carried to complete dryness after the evaporation, the baked chloride is much more easily re-dissolved than the phosphate under similar conditions. Finally, the hydrate is not hygroscopic after ignition. On the other hand, the phosphate precipitate is less liable to take up SiO_2 when unwittingly boiled in a new beaker, and is not so soluble in any accidentally added large excess of ammonia. In has also the advantage of giving a larger weight of precipitate for a corresponding percentage of metal. The authors' experience in working upon 0·5 gramme of chromium free steels, into which 6% of metal in the form of $K_2Cr_2O_7$ had been introduced, has been, that the hydrate results averaged 5·95% Cr, whilst the phosphate determinations indicated 6·05%. In working upon steels containing say 2% of chromium, duplicate estimations on different weights of drillings agree to about 0·02%. Mr. William Galbraith has stated in a paper to be subsequently referred to, that gravimetric estimations of

N

chromium are usually seriously high. Mr. Galbraith's view on this point is an altogether mistaken one. For more than twenty years the authors' experience of gravimetric estimations of chromium, made not only upon known quantities, but upon samples representing hundreds of tons of chrome pig-iron, and thousands of tons of chrome steel, has proved that properly-conducted gravimetric determinations of chromium invariably give accurate and concordant results.[1]

Determination of Chromium in Aluminium Steels.

When aluminium is present in a steel in which the chromium is being estimated by either of the foregoing methods, part of it will be found in the yellow solution of the chromates as sodic aluminate $(NaAl)_2O_4$, whilst a portion remains with the ferric oxide as Al_2O_3. Unless separated, the portion present with the chromium will be precipitated as hydrate or phosphate, thus giving too high a result. The separation is easily and completely effected thus: To the total yellow extract containing the precipitates of iron and manganese add 10 cc. of a saturated solution of re-sublimed ordinary ammonium carbonate $(3\ NH_3\cdot2\ CO_2\cdot H_2O)$, then pass through the liquid for at least fifteen minutes a brisk current of washed CO_2 generated from marble and hydrochloric acid. The aluminium is totally precipitated as an indefinite, basic carbonate, and is then filtered off with the

---

[1] As has already been pointed out by Mr. Stead, the precipitation of chromium by diffused $BaCO_3$ is valueless as a quantitative process.

iron and manganese. The principle of the reactions involved may be formulated as follows—

$$Na_2 CO_3 + (Al_2O_3, Na_2O) + 4\ AmHCO_3 + H_2O =$$
$$4\ NaHCO_3 + Am_2CO_3 + 2\ AmHO + Al_2O_3$$
$$2\ AmHO + CO_2 = Am_2CO_3 + H_2O$$

The sodic aluminate and the excess of normal sodium carbonate present in the liquid after the fusion form acid or bi-carbonate of soda (in which alumina is insoluble), together with normal ammonium carbonate and free ammonia, in which the alumina remains dissolved; but on the conversion of the free ammonia into ammonium carbonate by the passage of CO_2, the alumina is totally precipitated in combination with some carbonic acid.

Volumetric Determination of Chromium (Galbraith).

This process was devised some fifteen years ago by Mr. W. Galbraith for estimating the chromium in pig-iron, and that alloyed in small quantity with steel. For the latter purpose up to $0·25\%$ Cr, the method originally published, answered well, but when applied to chrome-pig or to steel containing a considerable percentage of the metal, the results obtained were always low, sometimes seriously so, from the following causes:

(a) In pig-irons the chromium present was not completely dissolved by the dilute sulphuric acid used for a solvent.

(b) No precaution was given with reference to the vital point of the volume to which the solution must be diluted, to ensure the oxidation of the chromic oxide [existing in the sulphate $(Cr_2O_3, 3\ SO_3)$] to chromic anhydride CrO_3.

(c) The amount of permanganate of potash specified was about six times too much.

The error introduced under heading (a) is too obvious to need explanation. The chromium missed under heading (b) escaped estimation, owing to the fact that in a not sufficiently diluted sulphuric acid solution some chromic oxide remained unoxidized to the acid-forming oxide. The loss under heading (c) was brought about by the unnecessarily large amount of manganic precipitate formed, carrying down with it some of the chromium. The above facts have since been recognized by Mr. Galbraith, and in the " Journal of the Iron and Steel Institute," 1893, No. 1, page 150, he amended his process for completely soluble steels as follows: " The process thus becomes—Dissolve in sulphuric acid (1 in 6), add permanganate, and boil till precipitate is black; then dilute and make alkaline with caustic soda; filter, wash, acidulate filtrate, and treat as before with ferrous salt and potassium bichromate."

The authors have been unable to work the amended process—(1) because the precipitate never becomes black, but is of a deep rich brown colour; (2) when working say upon 2 grammes of steel, on making the oxidized solution alkaline with sodic hydrate, the whole of the iron is thrown down, yielding a bulky precipitate, almost incapable of being properly washed.

Modified method.—The following modification worked out by one of the authors preserves the simplicity of the original process, and to a great extent eliminates its errors. The results obtained on strictly following out the empirical conditions herein laid down are practically accurate, at any rate in steels containing up to 3% of chromium.

Re-agent required.

Standard solution of $K_2Cr_2O_7$.—This is made by dissolving 2·8310 grammes of pure, recently dried crystals of potassium bichromate in distilled water, and making up the solution to 1000 cc. The liquid is then standardized by dissolving 0·1618 gramme of Swedish bar-iron (99·8% *Fe*) in 70 cc. of dilute sulphuric acid (1 in 7). On titrating the acid solution of ferrous sulphate with the ferricyanide indicator (see p. 84), exactly 50 cc. of bichromate solution should be required. The liquid is corrected for strength or weakness in the manner exemplified on p. 89.

The Process.

(Time occupied, about $1\frac{1}{2}$ hours.)

Weight taken.—Weigh out 2 grammes of the steel into a clean dry 10-oz. flask.

Dissolving—To 60 cc. of water contained in a small beaker add 10 cc. of pure, strong sulphuric acid, and pour the hot mixture into the flask. The contents of the latter, after covering the mouth with a watch-glass, are briskly boiled till the drillings are dissolved, and the acid has become so concentrated that white crystals of anhydrous sulphate of iron begin to precipitate.

Diluting.—Rinse the watch-glass, dilute the solution with 100 cc. of hot water, and bring the liquid to incipient boiling.

Oxidizing the chromium to CrO_3.—Remove the flask from the plate, dissolve in the solution, a few crystals at a time, pure potassium permanganate, well shaking round the fluid after each addition till the iron is oxidized to ferric sulphate, and a slight, pale-brown permanent precipitate is produced. About $1\frac{1}{4}$ grammes of the crystal will be required to reach this stage. Next add, weighed roughly, 0·2 gramme more of the permanganate crystals and shake the liquid round till they have dissolved, producing a dark brown precipitate; then rinse down from inside the neck of the flask any adhering fragments of permanganate; the contents of the flask are then boiled for five minutes and removed from the plate.

Filtering.—Allow the precipitate to settle somewhat, and, slowly at first, pour the solution through a *pure*[1] 110 mm. filter contained in a $2\frac{1}{4}''$ funnel. The rich purple-brown precipitate is then thrown upon the filter, the flask is well rinsed out, and the precipitate and paper are washed with hot water till the filtrate is colourless. The latter is received into a perfectly clean 14-oz. conical beaker. The filtration and washing occupy only from five to ten minutes.

Titrating.—When weighing out the chrome steel there

[1] Thick filters of impure paper are liable to reduce a little chromic acid to chromic oxide during the filtration, but the authors have not been able to detect any practical difference in the results obtained when ashless papers are used, and those registered on a filtrate passed —as suggested by Mr. Hogg—through recently-ignited asbestos. If the latter is used, 2·4 grammes of steel may be employed, using 0·25 gramme excess of permanganate, and titrating five-sixths of the total liquid. The latter is filtered through an asbestos plug packed in the shoulder of a small piece of combustion tubing 1″ in diameter, but drawn out at one end to an inside diameter of $\frac{1}{4}''$; as much as possible of the liquid is passed through the plug before throwing much precipitate upon it.

should also be weighed out into a clean, dry 12-oz. flask 0·1618 gramme of Swedish Lancashire hearth bar-iron, in which on analysis the iron by difference should be practically 99·8%. As soon as the filtration of the chromic solution is commenced, add to the flask containing the iron a mixture of 10 cc. of strong sulphuric acid with 60 cc. of water, and boil the contents of the flask, after covering the latter with a watch-glass. The known quantity of ferrous sulphate in sulphuric acid solution, which must be quite colourless, will thus be ready shortly after the washing is completed. When the last particle of iron is dissolved, remove the flask from the plate, and pour into it the perfectly clear chromic solution from the conical beaker, well rinsing out the latter.[1] The excess of iron is then determined by the standard bichromate solution, delivered from a 50 cc. burette, exactly in the manner described for manganese on p. 85; each cc. remaining in the burette equals 0·05% *Cr*. The 50 cc. of standard solution are therefore capable of estimating a maximum of 2·5% *Cr*. For steels up to 5% double the weight of iron (0·3236) is employed, then each cc. left out of 100 cc. of the bichromate solution also equals 0·05% *Cr*.

Example of Titration.

Working on the quantities first given, 23·2 cc. of the standard solution were required to oxidize the excess of ferrous iron, then 50—23·2 = 26·8, and 26·8 × ·05 = 1·34% of chromium.

---

[1] Never pour the iron solution into the chromic liquid, because the former may then become slightly oxidized by the air.

Theoretical Considerations.

The reason for boiling the sulphuric acid solution of the steel till sulphates precipitate, is to ensure the decomposition of separated flocks of black chromium carbide, which resists the attack of the more dilute acid. On adding the first and main portion of permanganate to the solution the iron is oxidized from ferrous to ferric sulphate thus—

$$2KMnO_4 + 10FeSO_4 + 8H_2SO_4 = 5Fe_2(SO_4)_3 + K_2SO_4 + 2MnSO_4 + 8H_2O$$

The last-added $\frac{3}{10}$ths of a gramme of permanganate by a reaction not well understood, oxidizes the chromium existing as chromic oxide Cr_2O_3—in the chromic sulphate $Cr_2(SO_4)_3 = (Cr_2O_3, 3\ SO_3)$—to potassium bichromate, $K_2Cr_2O_7$.

$$Cr_2(SO_4)_3 + 2KMnO_4 + 3H_2O = K_2Cr_2O_7 + 2MnO_2 + 3H_2SO_4$$

The reaction of the bichromate solution upon the acid ferrous sulphate is formulated on p. 88, and from the examples there given, the calculation of the standard solution used in the present case should be obvious. Some chemists use for ferrous iron a weighed quantity of ferrous sulphate or ammonio-ferrous sulphate crystals. Sometimes the salts are made up in dilute sulphuric acid solution (1 in 10) into standard liquids. The above proceedings involve a pre-supposition of the perfect purity of the bichromate. It is better therefore to standardize from pure metallic iron, concerning which no doubt can exist. When standard acid solutions of ferrous salts are employed, they should be frequently checked by a standard bichromate solution, to ascertain that no atmospheric oxidation has occurred. The weight of uneffloresced green crystals of ferrous sulphate ($FeSO_4$, $7 H_2O$) necessary to dissolve in dilute sulphuric acid as an equivalent for the weight of metallic iron used in the foregoing process will be 1·603 grammes. If made up into a standard solution 32·06 grammes of salt must be dissolved in about 700 cc. of cold dilute sulphuric acid (1 in 7), and the liquid made up to 1 litre. 50 cc. of this solution should be equivalent to 0·1618 gramme of Swedish iron. In the case of ammonio-ferrous sulphate ($FeAm_2(SO_4)_2$, $6 H_2O$), which is perhaps the better salt to employ, 2·261 grammes of crystals will be required per estimation, or if made up into a standard solution containing in 50 cc. ferrous sulphate equivalent to 0·1618 gramme of Swedish iron, 45·22 grammes of the salt must be contained in 1000 cc. of dilute sulphuric acid.

VOLUMETRIC DETERMINATION OF CHROMIUM (Stead[1]).

Mr. Stead has devised the following modification of the permanganate process, which in the authors' hands has yielded excellent results, closely agreeing with those obtained by the gravimetric processes and the preceding method when working upon completely soluble chrome steels.

The Process.

(Time occupied, about 1½ hours.)

Weight taken.—Weigh out 2 grammes of drillings into a 40-oz. flask.

---

[1] " Journal of the Iron and Steel Institute," 1893, No. 1, p. 158.

Dissolving.—This is effected exactly as in the process last described.

Diluting.—Take up the separated sulphates by diluting the solution with 300 cc. of hot water.

Oxidizing.—Bring the liquid to boiling, and add a warm saturated solution of potassium permanganate till a brown precipitate is produced, and the boiling liquid is decidedly and permanently coloured with permanganate.

Dissolving up the manganic precipitate.—Add little by little to the still boiling fluid strong *HCl* solution till the precipitate is dissolved, and a clear, rich yellow-red liquid is obtained: 70 to 90 cc. of the fuming acid will be required. Then add 100 cc. of hot water.

Boiling off the chlorine.—The liquid is now briskly boiled for about 20 minutes, till absolutely free from any smell of chlorine. The disengagement of the latter is facilitated by dropping into the flask a pinch of recently-ignited white sand.

Titrating.—The chlorine-free liquid is then added to an excess of ferrous sulphate, the liquid is titrated, and the percentage of chromium is calculated exactly as described for the last method, the dilute sulphuric being added to the iron contained in a 40-oz flask, when the operation of boiling off the chlorine is nearly completed.

Theoretical Considerations.

Most of the reactions are identical with those occurring in the last process. The precipitated MnO_2 is, however, in the present case converted into manganous chloride with evolution of chlorine, thus—

$$MnO_2 + 4\ HCl = MnCl_2 + 2\ Cl + 2\ H_2O$$

The sand mechanically assists the evolution of chlorine gas from the solution. If any free chlorine is left in the liquid it will oxidize the ferrous sulphate thus—

$$2\ FeSO_4 + 2\ Cl + H_2SO_4 = Fe_2(SO_4)_3 + 2\ HCl$$

of course giving a result higher than the truth, the oxidizing power of the chlorine being registered as due to chromic acid. The solution in the present process is largely diluted to avoid the reduction of some of the chromic acid to chromic chloride, which takes place in a liquid strongly acid with HCl thus—

$$K_2Cr_2O_7 + 14\ HCl = 2\ KCl + 2\ CrCl_3 + 3\ Cl_2 + 7\ H_2O$$

Vignal's Method.

A rapid and very extensively practised modification of the volumetric process for the estimation of chromium is the one due to Vignal. It differs from those just described in two essential points: (1) the iron is converted into the ferric condition by means of nitric acid before commencing the oxidation of the chromium with permanganate, and (2) the final titration is performed with a standard solution of potassium permanganate instead of bichromate.

A brief but sufficiently detailed account of the method is rendered under the analysis of high-speed steels on p. 250, where also the theoretical value of the modifications referred to are discussed.

Comparative Consideration of the Gravimetric and Volumetric Methods.

Where only few estimations have to be made, and time is not a condition of vital importance, the gravimetric is the most reliable process to employ, particularly in the analysis of steels containing a very high percentage of chromium, which are not completely dissolved by sulphuric acid, leaving a black residue of carbide of chromium. In disputed cases, volumetric results should be invariably confirmed by a carefully conducted direct assay. On the other hand, the volumetric process, certainly in steels containing up to 3% of chromium, gives practically accurate results, which have the advantage of being very promptly obtained, in a manner far less tedious than the careful operations necessary to yield accurate gravimetric results.

In order to check his working of the gravimetric process, the student should weigh out 2·4 grammes of a steel proved to be free from chromium, and add before dissolving in HCl say exactly 0·1 gramme of pure dry $K_2Cr_2O_7$. The weight of oxide or phosphate obtained should calculate out to 1·475% of metal. It should also be ascertained that the volumetric method is being carried out under correct conditions by taking 2 grammes of the chromium free drillings, and before dissolving in dilute sulphuric acid, adding from the burette say 25 cc. of the standard bichromate solution. On titrating the excess of ferrous iron left at the end of the operation, exactly 25 cc. of standard solution should remain in the burette, or, in Vignal's method, an amount of ferrous ammonium sulphate should be used up equivalent to 14·4 cc. of decinormal potassium permanganate.

DETERMINATION OF NICKEL (BREARLEY).

(Time occupied, 2 hours.)

Re-agents required.

Standard silver nitrate solution.—Dissolve 3·4 grammes of pure silver nitrate crystals in water, add a few drops of ammonia and make up to 1000 cc. Store the solution in a dark blue Winchester and label it

$$AgNO_3 \; 1 \; cc. = 0·000586 \; gramme \; nickel.$$

Standard Potassium cyanide solution.—Dissolve about 3 grammes of potassium cyanide in water containing a few cc. of ammonia and make up to 1000 cc. This solution is not permanent, and is standardized at each determination by means of the silver solution.

The Process.

Dissolving, etc.—Two grammes of the drillings are weighed out and placed in a 30-oz. registered conical flask, dissolved in 20 cc. of strong hydrochloric acid and the iron oxidized by the usual addition of a few cc. of strong nitric acid.

Neutralizing.—The acid solution is diluted to a bulk of

about 400 cc. with luke warm water and dilute ammonia
(1 to 3) added a little at a time with vigorous shaking
between each addition. When the liquid just begins to
darken in colour and before a permanent turbidity is
produced the addition of ammonia is stopped and a
saturated solution of ammonium carbonate is added also
a little at a time with vigorous shaking between each
addition. Each successive addition of the carbonated
alkali results in the formation of a brown precipitate
which dissolves on shaking, producing a solution growing
darker and darker in colour by each addition, and finally
appearing black in the bulk, although thin layers by
transmitted light exhibit a lemon-yellow tint. The
addition of ammonium carbonate is continued until a
permanent brown precipitate is produced. This is then
dissolved in from 10 to 20 cc. of the B. P. acetic acid by
shaking vigorously. The liquid is then diluted with
water nearly to a litre.

Precipitating the iron.—The flask is placed on the hot
plate and a thermometer inserted. The at first very
dark liquid will after a time become paler in colour and
at the same time develop a turbidity. If the preceding
neutralization has been carefully conducted, the turbidity
should not become apparent below 70° C. Should this
happen, however, the liquid is cleared by the addition of
two or three drops more of acetic acid, but it must be
remembered that the amount specified above (20 cc. at
the most) should not be exceeded. As the temperature
rises further, the turbidity becomes more pronounced, and
individual flocks of ferric hydrate can readily be dis-
tinguished. At or near the boiling-point, the precipitation of the iron is completed by the addition of ammonium
acetate. Great care is necessary at this point, because

the addition of an excess of this re-agent results in a loss
of nickel carried down with the iron precipitate. To
90 cc. of water add 10 cc. of the ammonium acetate
solution prepared by neutralizing ·880 ammonia with
B. P. acetic acid and mix. From 10 to 20 cc. of this
dilute ammonium acetate should be ample in effecting
complete precipitation of the iron, and on no account
must this amount be exceeded. The whole mixture is
now maintained at the boiling-point for about a minute
and then removed from the plate.

Fractional filtration.—Transfer the mixture to a graduated litre flask, wash out and make up to the mark with
hot water, the usual allowance being made for the
volume of the precipitate, note the temperature after
mixing, and filter off 500 cc. through a large funnel
fitted with a dry folded filter-paper. The filtrate, adjusted to 500 cc. at the previously noted temperature,
contains the nickel from 1 gramme of steel, and should
be absolutely free from iron. It contains the whole of the
manganese and nickel, and its colour will be determined
by the amount of the latter metal.

Titration of the Nickel.—The 500 cc. are transferred
to a clean 30 oz. registered flask and quickly cooled to
the laboratory temperature under the water tap. Two
cc. of concentrated sulphuric acid are added, and then
dilute ammonia until the solution is faintly but distinctly
alkaline. Several small crystals of potassium iodide are
now introduced and dissolved by shaking.

Two burettes are charged to the zero mark, one with
the standard silver nitrate solution, and the other with the
potassium cyanide solution. The flask containing the
nickel solution is placed under the silver nitrate burette
and about 3 cc. of the latter run in so as to produce a

yellowish turbidity due to the precipitation of silver iodide. The flask is then placed under the potassium cyanide burette and the latter solution delivered, not more than 2 cc. at a time, with shaking between each addition. The turbidity increases at first owing to the precipitation of nickel cyanide, but afterwards decreases again, becoming fainter and fainter until the solution becomes absolutely clear at the last careful addition of a few drops only of the potassium cyanide solution. The exact end point is obtained with the greatest exactitude because after having " cleared " with cyanide, the turbidity is at once reproduced by the addition of a drop or two of silver solution, and can be again discharged, the process being capable of repetition any number of times. The burette readings are then taken.

Standardizing the Cyanide Solution.—From 20 to 30 cc. of the standard silver nitrate solution are now run into the flask still holding the finished assay, and potassium cyanide again added in the same manner until the turbidity is just removed. The difference between the second pair of burette readings and the first represents the relative strengths of the cyanide and silver solutions.

Taking the latter solution as being accurate, sufficient data have now been obtained to furnish the desired result. If, however, it be deemed advisable to determine the strength of the cyanide directly in terms of metallic nickel instead of calculating through silver to nickel, a definite amount of a pure nickel salt should be introduced after the standardizing and a third pair of readings obtained. The authors recommend the use of a solution of recrystallized nickel ammonium sulphate; 6·735 grammes of the pure salt in 1000 cc. furnish a solution containing 1 milligramme of nickel per cc., and 20 cc. of such a solution is a convenient amount to use for standardizing the cyanide. An example of each method of calculation is appended.

Silver Nitrate readings.		Potassium Cyanide readings.	
0·0	Titration of	0·0	I.
2·6	assay.	35·2	
29·3	Standardizing.	60·6	
0·0	Titration of	0·0	II.
5·5	assay.	38·0	
26·5	Standardizing KCN with $AgNO_3$.	58·0	
29·7	Standardizing KCN with Ni = ·02 gramme.	93·4	

I. KCN $AgNO_3$

           60·6 cc.   29·3 cc.

           35·2   2·6

           25·4   26·7

$$1 \text{ cc. } KCN = \frac{26·7}{25·4} = 1·051 \text{ cc. } AgNO_3.$$

In the actual titration of the solution containing the nickel, 35·2 cc. KCN were used up on the unknown amount of nickel plus 2·6 cc. of the silver solution. From the above we have

$$35·2 \text{ cc. } KCN = 35·2 \times 1·051$$
$$= 37 \text{ cc. } AgNO_3$$
$$37 \text{ less } 2·6 = 34·4 \text{ cc. } AgNO_3$$

The actual amount of nickel is therefore

$$34·4 \times ·000586 = ·02016 \text{ gramme}$$
$$·02016 \times 100 = 2·016 \text{ per cent. nickel.}$$

II. $\qquad 21 \text{ cc. } AgNO_3 = 20 \text{ cc. } KCN$

$$1 \text{ cc. } = \frac{20}{21} = 0·95 \text{ cc. } KCN.$$

·02 gramme nickel $= (93·4 - 58)$ cc. KCN less the amount equivalent to $(29·7 - 26·5)$ cc. of $AgNO_3$.

$$·02 \text{ gramme nickel} = 35·4 - 3·2 \times ·95 \text{ cc. } KCN$$
$$= 32·4 \text{ cc. } KCN.$$

The assay itself gives $38 - 5·5 \times ·95 = 32·8$ cc. KCN. If therefore ·02 gramme nickel represents 32·4 cc. KCN, the nickel in 1 gramme of the steel is

$$\frac{·02 \times 32·8}{32·4} = ·02024 \text{ gramme.}$$

$$\text{Nickel} = 2·024 \text{ per cent.}$$

Theory of the Process.

The separation of nickel from large amounts of iron is based upon the fact that the latter when precipitated as ferric hydrate does not carry down with it any nickel when the requisite condition of feeble acidity is secured. It is well known that if ammonia is added in excess to a mixture of iron in the ferric condition with nickel, the precipated ferric hydrate invariably carries down with it (adsorbs) a certain amount of the nickel. The latter can be removed from the precipitate by the cautious addition of very dilute acid without dissolving an appreciable amount of the ferric hydrate, but the operation is only possible to skilled and experienced workers. By operating in the manner detailed above, however, the student should experience no difficulty in effecting a perfect separation of iron from nickel.

The theory of the neutralization of the acid solution containing the iron and nickel has been already dealt with to some extent in connection with the gravimetric determination of manganese. The substitution of ammonium carbonate for the hydrate in neutralizing enables one to generate a highly basic ferric chloride before the formation of a permanent precipitate. The deepening colour of the solution is due to the solution of increasing amounts of ferric hydrate in correspondingly decreasing amounts of ferric chloride. This action is facilitated by shaking and by the disintegration of the ferric carbonate, momentarily precipitated, into tiny particles of hydrated ferric oxide by the escaping carbon dioxide resulting from its spontaneous decomposition.

$$2 \ FeCl_3 + 3 \ Am_2CO_3 = Fe_2(CO_3)_3 + 6 \ AmCl$$
$$Fe_2(CO_3)_3 = Fe_2O_3 + 3 \ CO_2$$

When the precipitate finally refuses to dissolve, at least seven-eighths of the iron is in a state of loose combination with the remainder, and the clearing of the solution with a small amount of acetic acid yields, as far as concerns the iron, a condition approximating to the formula $FeCl_3 \cdot 7 Fe(HO)_3$. By boiling this soluble compound, it is decomposed with precipitation of the hydrate and partial hydrolysis of the chloride.

$$FeCl_3 + 3 H_2O = Fe(OH)_3 + 3 HCl.$$

The complete precipitation of the small amount of unchanged chloride is effected by the dilute ammonium acetate, a basic acetate being formed and a small amount of acetic acid generated. The conditions specified in the detailed account are chosen so as to produce the requisite degree of acidity, and these conditions ought not to be departed from.

The cyanometric determination of small amounts of nickel in the filtrate, after making alkaline, is perhaps the most accurate quantitative operation known to the authors. When potassium cyanide is added to a solution containing nickel and silver, the following reactions occur in the order given:

$$NiCl_2 + 2 KCN = Ni(CN)_2 + 2 KCl$$
$$Ni(CN)_2 + 2 KCN = Ni(CN)_2 \cdot 2 KCN$$
$$AgNO_3 + KCN = AgCN + KNO_3$$
$$AgCN + KCN = AgCN \cdot KCN.$$

The nickel is first converted to an insoluble cyanide which dissolves in excess of the re-agent to form a double cyanide, and until this reaction has been carried to completion the silver purposely added is not attacked. In its turn, this metal is also converted to a soluble double cyanide. The end [1] of the operation is determined by

[1] The sharpness of the end reaction is improved by the presence of ammonium sulphate. This salt can be added in the solid form or generated in the solution in the manner indicated.

the final decomposition of the silver iodide generated by the addition of potassium iodide before the titration is commenced.

$$AgNO_3 + KI = AgI + KNO_3$$
<small>The turbidity.</small>

$$AgI + 2\ KCN = AgCN \cdot KCN + KI.$$

From the above equations it is evident that twice as much potassium cyanide is consumed in converting an atomic weight of nickel to the double cyanide than in similarly converting one atomic weight of silver. Hence $Ag = 108$ is equivalent to $\frac{1}{2}\ Ni = 29 \cdot 3$. But 108 parts of Ag are contained in 170 parts of $AgNO_3$, so that by dissolving $3 \cdot 4$ grammes of silver nitrate, and diluting to 1000 cc., we have a solution each cc. of which contains $\cdot 00216$ gramme of the metal, and this amount is equivalent to $\cdot 000586$ gramme of nickel.

High Nickel Steels.

The separation of nickel from iron by the method just described is applicable to all percentages of nickel, so that the same original weight of drillings may always be taken. The solutions of silver nitrate and potassium cyanide at the strengths specified cannot, however, be advantageously used when the nickel in the filtrate (representing one gramme of material) exceeds 5 per cent. A measured fraction of the filtrate should therefore be used for the titration so as to comply with this condition. This procedure is better than that of dealing with a smaller amount of drillings.

High nickel steels invariably contain comparatively

large amounts of manganese, and this metal passes entirely into the filtrate with the nickel.[1] On making alkaline with ammonia the manganous hydrate partially precipitated may produce sufficient manganic hydrate by atmospheric oxidation during the titration to obscure the end reaction. In such an event, excess of potassium cyanide is added, and the whole solution then passed through a small pulp filter. The clear filtrate is then treated with silver nitrate so as just to reproduce the turbidity, and this is then finally discharged by a drop or two of cyanide.

Copper, if present in more than traces, is found in the filtrate with the nickel, and reacts with the potassium cyanide solution. It should be removed by passing a washed current of sulphuretted hydrogen through the acidified filtrate. The precipitated copper sulphide is filtered away, and the excess of sulphuretted hydrogen expelled by boiling before commencing the cyanometric determination of the nickel.

[1] An excellent modification of the gravimetric process for estimating manganese is the one here described for nickel. Four grammes of drillings are weighed out and the process carried out exactly as described, except that the ammonium acetate may be added in much larger amounts without any fear of loss of manganese. The 500 cc. of filtrate, containing the manganese from 2 grammes of steel may be at once cooled and treated with bromine and ammonia. There is no necessity for concentrating the liquid to eliminate traces of iron, as the filtrate is invariably free from it.

The method is applicable to manganese alloys also, a perfect separation of manganese from iron resulting at one precipitation even when as much as one gram of the richest alloy is taken for the analysis. The large amount of manganese in the filtrate is too cumbersome to deal with, however, and a fraction only should be taken for the subsequent precipitation with bromine and ammonia.

Gravimetric Determination of Aluminium (Arnold).

Aluminium steel, in the sense that the material contains a considerable percentage of the somewhat costly metal alloyed with the iron, can hardly be considered as a commercial product, but steels which have been treated to prevent blow-holes with a small percentage of aluminium, and consequently contain a few hundredths of 1% of that metal, are now of fairly frequent occurrence. The accurate determination of so small a quanty of aluminium associated with such a comparatively enormous mass of iron is a matter requiring considerable care and skill; the chemical reactions of the two metals being so closely analogous. The following process is designed for steels containing not more than $0·1\%$ of aluminium. It must not be applied without some modification (which will be referred to later on) to steels containing a considerable percentage of Al; neither is it suitable for chrome steels.

Re-agents required.

Strong sodic hydrate solution.—This may be prepared as required in a platinum dish from equal weights of the pure solid (made from sodium) and water.

Standard solution of sodium phosphate.—This solution must contain in 1 cc. (measured from a 1 cc. pipette) enough P_2O_5 to precipitate $0·1\%$ Al in 6 grammes of steel as phosphate. It is made by dissolving 7·87 grammes of crystallized ordinary phosphate of soda

($Na_2HPO_4 \cdot 12\ H_2O$) in hot water, and diluting the liquid when cold to 100 cc. It should be preserved in a well-stoppered bottle labelled with the strength of the solution.

The Process.

(Time occupied, about 1 day.)

Weight taken.—Weigh out into a 30-oz. registered flask 6 grammes of the steel.

Dissolving.—Add to the drillings 1 cc. of the standard sodium phosphate solution (*this must not be forgotten*) and 50 cc. of strong HCl solution. Place a watch-glass on the flask, heat quietly, and finally boil on the hot plate till the drillings have dissolved.

Diluting.—Then dilute with 200 cc. of hot water.

Neutralizing and reducing.—Bring the liquid nearly to boiling, and little by little, and finally drop by drop, constantly shaking the solution round, add dilute ammonia till a slight permanent precipitate is obtained; then add 25 cc. of strong H_2SO_3 solution, and boil till no smell of SO_2 is noticeable.

First precipitation.—Next, all the time keeping the pale-green liquid gently boiling, add slowly 5 cc. of 33% acetic acid solution, then, a few cc. at a time, 25 cc. of hot ammonium acetate solution, after which briskly boil for 2 or 3 minutes.

First filtration.—Remove the flask from the plate, allow the precipitate to settle somewhat, and then pour through an ashless filter 110 mm. in diameter, contained in a 2¼-in. ribbed funnel (to which is attached by means of india-rubber tubing the glass loop shown in Fig. 2), as much as possible of the liquid before throwing the precipitate on the filter. The filtrate should be at first quite clear and pale-green in tint, but it soon becomes dark coloured and turbid, a scum also forming on the filter-paper and in the flask. Drain as much as possible of the liquid into the filter, and let it all pass through, the filtrate may then be thrown away. No attempt must be made to wash either flask or precipitate.

First re-dissolving.—Remove the funnel (detach the looped glass), and place it in the neck of the flask in which the precipitation took place. Dissolve the precipitate in boiling hydrochloric acid contained in a beaker, and pour round the edges of the paper by means of a glass rod, using as little acid as possible. Wash the paper alternately with a little hot acid and cold water till free from iron salt; it may then be thrown away. Wash into the flask any splashings on the stem of the funnel, and remove the latter. Boil the solution till the scum on the sides of the flask is dissolved and the liquid a clear yellow.

Repetition of above operations.—Dilute with hot water to 200 cc., bring nearly to boiling, neutralize the dilute ammonia, reduce with sulphurous acid, add 5 cc. of acetic acid solution, and precipitate with ammonium acetate exactly as before. Filter off the precipitate, this time washing out the flask with hot water, slightly wash the precipitate, and allow it to drain. Place the funnel inside a 20-oz. beaker on a glass hanger, and dissolve up the precipitate in hydrochloric acid boiled in the flask in which the precipitation took place. Well rinse out the flask, and thoroughly wash the filter-paper as before, then remove the funnel and hanger.

Evaporating nearly to dryness.—To the contents of the beaker add 2 *drops* of strong nitric acid (to fully peroxidize the iron), put on the cover, and boil down to low bulk, then, removing the cover, *very gently evaporate almost to dryness.*

Precipitating the iron.—Take up the moist crystals of ferric chloride in 10 cc. of water, and wash every drop into a deep 3-in. platinum dish: the volume of the liquid should be about 25 cc. Next add 5 cc. of the strong solution of sodic hydrate, thoroughly but quickly stir the solution with a glass rod (of course well washing the latter), place the dish on a pipe-stem triangle on the hot plate, cover it with a 4-in. clock-glass, and maintain at a gentle boil for 15 minutes. Remove and allow to cool.

Filtering off the sodic aluminate.—Pinch up the edges of the platinum dish so as to form a temporary spout, and cautiously pour the solution and precipitate into a 60 cc. flask, into which every trace of solution must be washed out of the dish with cold water; dilute exactly to the mark, and thoroughly mix the contents of the flask, then, through a dry double filter contained in a 2-in. funnel, filter off 50 cc. of the clear liquid.

Precipitating of the aluminium.—Transfer the liquid from the 50 cc. flask into a 20-oz. beaker containing 25 cc. of strong HCl, add 10 cc. of a 10% solution of sodium phosphate, bring the liquid to a gentle boil, and then little by little add (down the lip of the beaker, the cover being kept on) dilute ammonia solution till the acid is neutralized, a white gelatinous precipitate thrown down, and a *faint* smell of ammonia is perceptible. Digest the contents of the beaker just short of boiling till the precipitate has gathered into flocks and the liquid is clear. Remove the beaker from the plate and allow the precipitate to settle.

Filtering.—Pass as much as possible of the clear liquid

through a 110 mm. paper contained in a 2-in. funnel, then, with the aid of a policeman and the wash-bottle jet, bring every particle of the precipitate on to the paper, and *thoroughly* wash the filter with almost boiling water till the washings fail to produce the slightest opalescence when added to a dilute solution of silver nitrate contained in a test tube.

When the precipitate has thoroughly drained, dry it in the usual manner, strongly ignite in a tared platinum crucible, and weigh the white residue when cold in the usual manner. Its formula is approximately $AlPO_4$, containing 22·2% of metallic aluminium. Calculate the percentage on 5 grammes of steel.

Blank determination.—It is highly advisable in this process to make on 6 grammes of a steel free from aluminium a determination of the extraneous metal present in the re-agents used or possibly taken up during the analysis; the weight obtained is of course deducted from that of the precipitate obtained from the aluminium steel.

Example of Calculation.

Feb. 9, 1891.
Crucible cast steel ingot No. 87 (to which was added 0·1°/₀ Al)
Weight of steel taken, 6 grammes.
Crucible + ppt = 28·6236
Weight of crucible = 28·6097

$$\frac{}{\cdot 0139}$$

Less blank = ·0027

·0112 gramme $AlPO_4$
22·2

224
224
224

5)·24864

·0497   say 0·05°/₀ Al.

Cases of Special Steels.

High silicon.—If a large percentage of silicon is present, it is best before proceeding with the analysis to evaporate the hydrochloric acid solution of the steel to dryness; take up in *HCl* and filter off the silica, which would otherwise obscure the correct neutralization of the solution. When reducing the filtrate, it is advisable to use 50 instead of 25 cc. of SO_2 solution, because more ferric chloride will be present.

Tungsten.—In the case of tungsten steels, it is necessary to add to the preliminary hydrochloric acid solution 10 cc. of strong nitric acid, evaporate to dryness, bake well, take up in *HCl*, and filter off the tungstic acid. This is most speedily and conveniently accomplished by taking originally 7·2 grammes of steel, making up the solution containing the tungsten precipitate to 90 cc., and filtering off 75 cc. which will contain the aluminium in 6 grammes of steel. As the iron in solution will be totally in the ferric condition, at least 100 cc. of sulphurous acid will be required to perfectly reduce the neutralized yellow ferric chloride to pale-green ferrous chloride.

Theory of the Process.

After the neutralization there is present a mixture of ferrous, manganous, aluminic, and ferric chloride; the last-named (formed by the action of the air, as described on p. 68) must be again reduced to the ferrous state. This is effected by the reaction given on p. 186.

On the removal of the free mineral acids by the addition of ammonium acetate (see p. 137), the aluminium is thrown down as the normal phosphate $AlPO_4$, which is insoluble in dilute acetic acid. The phosphoric acid present (as phosphate of soda and a little phosphate of iron from the steel) in excess of the amount required by the aluminium, throws down some ferrous phosphate $Fe_3(PO_4)_2$, and the amount of iron in the precipitate is also increased by the atmospheric oxidation of the ferrous acetate, which forms a scum of basic *ferric* acetate insoluble in acetic acid. On the second precipitation, however, the solution of iron being comparatively very dilute, the phosphate of alumina has associated with it a much smaller quantity of iron. This, however, must be totally separated by boiling the concentrated and nearly neutral solution of the two metals with an excess of caustic soda. Ferric hydrate is precipitated, and sodic aluminate remains in solution, thus—

$$FePO_4 + 3\ NaHO = Fe(HO)_3 + Na_3PO_4$$
$$2AlPO_4 + 8\ NaHO = (NaAl)_2O_4 + 2\ Na_3PO_4 + 4\ H_2O$$

The solution of aluminate of soda in excess of sodic hydrate gives no precipitate with ammonia till it has been decomposed with excess of hydrochloric acid, thus—

$$(NaAl)_2O_4 + 8\ HCl = 2\ NaCl + 2\ AlCl_3 + 4\ H_2O$$

The aluminic chloride is at once converted by the sodium phosphate present into aluminic phosphate (which remains dissolved in the excess of acid) thus—

$$AlCl_3 + Na_3PO_4 = 3\ NaCl + AlPO_4$$

When the excess of hydrochloric acid is neutralized, forming $AmCl$, and a faint excess of ammonia substituted,

the normal phosphate of alumina is precipitated by the
excess of phosphoric acid present; in the absence of
sufficient phosphoric acid a basic phosphate $Al_6P_4O_{19}$
similar to that of chromium is thrown down, but it is
less certain in composition than the salt of the metal last
named.

The success of the foregoing method depends in a
great measure upon having the phosphoric acid present
only *slightly* in excess of the amount required theoretically
to precipitate the aluminium. If a large excess of P_2O_5
is in the solution, so much ferrous phosphate is carried
down with the aluminium salt as to render the process
almost impracticable. The method can of course be
applied to steels containing high percentage of Al (see
analysis of ferro-aluminium, p. 286), if only the percentage
of the latter is roughly known. In a steel works the analyst
should have no difficulty in ascertaining the maximum
percentage possible, and a quantity of sodium phosphate
sufficient to precipitate that percentage should be added,
calculated on the much smaller weight of steel employed.
Unfortunately, however, some works managers who are
unacquainted with analytical chemistry, are possessed
with the curious idea that the best way to get accurate
reports is to keep the chemist as much as possible in the
dark concerning the calculated composition of the steels
sent up to the laboratory.

The principle of taking $\frac{5}{6}$ths of the liquid in order
to avoid a tedious and in this case somewhat dangerous
washing of the precipitate, has already been explained
with reference to the estimation of manganese on p. 81.
If the aluminium in 6 grammes of steel is contained in
a volume of liquid measuring 90 cc., then the metal in
5 grammes of steel will be contained in $\frac{5}{6}$ of $90 = 75$ cc.

ALTERNATIVE METHOD.

The Process.

Dissolving, etc.—To 10 grammes of the drillings in a 20-oz. beaker add 80 cc. of hydrochloric acid and heat till dissolved. Dilute with water and filter off silica, etc., retaining the filtrate and washings in a 30-oz. registered flask.

First precipitation.—Dilute to about 300 cc., add 10 cc. of a saturated solution of sodium phosphate in water, and neutralize with very dilute ammonia or with a solution of ammonium carbonate until a slight precipitate is obtained. Cautiously dissolve this in a few drops of hydrochloric acid, and add several drops more in excess. Now add 25 cc. of B.P. acetic acid, from 5 to 10 grammes of sodium thiosulphate dissolved in water, 5 cc. of ammonium acetate, and boil the liquid for half an hour, or until the escaping steam no longer smells of sulphur dioxide.

Filtration, etc.—Collect the precipitate on a pulp filter, wash well, dry and ignite at a low red heat until the filter is destroyed.

Second precipitation.—Brush the ignited residue into a small beaker and decompose it by beating with 10 cc. of strong hydrochloric acid. Dilute with water and pass the solution through a small filter paper to remove silica, washing thoroughly. The filtrate, collected in a small (10-oz.) conical flask, is diluted to about 100 cc., several drops of the saturated sodium phosphate solution added, the solution cautiously neutralized as above by ammonium carbonate, and the re-precipitation effected by means of 10 cc. of acetic acid and about 2 grammes of sodium thiosulphate.

Final filtration, etc.—After boiling well, the precipitated aluminium phosphate, associated with sulphur, is filtered off, washed, dried, ignited, and weighed. The residue is aluminium orthophosphate, $AlPO_4$, and it contains 22·2 per cent. of aluminium. It should now be perfectly white.

Theory of the Process.

The precipitation of phosphates of ferric iron, and of chromium and aluminium, in the presence of preponderating amounts of ferrous iron, has already been dealt with in connection with the determination of phosphorus in steel by the combined method. The phosphates of these three bases are precipitated without serious contamination with ferrous phosphate from solutions containing free but weak acid, such as acetic acid.

The original solution of the steel in excess of hydrochloric acid provides a solution containing the aluminium as a chloride, and most of the iron in the form of ferrous chloride. The solution contains a sufficient excess of free strong acid to prevent a precipitation of aluminium phosphate on the addition of the sodium phosphate solution, but, on neutralizing, this substance separates out. On taking it into solution again with acid, the original conditions are reverted to, except that now the amount of strong acid is very small. The addition of sodium thiosulphate decomposes this excess of acid, and at the same time liberates sulphur dioxide, the latter maintaining the iron, which would by the prolonged boiling be partially oxidized, in the ferrous condition. This is an important point, because the oxidation of the iron would result in the contamination of the precipitated phosphate of aluminium with unnecessarily large amounts of ferric phosphate. These reactions are set forth in the following equations:

$$Na_2S_2O_3 + 2\ HCl = 2\ NaCl + H_2O + SO_2 + S$$
$$Fe_2Cl_6 + SO_2 + 2\ H_2O = 2\ FeCl_2 + H_2SO_4 + 2\ HCl.[1]$$

It is necessary to again state the fact that the above operations have for their object the provision of a solution containing the whole of the iron in the ferrous condition, and a degree of acidity sufficient to prevent the formation of ferrous phosphate, whilst the phosphate of aluminium (and of chromium and ferric iron), being completely insoluble in weak acids, such as acetic acid, separate out.

$$AlCl_3 + Na_2HPO_4 = AlPO_4 + 2\ NaCl + HCl.$$

The second precipitation, after removal of the silica introduced by the first, is practically a repetition of the first, and has for its object the removal of traces of iron unavoidably carried down by an operation involving the separation of a few milligrammes of aluminium from nearly 10,000 milligrammes of iron.

Notes.

In ordinary steels, the only element which interferes with the above process is copper. This metal can be

[1] The mineral acid generated by this reaction is accounted for by the excess of sodium thiosulphate, and by the ammonium acetate added.

P

removed from the preliminary acid solution of the drillings by passing a washed current of sulphuretted hydrogen through it. After filtering out the copper sulphide the excess of sulphuretted hydrogen is expelled by boiling, and the process carried forward as usual. As an alternative, the following procedure may be adopted. After the first ignition of the impure phosphate of aluminium, dissolve as before in hydrochloric acid, filter out the silica, wash well, and to the filtrate and washings add dilute ammonia to alkalinity. Allow the precipitated phosphates of iron and aluminium to flock out and filter them off from the blue liquid containing the copper in solution. The precipitate is again dissolved in acid, and the separation of the aluminium from the iron carried out by a repetition of the thiosulphate precipitation exactly as described.

Steels containing chromium yield a mixture of chromium and aluminium phosphates, no matter how many times the precipitation is repeated. This case has already been dealt with on page 178. The following method of separating these metals also answers well. Fuse the ignited residue with four times its weight of sodium carbonate containing a few milligrammes of sodium peroxide, dissolve out with water, add dilute hydrochloric acid until acid, two or three drops of the sodium phosphate solution, and then 10 cc. of ammonium acetate. The chromium remains in solution as sodium chromate, and is thus removed from the precipitated aluminium phosphate.

VOLUMETRIC DETERMINATION OF COPPER (Arnold).

(Time occupied, about 3 hours.)

Re-agents required.

Standard solution of "Hypo."—Powder and dry (by pressing the spread-out salt between filter-paper) a few grammes of moist crystals of pure sodium hyposulphite (thiosulphate) $Na_2S_2O_3,5H_2O$. Weigh out 3·938 grammes of the salt into a litre flask, and dissolve in a few hundred cc. of cold distilled water, dilute to the mark, and thoroughly mix the liquid. The standard solution thus prepared should be preserved in the dark, otherwise it is liable to decompose with precipitation of sulphur. It is advisable to frequently make up a new solution.

Starch solution.—Make about one gramme of wheat or arrowroot starch into a thin paste with 5 cc. of water. Boil in a 20-oz. beaker about 100 cc. of distilled water. Remove it from the plate and pour into the hot water the 5 cc. of cold starch cream. Well mix the emulsion by shaking the beaker round, and *filter* off a portion of the clear liquid for use. This re-agent must be freshly made for each set of estimations.

Potassic iodide free from iodate.—To prove the freedom of the iodide (KI) from iodate (KIO_3), dissolve a crystal in a test tube containing 10 cc. of water; add 1 cc. of starch liquor, and then a few drops of acetic acid. No blue coloration should be developed.

Solution of sodium carbonate.—Saturate 250 cc. of cold

water with pure Na_2CO_3, filter for use, and store in a
green glass bottle fitted with an india-rubber stopper.

Electrotype copper.—Polish some electro-deposited
copper-foil with fine emery-cloth, and cut it up with a
pair of scissors into conveniently small pieces.

Standardizing the " Hypo" Solution.

Standard copper solution.—Weigh out exactly one
gramme of the pure copper into a 20-oz. beaker, put on
the cover, and add cautiously 10 cc. of nitric acid, sp. gr.
1·20. Heat gently to boiling on the hot plate, and when
the metal has all dissolved remove the cover, rinsing
any splashings on it and the sides of the beaker into the
solution. Next very quietly evaporate to low bulk till
cupric nitrate begins to crystallize out. Add 50 cc. of
water, and dissolve up every particle of the separated
salt, and then without loss transfer the blue liquid
to a litre flask. When cold dilute to the mark, and
thoroughly mix the solution. Keep in a stoppered bottle
labelled—" $Cu(NO_3)_2$. 50 cc. = 0·05 gramme of metallic
copper."

Titrating.—From a pipette deliver exactly 50 cc. of the
standard Cu solution into a 20-oz. beaker. Put on the
cover, and little by little, constantly shaking round the
beaker, add down the lip the strong solution of sodium
carbonate till no further evolution of CO_2 is noticed, and
the copper is all thrown down as a pale-blue precipitate.
Every trace of this is next dissolved up by gently boiling
with a *slight* excess of dilute acetic acid. Thoroughly
cool the liquid, and add about two grammes of potassium

iodide crystals, and shake round the beaker till they have dissolved. Fill up a 50 cc. burette with the "hypo" solution, and set the meniscus at zero. Then run the thiosulphate into the copper solution till the brown tint of the dissolved iodine has become much fainter; this should happen when about 45 cc. have been run in. Then add 2 cc. of clear strong starch liquor, when a dark-blue colour will be produced. Cautiously continue the addition of the "hypo" half a cc., and finally a few drops at a time, continually shaking round the contents of the beaker till the blue colour has been totally discharged. It should not reappear on the solution standing for a few minutes. The end of the reaction requires a little experience for its correct determination. It is best decided by noting when a few drops of liquid from the burette no longer produce a lighter patch or streaks in the surrounding liquid, which has for a background a precipitate of yellowish-white cuprous iodide CuI. If the solution of "hypo" is of correct strength, just 50 cc. should be required to discharge the colour of the iodide of starch. If the standard liquid is not exactly right, the student should have no difficulty in correcting it either for strength or weakness after referring to the examples given for adjusting the standard solution of $K_2Cr_2O_7$ on p. 89. The above titration must never be made when fumes of bromine vapour or of aqua regia (chlorine) are present in the air of the laboratory, because these elements at once liberate free iodine from a solution of KI, and thus render the accurate determination of the final point almost impossible. Nitrous acid and the nitrites must also be avoided in the re-agents used.

The Process for Steel.

Weight taken.—Weight out 10 grammes of drillings into a covered 20-oz. beaker.

Dissolving.—Add 60 cc. of strong hydrochloric acid. When the reaction has somewhat subsided, quietly heat on the plate till the steel has dissolved, and then boil the solution till most of the acid has been driven off, and crystals of ferrous chloride have commenced to separate, making the solution thick. Then cautiously add down the lip of the beaker 300 cc. of warm water, and heat if necessary till the whole of the separated ferrous chloride has re-dissolved; then remove from the plate. During this dissolution the cover should not be taken off.

Precipitating the copper.—Next, by means of a glass tube about 9 in. long (inserted under the cover down the lip of the beaker), pass through the solution for ten minutes a brisk current of washed H_2S gas (from a Kipp's apparatus well charged with FeS and slightly diluted HCl solution), when the dark precipitate should have flocked out, leaving a clear pale-green liquid somewhat opalescent with finely-divided sulphur. Detach the glass tube (from the india-rubber tubing of the washing cylinder) and leave it in the beaker.

Filtering.—When the precipitate has somewhat settled, guide the clear liquid by means of the tube into a 110 mm. pure filter contained in a 2¼-in. ribbed funnel supported in a conical beaker. When most of the filtrate has passed through the filter, throw on the dark CuS (mixed with sulphur, FeS, etc.), and rinse the beaker and tube free from every trace of iron solution, but do not attempt to detach any strongly adhering precipitate from either. Leave the tube in the beaker, and well wash the paper and sulphide of copper till free from iron salt with cold water containing some H_2S and 5 cc. of strong HCl solution per 100 of water. Finally wash once with cold water.

Dissolving up the precipitate.—Wash the funnel free from any splashings of ferrous chloride solution, and support it inside the beaker in which the precipitation took place on a glass hanger. *Cautiously* treat the filter with hot 1·20 nitric acid to dissolve up the precipitate, using as little acid as possible. It almost invariably happens that some crusts of sulphur, black with intermixed sulphides, remain insoluble. These, after the filter has been well washed with hot water, must be added to the copper solution by spreading out the paper on a beaker cover, and detaching them with the aid of a fine jet of water.

Separating co-precipitated iron.—Boil the nitric acid solution in a covered beaker till the crusts of sulphur are yellow; then add cautiously dilute ammonia till the acid is neutralized, and the deep blue liquid has a distinct smell of the alkali. Boil for two or three minutes, and filter off the copper solution into a clean 20-oz. beaker, collecting the precipitated $Fe_2(HO)_6$, SiO_2, sulphur, etc., in a 2-in. funnel containing a 90 mm. pure paper. The latter must be well washed with hot water, using, however, as little as possible.

Conversion of the copper into acetate.—To the covered beaker containing the ammonio-copper solution, add a few drops of strong nitric acid, till the deep blue of the liquid is changed to a pale greenish-blue tint, then boil down to about 10 cc. Next add, a few drops at a time, the strong solution of sodium carbonate till the deep azure blue colour is permanently reproduced. Then add, drop by

drop, acetic acid till it is again discharged, being replaced
by a much paler blue. Remove the beaker from the
plate, and place it in a bath of cold water till the contents
are cool.

Titrating the copper.—Next add to the cold liquid, the
bulk of which should not exceed 25 cc., about 2 grammes
of potassic iodide and titrate with hypo and starch liquor,
exactly in the manner already described for checking the
standard, only of course in the present case, the amount of
copper being unknown, great care must be exercised in
watching the yellowness of the solution so as not to overshoot the mark before adding the starch. The latter
could be put into the solution immediately after the dissolution of the iodide, but would then precipitate the
iodine in flocks of iodide of starch, which are not so
readily acted upon by the thiosulphate as when in solution,
which condition is ensured when only traces of iodine are
left at the time the starch is added.

Each cc. of hypo used equals 0.01% Cu on 10 grammes
of steel. Thus, if the reaction were finished when 9 cc.
had been run in, the copper present $= 0.09\%$; if 27 cc.
were required the copper $= 0.27\%$. If the whole 50 cc.
failed to discharge the colour of the starch solution, more
than 0.5% Cu was present in the steel. Such, however,
will never be the case in ordinary steels. When an experimental steel containing over 0.5 but under 1% of
copper has to be dealt with, take for the assay only 5
grammes of steel, when each cc. required will equal
0.02 or 50 cc. $= 1\%$ Cu. It is also easy to adjust the
strength of the thiosulphate solution to take any percentage of copper; the basis of the above process having
been originally devised for the analysis of copper alloys
by Mr. E. O. Brown.

Determination of Copper in Tungsten Steel.

In the case of tungsten steel, proceed to obtain the acid ferrous solution (from which to precipitate the CuS) free from this element in the manner described in the article on the estimation of aluminium on p. 204.

Theoretical Considerations.

The reactions taking place in titrating the standard copper solution will be first considered. On adding the Na_2CO_3 solution to that containing the nitrate of copper in which is a little free nitric acid, CO_2 is evolved, and sodium nitrate $NaNO_3$ is formed as the result of the neutralization of the acid. The excess of sodium carbonate then precipitates basic carbonate of copper $(CuCO_3, Cu(HO)_2)$. On the addition of an excess of acetic acid, the surplus sodium carbonate is converted into sodium acetate $Na(C_2H_3O_2)$, and the copper precipitate is dissolved up, forming cupric acetate $Cu(C_2H_3O_2)_2$ with evolution of CO_2.

The reactions occurring in the case of steel will now be dealt with. On dissolving up the drillings, the finely-divided copper diffused throughout the mass of the iron is attacked by the hydrochloric acid with formation of cupric chloride, $CuCl_2$.

The copper in the hydrochloric acid solution is separated from the soluble iron by the H_2S as a dark-brown sulphide insoluble in dilute acids, thus:

$$CuCl_2 + H_2S = CuS + 2\ HCl$$

By an analogous reaction the sulphide of copper is contaminated with a small quantity of co-precipitated FeS. On dissolving up the sulphides in nitric acid, they are oxidized by a complex reaction to cupric sulphate $CuSO_4$ and ferric sulphate $Fe_2(SO_4)_3$.

On adding an excess of ammonia to the nitric acid solution, the acid is neutralized with formation of ammonic nitrate $AmNO_3$, ferric hydrate $Fe_2(HO)_6$ is precipitated, whilst the copper remains dissolved in the excess of ammonia as a compound possessing the formula $(CuSO_4, 4 NH_3)$. On acidifying the liquid with nitric acid, the last-named substance is decomposed into a mixture of copper sulphate and ammonium nitrate, but it is again formed on the addition of excess of sodium carbonate, owing to the liberation of free ammonia from the ammonium nitrate, thus:

$$Na_2CO_3 + 2 AmNO_3 = 2 NaNO_3 + CO_2 + 2 NH_3 + H_2O$$

On acidulating with acetic acid, the ammonio-cupric compound is again decomposed with formation of cupric acetate and ammonium acetate and sulphate, thus:

$$(CuSO_4, 4 NH_3) + 4 C_2H_4O_2 = Am_2SO_4 + 2Am(C_2H_3O_2) + Cu(C_2H_3O_2)_2$$

The following reactions are common to the cases of the standard and the steel. On the addition of potassium iodide to the acetic acid solution of cupric acetate, the following changes take place:

$$Cu(C_2H_3O_2)_2 + 2 KI = I + CuI^1 + 2 K(C_2H_3O_2)$$

Cupric acetate and potassic iodide yield free iodine

---

[1] Theoretically the equations require doubling, but for simplicity are expressed in their lowest terms; the actual compounds are Cu_2I_2 and $Na_2S_4O_6$.

(which remains dissolved in the excess of KI added), cuprous iodide (a soiled white precipitate), and soluble acetate of potassium.

On running in the solution of thiosulphate to that containing the iodine, the following reaction ensues :

$$Na_2S_2O_3 + I = NaS_2O_3{}^1 + NaI$$

Sodium thiosulphate and iodine yield sodium tetrathionate and sodium iodide.

The starch indicator owes its colour to the formation of blue iodide of starch, a compound readily robbed of its iodine by hypo. It therefore only retains its tint as long as any *free* iodine is present, and consequently as soon as the latter is converted into the sodium salt the colour disappears.

On studying the above reactions, it will be seen that, firstly, each atom of copper weighing 63 liberates its equivalent of one atom of iodine, weighing 127 : and secondly, that each molecule of thiosulphate, weighing 248,[2] converts one atom of iodine into iodide of sodium : therefore 248 parts of the hydrated thiosulphate correspond to 63[3] parts of metallic copper. But in 50 cc. of the standard solution we have 0·1969 gramme $(\frac{9\cdot848}{50})$ of hypo.

$$\text{Then if 248 parts of hypo} = 63 \text{ parts } Cu$$
$$0\cdot1969 \quad ,, \qquad ,, \quad = x \quad ,,$$
$$\frac{0\cdot1969 \times 63}{248} = 0\cdot05 \text{ gramme } Cu$$

Or 1 cc. = 0·001 gramme Cu = 0·01% of 10 grammes.

---

[1] See note on previous page.

[2] The original salt contained five molecules of water, weighing 90.

[3] The atomic weights have been taken in round numbers, which in the present case are sufficiently accurate.

It is of great importance to separate the small quantity of iron precipitated with the copper, because ferric salts liberate iodine from potassic iodide, and their presence would therefore cause the result to come out higher than the truth.

In the preliminary solution of the steel the cover should not be removed from the beaker, so as to prevent as far as possible atmospheric oxidation of $FeCl_2$ to $FeCl_3$ (see p. 68). If much of the latter salt be present, a large quantity of sulphur is thrown down with the CuS by the reaction formulated in the following equation:

$$2\,FeCl_3 + H_2S = 2\,FeCl_2 + 2\,HCl + S$$

GRAVIMETRIC DETERMINATION OF COPPER.

(Time occupied, $1\frac{1}{2}$ hours.)

The Process.

Dissolving, etc.—To 5 grammes of the drillings, contained in a 20-oz. beaker add a previously-made mixture of 20 cc. strong sulphuric acid with 100 cc. of water, and heat quietly on the plate till the drillings are completely decomposed. Dilute with hot water to a volume of 350 cc. and then add a solution of 10 grammes of sodium thiosulphate in about 30 cc. of hot water. The whole mixture is then boiled until the liquid is almost clear.

Filtration.—The residue is filtered off through pulp and thoroughly washed with hot water, dried, ignited at a low temperature in a porcelain crucible and weighed. It contains the copper as a mixture of cupric oxide (CuO) with cuprous sulphide (Cu_2S), and impurities in the form of silica and ferric oxide.

Re-precipitation, etc.—Brush the ignited residue into a small beaker, add 10 cc. of hydrochloric acid and digest in order to decompose the copper compounds. To the solution, after dilution with an equal volume of water, add dilute ammonia to pronounced alkalinity and again filter off. Wash, dry, ignite and weigh as before. The residue contains the impurities of the original precipitate, and the difference between the two weighings represents the copper in the ammoniacal filtrate. This difference, multiplied by 0·798, gives the copper in the 5 grammes of steel.

Direct determination of the copper.—As a valuable check on the result obtained by the preceding treatment, the ammoniacal filtrate can be treated exactly as described under the preceding method. That is to say, it is acidified with nitric acid, treated with excess of sodium carbonate, re-acidified with acetic acid, the CO_2 expelled, the solution cooled and the copper determined after adding potassium iodide by titration with the standardized solution of sodium thiosulphate.

Theory of the Process.

Dilute sulphuric acid leaves most of the copper in steel in the metallic form when the metal is opened out, the iron of course passing into solution as ferrous sulphate. The traces of copper which may have passed into solution are precipitated by the addition of sodium thiosulphate.

A sparingly soluble cupric thiosulphate is first formed and this dissolves in excess of the thiosulphate forming a double thiosulphate of sodium and copper. In acid solution both these compounds quickly decompose on boiling with formation of free sulphuric acid and precipitation of sulphur and the sulphide of copper.

$$CuSO_4 + Na_2S_2O_3 = CuS_2O_3 + Na_2SO_4$$
$$2\ CuS_2O_3 + 2\ H_2O = Cu_2S + 2\ H_2SO_4 + S$$

The sulphur thus formed is augmented by the decomposition of some of the precipitant by the excess of sulphuric acid present.

$$Na_2S_2O_3 + H_2SO_4 = Na_2SO_4 + H_2O + SO_2 + S$$

The boiling after adding the thiosulphate hastens both these changes and at the same time causes the precipitated sulphur which at first imparts a milkiness to the solution to collect together in a granular form. This is filtered off with the metallic copper and the cuprous sulphide, and ignition removes it as sulphur dioxide. The percentage of copper in CuO, formed by the oxidation of the metallic copper in the muffle, is the same as in Cu_2S, viz., 79·8.

DETERMINATION OF IRON (Penny).

Re-agents required.

Standard solution of $K_2Cr_2O_7$.—Weigh out into a clean, dry 10-oz. beaker exactly 4·383 grammes of pure, dry, selected crystals of potassium bichromate. Dissolve the salt in about 250 cc. of hot water; when cold, transfer the solution to a litre flask, thoroughly washing out the beaker,

make up the liquid to the mark, and thoroughly mix the
solution by repeatedly inverting the stoppered flask. Keep
in a well-stoppered bottle labelled—" $K_2Cr_2O_7$ 1 cc. $= 1\%$
Fe on 0·5 gramme." Standardize and adjust the solution
in accordance with the directions given on pp. 88, 89.
0·501 gramme of the standard iron should require exactly
100 cc. of bichromate.

The Process.

(Time occupied, about 1 hour.)

Weight taken.—Weigh out into a clean, dry 10-oz. flask
exactly 0·5 gramme of the steel drillings.

Dissolving.—Add to the metal 25 cc. strong *HCl* mixed
with 15 cc. of water, cover the flask with a watch-glass,
and gently heat the liquid to boiling till the iron has dissolved, and only some black flocks of carbonaceous matter
remain.

Oxidizing the organic matter.—Rinse the watch-glass
with a little hot water, and add in three portions about 3
grammes of chlorate of potash crystals, boiling the liquid
between each addition, and especially after adding the
last gramme of salt.

Neutralizing.—The acid solution of perchloride of iron
is next neutralized with dilute ammonia (half 880, half
water) added little by little, the liquid being well shaken
between each addition, till a slight permanent precipitate
is obtained.

Reducing.—Pour down the sides of the flask about
25 cc. of a saturated solution of sulphurous acid, and
briskly boil the liquid till every trace of SO_2 has been

expelled, and the solution is of a faint, sea-green colour, quite free from any yellow tinge.

Titrating.—Add to the solution 10 cc. of dilute sulphuric acid: the iron is then determined by the standard solution of $K_2Cr_2O_7$, with a dilute solution of potassic ferricyanide as indicator, in the manner fully described on pp. 88, 89. Each cc. required = 1% *Fe*. Example:

0·5 gramme of a Bessemer spring steel required 98·2 cc. of the standard liquid: therefore the iron equalled 98·2%.

Theoretical Considerations.

These have been already dealt with on p. 89; the only point requiring mention is the fact, that in steel containing any appreciable percentage of carbon it would not be safe to dissolve the drillings in dilute sulphuric acid and directly titrate the solution, because the solid, residual carbonaceous matter which has escaped evolution in the form of hydrocarbons has a slight but distinct reducing action upon the bichromate solution, and would therefore cause the result registered to be somewhat high. The organic matter is decomposed by the mixture of chlorine and chlorine peroxide evolved from the chlorate of potash and HCl; but at the same time, the iron is oxidized to the ferric state, hence the necessity for reducing the nearly neutral liquid with sulphurous acid to the ferrous state (see p. 136). It is not often necessary to directly determine the iron in steel, the metal being usually taken by difference. In certain cases, however, it may be important to directly check the percentage present when making a complete analysis, in order to ensure that no appreciable percentage of any unestimated element has been overlooked.

In estimating iron it is important to bear in mind the fact, that in solutions of perchloride, from which a violent evolution of gas is proceeding, loss of iron may possibly occur during brisk boiling, on account of the volatilization of some ferric chloride with the gas.

DETERMINATION OF MOLYBDENUM (Ibbotson and Brearley [1]).

(Time occupied, 2 hours.)

The Process.

Dissolving, etc.—Two grammes of drillings are weighed out, placed in a small conical flask of 10-oz. capacity and covered with 20 cc. of strong hydrochloric acid. When the steel has nearly dissolved, the iron is oxidized by the addition of a few drops of strong nitric acid, and the solution boiled vigorously for a few minutes to expel nitrous fumes. If the solution is perfectly clear, proceed to the next operation; if, however, any solid matter is perceptible, filter this off through a small pulp filter, washing once only.

Separation of the iron.—The clear solution is transferred completely to a tap funnel clamped above a beaker or flask containing about 16 grammes of pure caustic soda dissolved in 250 to 300 cc. of water. This latter solution should be hot, and in it is placed the pulp filter

[1] "Chemical News," vol. 81, p. 269.

holding any solid matter which was filtered off, the pulp being then thoroughly broken up by shaking. The acid mixture containing iron and molybdenum is then allowed to run in rapid drops into the alkaline solution whilst the latter is briskly agitated. The mixture is transferred to a half-litre flask and made up to the mark with an allowance of 1 or 2 cc. for the volume of the precipitate. (It is usually unnecessary to make a temperature correction.) After thoroughly mixing, filter through two thicknesses of stiff filter paper and collect 250 cc. of the clear filtrate, containing the molybdenum in 1 gramme of steel.

Precipitating the molybdenum.—The alkaline filtrate is transferred to a 20-oz. beaker and two drops of litmus solution added. The solution is placed on the hot plate and hydrochloric acid is carefully added until acidity is just reached and then a further 5 cc. of the acid. The liquid is boiled vigorously for a minute to expel carbon dioxide, 30 cc. of ammonium acetate made as directed in the estimation of manganese on p. 70 added, and lastly 10 cc. of a clear solution of lead acetate of 4% strength.

Filtering, etc.—The precipitate of lead molybdate is filtered at once through pulp, washed with hot water and transferred as described on p. 9 to an unweighed porcelain crucible. It is then ignited near the front of the muffle, cooled, brushed out and weighed. Lead molybdate contains 26·16% of molybdenum.

Example.

Weight of $PbMoO_4 = 0\cdot1023$ gramme

$0\cdot1023 \times 26\cdot16 = 2\cdot676\%$

Theory of the Process.

The preliminary solution and oxidation generate molybdic acid, a trace of which may separate out. This is filtered off and placed in the strong solution of caustic soda, in which it at once dissolves, forming sodium molybdate:

$$H_2MoO_4 + 2\ NaHO = Na_2MoO_4 + 2\ H_2O$$

This same reaction takes place when the acid mixture containing the iron and molybdenum is run into the soda, the iron being completely precipitated as ferric hydrate at the same time:

$$FeCl_3 + 3\ NaHO = Fe(HO)_3 + 3\ NaCl$$

The necessity for slowly adding the acid mixture to an excess of caustic soda arises from the fact that in neutral or feebly alkaline solutions iron and molybdenum form insoluble basic molybdates of complex constitution. Thus when to an acid solution containing both of these metals an alkali is added, the neutral point is indicated by the precipitation of a basic ferric molybdate, $xFe_2O_3 \cdot yMoO_3$, and the addition of an excess of alkali, however great, does not effect the complete decomposition of this compound, particularly when, as in the analysis of a steel, the iron is the predominating metal. By running the acid solution of the metals a drop at a time into a large excess of the alkali, however, the molybdenum is fixed as sodium molybdate instantaneously, and ferric hydrate, uncontaminated with ferric molybdate, is precipitated. The hydrates of sodium and potassium are much more effective than their carbonates or than ammonium hydrate.

The precipitation of the molybdenum as lead molybdate has been dealt with already on p. 147.

DETERMINATION OF MOLYBDENUM IN SPECIAL STEELS.

The foregoing process is not interfered with by any of the elements usually present in steel except chromium and tungsten. The former is nearly all precipitated with the iron, but small quantities may pass into the filtrate as chromate and will impart a yellow colour to it. If, after acidification with hydrochloric acid, the yellow colour is not discharged, a few drops of sulphurous acid are added and the determination carried forward without any further trouble.

When tungsten is present, most of it will be found in the filtrate with the molybdenum and will be precipitated and weighed as an acid tungstate of lead along with the lead molybdate. In such cases the determination of the molybdenum is effected as follows.

The ignited precipitate is digested at the corner of the plate with strong hydrochloric acid until it is entirely decomposed and passes into solution. A few drops of strong nitric acid are then added and the whole mixture evaporated to pastiness. To the paste is added a mixture of 10 cc. of strong hydrochloric acid with 30 cc. of water, the liquid boiled and filtered. The tungsten remains as WO_3 on the filter; it is washed with water containing a few drops of hydrochloric acid, the washings being added to the main filtrate containing the molybdenum as molybdic acid along with the lead as chloride.

To the hot filtrate dilute ammonia is added until a faint but persistent milkiness is obtained, and then 20 cc. of ammonium acetate are added to effect complete precipitation of the molybdenum. The lead molybdate, now free from tungsten, is again filtered off, washed, ignited and weighed.

DETERMINATION OF VANADIUM.

(Time occupied, 1 day.)

Combined Method (Authors).

Dissolving, etc.—2·4 grammes of the drillings are placed in a 20-oz. beaker and covered with 40 cc. of 1·20 nitric acid, added a little at a time. When the violent action has subsided, the solution is evaporated as rapidly as possible to low bulk, and the subsequent heating conducted with the usual care necessary in order to secure at the bottom of the beaker, and with as few splashings on the sides as possible, a compact cake. This is then heated for half an hour strongly in the middle of the plate and then allowed to cool. By means of a pointed glass rod or steel spatula, the residue is detached as far as possible from the beaker and transferred to a clean dry porcelain mortar. About 5 cc. of strong hydrochloric acid are then put in the beaker, the cover replaced and the beaker placed at the corner of the plate until the acid has dissolved all the splashings from the sides. The solution is then rinsed into a deep 3 inch platinum basin and the liquid evaporated to dryness on the plate. In the meantime the main residue in the porcelain mortar is reduced to an impalpable powder and intimately mixed with 12 grammes of dry sodium carbonate and the same weight of sodium nitrate. When the solution in the platinum dish has reached dryness, the mixture in the mortar is added and the usual fusion of the whole mass proceeded with. This can be readily carried out over a powerful bunsen of the " Mecker " type, but care should be taken when the mass has nearly liquefied to maintain a continuous motion of the melt by holding the dish with the tongs and imparting a circular movement to it, taking care that the flame reaches well up the sides.

Extraction, etc.—When cold, the dish is placed in a 20-oz. beaker and covered with hot water. The subsequent treatment, up to the end of the fractional filtration (from 300 to 250 cc.), is conducted as already described under the gravimetric estimation of chromium on p. 167.

Evaporation to low bulk.—The 250 cc. of filtrate, representing 2 grammes of steel, are transferred to a 40-oz. beaker. A yellow colour indicates the presence of chromium, but strongly alkaline solutions of vanadates are colourless. To the alkaline solution dilute sulphuric acid (1 to 3) is cautiously added, until a drop of the solution gives an acid reaction with litmus paper; an excess of 30 cc. of the dilute acid is then added at once. In the absence of chromium, the presence of vanadium in the colourless filtrate from the fusion is betrayed by the development of a yellow colour on the addition of the acid. The yellow colour increases in intensity as more acid is added up to the neutralization point and decreases afterwards with the formation of an almost colourless solution again. These colour changes are entirely masked in the presence of chromium by the change of the yellow sodium chromate to dark green chromium sulphate through the agency of the oxides of nitrogen liberated. The acid solution is now boiled vigorously and evaporated to low bulk in order to expel all free nitric acid. If difficulty is experienced by the separation of solid sodium sulphate towards the end of the evaporation, the contents of the beaker should be transferred to a capacious platinum dish and the evaporation completed over a rose burner, with constant stirring of the semi-solid mass until thick fumes of sulphur trioxide are evolved copiously.

Titration.—After cooling, water is added to the residue and heat applied to effect complete solution. The solution is then rinsed into a 30-oz. registered flask and diluted to about 250 cc. with water. Sulphurous acid (20 cc.) is then added, and the flask, after introducing a filter plate to facilitate the expulsion of the excess of sulphur dioxide and prevent bumping, set on the plate. When the smell of sulphur dioxide is no longer perceptible in the escaping steam, the fairly blue solution (chromium being absent) is cooled off rapidly under the water tap. A centinormal solution (made as wanted from a deci-normal), of potassium permanganate is added, a few drops at a time, from a burette, until a faint pink tint persists for 3 minutes after the final addition. Each cc. of centi-normal permanganate represents 0·000512 gramme of vanadium.

The end point of the reaction when chromium is present is manifested by a change from the green colour of chromium salts to a peculiar purple tint.

Theory of the Process.

The basic vanadate of iron formed by baking the preliminary nitric acid solution of the steel is decomposed by the fusion and sodium orthovanadate formed. The chemical changes occurring in the case of the other elements have already been dealt with on p. 171.

$$V_2O_5 + 3\ Na_2CO_3 = 2\ Na_3VO_4 + 3\ CO_2$$

On acidification of the filtrate, the orthovanadate is first changed to metavanadate of sodium and the latter then decomposed with formation of vanadic acid.

$$Na_3VO_4 + H_2SO_4 = Na_2SO_4 + NaVO_3 + H_2O$$
$$2\ NaVO_3 + H_2SO_4 = Na_2SO_4 + V_2O_5 + H_2O$$

The reduction of vanadic acid and soluble vanadates in acid solution to the characteristic blue solutions so much like those of copper salts involves a change from V_2O_5 to V_2O_4, and the subsequent titration with permanganate effects the converse change

$$V_2O_5 + H_2SO_3 = V_2O_4 + H_2SO_4$$
$$5\ V_2O_4 + K_2Mn_2O_8 + 3\ H_2SO_4 = 5\ V_2O_5 + K_2SO_4 + 2\ MnSO_4 + 3\ H_2O$$

From the last equation it is evident that 10 atoms of vanadium (weight 512) correspond to one molecule of permanganate (weight 316), and as a centinormal solution of the latter contains 0·316 gramme of the salt in 1,000 cc., each cc. therefore containing 0·000316 gramme, we have the relation

1 cc. $\dfrac{N}{100}$ permanganate $= 0\cdot000512$ gramme vanadium.

In an actual case, 9·3 cc. of the permanganate were used, giving ·000512 × 9·3 = ·0047616 gramme *V* from 2 grammes of steel. Hence

$$·0047616 \times \frac{100}{2} = 0·238\% \text{ of vanadium.}$$

Dilute solutions of potassium permanganate in the cold exert no oxidizing effect on solution of chromium salts, so that the latter exert no influence, except in so far as to make the end point less readily discernible on account of their strong colour.

COLORIMETRIC METHOD.

(Time occupied, $\frac{1}{2}$ hour.)

Re-agents required.

Standard solution of vanadium.—This is readily prepared from pure ammonium metavanadate, a white amorphous powder, sparingly soluble in water. From the formula NH_4VO_3, it will be found to contain 43·7 % of vanadium and commercial samples are purchasable which yield a percentage of 43·5, the impurity consisting usually of a trace of ammonium chloride. It should be assayed for vanadium by weighing off accurately 0·25 gramme of the salt, transferring to a conical flask, dissolving in 250 cc. of hot water with 10 cc. of sulphuric acid and reducing with 20 cc. of strong sulphurous acid solution. The excess of sulphur dioxide is then completely expelled by boiling, and the solution titrated after cooling to the ordinary temperature with a reliable solution of potassium permanganate of decinormal strength. The colour changes during the titration from a blue indistinguishable from that of strong copper sulphate solution through various shades of green up to a full yellowish brown, are very striking. A pink colour persisting for 3 minutes marks the end of the reaction. By reducing again with sulphurous acid, the operation can be repeated, and this process can be again repeated many times, until the solution becomes so loaded with manganese and potassium sulphates as to make the boiling very difficult, if not impossible. As each cc. of $\frac{N}{10}$ $KMnO_4$ represents 0·00512 gramme of vanadium, the amount of this metal in the 0·25 gramme of ammonium metavanadate is easily calculated.

From the result of the above assay, the calculated amount of ammonium metavanadate is weighed off, transferred to a 250 cc. flask, dissolved in about 200 cc. of hot water, the solution cooled and made up to the mark. The amount to be weighed off should contain 0·1 gramme of vanadium, so that each cc. of the solution will contain 0·0004 gramme of vanadium. Approximately 0·23 gramme of the commercially pure salt will be required.

Solution of hydrogen peroxide.—Weigh off roughly 7 grammes of sodium peroxide and sprinkle it a little at a time into a beaker standing in cold water and containing 250 cc. of nitric acid of s.g. 1.20. Dissolve by stirring.

The Process.

Dissolving, etc.—Weigh off 1 gramme of the sample and the same weight of a steel, free from vanadium, of approximately the same carbon contents. Dissolve each

in 20 cc. of 1·20 nitric acid, and when dissolved, expel all
nitrous fumes by boiling. Add a solution of potassium
permanganate (of any strength) a few drops at a time
until a brown precipitate is obtained which persists in
the boiling solution. Now add sulphurous acid solution
in drops until the liquid is cleared, and then a further
2 or 3 cc. Boil vigorously to expel the excess of sulphur
dioxide and transfer each solution, assay and standard,
separately to a 100 cc. graduated flask. Cool under the
tap to the normal temperature, and dilute with cold water
so as to make the flasks about two-thirds full. Now add
carefully, a drop at a time, a solution of potassium permanganate, shaking after the addition of each drop, until
it is judged that a further drop would produce a permanent colour. If by chance too much permanganate
should be added, the colour must be again discharged by
the very careful addition of a highly dilute solution of
sulphurous acid. The pale yellowish green liquids are
now diluted to the mark.

Comparison of colours.—The solutions are then transferred to tall narrow beakers of about 200 cc. capacity,
and the beakers placed on a white tile or a sheet of white
paper. To each is then added 10 cc. of the sodium
peroxide solution, whereupon the vanadium sample
develops a characteristic brown colour. This brown
colour is then matched by delivering from a burette the
standard vanadium solution, a cc. at a time at first, and
smaller amounts towards the end, into the vanadium-free
solution. For each cc. of vanadium solution added, a cc.
of distilled water must be added to the assay solution so
as to maintain the same volume of liquid in each. The
equality of the colour intensities is best judged by looking
vertically into the solutions.

In a specific case, 6·2 cc. of the standard vanadium solution were used up in matching the colour yielded by a certain vanadium steel, 1 gramme of each steel (standard and sample), being weighed off originally. Hence 1 gramme of the steel contains ·0004 × 6·2 = ·00248 gramme V.

Percentage of vanadium = 0·248

Theory of the Process.

Solutions of vanadic acid or of soluble vanadates yield in nitric or sulphuric acid solution a brown colour of unknown constitution,[1] the depth of which for small quantities of vanadium is proportional to the amount of this metal present.

The preliminary operations have already been explained elsewhere. It will be noticed that they have for their object the generation in the solution of the higher oxide of vanadium, and the preparation of a solution as free from colour as possible. For both reasons the carbonaceous matter is therefore destroyed, and to comply with the first requirement, potassium permanganate is added to the cold solution to oxidize V_2O_4 formed by the addition of H_2SO_4 up to V_2O_5 again.

Special Steels.

In ordinary steels, the colorimetric process just described yields accurate results, and is on this account to

The colour is probably due to the formation of a salt of per-be recommended before the tedious but equally accurate process described under the title of " combined method." The method is, however, not workable in the presence of titanium, for hydrogen peroxide produces a yellow colour with traces of titanic acid. Steels containing nickel and chromium, and which therefore yield coloured solutions after the preliminary solution, oxidation, etc., can be assayed with a fair degree of accuracy by selecting a standard steel containing approximately the same amounts of these elements, but free from vanadium, and proceeding. It is even permissible to introduce these elements in the form of a weighed amount of one of their salts into a solution obtained from a standard steel not containing them, so as to imitate the colour of the assay before the addition of the peroxide. The case of chromium requires a further note.

When permanganate is added to the hot nitric acid solution of the steel so as to destroy the carbonaceous matter, a permanent brown precipitate of peroxide of manganese will obviously not be obtained until the chromium has been oxidized to chromic acid. When therefore the precipitate is dissolved in sulphurous acid, sufficient of this re-agent should be added to reduce the chromic acid again completely to a chromium salt before proceeding.

Certain chromium steels cannot be decomposed with 1·20 nitric acid. This difficulty is overcome by adding first 10 cc. of dilute sulphuric acid (1 acid, 3 water), and when the steel has almost dissolved, 10 cc. of nitric acid, 1·20.

DETERMINATION OF TITANIUM.

(Time occupied, $\frac{1}{2}$-hour.)

The small percentages of titanium purposely introduced into steel are just as accurately determined by a rapid colorimetric method as by the troublesome gravimetric methods usually applied.

Re-agents required.

Standard solution of titanium.—Exactly 0·1668 gramme of pure oxide of titanium (TiO_2) is weighed off and thoroughly fused in a platinum crucible with ten times its weight of sodium carbonate. The melt is boiled out with a small quantity of water so as to detach it as completely as possible from the crucible, and the insoluble sodium titanate then taken into solution by the cautious addition of strong sulphuric acid. The clear solution is transferred to a 250 cc. flask, cooled and diluted to the mark with sulphuric acid and water. This operation must be performed carefully, because if too much water is used titanic acid separates out. The best proportions for keeping it in solution are approximately three parts strong acid to one of water. Each cc. of the solution contains 0·0004 gramme titanium.

Solution of hydrogen peroxide.—Prepare this exactly as described under the corresponding colorimetric process for vanadium.

The Process.

This needs no description, as the details are exactly the same as for vanadium, the standard solution of titanium prepared as above being used for matching the colour obtained from the steel under examination.

Notes.

The colour yielded in acid solution by titanic acid and hydrogen peroxide is yellow, and therefore paler than the colour yielded by vanadium. The reaction is an extremely sensitive one, however. The colour is generally understood to be due to the formation of a higher oxide TiO_3. The test is obviously of no value in the presence of vanadium.

DETERMINATION OF TANTALUM (Authors).

The introduction of tantalum into steel is a recent innovation, and its effect is at the present time the subject of investigation. The process described below for its estimation was worked out on an experimental steel specially made from a rich ferro-tantalum, and is submitted as being likely to prove satisfactory, not only in the case of the mild steel obtained (carbon $0·2\%$), but in general.

The attention of the student is directed to the following experiments, which were made in order to arrive at a generally satisfactory method for the determination of tantalum :

I. Five grammes of drillings were treated exactly as in the estimation of silicon by opening out with hydrochloric acid, baking, extracting with acid, diluting with water and filtering. The washed residue, consisting of silica and tantalic oxide was strongly ignited and treated with hydrofluoric acid to remove silica. The residue, calculated to tantalum, yielded 0·33% of the metal.

II. Five grammes of drillings were dissolved in dilute sulphuric acid (1 acid, 6 water). The black residue, more volumious than an ordinary steel of the same carbon contents would leave, was filtered off, well washed with dilute hot hydrochloric acid, finally with water, ignited and weighed. After treatment with HF the residue calculated out to 0·32% tantalum.

III. Five grammes of drillings were dissolved in a mixture of 40 cc. of strong hydrochloric acid with an equal bulk of water. The residue was at once filtered off and treated as in II, yielding 0·34% of tantalum. The filtrate was evaporated to dryness, the residue baked, extracted with strong hydrochloric acid, the solution diluted and at once filtered and treated as before. A further amount of tantalum was obtained, bringing the total to 0·402%.

IV. Five grammes of drillings were dissolved in aqua regia, the solution evaporated to dryness, the residue baked strongly, extracted with 20 to 30 cc. hydrochloric acid, the liquid diluted with water up to 500 cc. and allowed to stand over night. The residue was filtered off and treated as before, yielding 0·48% of tantalum.

V. Two grammes of the drillings were dissolved in 40 cc. of nitric acid s.g. 1·20. The solution was evapor-

ated to low bulk and then transferred to a large platinum
dish, in which the evaporation was continued to dryness,
the mass being finally baked strongly. The dried residue
was then intimately mixed with 10 grammes of pure
finely powdered acid potassium sulphate, and the whole
mixture heated to fusion over the bunsen. The liquid
mass was brought to thorough homogeneity by swimming
the melt well up the sides of the dish under a powerful
" Mecker " burner. After cooling, the residue was dissolved out by prolonged digestion with dilute hydrochloric acid until the insoluble residue of silica and
tantalic acid was judged to be white. The extract was
copiously diluted and allowed to stand for several hours.
The residue was filtered off and treated as before, and
exhibited a slight pink tinge, evidently due to a trace of
iron. It was covered with an equal bulk of powdered
$HKSO_4$ and the preceding treatment repeated, yielding
finally 0·49% of tantalum.

VI. Five grammes of the drillings were placed in a
conical flask and covered with 300 cc. of a saturated
solution of cupric ammonium chloride containing 5% of
hydrochloric acid. In order to expedite the decomposition of the steel, a brisk current of air was drawn through
the liquid by means of a filter pump. The carbonaceous
residue was filtered off, washed with 10% hydrochloric
acid, and ignited. To eliminate the iron present in the
residue, the latter was fused with $HKSO_4$, and the treatment described in IV repeated. After the removal of
silica with HF the pure white residue of Ta_2O_5 calculated
out to 0·49% tantalum.

R

Consideration of Results.

From the foregoing experiments it is evident that when a steel containing tantalum is dissolved in dilute hydrochloric or sulphuric acid, much but not all of the tantalum is left with the insoluble residue. The authors have reason to believe that the proportion would be greater in the cases of harder steels. The subsequent evaporation of the filtrate, baking of the residue, etc., cannot be made to furnish the remainder of the tantalum, unless, as is described under IV, the acid extract is very largely diluted and allowed to stand for a long time.

The method described under V, although tedious, undoubtedly yields the correct figure when the process is carefully conducted by skilled operators; and since method VI evidently leads to a successful issue and is much more easily carried out, the authors have no hesitation in recommending it.

The Process.

Dissolving.—Five grammes of drillings are weighed off, transferred to a conical flask, and 300 cc. of a saturated solution of cuprammonium chloride, together with 15 cc. of strong hydrochloric acid added. The flask is either closed with a solid bung and the contents shaken until the drillings have entirely disappeared, or it is closed with a bung pierced with two holes carrying glass tubing, arranged as in an ordinary wash bottle, and a rapid current of air drawn through the liquid by means of the filter pump. The object in either case is to facilitate the solution of the metallic copper precipitated on the surfaces of the drillings by keeping the latter in motion.

The time occupied in dissolving depends also upon the shape and size of the drillings as also upon the amount of carbon in the steel.

Filtration.—The residue, containing the whole of the carbon of the steel associated with the tantalum and some iron, is filtered off and well washed with hot 10% hydrochloric acid and finally with water. It is then dried and ignited in a shallow platinum dish.

Fusion of the residue.—Sufficient pure powered acid potassium sulphate is then added to more than cover the residue, and, without mixing, the dish is held in a bunsen flame by the tongs. To the accompaniment of a copious evolution of sulphur trioxide, the mass is thus reduced to a perfect melt, which is run well up the red-hot sides of the dish by communicating to the latter a sweeping circular motion.

Extraction, etc.—When cold the dish is placed in a 20-oz. beaker and just covered with hot water. The mass quickly dissolves away from the dish, which is then lifted out and washed. To ensure complete purification of the insoluble residue from the last traces of iron, several cc. of strong hydrochloric acid are added and the mixture once more brought to boiling before the final filtration. The residue after being washed on the filter-paper with 10% hydrochloric acid is dried and ignited as strongly as possible for ten minutes. The mixture of pure tantalic oxide and silica is then treated as usual with a few drops of hydrofluoric acid and the tantalum percentage calculated from the difference. Ta_2O_5 contains $82 \cdot 0\%$ of tantalum.

Theory of the Process.

The reactions involved in the preliminary decomposition of the steel with the double chloride of copper and ammonium have already been dealt with in connection with the estimation of carbon on p. 34, where sodium chloride was used instead of ammonium chloride.

By the ignition, the carbon is eliminated as carbon dioxide and the double carbide of iron and tantalum decomposed with formation of the oxides of the metals. The fusion of the oxides with $HKSO_4$ at a red heat converts the ferric oxide into soluble ferric sulphate, and leaves the tantalic oxide (Ta_2O_5) in the form of a perfectly white amorphous solid, insoluble in hydrochloric or hydrofluoric acid.

HIGH-SPEED STEELS.

The introduction of chrome-tungsten steels for twist drills, turning tools, etc., has made it necessary to devote a special section to their analysis, even although the modifications of the ordinary methods of analysis demanded by the presence of comparatively large amounts of chromium and tungsten have been dealt with as they arose.

THE COMPLETE ANALYSIS OF HIGH-SPEED STEELS.

Determination of Carbon.

Carbon in high-speed steels cannot be accurately determined by preliminary decomposition with copper solutions and subsequent combustion of the dried residue. The direct combustion with oxide of manganese in a stream of oxygen yields accurate results.

Determination of Tungsten, Silicon, and Manganese.

Decomposition, etc.—Weigh off 2·2 grammes of drillings and transfer to a beaker (of about 350 cc. capacity) without a lip. Add 70 cc. of strong hydrochloric acid, and slowly bring the mixture just to the boiling point. Remove the beaker to a less hot part of the plate and continue the digestion just short of boiling point until the action nearly ceases. Now add, little by little, 4 cc. of concentrated nitric acid with constant shaking. The steel should now be completely decomposed without any separation of tungstic oxide. During the preceding operations the beaker should be kept covered as much as possible to maintain the strength of the hydrochloric acid. The cover is now pulled aside slightly, and the solution evaporated to pastiness, a hot mixture of 10 cc. hydrochloric acid with 40 cc. of water added, and the contents of the beaker boiled for half a minute to effect complete solution of the ferric chloride.

First filtration.—Allow the separated tungstic oxide to settle and filter through a pulp filter, washing well with 5% hydrochloric. The residue (I) is set aside.

Evaporation.—The filtrate, which is collected in a beaker, is now evaporated to complete dryness, but the dry mass must not be baked strongly or it will re-dissolve with great difficulty. Add 30 cc. of strong hydrochloric acid and evaporate to pastiness as before. Boil, as before, with 50 cc. of the dilute acid (1 to 4) and allow to settle.

Second filtration.—Filter again through pulp, receiving the filtrate in a 30-oz. registered flask. The residue (II) is treated as follows:

Ignition, etc.—The residues I and II are partially dried and ignited strongly in a weighed shallow platinum dish. The weight represents the tungstic oxide, the silica, and possibly also traces of ferric and chromic oxides. The weighed residue is treated with a few drops of hydrofluoric acid, the excess of the latter removed on the plate, and the residue again strongly ignited. The loss in weight represents the silica.

After expulsion of the silica, the residue is covered with an equal bulk of pure dry sodium carbonate and the dish, without mixing the contents, placed in the muffle. The whole mass quickly fuses and the dish is then removed, cooled off, placed in a beaker and covered with hot water. When all solid matter has apparently dissolved, the dish is removed and washed, and the solution allowed to stand. A small residue of ferric oxide almost invariably settles out and is filtered off, washed, dried, ignited and weighed. Its weight is deducted from that of the tungstic oxide.

Should the filtrate containing the tungsten as sodium tungstate exhibit a yellow colour, the original residue (I) contained a small quantity of chromic oxide. The amount of this is quickly ascertained by adding sulphuric acid to acidity, then a few cc., carefully measured, of an approximately decinormal ferrous ammonium sulphate, which has been standardized with a reliable decinormal permanganate solution, and finally permanganate itself from a burette to determine the excess of ferrous iron.

1 cc. $\frac{N}{10}$ $KMnO_4$ represents 0·00254 gramme Cr_2O_3.

Example of Calculation.

Weight I = 23·5770 grammes.
dish = 23·2568
‾‾‾‾‾‾‾‾
0·3202 = weight of $WO_3 + SiO_2 +$ traces of Fe_2O_3
and Cr_2O_3.

Weight II = 23·5710
23·5770 − 23·5710 = 0·0060 gramme of silica.

Silicon per cent = $\dfrac{·006 \times ·467 \times 100}{2·2} = 0·1^{22}$

Weight II = 23·5710
　dish = 23·2568

$$0·3142 = WO_3 + Fe_2O_3 + Cr_2O_3$$
$$0·0020 = \text{weight of } Fe_2O_3 \text{ found after fusion}$$
$$\overline{0·3122 = WO_3 + Cr_2O_3}$$

$\dfrac{N}{10}$ Ferrous ammon. sulphate solution added = 3 cc.

$\dfrac{N}{10}$ potassium permanganate ,, = 2·6 cc.

$0·4 \times ·00254 = ·001$ gramme Cr_2O_3.
$·3122 - ·001 = 0·3112$ gramme WO_3.
$$\dfrac{0·3112 \times ·793 \times 100}{2·2} = 11·2 \text{ per cent. tungsten.}$$

The manganese is next determined on the second filtrate, collected in the registered flask. (If more than 2 milligrammes of ferric oxide are found in the tungstic oxide, they should be dissolved in hydrochloric acid and the solution rinsed into the registered flask containing the filtrate for the manganese estimation.) This filtrate is partially neutralized with ammonium hydrate, and afterwards with ammonium carbonate, exactly as described under the determination of nickel on p. 190. After precipitating with ammonium acetate and making up to 1000 cc., 500 cc. of filtrate, containing the manganese from 1·1 grammes of steel, are collected, cooled and precipitated with bromine and ammonia. The hydrated peroxide of manganese is filtered off, washed and ignited. *It is invariably contaminated with chromium.* It is therefore brushed into a 10-oz. conical flask and heated with 5 cc. of strong hydrochloric acid until dissolved. Three or four drops of concentrated sulphuric acid are then cautiously added and the mixture evaporated to complete expulsion of the hydrochloric acid as indicated by a

copious evolution of sulphur trioxide fumes. After cooling, 20 cc. of 1·20 nitric acid are added and the manganese estimated in the solution by the bismuthate
process described fully on p. 92.

Determination of Phosphorus.

Dissolve 2 grammes of the drillings in 20 cc. nitric acid
and 25 cc. of hydrochloric acid, evaporate to pastiness and
boil with 50 cc. dilute hydrochloric, as already described
under the estimation of tungsten. Filter, wash with 5%
acid, evaporate filtrate and washings to dryness, bake
very gently, take up with 30 cc. hydrochloric acid, and
evaporate to low bulk. Now add 15 cc. strong ammonia,
then strong nitric acid a little at a time until the precipitate just dissolves, and finally about 2 cc. in excess.
Cool, if necessary, to about 70° C., precipitate with 30 cc.
of molybdate re-agent, and finish the estimation in one of
the ways already described.

Determination of Sulphur.

Dissolve 6 grammes of the drillings in 24 cc. concentrated nitric acid and 30 cc. concentrated hydrochloric
acid. Evaporate to pastiness, boil with dilute hydrochloric acid as before, and transfer to a graduated flask of
120 cc. capacity. Cool, make up to the mark and transfer to a small beaker to allow the tungstic oxide to
settle. Filter off exactly 100 cc. of the clear solution
through a dry paper and determine the sulphur in it
by precipitation as barium sulphate.

Phosphorus may, if thought desirable, be estimated in the filtrate from the $BaSO_4$ without separating the excess of barium chloride.

Determination of Molybdenum.

Two grammes of the drillings are opened out exactly as for tungsten, and the tungstic oxide filtered off and washed. The acid filtrate is concentrated to about 30 cc. and neutralized partially by a solution of sodium hydrate, care being taken to stop the addition of the alkali before the solution commences to darken in colour. The liquid is then run from a tap funnel into excess of caustic soda, and the determination carried out as already described on p. 225.

The filtrate from the ferric hydrate may be coloured yellow, indicating the presence of sodium chromate. This contingency has been provided for also on p. 228.

Determination of Chromium.

To 2 grammes of drillings, contained in a 10-oz. conical flask, add 50 cc. of dilute sulphuric acid (1 acid to 5 water). When the drillings have nearly all dissolved add 5 cc. concentrated nitric acid and boil to expel all nitrous fumes. Dilute to about 200 cc. with hot water and heat to boiling. Add little by little a strong solution of potassium permanganate (25 grammes per litre) until the chromium is oxidized and the permanganate is in slight excess as indicated by the appearance of a turbidity, and then add 2 cc. more. Boil for about eight minutes, add a few milligrammes of solid manganous sulphate, and continue the boiling two minutes longer. Allow the precipitated manganese dioxide to settle, and filter through asbestos, washing with hot water. Cool the solution and titrate by adding first an excess of standardized ferrous ammonium sulphate solution, and then decinormal potassium permanganate for measuring the excess of ferrous iron added. The end point of the reaction is easily seen even in solutions containing as much as a decigramme of actual chromium.

The smallest excess of permanganate converts the clear green colour of the chromic sulphate to a peculiar purplish green.

$$1 \text{ cc. } \frac{N}{10} KMnO_4 = \cdot001736 \text{ gramme Chromium.}$$

Example of Calculation.

In an actual case, 50 cc. of ferrous solution (approximately $\frac{N}{10}$) were added to the filtrate, and the excess found to correspond to 9·8 cc. of potassium permanganate $\left(\frac{N}{10}\right)$. The 50 cc. of ferrous solution were found, on standardizing, to be equivalent to 49·4 cc. of the permanganate. We have therefore an amount of chromium corresponding to 49·4 − 9·8 cc. of $\frac{N}{10}$ permanganate. Hence the chromium from 2 grammes of steel amounts to

$$(49\cdot4 - 9\cdot8) \times \cdot001736 = \cdot0687 \text{ gramme}$$
$$\text{Percentage} = \cdot0687 \times 50 = 3\cdot435.$$

Notes and Theoretical Considerations.

Very few points call for special notice in connection with the analysis of high speed steels as just described.

It most frequently happens that the analyst is called upon to estimate only the most essential constituents of a high speed steel, viz.: carbon, tungsten, chromium and (if present) molybdenum. In such cases the rapid method for the estimation of tungsten, described in detail on p. 164, may be applied, care being taken to note the presence of chromium in the filtrate from the sodium carbonate fusion, and to determine its amount.

The modified form, described above, of the ordinary volumetric process for estimating chromium calls for a brief notice. The use of nitric acid in effecting complete solution after the preliminary treatment with dilute sulphuric acid at once converts the iron present into the ferric condition, and thus lessens considerably the amount of permanganate which would otherwise be required, and the precipitated oxide of manganese is filtered more readily after this treatment. The small amount of manganese sulphate added just before filtration is for the purpose of ensuring the complete decomposition of the excess of permanganate added.

$$2 \, KMnO_4 + 3 \, MnSO_4 + 2 \, H_2O = K_2SO_4 + 2 \, H_2SO_4 + 5 \, MnO_2.$$

Needless to say, the titration of the chromium can be carried out by means of a suitable amount of pure bar iron dissolved in sulphuric acid and a standard solution of potassium bichromate.

ANALYSIS OF PIG-IRON.

Sampling.

Gray irons.—In these the pigs should be broken, and the drillings taken from different parts of the fracture; the danger of getting into the sample sand from the outside of the pig is thus reduced to a minimum.

Mottled and white irons.—These may either be drilled at a slow speed, with a drill made from high quality water-hardening tungsten steel, quenched out at a moderate red heat, or small pieces of the sample may be crushed in the steel mortar, and passed through a sieve of sixty meshes to the inch.

Determination of Carbon.

Total carbon.—This is determined working on 1 gramme of the sample, exactly as described for steel on p. 24, but the temperature of the combustion should be as high as possible, to ensure burning off every particle of the graphite. The direct combustion also answers admirably for pig irons.

Graphitic carbon.—This is determined on 1 to 3 grammes of the sample, in the manner described for the weight 3 grammes has reference to irons. In highly silicious irons, in

Notes and Theoretical Considerations.

Very few points call for special notice in connection with the analysis of high speed steels as just described.

It most frequently happens that the analyst is called upon to estimate only the most essential constituents of a high speed steel, viz.: carbon, tungsten, chromium and (if present) molybdenum. In such cases the rapid method for the estimation of tungsten, described in detail on p. 164, may be applied, care being taken to note the presence of chromium in the filtrate from the sodium carbonate fusion, and to determine its amount.

The modified form, described above, of the ordinary volumetric process for estimating chromium calls for a brief notice. The use of nitric acid in effecting complete solution after the preliminary treatment with dilute sulphuric acid at once converts the iron present into the ferric condition, and thus lessens considerably the amount of permanganate which would otherwise be required, and the precipitated oxide of manganese is filtered more readily after this treatment. The small amount of manganese sulphate added just before filtration is for the purpose of ensuring the complete decomposition of the excess of permanganate added.

$$2\ KMnO_4 + 3\ MnSO_4 + 2\ H_2O = K_2SO_4 + 2\ H_2SO_4 + 5\ MnO_2.$$

Needless to say, the titration of the chromium can be carried out by means of a suitable amount of pure bar iron dissolved in sulphuric acid and a standard solution of potassium bichromate.

ANALYSIS OF PIG-IRON.

Sampling.

Gray irons.—In these the pigs should be broken, and the drillings taken from different parts of the fracture; the danger of getting into the sample sand from the outside of the pig is thus reduced to a minimum.

Mottled and white irons.—These may either be drilled at a slow speed, with a drill made from high quality water-hardening tungsten steel, quenched out at a moderate red heat, or small pieces of the sample may be crushed in the steel mortar, and passed through a sieve of sixty meshes to the inch.

Determination of Carbon.

Total carbon.—This is determined working on 1 gramme of the sample, exactly as described for steel on p. 24, but the temperature of the combustion should be as high as possible, to ensure burning off every particle of the graphite. The direct combustion also answers admirably for pig irons.

Graphitic carbon.—This is determined on 1 to 3 grammes of the sample, in the manner described for ... he weight 3 grammes has reference to ... e irons. In highly silicious irons, in

Notes and Theoretical Considerations.

Very few points call for special notice in connection with the analysis of high speed steels as just described.

It most frequently happens that the analyst is called upon to estimate only the most essential constituents of a high speed steel, viz.: carbon, tungsten, chromium and (if present) molybdenum. In such cases the rapid method for the estimation of tungsten, described in detail on p. 164, may be applied, care being taken to note the presence of chromium in the filtrate from the sodium carbonate fusion, and to determine its amount.

The modified form, described above, of the ordinary volumetric process for estimating chromium calls for a brief notice. The use of nitric acid in effecting complete solution after the preliminary treatment with dilute sulphuric acid at once converts the iron present into the ferric condition, and thus lessens considerably the amount of permanganate which would otherwise be required, and the precipitated oxide of manganese is filtered more readily after this treatment. The small amount of manganese sulphate added just before filtration is for the purpose of ensuring the complete decomposition of the excess of permanganate added.

$$2\ KMnO_4 + 3\ MnSO_4 + 2\ H_2O = K_2SO_4 + 2\ H_2SO_4 + 5\ MnO_2.$$

Needless to say, the titration of the chromium can be carried out by means of a suitable amount of pure bar iron dissolved in sulphuric acid and a standard solution of potassium bichromate.

ANALYSIS OF PIG-IRON.

Sampling.

Gray irons.—In these the pigs should be broken, and the drillings taken from different parts of the fracture; the danger of getting into the sample sand from the outside of the pig is thus reduced to a minimum.

Mottled and white irons.—These may either be drilled at a slow speed, with a drill made from high quality water-hardening tungsten steel, quenched out at a moderate red heat, or small pieces of the sample may be crushed in the steel mortar, and passed through a sieve of sixty meshes to the inch.

Determination of Carbon.

Total carbon.—This is determined working on 1 gramme of the sample, exactly as described for steel on p. 24, but the temperature of the combustion should be as high as possible, to ensure burning off every particle of the graphite. The direct combustion also answers admirably for pig irons.

Graphitic carbon.—This is determined on 1 to 3 grammes of the sample, in the manner described for the weight 3 grammes has reference to irons. In highly silicious irons, in

Notes and Theoretical Considerations.

Very few points call for special notice in connection with the analysis of high speed steels as just described.

It most frequently happens that the analyst is called upon to estimate only the most essential constituents of a high speed steel, viz.: carbon, tungsten, chromium and (if present) molybdenum. In such cases the rapid method for the estimation of tungsten, described in detail on p. 164, may be applied, care being taken to note the presence of chromium in the filtrate from the sodium carbonate fusion, and to determine its amount.

The modified form, described above, of the ordinary volumetric process for estimating chromium calls for a brief notice. The use of nitric acid in effecting complete solution after the preliminary treatment with dilute sulphuric acid at once converts the iron present into the ferric condition, and thus lessens considerably the amount of permanganate which would otherwise be required, and the precipitated oxide of manganese is filtered more readily after this treatment. The small amount of manganese sulphate added just before filtration is for the purpose of ensuring the complete decomposition of the excess of permanganate added.

$$2\ KMnO_4 + 3\ MnSO_4 + 2\ H_2O = K_2SO_4 + 2\ H_2SO_4 + 5\ MnO_2.$$

Needless to say, the titration of the chromium can be carried out by means of a suitable amount of pure bar iron dissolved in sulphuric acid and a standard solution of potassium bichromate.

ANALYSIS OF PIG-IRON.

Sampling.

Gray irons.—In these the pigs should be broken, and the drillings taken from different parts of the fracture; the danger of getting into the sample sand from the outside of the pig is thus reduced to a minimum.

Mottled and white irons.—These may either be drilled at a slow speed, with a drill made from high quality water-hardening tungsten steel, quenched out at a moderate red heat, or small pieces of the sample may be crushed in the steel mortar, and passed through a sieve of sixty meshes to the inch.

Determination of Carbon.

Total carbon.—This is determined working on 1 gramme of the sample, exactly as described for steel on p. 24, but the temperature of the combustion should be as high as possible, to ensure burning off every particle of the graphite. The direct combustion also answers admirably for pig irons.

Graphitic carbon.—This is determined on 1 to 3 grammes of the sample, in the manner described for steel on p. 52, the weight 3 grammes has reference to faintly mottled white irons. In highly silicious irons, in which the silica is not completely soluble in dilute nitric acid, it is necessary to make the preliminary solution in hydrochloric acid evaporate to dryness, take up in hydrochloric acid, and collect the total residue on the asbestos plug. The latter is washed free from iron with hydrochloric acid and water, and is then treated with moderately strong caustic potash solution to dissolve up most of the silica. The residual graphite is then washed with hydrochloric acid and water till free from potash. The foregoing procedure is necessary, because gelatinous silica, as separated from nitric acid solution, would clog up the filter to such an extent that the filtration might occupy several hours. The result may be a little high owing to the presence with the graphite of traces of unevolved combined carbon.

Combined carbon.—This may be estimated by colour in the manner described for graphite steels on p. 50. It is, however, most accurately measured by deducting the percentage of graphite by combustion from that of the total carbon.

The estimation of the remaining elements found in pig-irons will be dealt with under separate headings, having reference respectively to the cases of non-titanic and titanic metals.

ANALYSIS OF NON-TITANIC IRONS.

Determination of Silicon.

This is carried out much in the same manner as that described for steel on p. 65, but, as a rule, only 1 gramme need be taken for analysis.

Boiling the insoluble residue with aqua regia.—After taking up the soluble portion of the cake resulting from the evaporation of the original hydrochloric acid solution to dryness in 50 cc. of strong *HCl*, 10 cc. of strong nitric acid are also added, and the liquid is boiled down to 25 cc. before diluting for filtration. This precaution is taken to decompose and render soluble some compound of iron which, particularly in the case of phosphoric irons, is apt to obstinately attach itself to the graphite and silica, the consequence being that the final residue is impure, and red with oxide of iron after ignition.

Washing.—The washing of the residue also must be very thorough, the silica and graphite on the filter being repeatedly treated alternately with fairly strong, hot hydrochloric acid and cold water till every trace of iron is removed.

Igniting.—The ignition in the case of graphitic iron usually occupies at least 20 minutes in a hot muffle before the last traces of graphite are burnt off. The final residue should be snow-white, and quite free from gray patches or any red tinge.

THE " NITRO-SULPHURIC ACID PROCESS." (Drown.)

(Time occupied, about 1½ hours.)

In this method the pig iron or steel is opened out with a mixture of nitric and sulphuric acids with water. A stock mixture may be made up by adding to 1,000 cc. of water about 250 cc. of strong sulphuric acid and 450 cc. of strong nitric acid.

The Process.

Weight taken.—In the case of pig irons, weigh off 1 gramme, transfer to a 20 oz. beaker and add about 25 cc. of the above mixture. For steels the usual weight of 4·67 grammes are treated in a 40 oz. beaker with 80 to 90 cc. of the nitro-sulphuric acid mixture.

Evaporation, etc.—Immediately after the first violent action has subsided, place the beaker in the middle of the plate and evaporate as quickly as possible. It is often possible to evaporate, without any spitting, to the copious evolution of thick fumes of sulphur trioxide indicating the end of the operation. If, however, the yellow solid mass is projected from the bottom of the beaker before the appearance of SO_3 fumes, the beaker must be removed to the corner of the plate and the cover removed. The heating must then be continued at the lower temperature, the beaker being gradually pushed towards the centre of the plate, a little at a time accordingly as it is found safe to do so.

Dissolving.—When, as stated above, thick choking fumes of sulphur trioxide are copiously evolved, the beaker is removed and allowed to cool slightly. When the bottom is still too hot to be touched by the fingers except momentarily, hot water is added from the wide end of the wash bottle; the cover being slightly pushed aside for this purpose. For pig irons add water to about 20 cc., and then 10 to 15 cc. of strong hydrochloric acid; in the case of steels add water to about 50 cc., and then 30 to 40 cc. of the strong acid. Boil up well to dissolve the cake of ferric sulphate.

Filtration, etc.—The filtration and washing are then conducted with the precautions specified already.

Theoretical Considerations.

These call for very little treatment. The iron is of course at once converted to a ferric salt by the acid mixture used. The subsequent drastic evaporation completely expels every trace of nitric acid and water, and the strong sulphuric acid finally dehydrates the silicic acid yielding insoluble silica.

$$H_4SiO_4 = SiO_2 + 2\,H_2O.$$

This reaction corresponds to the one brought about in the hydrochloric acid method by baking the dry residue of chlorides.

Determination of Manganese.

This is estimated by the ammonium acetate process in the manner described for silicious steels on p. 82, or by the modification of it described under the estimation of nickel, or more rapidly still by the bismuthate process after filtering off the graphite.

Determination of Sulphur.

This is determined by the aqua regia process, exactly as described for steel on p. 108.

Determination of Phosphorus.

This point requires from the analyst careful consideration as to the weight of metal to be employed for the analysis, because, although 0.1% phosphorus is a somewhat high percentage to occur in steel, in the case of pig-iron as much as 4% of the element may be present in irons to be converted into steel by the basic process. The authors are of opinion, that when the metalloid is to be weighed as ammonio-phospho-molybdate, a quantity of drillings yielding not more than about 0·3 gramme of precipitate should be weighed out, otherwise the yellow compound may not be strictly to formula. The following table will form a rough guide as to the weight of metal conveniently taken for every class of pig-iron, from Swedish pigs smelted from Daunemora magnetite to the most impure iron reduced from the deposits of brown hematite occurring in North Lincolnshire and Northamptonshire.

Approximate % Phosphorus in Iron.	Weight taken for analysis, grammes.		Approximate weight of precipitate obtained.	
	Process.		Process.	
	Molybdate.	Combined.	Molybdate.	Combined.
4·00	—	0·25	—	0·032
2·00	0·20	0·50	0·31	0·032
1·00	0·50	1·00	0·31	0·032
0·50	1·00	2·00	0·31	0·032
0·25	2·00	4·00	0·31	0·032
0·10	3·00	6·00	0·18	0·021
0·05	4·00	8·00	0·12	0·014
0·02	5·00	10·00	0·06	0·007

In the "lead molybdate" process the same weight as for steels is taken for percentages of phosphorus up to 0·1. Between ·1 and ·5%, one gramme is sufficient, and near the upper limit it is advisable to introduce a further alteration. When the yellow precipitate is dissolved in ammonia, the filtrate should be made up to a definite volume and a fractional part of this carried forward.

The highest percentages demand correspondingly smaller amounts of drillings, together with the fractionation of the ammoniacal solution of the yellow precipitate. The graphite should be filtered out after the preliminary solution of the drillings in 1·20 nitric acid.

In chemical analysis it should always be borne in mind, that although, *cæteris paribus*, a heavy precipitate reduces the errors of analysis, there are often other considerations to take into account, such as the bulk of the precipitate to be dealt with with reference to convenience as to filtration, thorough washing, ignition, etc.

The Processes.

These differ little from those described for the analysis of steel by the long molybdate and combined methods respectively dealt with on pp. 139, 141. It is, however, absolutely necessary, after dissolving up the dry oxide of iron in hydrochloric acid, to again evaporate to dryness, and take up in hydrochloric acid, thus rendering the silica insoluble before diluting the liquid and filtering off the silica and graphite, otherwise the gelatinous silica will seriously clog the filtration of the solution ultimately to be neutralized and reduced in the preliminary process described on p. 133, in which it is of course necessary to add sufficient ferric chloride to precipitate the whole of the phosphoric acid as ferric phosphate, together with some basic peracetate of iron.

The case of the lead molybdate process has already been dealt with. The authors do not recommend the volumetric method for pig-irons unless they contain small amounts of phosphorus, when the method described for steels can be strictly followed after removing the graphite by filtration.

Determination of Phosphorus in Chrome pig-irons.

In the case of chrome pigs the preliminary solution of the iron should be made in aqua regia, because nitric acid leaves a large insoluble metallic residue possibly containing phosphorus. There is usually also some insoluble metallic residue after the evaporation with aqua regia, but it is, as a rule, free from phosphorus.

Determination of Chromium.

Sampling.—The chromium in specially smelted chrome pig-iron usually occurs alloyed in proportions of from 6 to 12%. These irons are generally white, and perfectly clean-broken fragments from the pigs must be crushed and passed through a sieve of 90 meshes to the inch before using for analysis.

Method of estimation. — If the iron is low in phosphorus the chromium is best determined by the gravimetric hydrate method described for steel on p. 166. If, however, the pig is phosphoric, the chromium must be estimated as phosphate by the process given on p. 173.

Determination of Copper.

Copper is determined by the volumetric process described for tungsten steels on p. 217, or by the gravimetric process. In the latter method, it is not necessary to ignite the first precipitate to the complete oxidation of the graphite, if after treatment of the ignited residue with *HCl*, the graphite be removed by filtration and the copper determined in the filtrate volumetrically.

Determination of Arsenic.

Arsenic is determined in pig-irons by the method applied to the case of steels on p. 155 after certain preliminary operations. Dissolve 6 grammes in 1·20 nitric acid, evaporate to dryness, dissolve in cold hydrochloric acid, dilute to 300 cc. and filter off 250 cc. from the graphite and silica. Neutralize and reduce with sulphurous acid, boil off the excess, cool rapidly, add 10 cc. of hydrochloric acid and then the zinc sulphide. Collect the arsenic sulphide and proceed.

Analysis of Titanic Pig-irons.

Determination of Silicon.

In irons containing titanium, some TiO_2 is usually found with the ignited silica. This impurity must be separated by thoroughly fusing the residue in a platinum

follows: the ignited residue of silica and phosphotitanate of iron from which the graphite has been burnt off, is fused with an excess of Na_2CO_3, the fusion being extracted with hot water and filtered; the filtrate from the insoluble titanate of sodium and oxide of iron will contain the phosphorus in solution as sodium phosphate. The clear liquid is made slightly acid with HCl, and a few cc. (say two to ten, according to the richness of the iron in phosphorus) of the standard solution of ferric chloride referred to on p. 132 are added. The acid liquid is heated, made alkaline with ammonia, and boiled. The precipitated phosphate of iron is filtered off, washed with hot water, dissolved in HCl, and the solution is evaporated to dryness. The dry residue is taken up in hydrochloric acid, and the insoluble silica is filtered off; the filtrate containing the phosphoric acid is added to the main solution, in which the phosphorus is then determined as usual.

ANALYSIS OF SPIEGELEISEN AND FERRO-MANGANESE.

These always consist essentially of iron, manganese, and carbon, but also contain on an average 0·75% Si, 0·02% S, 0·25% P, and often a little copper. These four elements are estimated by the respective methods described for steel on pp. 65, 117, 143, 211. The term Spiegeleisen (German, looking-glass iron) is usually contracted to spiegel, and denotes an alloy having a fracture consisting of large bright plates, and containing up to about 30% of manganese. When the percentage of this metal rises much above this quantity the alloy assumes a granular fracture, and is then known as ferro-manganese. In these alloys, as a rule, the carbon rises with the percentage of manganese, so that in spiegel containing about 15% *Mn* the carbon is usually about 4·25%. In ferro-manganese containing about 50% *Mn*, the carbon averages 5·5%, and in an alloy containing 80% *Mn* the carbon approximates 6·75%. In spiegel the carbon exists as a double carbide of iron and manganese, in rich ferro-manganese as carbide of manganese.

Determination of Carbon.

The carbon should be estimated by combustion, either by the method described for steel on p. 29 *et seq.*, or by the direct method in a current of oxygen, the powdered alloy alone being used in the case of spiegels, and mixed with red lead in the case of richer alloys.

Rapid Indirect Estimation of Manganese.

In well-organized Bessemer and open-hearth steel large quantities of spiegel and ferro-, it is usual to approximately check alloys before unloading from the metal yard. Hence, a delivery used in a day, necessitating inations.

.. each truck six bright pieces as big as a walnut. These pieces are in pairs, and representative portions from each are crushed up together in a steel mortar, passed a sieve of ninety meshes to the inch, and the insolub us obtained is placed in a dry, numbered sample in the or

tube. Thus on the contents of each truck three determinations are made, and an average assay of the six
samples is obtained.

The Process.

(Time occupied, about ¾ hour.)

Weight taken.—Weigh out into a clean, dry 10-oz.
flask, exactly 0·5 gramme of the sample.

Dissolving.—Add 100 cc. of pure dilute sulphuric acid,
one in seven, cover the flask with a watch-glass, bring
the liquid to boiling, and keep it so for twenty minutes,
or till the alloy has completely dissolved, and no further
evolution of hydrogen is observed.

Titrating the iron.—Rinse the watch-glass, and determine the percentage of iron present by titrating the
solution of $FeSO_4$ in the manner described on p. 85 with
the standard bichromate specified on p. 222. Each cc.
required = 1% Fe.

Calculating the manganese by difference.—To the percentage of iron obtained add the average percentage of
elements other than iron and manganese (as indicated in
the following table), deduct the sum from 100, and the
difference is the approximate percentage of manganese.

% Fe.	Sum of the % of impurities.	% Mn.
12·5	7·5	80·0
28·0	7·0	65·0
43·5	6·5	50·0
59·0	6·0	35·0
79·5	5·5	15·0
85·0	5·0	10·0

Example.—The sulphuric acid solution of 0·5 gramme of ferro-manganese required 46·8 cc. of the standard bichromate to completely oxidize the iron to ferric sulphate : then $46·8 + 6·5 = 53·3$, and $100 - 53·3 = 46·7\% Mn$. It will be obvious, that the results thus obtained are always liable to two sources of error, namely, the percentage of impurities may vary somewhat, giving a + or − error, and some solid carbonaceous flocks, and un-evolved greasy hydrocarbons, which always remain in the flask, have a slight reducing action on the bichromate, thus producing a − error. However, the authors' experience of the process has been, that the percentages of manganese registered are seldom more than 1% from the truth, an error of no great practical importance to the steel-maker.

Volumetric Determination of Manganese in Spiegel and Ferro-manganese (Pattinson).

Re-agents required.

Standard solution of $K_2Cr_2O_7$.—This is made up in the manner described on p. 84 by dissolving 8·9225 grammes of the salt in 1000 cc. of water. The solution is standardized in the manner described on p. 85 by titrating a dilute sulphuric acid solution of 0·51 gramme of Swedish bar-iron, which should require exactly 50 cc. of the bichromate to peroxidize it.

$CaCO_3$ diffused in water.—Place in a Winchester quart 250 grammes of pure precipitated chalk ; add two litres of distilled water, and well shake the bottle before pouring off into a beaker a portion of the white fluid as required for use.

The Process for Spiegeleisen.

Weight taken.—Weigh out into a 20-oz. covered beaker 0·5 gramme of the finely-divided alloy. Also weigh out into a dry 12-oz. *very wide-necked* flask 0·51 gramme of standard Swedish iron.

Dissolving.—Pour down the lip of the beaker 25 cc. of strong *HCl*, and gently boil on the plate till the metal has all passed into solution, then add 1 cc. of strong nitric acid, boil, and finally evaporate quietly to a very low bulk (not more than 5 cc.).

Neutralizing.—Remove the beaker from the plate, carefully rinse the cover and sides of the vessel, replace the former, and little by little pour down the lip of the beaker the water containing chalk in suspension, constantly shaking round the solution till the free acid is neutralized and a faint red permanent precipitate remains.

Oxidizing and precipitating hydrated MnO_2.—Next add 50 cc. of a saturated aqueous solution of bromine, and then 300 cc. of nearly boiling distilled water; then little by little, with constant stirring, add a few cc. of the chalk and water, till on the neutralization of the hydrobromic acid a bulky brown precipitate is obtained.

Filtering and washing the precipitate.—Collect the hydrate on a 3-in. ribbed funnel containing a thick German paper, cut so as to project very slightly over the edge. Every particle of precipitate is washed from the rod and beaker, and the filter and its contents are *most thoroughly washed with a jet of nearly boiling water till quite free from hypobromites, etc.*

Titrating.—At the commencement of the washing, add

to the flask containing the iron a mixture of 10 cc. of strong H_2SO_4 and 60 cc. of water, and boil the covered flask on the plate till the last particle of iron has dissolved. Remove from the plate, rinse the cover, and very cautiously slide bodily into the acid solution of $FeSO_4$ the paper containing the manganic precipitate. Shake round the contents of the flask till the paper is in pulp, and the dark precipitate has entirely dissolved. The amount of unoxidized iron is then determined in the usual manner by the standard solution of bichromate and the ferricyanide indicator. The number of cc. required subtracted from 50 gives the percentage of manganese present.

Example.—A sample of German spiegel required 35·2 cc. of the standard solution: therefore, $50 - 35·2 = 14·8\%$ manganese.

Theoretical Considerations.

The general principles involved in this process are almost identical with those fully dealt with in describing the Ford and Williams method for the volumetric estimation of manganese in steel on p. 83.

The last-named process may indeed be used for spiegel, but not for ferro-manganese. But when dealing with such highly manganiferous alloys, Pattinson's process is to be preferred. The oxidation of the manganous oxide to the hydrate of the peroxide is brought about in the neutral solution by the bromine water, but the metal is only entirely thrown down in the form of hydrated dioxide in a hot, dilute solution, containing a considerable excess of ferric iron; the latter condition is of course always

present in the case of spiegel. If the precipitate is not
freed by thorough washing from bromine and calcium
hypobromite, these substances will oxidize the iron, be
registered as MnO_2, and so give a high result.

The Process for Ferro-manganese.

Two slight but essential alterations must be made in
the foregoing process when dealing with very rich manganese alloys. First, in order to ensure the presence of
sufficient iron, only 0·25 gramme of the alloy is weighed
out for the analysis, and the finely-divided metal is dissolved up with the addition of half a gramme (weighed
roughly) of Swedish iron. To allow for the manganese
present in the latter, $0·2\%$ ($= 0·1\%$ in each 0·25 gramme)
must be deducted from the percentage registered. Second,
as only 0·25 gramme of alloy is employed for the assay,
the result obtained must be multiplied by two.

Example.—On titration, a sample of rich ferro-manganese required 9·8 of bichromate solution, then 50 −
9·8 = 40·2 and (40·2 × 2) − 0·2 = 80·2% *Mn.*

THE BISMUTHATE PROCESS.

The bismuthate process of manganese alloys is doubt-
less the most reliable of all, and may be worked in very
little more time than it occupies when applied to steel.

The Process.

Weight taken.—For spiegel weigh off 0·55 gramme,
and for ferro-manganese 0·275 gramme.

Dissolving, etc.—Add 50 cc. of nitric acid (1·20) and boil until decomposed. Sodium bismuthate is then added a little at a time until the carbonaceous matter has been destroyed and a permanent precipitate of manganese dioxide is obtained. The latter is then just taken into solution with sulphurous acid and the whole liquid rinsed into a 250 cc. flask, cooled and diluted to the mark.

Oxidation, etc.—50 cc. of the solution are measured off and mixed with 30 cc. of nitric acid s.g. 1·20. The mixture is then shaken with 2 grammes of sodium bismuthate, and the assay completed exactly as described under the corresponding process for steels on p. 90, except that the filtrate and washings should be copiously diluted with water before titrating.

In the subsequent calculation it must be remembered that the weights represented by the amount of solution oxidized are 0·11 gramme for spiegel and 0·055 gramme for ferro-manganese.

Notes.

Comparatively large amounts of bismuthate will be used up in destroying the carbon in the hot solution on account of the large amount of this element contained by rich manganese alloys.

A considerable excess of free nitric acid is purposely added to the solution before the addition of bismuthate. Neglect of this would result in an incomplete oxidation, part of the manganese being oxidized to MnO_2 only, and this would be left on the filter.

After washing the filter with the dilute acid until the washings are colourless, it is generally found that the residue, after allowing to stand, will again yield coloured washings. The amount of manganese thus left behind is, however, negligible, representing at the most only three-tenths of a cc. of decinormal permanganate.

The preliminary decomposition of the alloy may in some cases be difficult to effect with nitric acid. Silico-spiegels, for instance, are not readily decomposed in the manner specified. In such cases sulphuric acid, with the addition of hydrofluoric acid from time to time to decompose silica, is used instead, and 1·20 nitric acid subsequently added before the oxidation.

Gravimetric Determination of Manganese in Spiegel and Ferro-manganese.

(Time occupied, about 1 day.)

Weight taken.—Weigh out into a 20-oz. breaker 0·5 gramme of spiegel or 0·2 gramme of ferro-manganese. To the latter it is convenient to add about $\frac{2}{10}$ gramme of Swedish iron.

Dissolving.—Dissolve the metal by boiling with 25 cc. of strong *HCl*, then add 1 cc. of strong nitric acid, boil well, and dilute to 200 cc. with nearly boiling water.

Neutralizing and precipitating the iron.—The solution is neutralized with dilute ammonia, and the iron precipitated with 20 cc. ammonium acetate in the manner described on p. 72, but in the present case fractional filtration is not employed.

Re-dissolving and re-precipitating the iron.—The basic ferric acetate is collected on a German paper (previously well washed with hot dilute *HCl* and water) contained in

a 3-in. ribbed funnel. The beaker is well washed out, and
the precipitate is allowed to drain, the filtrate being
received in a clean 40-oz. beaker. The funnel containing
the iron is next supported on a hanger inside the beaker
in which the precipitation took place, and is re-dissolved
in the smallest possible quantity of hot *HCl*, the paper
being washed in cold water till free from any yellow
tinge. The acid solution of ferric chloride is boiled down
to about 15 cc., when the liquid is diluted, neutralized,
and the iron is precipitated exactly as before. The filtrate is added to that containing the bulk of the manganese (which should in the meantime have been quietly
boiled down). The beaker is well rinsed out, and the
precipitate is slightly washed with hot water.

Precipitating the manganese.—The two filtrates are
boiled down to about 200 cc. to separate traces of iron,
and the liquid is filtered into a 30-oz. registered flask;
the manganese is then precipitated from the cold solution with bromine and ammonia exactly as described on
p. 73.

Igniting, weighing, etc.—When the solution is crystal
clear, every particle of the bulky precipitate of manganese dioxide is collected on a 125 mm. pure paper, and is
well washed with hot water, and after thoroughly drain-
weighed in the usual manner.
must be carefully ignited,
idue when dealing with such
ts of oxide will not contain
ering has shown that it may
as much as 74% of metal.[1]
off, the crucible should be
the muffle for about half an
pa. this for Aft in washing.
s," 1881, No. 1121.

hour; it is then allowed to become quite cold in the desiccator before re-weighing. The weight of precipitate obtained in the case of spiegel when working on 0·5 gramme of the sample is multiplied by 144, and in the case of ferro-manganese when working on 0·2 gramme of metal by 360; the result obtained is the manganese %.

Theoretical Considerations.

The principles of the foregoing method are identical with those described on p. 78 *et seq.* for steel analysis. In the present case, however, it is necessary to re-precipitate the iron[1] to ensure the separation of a small amount of manganese (about 1%), almost invariably carried down on the first precipitation. It will be obvious that when working upon such comparatively small original weights it is necessary to exercise the greatest care during analysis to avoid the introduction of any manipulative errors, because the latter would be respectively multiplied by two and five instead of being diminished by distribution over a large original weight. The addition of a little Swedish iron to the ferro-manganese enables the neutralizing operation to be carried out with greater certainty than when only the small amount existing in the sample *per se* is present.

ANALYSIS OF FERRO-CHROME.

An accurate complete analysis of this material is a matter presenting considerable difficulties. The rich

---

[1] See footnote to nickel determination, p. 198.

T

alloy used for the manufacture of special steels contains from 40 to 65% of chromium, and 7 or 8% of carbon, and is not completely soluble in acids. Recently very rich alloys have been placed on the market containing very little carbon and they are readily soluble in acids, thus making their analysis much easier.

Sampling.—Representative pieces must be reduced to a granular condition by crushing in a steel mortar, and passing through a sieve of 90 meshes to the inch. The comparatively coarse metallic powder thus obtained then requires to be converted into an impalpable flour by treating it a few tenths of a gramme at a time in an agate mortar. The success of the analysis depends in a great measure upon having the alloy in an excessively fine state of division, necessitating a very tedious pulverizing operation to obtain enough of the floured material for a complete analysis, as at least 5 grammes will be required.

DETERMINATION OF CHROMIUM.

Gravimetric Process.

This is carried out by the hydrate method described on p. 166, by mixing in a 3-in. platinum dish ·12 gramme of the metallic flour with 5 grammes of the fusion mixture, and maintaining the fused mass in a liquid state over a powerful Bunsen for half an hour, when the chromium will be completely converted into alkaline chromate. The process when skilfully carried out gives accurate results, but the small original weight necessarily taken to obtain a readily washed precipitate makes a small manipulative error serious. Hence it is, as a rule, best to use one of the volumetric processes next dealt with, which have the additional advantage of being quickly carried out.

Volumetric Method (Clark and Stead).

Re-agents required.

Tribasic dry fusion mixture.—Intimately mix and bottle for use:

50·0 grammes pure calcined magnesia (MgO).

12·5 grammes pure K_2CO_3.

12·5 grammes pure Na_2CO_3.

Standard solution of $K_2Cr_2O_7$. — Dissolve 14·155 grammes of pure bichromate in 1000 cc. of water.

The Process.

(Time occupied, about 3 hours.)

Weight taken.—Weigh out into a $2\frac{1}{2}$-in. diameter flat platinum dish 0·5 gramme of the floured alloy, and by means of a glass rod *very intimately* mix with 10 grammes of the tri-basic re-agent. Carefully brush any adhering powder from the rod into the dish, and then gently tap down the mass.

Dry fusion.—Having heated the dish for a few minutes in the middle of the hot plate to drive off any hygroscopic moisture, introduce it into the muffle, and heat in the hottest part for two hours, when the metal will have become completely oxidized to chromate.

Extracting the fusion.—Introduce the dish when cold into a clean 20-oz. covered beaker, and pour down the lip a mixture of 25 cc. strong sulphuric acid with 150 cc. of water. Heat till all soluble matter has passed into solution, and only a small residue of oxide of iron remains; the dish is then washed and removed. The liquid should be of a clear yellow colour.

Titrating.—When the extraction is commenced weigh out into a 20-oz. dry flask 1·618 grammes of Swedish iron, and dissolve in a mixture of 20 cc. strong sulphuric acid and 120 cc. of water. When the solution is complete, rinse the watch-glass, and transfer to the flask every trace of the yellow liquid in the beaker. The excess of ferrous iron is then determined as on p. 183. The number of cc. used subtracted from 100 gives the percentage of chromium present; in other words, each cc. left corresponds to 1% of chromium.

Example.—A sample of Hanoverian ferro-chrome required on titrating back 35·7 cc. of bichromate, then $100·3 - 5·7 = 64·3\%\ Cr$.

Theoretical Considerations.

The theoretical principles involved in this process are almost identical with those described on p. 184 in connection with the volumetric estimation of chromium in steel. On extracting the dry fusion from which nitrates were absent, the chromic acid CrO_3 remains unreduced by the dilute sulphuric acid employed, whereas, had nitrates been present in the wet process, the anhydride would have been at once reduced to chromic oxide Cr_2O_3, which change in the present case is brought about by the ferrous iron, the oxygen yielded and consequently the chromium present being measured by difference on estimating the excess of FeO by the standard solution of $K_2Cr_2O_7$.

The Sodium Peroxide Method.

(Time occupied, $\frac{3}{4}$ hour.)

Weight taken.—Weigh out 0·5 gramme of the finely floured alloy into a large nickel crucible, and by means of a rounded glass rod mix it with about 4 grammes of sodium peroxide.

Fusion.—Hold the crucible, by means of a pair of tongs, in an ordinary bunsen flame until the mixture just melts. This may happen suddenly with deflagration and consequent loss if due vigilance is not exerted. The molten mass is then kept in constant circular motion for at least three minutes, the crucible being held in the flame so that the latter reaches well up the sides. A dull red heat only need be maintained throughout; a higher temperature is not only unnecessary, but it entails greater loss of nickel from the crucible which suffers considerable loss in weight under any circumstances.

Extraction.—When cold, wipe the outside of the crucible and place it in a 20 oz. beaker with 150 to 200 cc. of water. Heat the solution, and when the vigorous effervescence ceases, remove the crucible, well washing it inside and out. Maintain the liquid in ebullition for five minutes and then remove from the plate. Push the cover glass aside and add, a little at a time, dilute sulphuric acid (1 to 4) until its addition causes no further

violent action, by which time the solution is freely acid.
Place the beaker on the plate again and boil until the
solution is perfectly clear. Black oxide of nickel is last
of all to pass into solution, and it may be found necessary
to add more dilute sulphuric acid to thoroughly clear the
liquid.

Titration.—The rich orange solution containing the
chromium is then titrated exactly as just described in
the preceding method of Clark and Stead, or by means
of potassium permanganate as described under the determination of chromium in "self-hard alloys" on p. 291.
Before commencing the titration, the bottom of the
beaker containing the acid extract should be carefully
examined for tiny particles of the undecomposed alloy.
If these are found, the assay should be rejected and a
new one begun. Attention to the details of conducting
the fusion should never bring about this undesirable
result.

Theoretical Considerations.

Sodium peroxide, Na_2O_2, at a red heat readily effects
the decomposition of many highly refractory alloys, ores,
etc., one oxygen atom from each molecule of the peroxide being available for oxidizing purposes. In the case
of ferrochromes the resulting products will therefore be
primarily ferric oxide and sodium chromate. The carbon
is oxidized to carbon dioxide, the manganese to sodium
manganate, and the minor constituents to the usual
oxidized products. Nickel from the crucible enters the
melt as the black oxide. Extraction with water decomposes the excess of peroxide with formation of hydrogen

peroxide and boiling decomposes the latter with expulsion of oxygen.

$$Na_2O_2 + 2 H_2O = 2 NaHO + H_2O_2$$
$$H_2O_2 = H_2O + O$$

The boiling is an important point, because undecomposed hydrogen peroxide would on subsequent acidification exert a reducing action on the sodium bichromate. It also serves to decompose the sodium manganate leaving manganese dioxide with the oxides of nickel and ferric iron. The insoluble oxides are finally dissolved in sulphuric oxide with generation of oxygen in the cases of the manganese and nickel.

$$MnO_2 + H_2SO_4 = MnSO_4 + H_2O + O$$
$$Ni_2O_3 + 2 H_2SO_4 = 2 NiSO_4 + 2 H_2O + O$$

The acidification converts the sodium chromate to bichromate.

$$2 Na_2CrO_4 + H_2SO_4 = Na_2Cr_2O_7 + Na_2SO_4 + H_2O$$

The remaining operations have already been discussed.

The determination of the other constituents of ferrochrome present no special difficulties in the case of completely soluble alloys, and need not be described here. The more refractory alloys, however, require further consideration.

Determination of Silicon.

(Time occupied, about 4 hours.)

The determination of silicon is carried out working upon 2 grammes of the floured alloy in the manner described for chrome steels on p. 67. As an alternative, the process devised by Tate may be adopted.

Fuse 2 grammes of the floured alloy with 10 to 12 grammes of sodium peroxide in the manner already described. After extracting with water, transfer the solution to a large dish (preferably of nickel or silver) and add hydrochloric acid until the solution is nearly neutral. The solution is then evaporated to dryness, and the dry residue treated with about 50 cc. of strong sulphuric acid. The mixture is heated until copious fumes of sulphur trioxide escape, by which time the hydrochloric acid has been expelled completely together also with most of the chromium as the volatile chlorochromic acid. After cooling, add 200 cc. of water cautiously, and boil to dissolve up soluble sulphates. The silica is collected and weighed as usual. It is usually contaminated with chromium, and must be purified in the manner described on p. 67, or its weight determined, after treatment in the usual manner with hydrofluoric acid, by difference. The results obtained by this process must not be accepted without performing a blank experiment on the re-agents used, and making a correction for the amount of silicon yielded by them and by the vessels in which the operations are performed.

Determination of Sulphur.

This may be determined with sufficient accuracy for practical purposes by treating 3·6 grammes of the alloy which has passed through the 90-mesh sieve with 100 cc. of aqua regia. The solution is boiled down to low bulk in a 20-oz. covered beaker, the evaporation is then gently continued to complete dryness. The dry mass when cool is taken up in *HCl*, evaporated to low bulk, transferred to a 60 cc. flask, and 50 cc., corresponding to 3 grammes of alloy, are filtered off in the usual manner, and the sulphur is estimated by the gravimetric process described for steel on p. 108. The insoluble residue remaining with the $\frac{1}{6}$ of unfiltered solution is, as a rule, practically free from sulphur.

Determination of Phosphorus.

3·6 grammes of the alloy, after being passed through the 90-mesh sieve, are treated as in the case of the sulphur determination. The 50 cc. of liquid containing the phosphorus in 3 grammes of the alloy, are evaporated to low bulk, made alkaline with ammonia, acid with 1·42 nitric acid, and the phosphorus is approximately determined as ammonio-phospho-molybdate in the manner described on p. 126.

Determination of Manganese.

Fusion, etc.—Fuse 1·1 gramme of the floured alloy as described previously with 6 to 8 grammes of sodium peroxide.

Extraction, etc.—Extract with 400 cc. of water and boil well, to decompose the sodium manganate into manganese dioxide.

Filtration, etc.—The solution is allowed to stand until the oxides settle well to the bottom of the beaker, and the yellow supernatant liquid is then poured through an

asbestos filter without disturbing the residue more than
necessary. The latter is then repeatedly washed by decantation with water until the washings are colourless.

Titration.—The asbestos filter is returned to the
beaker containing the bulk of the insoluble residue and
30 cc. of nitric acid of s.g. 1·20 added; and the mixture
heated. A solution of ferrous sulphate is then added, a
little at a time, with stirring between each addition, until
the oxides pass completely into solution. The determination of the manganese is then carried out by the bis-
multhate process exactly as described for steel.

Determination of Carbon.

As ferro-chrome is not attacked by the usual copper
solutions, the direct combustion process is alone available for the determination of carbon in the alloy.

The Process.

Weight taken.—This varies with the amount of carbon in the alloy. Completely soluble alloys always
contain small amounts of carbon, and 2·727 grammes of
the finely divided material may be taken. The re-
...tle alloys (60 — 65% Cr) frequently contain
...bon, and 1 gramme is an ample
...ghed alloy to the shaking-
5 to 10 grammes of special
e from blank. Mix well.
er the mixture to a porcelain
sorption train is in position,
to position and quickly replace

the bung. The burners under that part of the tube which takes the boat must be shut off until the foregoing operation has been performed, unless it is known for certain that the alloy does not contain more than $1\frac{1}{4}$ per cent. of carbon, in which case that part of the tube can be heated before introducing the boat. The copper oxide spiral is of course heated to full redness at that end adjacent to the potash bulbs, but the temperature near the nose of the inserted boat requires careful manipulation. As soon as the alloy begins to react with the red lead, there is a greater or less evolution of gas according as there is much or little carbon in the alloy, and it is until this evolution of gas has occurred that the heating must be carefully controlled. The burners under the boat may then be lighted, the aspirator tap opened to the full, and oxygen admitted. The remaining operations have been described under the direct combustion of steels.

To prevent the splashes thrown out of the boat from soiling the tube it is advisable to cover the boat loosely with a lid of well-ignited asbestos paper.

Example.—1 gramme alloy, 5 grammes red lead.

Increase in weight of absorption bulbs was 0·2952 gramme. Blank from 5 grammes of red lead = 0·0042, hence actual weight of CO_2 evolved = 0·2910 gramme.

Carbon per cent. = 0·2910 × 27·27 = 7·93.

Analysis of Metallic Chromium.

Fused metallic chromium, containing up to 98 per cent. of actual Cr, is now an important commercial product.

bustion at the highest temp
amounts to less than 0·5 pe

Modern ferro-silicons ma
cent. of silicon, the older vari
use prior to the application
much poorer (10 to 15 per
principally as graphite in ferro
2 per cent. A notable featur
high-grade alloys is the almo
aluminium and calcium, and
occurrence to find magnesium

Low-grade

Ferro-silicons containing le
decomposed by acids, and tl
difficulty

about 150 cc. Filter off the silica, wash, dry, and ignite. The weighed residue is then purified either by fusion with acid potassium sulphate, or the actual amount of SiO_2 determined by the loss of weight due to a treatment with pure hydrofluoric acid and ignition. The filtrate from the silica invariably contains a further small amount, and this is obtained by the ordinary method of evaporation, baking, etc.

Determination of Carbon.

Carbon is determined by direct combustion in a stream of oxygen.

Determination of Manganese, Sulphur, and Phosphorus.

For the manganese determination, decompose 2·4 grammes of the alloy as above in the silicon determination, using twice the amount of acids. Dilute to 300 cc. and filter off 250 cc. Determine the manganese in the filtrate by making an acetate separation of the iron, and precipitating with bromide and ammonia. The ignited Mn_3O_4 should be treated with hydrofluoric acid to remove silica.

For the sulphur determination decompose 2·4 grammes as before, fractionate, add a crystal of potassium nitrate to the filtrate, and determine the sulphur by the gravimetric process for steels.

For the phosphorus determination, proceed as for

sulphur, evaporate the filtrate to dryness, and treat the residue according to the method selected for the determination of phosphorus.

High-grade alloys.

These alloys cannot be decomposed satisfactorily by acids. Perhaps the most straightforward method the student can use is to treat the material as though it were a "refractory," and decompose it as described under the analysis of refractory materials on p. 366. It must not be forgotten that the filtrate from the silica may contain, besides iron, aluminium, calcium, and magnesium. Titanium, if present, will be found with the iron and aluminium.

The small amounts of sulphur and phosphorus may safely be ignored in reporting an analysis of a high-grade ferro-silicon. For exact purposes the alloy is opened out as for a refractory, and these elements determined on the filtrate from the silica. For this purpose it is divided into two parts, the sulphur determined gravimetrically in one, and the phosphorus in the other by dissolving up the iron and aluminium precipitate (which contains all the phosphorus) in 1·20 nitric acid, and finishing by the "lead molybdate method."

Carbon is determined by direct combustion in a stream of oxygen.

ANALYSIS OF FERRO-ALUMINIUM.

The alloy used in steel and iron foundries seldom contains more than 10% of aluminium. It is often very impure, and its general analysis is carried out as in the case of pig-iron.

Determination of Aluminium.

(Time occupied, about 1 day.)

Weight taken.—Weigh out into a 20-oz. beaker 0·6 gramme of the finely-divided alloy, passed through a sieve of 90 meshes to the inch.

Dissolving.—Dissolve the metal in 30 cc. of strong HCl; evaporate to dryness, and take up in HCl.

Filtering off the insoluble residue.—The solution is diluted and made up to 60 cc., and 50 cc. of filtrate collected after passing through a dry filter paper.

Precipitation as phosphate.—The solution is transferred to a 30-oz. registered flask, diluted to about 300 cc., about 2 grammes of sodium phosphate added, and the aluminium precipitated as phosphate, after neutralizing, by means of sodium thiosulphate and acetic acid, as described for steel.

After ignition, the $AlPO_4$ is re-dissolved in HCl, sodium phosphat again added and the precipitation repeated. The ignited precipitate now consists of pure aluminium orthophosphate, $AlPO_4$.

Analysis of Aluminium Metal.

This product is now obtained so pure that the presence of more than 1% of foreign elements is unusual. The latter consist mainly of iron and silicon.

Determination of Silicon.

Silicon is determined on 2·4 grammes of drillings exactly as in the case of steel, but before filtering the solution containing the chlorides of aluminium and iron, it is evaporated to low bulk with the previous addition of two drops of strong HNO_3. The concentrated liquid when cold is washed into a 60 cc. flask, diluted to the mark, thoroughly mixed, and 50 cc. of the fluid are filtered into a graduated flask. The solution thus obtained, containing the iron in 2 grammes of aluminium, is set aside to be used for the determination of the iron in the manner described in the next article. The filtration of the SiO_2 is then continued in the usual manner. It is washed, dried, ignited, and weighed, and the percentage of silicon is calculated on 2·4 grammes.

Determination of the Iron.

On a convenient known volume measured from the 50 cc. of acid solution containing the iron in 2 grammes of aluminium obtained as described in the last article, the percentage of iron present is determined colorimetrically by means of the alkaline sulphocyanide by the process described on p. 75.

ANALYSIS OF FERRO-TUNGSTEN.

This alloy may or may not contain chromium. The ferro-tungstens now so extensively used in the manufacture of high-speed steels contain between 10 and 20%

of chromium, and methods for their complete analysis are appended. The same methods may be applied to the analysis of ferro-tungstens free from chromium, but as the latter are much more easily decomposed by acids, the determinations can be made by precisely the same methods as described under the analysis of steel, due provision being made for the presence of tungsten.

The tungsten in non-chromiferous alloys can be determined by either of the methods described for its determination in steel, and the rapid method in particular is very satisfactory even when worked without evaporating beyond the point at which tungstic oxide separates out. The amount of tungstic oxide left in solution after copious dilution with hot water is practically negligible.

COMPLETE ANALYSIS OF CHROMIFEROUS FERRO-TUNGSTENS. "HIGH-SPEED ALLOYS."

In the manufacture of high-speed steels, the necessary amount of tungsten and chromium, instead of being introduced separately in the form of tungsten metal and rich ferro-chrome respectively, is not infrequently added in the form of an alloy made separately. The details of a method for a complete analysis of such an alloy are appended accordingly.

Determination of Carbon.

Carbon is determined exactly as described under the direct combustion of steels. Instead of prepared trimanganic tetroxide, special red lead yielding a small

u

blank may be used with the alloy, and yields excellent results. In either case the alloy should be finely powdered.

Determination of Silicon, Tungsten, and Manganese.

Subject to the following emendations, these elements are determined as described under the analysis of high-speed steels.

To ensure the conversion of all the tungsten to tungstic oxide and the solution of all the iron, the finely divided alloy should be digested with the hydrochloric acid until all action ceases, and then digested several hours longer after adding the nitric acid. It is convenient to allow the digestion to take place over night by placing the beaker over a small safety burner. In the morning, the iron is entirely in solution and the tungstic oxide possesses a clean orange yellow colour. A dark green colour indicates unsatisfactory decomposition, and the WO_3 invariably contains in such a case comparatively large amounts of iron.

From this stage proceed as for steels.

The estimation of manganese calls for further notice. After neutralizing with ammonium carbonate up to the formation of a permanent precipitate, the latter defies solution in the usual amount of acetic acid in the comparatively cold solution. This need occasion no trouble, for on heating, the precipitate thins out as the temperature rises, and ultimately dissolves, and the ferric hydrate finally separates out completely as the boiling point is reached, just before which the ammonium acetate has been added freely.

Determination of Sulphur and Phosphorus.

Proceed as described under high-speed steels.

Determination of Chromium.

One gramme of the alloy, passed through a sieve of 90 meshes to the inch, is thoroughly mixed in a nickel crucible with about 8 grammes of sodium peroxide. The crucible is held in a pair of tongs and the contents maintained in fusion in the manner detailed under the estimation of chromium in ferro-chrome for about ten minutes at a barely visible red-heat. After cooling, the outside of the crucible is wiped, and the crucible placed in a 20-oz. beaker along with a filter plate. Water is then added so as nearly to cover the crucible, and the solution heated until effervescence ceases and the melt is dissolved from the sides of the crucible. The latter is then lifted out, rinsed inside and out, and the contents of the beaker boiled for ten minutes.

The extract is transferred to a 600 cc. flask, thoroughly cooled, made up to the mark, transferred to a beaker, and allowed to settle. From dry ignited asbestos fibre a filter is then prepared by means of the clear supernatant liquid and 400 cc. of the latter then carefully poured through, so as to disturb the slimy residue as little as possible. Transfer the filtrate, containing the chromium as sodium chromate from two-thirds of a gramme of the alloy, to a 30-oz. registered flask, and add dilute sulphuric acid to acidity. Titrate the solution by adding an excess of ferrous ammonium sulphate and then $\frac{N}{10}$ potassium permanganate as before. An amount of ferrous ammonium sulphate sufficient to account for alloys containing up to 18% of chromium may be required, but it is advisable to remove a tiny drop of the solution and determine when an excess has been added by means of the spot test with potassium ferricyanide.

Notes.

As an alternative method for the estimation of manganese, in these alloys, the insoluble residue obtained as above by the sodium peroxide fusion for chromium may be dealt with as follows:

Thoroughly wash the insoluble residue, consisting principally of ferric oxide, manganese dioxide and nickelic oxide, by decantation with hot water containing a little ammonium carbonate until the washings are colourless. Dissolve the residue in 30 cc. of hot nitric acid (1·20), with the assistance of a few cc. of a solution of sulphurous acid. When cold, add sodium bismuthate and finish the assay as described previously. The end point is slightly obscured by the presence of green nickel nitrate in the solution.

When, as indicated under high-speed steels, a complete analysis of the alloy is not required, the tungsten may be much more quickly determined by opening out with hydrofluoric and nitric acids in the manner fully described under the assay of tungsten metal for total tungsten on p. 293. In the case of a chromiferous alloy, it is always necessary, however, to examine the ignited WO_3 for chromium as well as iron, and to deduct the amount of the latter after determining it in the manner already indicated.

ANALYSIS OF METALLIC TUNGSTEN.

The metal in the form of a heavy gray powder is now obtainable, registering up to 98% of tungsten.[1] The assay for the total metal is made on ·6 gramme of the floured substance weighed out into a platinum dish, after cautious ignition in the muffle or over a powerful Bunsen flame (to convert the metal into oxide) by the process described on p. 355 for wolfram.

The total tungsten is also accurately determined by the following method, which, as already stated, is applicable to ferro-tungstens, chromiferous and non-chromiferous.

The Process.

Weigh one gramme of the metal, and transfer to a deep platinum dish provided with a lid. Add about 10 cc. of pure hydrofluoric acid, replace the lid, and warm. Remove from the plate and place the dish on a clean white tile. Now add three or four drops only of strong nitric acid by pushing the lid slightly aside, replacing it rapidly after the addition of the acid. When the violent action, accompanied by the evolution of nitrous fumes, subsides, repeat the addition of the nitric acid and continue these separate additions until the last one produces no visible or audible action. It is important to add the acid in very small amounts at a time, because if added all at once, the contents of the dish would inevitably overflow. After making certain that no loss has been

---

[1] Small quantities of niobium are sometimes present.

sustained by an inspection of the white tile, remove and wash the lid of the dish and place the latter on the hot plate or at such a height over a rose burner that the evaporation proceeds without ebullition. When this process has proceeded for about ten minutes, add cautiously, partially replacing the lid for the purpose, 5 cc. of concentrated sulphuric acid. The evaporation is continued until fumes of sulphur trioxide indicate the complete expulsion of the excess of nitric and hydro-fluoric acids. The dish is set aside to cool and the residue drenched with 10 cc. of strong hydrochloric acid added with the utmost care to prevent loss by splashing. The mixture is then diluted with an equal bulk of water and transferred as completely as possible with the assistance of hot wash water and a policeman to a beaker. The precipitate and liquid, now measuring at least 50 cc., are heated to boiling and the beaker then set aside. (It is generally to be noticed that an iridescent film obstinately adheres to the platinum basin; this may, for the time being, be neglected.) Filter off the WO_3, wash with 5% hot hydrochloric acid, and transfer to a platinum dish or crucible for ignition. The coloured film alluded to is then removed by wiping with a small piece of ashless filter paper moistened with a drop of ammonia, and this is ignited with the main precipitate.

The ignited tungstic oxide contains generally a few milligrammes only of ferric oxide; it is obviously free from silicon. The iron is determined and allowed for exactly as described previously.

Examination of the Metal for Sodium Tungstate and for Oxides.

Although the total yield of tungsten in commercial metals may seem fairly satisfactory, it does not follow that the whole of it represents actual reduced metal. The high atomic weight of tungsten renders possible the presence of the considerable percentage of oxides without apparently seriously impairing the value of the product as determined by assay. The authors some years ago found an alleged sample of metallic tungsten to contain over 25% of oxides. The material when reduced in dry hydrogen gave off water in well-defined fractions, corresponding to the sequence of the reduction of the oxides. First, at a low red heat, the powder assumed a deep, brilliant blue colour, due to the reduction of the WO_3 present to the blue oxide $(2 WO_3 + WO_2)$, and drops of water speedily collected in the cooler portion of the combustion tube. Second, as the temperature rose, the blue changed to a rich purplish-brown, corresponding to the production of the oxide WO_2, more water being given off. It was found impossible to complete the reduction of the brown oxide to metal at the highest temperature of the Hoffman furnace. For this purpose the material must be heated to a white heat in a porcelain tube in a current of hydrogen. A crude but useful qualitative test for oxides is to gently boil 10 grammes of the metallic powder with 10 cc. of strong *HCl*; the metal is allowed to settle, and the nearly clear supernatant liquid is decanted off into a 50 cc. measure. On filling up the latter with distilled water, if any considerable quantity of oxides are present, a blue colour will be developed, and after a little time, a deep blue, greenish, or yellowish precipitate of the oxides of tungsten will precipitate from the solution.

No satisfactory method exists for the accurate determination of the separate oxides of tungsten in tungsten metal. An approximation to the total amount of tungsten existing in an oxidized form is furnished by the following processes.

I. Digest a weighed amount of the powder with strong hydrochloric acid (10 cc. per gramme of powder) for 10 minutes and filter. Evaporate the filtrate nearly to dryness, dilute with water and filter off the tungstic oxide.

II. Digest the residue from the above treatment for 10 minutes with a weak solution of caustic soda (approximately decinormal) and filter. Nearly neutralize the filtrate with dilute nitric acid and precipitate with mercurous nitrate and mercuric oxide as directed under the assay of wolfram. The total weight of WO_3 found by the two extractions includes the tungsten which exists in the powder as sodium tungstate. This constituent can be determined separately, if desired, by exhausting a powder with water only and precipitating the filtrate with mercury salts as before. The weight of WO_3 obtained, multiplied by 1·267 gives the sodium tungstate, Na_2WO_4.

ANALYSIS OF FERRO-NICKEL.

The general analysis of this material is carried out as though dealing with a pig-iron. In the determination of manganese the precautions described on p. 82 must be observed. Or, after precipitating the manganese with bromine and ammonia, the precipitate can be re-dissolved in *HCl*, evaporated to fumes with H_2SO_4, and the bismuthate process applied.

Determination of Nickel.

The determination of nickel in ferro-nickel is carried out exactly as described for steels, a fractional part of the filtrate from the iron being used for the titration with potassium cyanide.

ANALYSIS OF METALLIC NICKEL.

This product when in cubes may contain some un-reduced oxide, and more or less carbon, silicon, copper, manganese, sulphur, iron, and cobalt are usually present. The metal last named may be safely ignored in steel works' practice, any small amount present being co-pre-cipitated with the nickel and recorded as such. Ingot nickel may be drilled for analysis, but if in the form of cubes or large shots, if possible one or two lbs. of the latter should be fused in a clay crucible and cast into a small ingot for drilling; otherwise the metal is very awkward to sample for analysis, the only way being to dissolve up one or two weighed cubes or a few shots in *aqua regia:* several grammes may be thus totally dis-solved, but only after prolonged digestion. The liquid is evaporated to dryness, the mass taken up in *HCl*, and the solution when cold is made up to exactly 250 cc., the liquid being thoroughly mixed. From this a volume of filtered solution corresponding by calculation to the desired weight of actual metal is carefully measured out for analysis from a delicately graduated burette.

Electrolytic Determination of Nickel.

(Time occupied, about 1½ days.)

Weight taken.—Two grammes of metal are weighed or measured into a 20-oz. covered beaker.

Dissolving.—The drillings are dissolved by boiling with 30 cc. of *aqua regia.* The solution is evaporated to dryness, and re-dissolved in 50 cc. of dilute sulphuric acid one in six. The solution is again concentrated till white fumes of sulphuric acid are evolved; the contents of the beaker are cooled, and 40 cc. of cold water are next cautiously added down the lip of the covered beaker, and the contents of the vessel are boiled till every trace of the precipitated sulphate of nickel has passed into solution. The liquid is then diluted to 150 cc. with nearly boiling water.

Separating the copper.—The copper is next precipitated as CuS by passing through the hot liquid a brisk current of washed H_2S for about fifteen minutes. The precipitate is filtered off on a 90 mm. pure paper, the latter and its contents being well washed with water containing H_2S and about 1% sulphuric acid. The filtrate and washings are received into a clean 30-oz. registered flask.

Separating the manganese and iron.—Cool the acid filtrate, add 2 cc. of bromine, and shake round until it has dissolved. Then add 50 cc. of strong ammonia, shake the solution vigorously round, and digest the deep blue liquid till the hydrates of manganese and iron have flocked out. Collect the precipitate on a 90 mm. pure filter, and wash the latter thoroughly with hot water. The filtrate and washings are received into a 300 cc. graduated flask, and when cold, are made up to the mark and thoroughly mixed.

Removing ammonium bromide.—Carefully measure off from a burette 37·5 cc. of the blue solution corresponding to 0·25 gramme of metal into a 4-in. porcelain dish, quietly evaporate on a sand-bath till the salts begin to separate, add 50 cc. of dilute sulphuric acid, and again

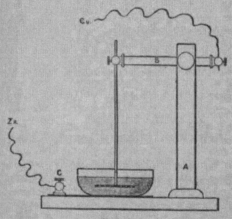

Fig. 15.

evaporate till white fumes are evolved. The precipitated sulphate of nickel is re-dissolved in the smallest possible quantity of water, is transferred without loss to a 3-in. deep platinum basin previously cleaned both inside and out, heated in the air-bath, and cooled and weighed.

Depositing the nickel. — The liquid is then made strongly alkaline with ammonia, when the total bulk should be about 30 cc., and the nickel is electro-deposited by connecting it over-night with the arrangements sketched in Fig. 15. The wooden stand A carries a brass rod B with brass screws at each end; the platinum basin is placed on a bright platinum plate on the base of the stand connected with the binding screw C. One end of the brass rod carries a stout platinum wire attached to a perforated platinum plate, the latter being immersed in the alkaline solution of nickel sulphate. A battery of three or four pint Daniell cells, well charged in the shelves with crystals of cupric sulphate, will be required.[1] The copper terminal of the battery is attached to the brass rod, whilst the zinc pole is coupled up with the screw C by means of stout insulated copper wire. In a few hours the whole of the nickel should be deposited as a closely adherent bright regular lining in the tared dish. The complete deposition of the nickel is proved by bringing a very small drop of the ammoniacal liquid (taken up in the capillary tube at the end of a drawn-out $\frac{1}{8}$-in. glass tube) into contact with a small drop of a saturated solution of H_2S water placed on a white slab. As long as any nickel remains in solution a brown colour is produced.

Weighing the nickel.—When the deposition is complete, the dish is withrawn and thoroughly washed with nearly boiling distilled water. It is dried in the air-bath at 100° C., cooled in the desiccator, and re-weighed. The increase over the first weighing multiplied by 400 gives the percentage of nickel.

[1] Where possible, electrolysis should be effected from storage cells, the most favourable strength of current previously determined by experiments being maintained by the interposition of a suitable galvanometer in the circuit.

Rapid Method.

The foregoing method is tedious, and the result obtained is usually slightly low, owing to the precipitates of copper and manganese carrying down with them traces of nickel. In the majority of cases, sufficiently accurate results may be obtained by dissolving 2 grammes of the nickel in dilute sulphuric acid, evaporating the solution till copious white fumes appear, and then, with the usual precautions, obtaining the sulphate in a volume of 300 cc.; 37·5 cc. of the filtered liquid are then electrolyzed as before described. The metal obtained may be slightly contaminated with copper and iron, but the manganese will be precipitated in the solution as hydrated peroxide.

Determination of Impurities.

The impurities in commercial metallic nickel are determined by the methods already described in connection with steel. The iron, however, may be estimated colorimetrically with an alkaline sulphocyanide, being previously precipitated as hydrate by means of ammonia, and then obtained in dilute *HCl* solution. The details of this process will be sufficiently obvious after reading the method described on p. 75, the result being calculated to metallic iron.

Carbon is estimated by combustion by the cupric chloride process. Heat will be required for dissolving the nickel, and no copper will be precipitated owing to the formation of a soluble double sub-chloride.

Silicon is determined on the residue obtained after the evaporation to dryness in *aqua regia*.

Copper is estimated after precipitation with H_2S from a dilute HCl or H_2SO_4 solution by the process described on p. 211.

Manganese is best determined by the bismuthate process on the precipitate obtained with bromine and ammonia, after re-dissolving in HCl, and evaporating to fumes with sulphuric acid.

Sulphur is estimated by the *aqua regia* process.

ANALYSIS OF FERRO-MOLYBDENUM.

Determination of Carbon, Silicon, Manganese, Sulphur, and Phosphorus.

Carbon is determined by direct combustion in oxygen, after mixing the alloy with red lead. (This re-agent could be dispensed with altogether as ferro-molybdenum is easily oxidized in a stream of oxygen, but molybdic oxide sublimes and covers the inside of the tube just beyond the red-hot portion.) The reaction with red lead is sometimes very energetic, and beads of metallic lead are formed which occasionally pierce the bottom of a porcelain boat and attack the tube. It is advisable, therefore, to line the inside of the boat with a thin layer of freshly ignited asbestos before introducing the assay.

Silicon is determined exactly as in steels, and phosphorus preferably by the combined method described for steels. Sulphur and manganese should be determined gravimetrically by the usual methods.

Determination of Molybdenum.

0·5 gramme of the alloy is dissolved in hydrochloric acid, and the iron oxidized with nitric. The solution is evaporated to dryness and the residue, without baking, is dissolved again in hydrochloric acid. If much silica remains, filter through a small pulp filter, and after washing, put the filter bodily into the strong solution of caustic soda. The filtrate and washings are then partially neutralized with caustic soda solution, and the mixture delivered exactly as described under the determination of molybdenum in steel, into the caustic soda solution. The remaining operations are then performed exactly in the manner and order specified.

The approximate percentage of molybdenum in the alloy is generally known beforehand, and the amount weighed off, or the amount of alkaline filtrate from the ferric hydrate should be arranged to provide from 0·1 to 0·15 gramme of actual molybdenum for precipitation as molybdate.

The precipitate obtained from large amounts of molybdenum by means of lead acetate may not conform to the formula $PbMoO_4$, as it is frequently basic. This is not so when the above amounts are selected, and when the precipitation is carried out exactly as described under the analysis of steel. By redissolving the ignited precipitate in hydrochloric acid with a few drops of nitric acid, diluting copiously, adding ammonium hydrate until a faint permanent opalescence is obtained, then an excess of ammonium acetate, and finally two drops only of the 4% lead acetate solution, pure lead molybdate is precipitated,

and its weight should not differ from the one previously
obtained except to the extent of legitimate manipulative
error. A loss of weight not thus explainable indicates
that the original precipitate was basic.

Molybdenum Powder.

Molybdenum powder is analyzed by the same methods
as applied to ferro-molybdenum.

In determining the chief constituent a slight modification may be introduced with advantage. After extracting
the evaporated acid solution with hydrochloric acid and
filtering, the residue on the filter should be dried, transferred to a nickel crucible, covered with sodium peroxide
and heat cautiously applied to burn the pulp and fuse the
residue. On extracting with water, the filtrate from any
insoluble residue is added to the main solution obtained by
making it strongly alkaline and removing the slight precipitate of ferric hydrate.

Molybdenum powders can be opened out by most of
the usual fusion mixtures containing some oxidant, but
care should be taken to apply heat cautiously at first to
prevent loss of MoO_3 by volatilization.

ANALYSIS OF FERRO-VANADIUM.

Alloys of iron and vanadium frequently contain comparatively large amounts of phosphorus, aluminium and
copper in addition to the chief constituent and the usual
impurities.

Determination of Carbon, Silicon, Sulphur, and Manganese.

Carbon is determined by direct combustion in a stream of oxygen. Silicon is determined by the methods applicable to steel. The ignited silica may not be quite free from vanadium, and its exact amount should therefore be obtained by difference after *HF* treatment. Sulphur is determined gravimetrically as in steel. The solution from which $BaSO_4$ is precipitated must contain more free acid than in the case of steel to avoid precipitation of barium as vanadate. Manganese is determined preferably by the bismuthate process.

Determination of Copper.

Dissolve the powdered alloy in 1·20 nitric acid (20 cc. per gramme of alloy), add 10 cc. of sulphuric acid and evaporate to fumes of sulphur trioxide. Cool and dissolve up the residue in 50 cc. of water. Without filtering off silica, add 20 cc. of a saturated solution of sulphur dioxide and 2 grammes of potassium iodide. If free iodine separates, add more sulphurous acid to dissolve it and bring the liquid to the clear blue colour of hypovanadic solutions, and digest until the precipitated cuprous iodide settles. Filter off the latter and wash with water containing sulphurous acid until the washings are colourless. Place the filter and its contained precipitate in a beaker and decompose the cuprous iodide by boiling with 20 cc. of nitric acid (1·20) until all iodine is expelled and

x

a pale blue solution of cupric nitrate obtained. Strain off the filter paper (and silica) through a small pulp filter, wash well, and add ammonia to the filtrate until alkaline. The dark blue solution thus obtained should be free from any trace of precipitate. It is made acid with acetic acid, excess of potassium iodide added, and the liberated iodine titrated with a standard solution of sodium thiosulphate exactly as described under the determination of copper in steel.

Determination of Aluminium.

Dissolve 2 grammes of the powdered alloy in a 10-oz. registered flask in a mixture of 60 cc. of water with 10 cc. of strong sulphuric acid. Filter, wash, and dilute the filtrate to 200 cc. Add one gramme of sodium phosphate, neutralize to a faint precipitate, re-dissolve in hydrochloric acid, add several grammes of sodium thiosulphate and 30 cc. of acetic acid. Boil for twenty minutes, filter, wash and ignite. Re-dissolve in hydrochloric acid, add ammonia till strongly alkaline, and digest. Filter off the precipitated aluminium phosphate and reject the filtrate containing the copper.

Re-dissolve the precipitate in hydrochloric acid, add ammonia until alkaline and 2 grammes of ammonium phosphate. Boil for ten minutes and filter off the $AlPO_4$ containing a trace of iron. The vanadium is now completely separated. If the colour of the ignited precipitate suggests the presence of more than a trace of iron, re-dissolve and re-precipitate by means of sodium thiosulphate in the usual manner.

Determination of Phosphorus.

Phosphorus can be determined in ferro-vanadium alloys by any of the ordinary methods. The precipitate obtained with ammonium molybdate is much deeper in colour than pure ammonium phospho-molybdate, and it contains vanadium in small quantities. By weighing it as obtained or after its conversion to lead molybdate the results are nevertheless low, although sufficiently accurate for practical purposes. A more exact result is secured by precipitating in the cold from a nitric acid solution to which has been added sufficient ferrous iron to reduce the vanadic to hypovanadic acid, and allowing about an hour for the yellow precipitate to settle.

Determination of Vanadium.

Method I.

Dissolve 0·6 gramme of the alloy in 10 cc. of 1·20 nitric acid in a deep platinum dish covered with a lid until decomposition is complete. Evaporate to dryness and bake strongly on the hottest part of the plate so as to make the residue capable of being detached almost entirely and pulverised by means of a rounded glass rod. Intimately mix it with 3 grammes of sodium carbonate and the same weight of finely-powdered sodium nitrate, and fuse the mixture over a powerful bunsen flame until a thoroughly homogeneous liquid melt is secured. Allow to cool, boil out with water, transfer to a 300 cc. flask, cool, dilute to the mark, and filter off

250 cc. through a double thickness of dry filter paper. The filtrate is then treated in one or other of the following ways, according to whether a volumetric or a gravimetric estimation of the vanadium is desired.

(a) *Volumetric.*—Acidify the filtrate with sulphuric acid, evaporate to fumes of SO_3, dilute, reduce with SO_2, boil off the excess, and titrate the cooled solution with $\frac{N}{10}$ potassium permanganate, each cc. of which registers 0·00512 gramme of vanadium.

(b) *Gravimetric.*—Bring the filtrate to boiling-point and add 1·20 nitric acid a little at a time until a drop of the solution reacts acid when applied to litmus paper. Then add 20 cc. of ammonium acetate and a solution of lead acetate of any convenient strength until it produces no further precipitate. Boil for two minutes, filter, wash with hot water, dry and ignite at a low red heat until the filter is completely destroyed. The ignited precipitate corresponds almost exactly to the formula $2\,Pb_3V_2O_7 \cdot PbO$, and contains 13·8 per cent. of vanadium.

Method II.

Dissolve 0·5 gramme of the alloy in dilute sulphuric acid (1 part acid to 6 parts water), and oxidise the iron (and vanadium) by the addition of a few cc. of strong nitric acid. Boil well and add a solution of potassium permanganate until the carbonaceous matter is destroyed. If a precipitate of manganese dioxide forms, dissolve it with a few drops of a solution of ferrous sulphate, then thoroughly cool the liquid. Now add, a little at a time, a solution of potassium permanganate until

t persists, thereby ensuring the existence of the
m as vanadic acid (V_2O_5). From a burette,
with a decinormal solution of ferrous ammonium
e, which has been carefully standardized with a
n of permanganate of the same strength, de-
he contents carefully into the assay. After each
addition make the usual spot test on a white slab
ning drops of a very dilute solution of potassium
ranide. The titration is finished when a drop of the
gives an immediate blue colour.

cc. $\frac{N}{10}$ ferrous ammonium sulphate $= 0\cdot00512$

nme vanadium.

ANALYSIS OF FERRO-TITANIUM.

Alloys of iron and titanium can generally be decom-
sed with the usual acids and the ordinary processes
r the determination of silicon, sulphur, and manganese
plied. Carbon is determined by direct combustion in
stream of oxygen.

Determination of Titanium and Iron.

Mix 0·6 gramme of the finely-divided alloy with a
large excess of powdered acid potassium sulphate, and
fuse the mixture to a homogeneous melt over a hot
bunsen flame. When cold add water, and digest until
everything is detached from the platinum dish, and then
add sufficient sulphuric acid (about 15 cc.) to take all
into solution except silica. The latter is removed by

filtration, washed, and ignited. After weighing (if thought necessary) it is fused again with a small quantity of acid potassium sulphate and boiled out with water and a few drops of sulphuric acid. The filtrate from the silica, now pure, is added to that from the first fusion. The mixed filtrates are then diluted to 300 cc., and the solution divided into three equal parts.

I. Add ammonium hydrate until a faint precipitate is formed, and then excess of sulphurous acid. In this way the iron is reduced, leaving the titanium unattacked. Boil off the excess of sulphur dioxide and determine the iron by titration with a standard solution of potassium permanganate.

II. Neutralize with ammonia up to the formation of a slight precipitate, clear the solution with a few drops of hydrochloric acid, and add about 15 grammes of sodium thiosulphate dissolved in water. Boil for twenty minutes, filter, wash with water containing acetic acid, ignite very strongly and weigh as TiO_2.

III. The third portion of the original filtrate can be used for an approximately accurate determination of both elements, iron and titanium. The method depends upon the fact that sulphuretted hydrogen or sulphur dioxide reduce the iron only, and nascent hydrogen reduces both the iron and the titanium.

Dilute the 100 cc. representing 0·2 gramme of the alloy to about 200 cc. and pass a current of washed sulphuretted hydrogen through the solution to saturation. Boil to the complete expulsion of the excess of H_2S, cool as quickly as possible, and titrate the iron with a standard solution of potassium permanganate. Cover the flask with an inverted crucible lid carrying several rods of pure zinc arranged to dip into the solution, add a few cc. more of sulphuric acid, and boil gently for forty-five minutes. Remove the zinc rods, and again titrate the solution with permanganate. The difference between the cc. used in the two titrations represents the titanium.

1 cc. of $\frac{N}{10}$ $KMnO_4 = 0.00024$ gramme Titanium.

Determination of Phosphorus. (Pattinson).

Dissolve 2 grammes of the alloy in 1.20 nitric acid, evaporate to dryness and dissolve the residue in hydrochloric acid. Add ammonia until a faint precipitate is formed, and then sufficient sulphurous acid to reduce the iron. Now add about 1 gramme of potash alum, and then ammonium hydrate to the formation of a sufficiently large precipitate of aluminium phosphate to contain the whole of the phosphorus, but not large enough to incorporate more than traces of iron. Filter off, wash, dry, and ignite. Fuse the residue with a large excess of sodium carbonate, digest the cooled melt with water, and filter off any residue of ferric oxide and sodium titanate. The sodium phosphate in the filtrate is collected by adding a few cc. of ferric chloride solution, filtering and dissolving in nitric acid. The determination is then carried to completion by one or other of the ordinary methods.

ANALYSIS OF FERRO-TANTALUM.

The essential constituents of ferro-tantalum, viz., carbon, iron, and tantalum, are readily determined by the following methods:

Determination of Carbon.

One gramme of the alloy, finely powdered, is mixed with ignited manganese dioxide, and the mixture burnt in a stream of oxygen, as already described.

Determination of Tantalum, Iron, and Manganese.

One gramme of the finely-divided alloy is placed in a deep platinum dish, and opened out with hydrofluoric acid and strong nitric acid, exactly as described in connection with tungsten powder. When the nitric acid ceases to produce any further visible action, all the alloy will be found to have disappeared except a small residue much blacker in colour than the original alloy. The mixture is heated gently on the plate for about half-an-hour, after which 5 cc. of strong sulphuric acid are added, and the evaporation continued until copious fumes of sulphur trioxide escape.

The semi-solid mass, after becoming cold, is covered with about 8 grammes of pure acid potassium sulphate, and the mixture heated over a bunsen flame until it is reduced to a thick liquid. The dish is then held well down in the flame by the tongs, and the liquid melt kept in motion for two minutes, after which it is allowed to cool.

The residue is boiled out with a mixture of equal parts of strong hydrochloric acid and water, and the tantalic oxide filtered off, washed well with hot dilute acid, and finally with water, ignited strongly and weighed.

$$Ta_4O_5 \times 0.82 = \text{Tantalum}.$$

The filtrate (and washings) from the tantalic oxide is neutralized, and the iron precipitated as basic acetate, leaving a filtrate in which the manganese is determined as usual. The basic acetate of iron is re-dissolved in acid, neutralized, reduced, and the iron determined by titration with a standard solution of potassium bichromate.

SECTION II. ORES.

THE industrial ores of iron may be roughly divided into three classes:

1. Ferric oxides. Type, hematite $Fe_2O_3 = Fe$ 70%, O 30%.

2. Ferroso-ferric oxides. Type, magnetite Fe_3O_4 or $(FeO, Fe_2O_3) = Fe_2O_3$ 69%, FeO 31%, Fe 72·4%.

3. Ferrous carbonates. Type, clay ironstone $FeCO_3$ or $(FeO, CO_2) = FeO$ 62%, CO_2 38%, Fe 48·2%.

(Calcined clay iron-stone may be regarded as an artificial hematite.)

These ores, it need hardly be stated, are, so far as commercial quantities are concerned, never to formula. They always contain more or less of the following impurities—silica SiO_2, alumina Al_2O_3, manganous oxide MnO, peroxide of manganese MnO_2, phosphoric acid P_2O_5, sulphuric acid SO_3, iron pyrites or ferric sulphide FeS_2, lime CaO, magnesia MgO, moisture and combined water H_2O, and organic matter; often, also, titanic acid TiO_2 is present. There may sometimes exist in the ore either the oxides or sulphides of the following metals; chromium, arsenic, copper, nickel, lead, zinc, barium, vanadium, potassium, and sodium.

The foregoing, in addition to CO_2, FeO, and Fe_2O_3,

314

constitute a formidable-looking list, and if it were necessary in practical work to follow the elaborate scheme of
analysis sometimes formulated, of estimating every trace
of every element, and assigning to it its actual form of
existence in the ore, the world would have to wait for its
iron. In the great majority of cases it is only requisite
to determine as nearly as possible the following substances:

Iron, existing as Fe_2O_3.

Iron, existing as FeO.

Manganese, best calculated to MnO_2 in oxides, and to
MnO in carbonates.

Silicious residue, sometimes reported as SiO_2, but often
impure, containing small quantities of oxide of iron,
alumina, titanic acid, lime, magnesia, and rarely potash
and soda.

Phosphorus, existing as P_2O_5.

Arsenic.

Sulphur, existing partly as SO_3 (in which form it is
usually reported), but sometimes chiefly as FeS_2.

Alumina, Al_2O_3.

Lime, CaO.

Magnesia, MgO.

Carbonic acid, CO_2.

Hygroscopic moisture.

Combined water and organic carbon.

After describing fully the methods by which the items
in the above list are estimated, the authors will deal more
briefly with the determinations of chromium, copper, and
nickel, the analysis of the silicious residue, the approximate estimation of titanic acid, and the alkalies.

Sampling the Ore.

It is far easier to make an accurate analysis of the ore than to ensure the selection of an absolutely representative sample. This must depend in a great measure upon the judgment of the analyst when this duty devolves upon him. It is only possible to advise a judicious selection of representative pieces from different parts of the parcel, and again taking from these smaller pieces, and crushing and mixing the whole of the latter. Of course, aggregated crystals of quartz, calcite, pyrites, apatite, etc. must be avoided, and yet the attempt must be made to obtain a fairly representative percentage of these in the sample. The latter, after being coarsely powdered in a large clean iron mortar, should at once be placed in a well-stoppered, wide-mouthed bottle.

DETERMINATION OF MOISTURE.

(Time occupied, about 1 day.)

This constituent being liable to change in a warm laboratory, should be determined at once. Clean a shallow platinum or porcelain dish about 3 in. in diameter, heat it slightly, and allow to cool in the desiccator. When cold, introduce about 20 grammes of the ore, and ascertain the exact weight of the dish + ore. Place them in an air-bath, and heat for several hours at 100° C., till the weight of two consecutive weighings made at an interval of an hour are practically identical, the dish and its contents before each weighing having been of course allowed to go quite cold in the desiccator: the difference between the original and final weighings is hygroscopic water.

The whole of this dry ore may now be finely pulverized in a Wedgwood ware mortar, passed through a 90 mesh sieve, transferred to a dry, wide-mouthed stoppered bottle, and be employed throughout for the determination of the other constituents, the percentages of which will have reference to the ore dried at 100° C., and not to the original sample, upon which, however, the results may be ultimately calculated if desired.

DETERMINATION OF THE TOTAL IRON.

For hematites, magnetites, and clay ironstones practically completely decomposed by hydrochloric acid, and containing only a small percentage of organic matter, this is a rapid process occupying only about an hour, and is applicable to the great majority of ores.

The Method.

Weight taken.—Carefully weigh out and transfer to a clean, dry 10-oz. flask 0·5 gramme of the finely-divided ore.

Dissolving.—Add 25 cc. of strong hydrochloric acid, put a watch-class on the flask, and boil till the insoluble residue is fairly white. In ores high in silica the flask is best heated on a pipe-stem triangle, otherwise the flask is liable to bump or spit.

Oxidizing organic matter.—If the ore contains any appreciable percentage of organic matter, cautiously add to the solution about a gramme of chlorate of potash crystals, and continue the boiling till the smell of the liberated chlorine has disappeared.[1]

Neutralizing.—Rinse the cover and inside of the flask with distilled water, and slowly add dilute ammonia solution, constantly shaking round the flask till a faint permanent precipitate is obtained.

Reducing.—Next pour round the inside of the flask 25 cc. of strong sulphurous acid solution and then 50 cc. of water. Boil the diluted solution till *free from every trace of* SO_2. The liquid should have a faint sea-green colour quite *free from any tinge of yellow*.

Titrating.—Add to the ferrous solution 10 cc. of dilute sulphuric acid (1 in 7), remove the flask from the plate, and determine the iron present in the manner set forth on p. 85 by means of the standard solution specified on p. 222. Each cc. of bichromate used = 1% of metallic iron in the half gramme of ore. If the material under examination is a hematite or magnetite, 50 cc. of the standard solution may as a rule be at once run into the flask, as in such ores the metal does not usually fall below 50%. If an uncalcined clay ironstone or a spathic carbonate is being analyzed, it is generally safe to run in 30 cc. without over-shooting the mark.

---

[1] This treatment will not suffice for black-band ores, the analysis of which will be dealt with later on.

Theory of the Process.

The hydrochloric acid converts the oxides of iron into their respective chlorides, thus—

$$FeO + 2\ HCl = FeCl_2 = H_2O$$
$$Fe_2O_3 + 6\ HCl = 2\ FeCl_3 + 3\ H_2O$$

From carbonated ores the CO_2 is evolved thus—

$$FeCO_3 + 2\ HCl = FeCl_2 + CO_2 + H_2O$$

The addition of the $KClO_3$ to the HCl causes an evolution of a mixture of chlorine and its oxides, which in the presence of organic matter and water liberate from the latter nascent oxygen, which converts the carbonaceous matter (when only moderate in quantity) into CO_2 and water.

Otherwise readily oxidized organic matter might have a reducing action on the bichromate, and so cause the result to be registered somewhat too high. The reasons for neutralizing the solution before reduction, and for adding a little sulphuric acid before the titration, have already been given respectively on pp. 136, 87, whilst the theory of the titration itself has been fully explained on p. 88. The reducing action of the SO_2 is formulated on p. 136.

DETERMINATION OF FERROUS OXIDE.

The exact amount of FeO present in an ore can only be estimated when peroxide of manganese is absent. The latter compound oxidizes or chlorinizes acid solutions of ferrous salts to the ferric condition, thus—

$$MnO_2 + 4\ HCl + 2\ FeCl_2 = MnCl_2 + 2\ FeCl_3 + 2\ H_2O$$

or

$$MnO_2 + 2\ H_2SO_4 + 2\ FeSO_4 = MnSO_4 + Fe_2(SO_4)_3 + 2\ H_2O$$

Therefore in ores containing MnO_2 the percentage of FeO registered will be more or less low.[1]

On the other hand, in ores containing much carbonaceous matter and no dioxide of manganese, the result obtained may be high, owing to the action of any easily oxidized organic matter in reducing the bichromate solution, when the oxygen thus absorbed would be recorded as due to the oxidation of ferrous salt. It is usual to make an approximate estimation of ferrous iron so as to balance the analysis in the cases of magnetites, raw carbonates, calcined carbonates (in which to some extent the FeO is a measure of the thoroughness of the calcination, after which operation the iron should exist almost totally in the ferric condition), and in certain brown hematites (such as those of Northamptonshire), which have resulted from the more or less complete decarbonation and oxidation of original deposits of impure ferrous carbonate. In red ores and in most brown hematites the estimation of FeO is not often a matter of any importance.

Apparatus required.

Fit a 10-oz. flask with a clean india-rubber stopper perforated with one hole, in which is inserted a piece of glass tubing $2''$ long by $\frac{1}{2}''$ inside diameter. Upon this slip a piece of india-rubber tubing $3''$ long, and closed at one end with about $\frac{3}{4}''$ of glass rod. In the space between the glass tube and the rod there must be cut very cleanly,

---

[1] Conversely it follows, that in the presence of ferrous iron it is not possible to accurately determine the percentage of dioxide of manganese present, when measured by the chlorine evolved on treating the ore with hydrochloric acid, thus—

$$MnO_2 + 4\ HCl = 2\ Cl + MnCl_2 + 2\ H_2O$$

with a keen penknife, a vertical slit about $\frac{1}{2}''$ long. This is best made whilst the india-rubber tubing is distended on a piece of glass rod. The opening acts as a valve allowing gases evolved from the interior of the flask to escape into the air, but preventing the latter from entering the flask, thus avoiding during the dissolution any atmospheric oxidation of the ferrous salt.

The Process.

(Time occupied, about half an hour.)

Weight taken.—Place exactly half a gramme of the very finely-divided ore in the clean and dry 10-oz. flask. Next add 2 or 3 tenths of a gramme of pure dry sodium carbonate (Na_2CO_3).[1]

Dissolving.—Add 25 cc. of strong *HCl*, and quickly insert the india-rubber stopper and valve. Heat the contents of the flask as rapidly as safely possible, and maintain at a gentle boil till the insoluble matter is fairly white, then take off the plate.

Diluting.—Remove the stopper, and add promptly 100 cc. of recently-boiled water, then rinse the stopper and sides of the flask.

Titrating.—Test a drop of the solution with a drop of the very dilute solution of potassic ferricyanide placed on the white slab to see if the blue colour indicative of the presence of *FeO* is produced; if not, the iron in solution exists totally as ferric chloride. If, however, the ferri-

---

[1] This on the addition of the acid expels the air in the vicinity of the liquid, thus reducing the chances of atmospheric oxidation of the latter.

Y

cyanide shows that ferrous iron is present, proceed to titrate the liquid exactly as in the case of the assay for the total iron. The volume of bichromate used will vary with different ores. Certain very pure spathose ores may require 45 cc., equivalent to 45% of metal, or about 58% of *FeO*. Magnetite will not often require much more than 20 cc., equal to 20% *Fe*, or about 25% *FeO*, whilst hematites or calcined carbonates may not take more than 1 cc., showing that only about $1\frac{1}{4}$% of *FeO* is present.

Conversion of cc. $K_2Cr_2O_7$ to % FeO.—To convert the cc. of standard solution required, which are each equivalent to 1% of metallic iron, to their corresponding percentage of *FeO, multiply by* 1·2857.

Calculation of the Ferric Oxide.

The total iron having been determined, and (approximately) the metal existing in the ferrous state, the difference between the two is necessarily (approximately) the iron present as ferric oxide. Therefore from the number of cc. required by the total iron, subtract the volume run in for the ferrous iron; the remainder is the percentage of metal existing in the ferric condition. This multiplied by 1·4286 gives the percentage of Fe_2O_3. The following example will show how the above factors are obtained:—

$$FeO = \begin{cases} Fe = 56 \\ O = 16 \end{cases} \quad \begin{array}{l} \text{Then } \frac{72}{56} = 1\cdot2857, \\ \text{or } 56 \times 1\cdot2857 = 72 \end{array}$$

$$\overline{\underline{72}}$$

Example showing Titrations of a Swedish Magnetite.

cc. taken by total iron $= 55\cdot3 = {}^o/_o Fe.$

" " ferrous " $= 18\cdot9 = $ "

" " ferric " $= 36\cdot4 = $ "

$18\cdot9 \times 1\cdot2857 = 24\cdot34 = {}^o/_o\ FeO.$

$36\cdot4 \times 1\cdot4286 = 52\cdot00 = {}^o/_o\ Fe_2O_3.$

DETERMINATION OF TOTAL IRON IN RAW BLACK-BAND ORES.

The variety of ferrous carbonate known by the above name contains a large quantity (up to 25%) of carbonaceous matter. To ensure an accurate estimation of the total metal it contains, the process used for ordinary ores requires modifying in the manner about to be described.

The Process.

(Time occupied, about 2 hours.)

Weight taken.—Weigh out into a platinum crucible exactly 0·5 of the finely-divided black ore.

Calcining.—Cover the crucible, and place it on a pipe-stem triangle resting upon a tripod; then cautiously heat the crucible by means of a Bunsen burner till the organic matter has burnt off.

Dissolving.—Place the crucible and cover in a 20-oz. beaker containing 50 cc. of nearly boiling strong hydrochloric acid solution, and boil till the whole of the Fe_2O_3 has passed into solution, then wash, and remove the cover and crucible, and quietly evaporate to low bulk, say 10 cc.

Treatment of the solution.—Transfer the liquid without loss to a 10-oz. flask; it is then neutralized, reduced, acidified, titrated, and the percentage of iron is read off exactly as described on p. 322 for the estimation of ores practically free from organic matter.

DETERMINATION OF FERROUS OXIDE IN RAW BLACKBAND ORES.

Apparatus required.

Fit up a 120 cc. graduated flask with an india-rubber stopper and valve in the manner described on p. 320.

The Process.

(Time occupied, about 1 hour.)

Weight taken.—Weigh out into the dry flask exactly 0·6 gramme of the finely-divided ore together with a little pure sodium carbonate.

Dissolving.—Add 25 cc. of strong hydrochloric acid, insert the stopper, and cautiously boil the contents of the flask till it is judged that all soluble matter has dissolved.

Diluting.—Next remove the stopper, add 95 cc. of recently-boiled water, loosely replace the stopper, and cool the flask and its contents under the tap: when cold, rinse the stopper and neck of the flask till the wash-water brings the solution to the mark. Close the flask with a plain india-rubber stopper, and thoroughly mix the contents by repeated inversions.

Filtering off the organic matter.—Allow the insoluble matter to settle, and filter off exactly 100 cc. of the solution through a dry 110 mm. filter into a graduated flask. Transfer this without loss, using recently-boiled wash-water, to a 10-oz. flask.

Titration.—This is carried out and the result calculated to *FeO* exactly as described on p. 322.

Theoretical Considerations.

The foregoing process is not strictly accurate. A little ferrous iron is unavoidably converted during the operations to the ferric state; but on the other hand, it is probable that any organic matter in the solution reduces some of the bichromate, thus possibly producing a compensating error. The reason for using throughout the analysis recently well-boiled water is, that it is for the time being free from dissolved oxygen, which if present would oxidize the ferrous salt.

DETERMINATION OF TOTAL IRON IN ORES NOT COMPLETELY SOLUBLE IN HYDROCHLORIC ACID.

Re-agent required.

Acid potassium sulphate.—This salt may sometimes be purchased pure and free from water, but to be quite sure of its purity it is best made in the laboratory. It is prepared in the following manner: Introduce into a large porcelain basin 100 grammes of pure powdered potassium nitrate and 60 cc. of pure concentrated sulphuric acid. Place the basin on a tripod, and cautiously heat over a Bunsen, gradually increasing the temperature until no more fumes of nitric acid are evolved, and white fumes of sulphuric acid begin to appear. Allow the liquid sulphate to cool till it begins to solidify, then break up the semi-solid mass with a glass rod. When cold, place the acid salt in a large platinum dish, supported on a pipe-stem triangle placed on a tripod, and again quietly fuse the salt, so as to drive off the last traces of water and free sulphuric acid. Be careful, however, not to raise the temperature sufficiently to drive off the combined sulphuric acid. The fused mass is allowed to solidify, and when cold is powdered and preserved for use in a stoppered bottle. It should be pure white in colour.

The Process.

(Time occupied, about 1 hour.)

Weight taken.—Weigh out into a 3-in. platinum dish 0·5 gramme of the finely-divided ore, and intimately mix it with 6 grammes of the powdered acid sulphate.

Fusing.—Heat the covered dish gently over the Bunsen till fusion takes place, and then raise the heat to redness, continuing the fusion for 15 min. The lamp is then removed. When cold, the dish and cover are boiled in a 20-oz. beaker containing 50 cc. of water mixed with 2 or 3 cc. of strong sulphuric acid, till the mass of sulphates is completely dissolved out from the insoluble silica, the dish and cover being then removed.

Treatment of the solution.—The acid liquid is transferred without loss to a 10-oz. flask, is neutralized, reacidified, acidified, and titrated in accordance with the instructions given on p. 318.

Theory of the Process.

When strongly heated, the acid sulphate gives off free sulphuric acid by the reaction formulated on p. 69. The acid, at the comparatively high temperature of the fusion, readily attacks the oxides of iron present, thus—

$$FeO + H_2SO_4 = FeSO_4 + H_2O$$
$$Fe_2O_3 + 3\ H_2SO_4 = Fe_2(SO_4)_3 + 3\ H_2O$$

The ferrous and ferric sulphates, together with the co-produced normal potassium sulphate, readily dissolve in the acidulated water. The SiO_2 is left insoluble, but the other bases pass into solution as $MnSO_4$, $Al_2(SO_4)_3$, $CaSO_4$, $MgSO_4$, etc.

DETERMINATION OF FeO IN INSOLUBLE ORES.

Apparatus required.

Fit up the apparatus sketched in Fig. 16: A is a per-fectly flat fire-clay plate 6″ sq. + ¼″ thick, and perforated in the centre with a hole 2½″ in diameter. In this rests a covered 3″ platinum dish, over which is inverted a suf-ficiently large fire-clay crucible, B, in the bottom of which a hole has been drilled, into which has been cemented a bent glass tube ¼″ inside diameter. The cement with which to fix this in is made by kneading to a very stiff dough a little finely-ground ganister with thick liquid silicate of soda. On leaving the fitted crucible for a few hours on the hot plate, the cement sets harder than the burnt fire-clay itself.

The Process.

(Time occupied, about 2 hours.)

Weight taken.—Intimately mix 0·5 gramme of the ore

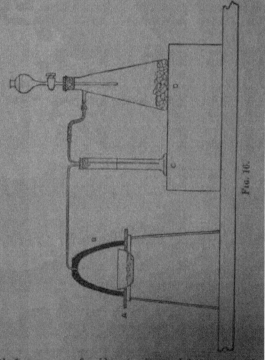

Fig. 16.

with 6 grammes of acid pota......................
process last described. Place

of the perforated plate, and support the latter on a
d. The fire-clay crucible is then inverted over the
and the glass bend is connected with an apparatus
ving CO_2 washed by passing it through a cylinder of
er. Fig. 16 c is a washing cylinder; D a filter-pump
el containing marble and water, into which hydro-
oric acid is delivered as required from a separator.
as the gas for several minutes, till it is judged that the
: in the dish and its vicinity is expelled, then, very
utiously as first, heat the bottom of the dish with a
nsen burner for the same length of time as that occu-
ied in the fusion for estimating the total iron; then take
way the lamp, and allow the dish and its contents to
cool in the current of CO_2.

Dissolving.—The fused mass is extracted in a covered
beaker by heating with dilute sulphuric acid, the cover
and crucible are rinsed with recently boiled water, and
are then removed.

Titration.—Next, without loss of time, the acid solution is titrated in the beaker with the standard bichromate solution, and the cc. required are converted to FeO
by multiplying them by 1·2857.

Theoretical Considerations.

The result obtained by the foregoing process is only
approximate, being always somewhat low from a slight
oxidation of the $FeSO_4$ to $Fe_2(SO_4)_3$ by the action of the
air, the — error being of course increased if peroxide of
manganese was originally present for the reason specified
on p. 320. The object of carrying out the fusion in an
atmosphere of CO_2 is of course to reduce the atmospheric
oxidation to a minimum.

dard bichromate solution to oxidize the excess of ferrous iron; then $100 - 89 = 11$, and $11 \times \cdot02 = 0\cdot22$ Mn, and $0\cdot22 \times 1\cdot582 = 0\cdot35\%$ MnO_2^1.

Gravimetric Method.

(Time occupied, about $\frac{3}{4}$ day.)

Weight taken.—Weigh out $2\cdot88$ grammes of the ore into a 20-oz. covered beaker.

Dissolving.—Digest with 50 cc. strong HCl till the residue is nearly white; then oxidize any ferrous iron by boiling for a minute or two with 2 cc. strong nitric acid.

Remaining operations.—Make up when cold to from 60 to 60·5 cc., according to the amount of silicic residue present. Filter off 50 cc., and treat the solution thus obtained containing $2\cdot4$ grammes of ore exactly according to the process described for the gravimetric estimation of manganese in steel. The result may be a little high, owing to the final residue of Mn_3O_4 containing traces of Al_2O_3, ZnO, and $BaSO_4$.

The Bismuthate Method.

$1\cdot32$ grammes are treated as above to eliminate SiO_2, etc. The fractionated solution, representing $1\cdot1$ gramme of ore, is then evaporated with a few cc. of strong H_2SO_4 until it fumes copiously. The liquid is then diluted with 30 cc. $1\cdot20$ nitric acid and treated as for steels.

Determination of Manganese in Organic Ores.

In black-band ores 2·88 grammes of the ore are dissolved in *HCl* after a previous calcination as described on p. 323. The remaining operations are identical with those just described.

Determination of Manganese in Insoluble Ores.

The manganese in iron ores insoluble in *HCl* is estimated by fusing 2·88 grammes with acid potassium sulphate. The mass is extracted in dilute *HCl*; when cold, the solution is made up to known bulk, five-sixths are filtered off, and the estimation is proceeded with by the acetate process as usual, the result being calculated on 2 grammes. The fused mass may also be extracted with dilute nitric acid, and after fractionating, the manganese determined by the bismuthate process.

Determination of Crude Silica.

(Time occupied, about 3 hours.)

Weight taken.—Weigh out 2 grammes of the finely-divided ore into a 20-oz. covered beaker.

Dissolving.—Add 40 cc. strong *HCl*, boil cautiously, and eventually quietly evaporate to complete dryness with the cover off.

Remaining operations.—The dry mass is re-dissolved in *HCl*, and the insoluble residue is estimated exactly in the manner described for the determination of silicon in steel on p. 65.[1]

Example.—Analysis of Rubio brown hematite. Weight taken, 2 grammes of ore dried at 100° C.

Weight of crucible + residue = 27·9338
Weight of crucible = 27·6309
——————
·3029 gramme SiO_2.
——————

$$\frac{·3029 \times 100}{2} = 15·14\%$$

DETERMINATION OF P_2O_5 IN NON-ARSENICAL ORES.

Weight taken.—The amount of ore weighed out and the process to be used must be decided after reading the remarks and inspecting the table on p. 258.

Dissolving.—The ore is dissolved by boiling with strong HCl. The solution is evaporated to complete dryness, the mass is taken up in strong HCl, made up when cold to 60 cc., and ⅝ths of the solution is filtered off.[2]

Remaining operations.—The liquid obtained as above is then—

(a) Diluted, reduced, and the phosphoric acid precipitated as $FePO_4$. The precipitate is then dissolved in accordance with the method to be employed; or

[1] When it is necessary to obtain the silica quite free from impurities, it must be fused and obtained pure by the process given for ganister on p. 366.

[2] In the case of ores containing titanic acid, it is essential to examine the washed insoluble residues for phosphoric acid, which, if present, is estimated by the method given for titanic pig-irons on p. 262.

(*b*) It is evaporated to low bulk, and estimated by the rapid process described for steel on p. 126.

The pyrophosphate contains 63·79, the yellow precipitate 3·75% of P_2O_5, and $PbMoO_4 \times 0·0161 = P_2O_5$.

Examples.

Analysis of Dannemora magnetite.

Weight of dry ore taken 12 grammes.

Weight of dish + yellow ppt. = 33·6295
Weight of dish = 33·6122

$$\overline{·0173}$$

$$\frac{·0173 \times 3·7}{10} = 0·006\% \ P_2O_5.$$

Analysis of Northampton brown hematite.

Weight of raw dry ore taken 1·2 grammes.

Weight of crucible + $Mg_2P_2O_7$ = 27·9324
Weight of crucible = 27·9006

$$\overline{·0318} \text{ gramme } Mg_2P_2O_7$$

Correction for solubility + ·0010

$$\overline{·0328}$$

$$\frac{·0328 \times 63·79}{1} = 2·09\% \ P_2O_5.$$

DETERMINATION OF ARSENIC AND P_2O_5.

Weigh out 6 grammes of the finely divided ore into a 20-oz. covered beaker, add 10 cc. strong nitric acid, and to avoid bumping, heat on a pipe-stem triangle. When the evolution of any CO_2 has ceased the cover is removed, and the contents of the beaker are quietly evaporated to complete dryness, the mass being heated in the centre of the hot plate till any nitrates formed are decomposed. The soluble portion of the dry mass is then dissolved at the lowest possible temperature in 40 cc. of HCl; 50 cc. of the clear solution, corresponding to 5 grammes of ore, are separated in the usual manner by fraction filtration. The liquid is then diluted, neutralized, reduced with H_2SO_3, the excess of SO_2 boiled off, the solution cooled rapidly, and the arsenic precipitated as sulphide by adding about 0·5 gramme of pure precipitated zinc sulphide with 5 to 10 cc. of hydrochloric acid. The liberated H_2S is retained under slight pressure by closing the flask. The precipitate is then dealt with in accordance with the instructions given for the determination of arsenic in steel.

Determination of Sulphur.

Sulphur is estimated by the *aqua regia* method described for steel on p. 108.

Examination of the insoluble residue.—When absolute accuracy is required the washed insoluble residue is fused with 6 grammes of the fusion mixture specified on p. 166. The fusion is extracted with hot water, made up when cold to as small a definite volume as possible, five-sixths of the clear liquid is filtered off, acidified with HCl, and evaporated to dryness; the dry mass is taken up in HCl and water, the SiO_2 is filtered off, washed, and the SO_3 is precipitated by boiling the filtrate after evaporating to 100 cc. by addition of $BaCl_2$. The resulting $BaSO_4$ is estimated as usual, and the percentage of sulphur contained therein is added to the main quantity. This examination of the insoluble residue is more particularly necessary in the case of ores containing barium, because in such the residue is very liable to contain $BaSO_4$, which the fusion coverts into insoluble BaO and Na_2SO_4 soluble in water. In the foregoing process a blank estimation of the sulphur in the fusion mixture is of course made, and the $BaSO_4$ obtained deducted.

DETERMINATION OF ALUMINA.

(Time occupied, about 1 day.)

Weight taken.—Weigh out 1·44 grammes of ore into a 20-oz. covered beaker.

Dissolving and separating the SiO_2. Dissolve in 30 cc. of strong HCl, evaporate to dryness, take up in 20 cc. of HCl, and obtain 50 cc. of clear solution containing 1·2 grammes of ore by fractional filtration.

Remaining operations.—The yellow liquid is transferred without loss to a 30-oz. registered flask, 3 cc. of a saturated solution of sodium phosphate are added, the solution is diluted to 200 cc., neutralized with dilute ammonia, reduced with H_2SO_3, precipitated with ammonium acetate, and the alumina is determined in exact accordance with the instructions given on p. 200 *et seq.*[1] for the estimation of aluminium in steel. The ignited precipitate contains 41·85% of Al_2O_3. The foregoing process gives only the soluble alumina present in the ore: when great accuracy is required the insoluble residue must be analyzed by the process described on p. 347, and any alumina contained therein be added to the main quantity. In ores containing soluble titanic acid or

[1] It is also advisable to re---- ---- he phosphate before weighing the ---- ---- described ---- nium on p. 287.

chromic oxide, the aluminium phosphate will be more or less contaminated with these substances.

Example.

A sample of Yorkshire clay ironstone gave on analysis the following result:

Weight taken 1·44 grammes.
Weight of crucible + $AlPO_4$ = 32·3962
Weight of crucible = 32·2816

·1146 gramme $AlPO_4$.

$$\frac{\cdot 1146 \times 41 \cdot 85}{1} = 4 \cdot 8\% \ Al_2O_3.$$

DETERMINATION OF LIME AND MAGNESIA.

(Time occupied, about 1½ days.)

Weight taken.—Weigh out into a 20-oz. beaker 1·2 grammes of the finely-divided ore, or in the case of a carbonate 2·4 grammes should be employed.

Dissolving.—Add 40 cc. strong HCl, boil down on the hot plate, add 2 cc. strong nitric acid, and then evaporate the contents of the beaker to complete dryness with the cover off. When cool, the mass is re-dissolved in about 30 cc. strong HCl, and the solution is quietly evaporated down to about 10 cc.

Fractional filtration.—The solution and residue are transferred without loss to a 60 cc. graduated flask, and the liquid when cold is made up to the mark, well mixed, and 50 cc., corresponding to 1 gramme of ore, are filtered off through a dry paper into a graduated flask.[1]

[1] The insoluble residue may be fused and tested for lime and magnesia, but as a rule it will be found to be practically free from these oxides.

z

First precipitation of Fe_2O_3 and Al_2O_3.—The 50 cc. of solution are transferred to a 20-oz. beaker, and diluted with warm water to about 200 cc. Next add, little by little, with constant stirring, dilute ammonia, till the liquid is faintly alkaline. The solution is then boiled, and is finally digested for a few minutes on the corner of the plate.

First filtration.—The precipitate is collected on a well-fitting, thick German filter-paper, contained in a 3-in. funnel, the paper having been previously well washed with hot HCl and water. The filtrate is collected in a clean 20-oz. beaker. The precipitation beaker is well rinsed out, and the precipitate is slightly washed with hot water, and allowed to drain well; the clear filtrate is then put on a hot plate to concentrate by evaporation.

Re-dissolving.—The funnel is supported on a hanger inside the beaker in which the precipitation took place, and the hydrates (and phosphates) of iron and aluminium are re-dissolved in moderately strong hot HCl. The paper having been washed free from iron alternately with hot acid and cold water, is put aside under cover till required for the second filtration.

Second precipitation and filtration.—The yellow solution is boiled down in the covered beaker to 5 cc. It is then diluted and precipitated with dilute ammonia exactly as before. The precipitate is collected on the previously used paper, and washed with hot water, the filtrate being received in a beaker containing the concentrated first filtrate. The double filtrate is then boiled down in a covered beaker to about 150 cc.

Separating the manganese and nickel.—Add to the liquid 10 cc. of dilute ammonia, and pass a current of washed H_2S through the boiling liquid for some minutes, to precipitate as sulphide any manganese and nickel not carried down with the iron and aluminium. The sulphides are allowed to settle, are filtered off, and washed with water containing a little ammonia and H_2S solution, the filtrate and washings being collected in a clean 20-oz. beaker. The latter is then covered, and its contents are brought to boiling. (In ores containing only small percentages of manganese the foregoing precipitation may be omitted, because when only a few tenths per cent. are present the manganese is all carried down as hydrate with the iron and alumina.)

Precipitating the CaO.—Next add to the boiling fluid down the lip of the beaker 10 cc. of a saturated solution of ammonium oxalate, and sufficient dilute ammonia to make the liquid distinctly alkaline. Boil for fifteen minutes, digest for at least an hour, remove the beaker from the plate, and allow the precipitated oxalate of calcium to settle thoroughly.

Filtering off and weighing the CaO.—The precipitate is collected on a 110 mm. paper contained in a 2½-in. plain funnel, the filtrate containing the magnesia being received into a clean 20-oz. beaker. The precipitate and paper must be thoroughly washed with hot water; they are then dried, strongly ignited in a tared platinum crucible, which when cold is quickly re-weighed, the residue of *CaO* being very hygroscopic.[1]

Estimating the magnesia.—To the filtrate and washings from the lime add 50 cc. strong nitric acid, and gently boil and evaporate the contents of the covered beaker

[1] As a check the *CaO* may be converted into *CaSO₄* by adding to the crucible 1 cc. of dilute sulphuric acid, evaporating to dryness, gently igniting, and when cold re-weighing. The precipitate contains 41·2% *CaO*.

down to low bulk, say 5 cc. Next add 5 cc. of a 10% solution of ammonium or ordinary sodium phosphate and 2 cc. of HCl, and then cautiously dilute ammonia in slight excess. The volume of the liquid is then made up to 50 cc. with strong ammonia solution; the liquid is allowed to stand for some hours, being occasionally briskly shaken round. The precipitate is collected on a 90 mm. pure paper, and is washed, dried, ignited, and weighed as $Mg_2P_2O_7$ in exact accordance with the instructions given on p. 138. The residue contains 36·2% MgO.

Example.

Sample of Ulverston red hematite.

Weight taken 1·2 grammes.

Lime.   Weight of crucible + CaO = 27·3962
Weight of crucible = 27·3846

·0116 gramme CaO.

$$\frac{·0116 \times 100}{1} = 1·16\% \ CaO.$$

Magnesia.   Practically absent = Trace MgO.

Theoretical Considerations.

The filtrate from the insoluble residue contains ferric, alumunic, calcic, magnesic, and manganous chlorides, and if present, cupric and nickelous chlorides; the whole of the phosphoric acid is also in solution. If present, there will likewise be dissolved in the liquid a portion of the titanic acid, and possibly chromic chloride, but only traces of arsenic acid, most of the latter having been volatilized as chloride. The solution is eva'   low bulk

avoid the presence in the filtrate of an unwieldy excess of $AmCl$ in the final evaporation to low bulk to determine the magnesia. On precipitation with ammonia the hydrates of ferric iron and aluminium carry down with them the whole of the P_2O_5, TiO_2, and Cr_2O_3 which may happen to be in solution. Also, the hydrates of nickel, manganese, and copper may be wholly or partially carried down. Unfortunately small portions of the lime and magnesia are also precipitated, hence the necessity for a second separation. The $AmCl$ in the filtrate containing the lime and magnesia retains the latter in solution as a soluble double chloride $AmMgCl_2$, whilst on the addition of ammonium oxalate the calcium is precipitated thus—$Am_2C_2O_4 + CaCl_2 = CaC_2O_4 + 2\ AmCl$. Ammonium oxalate and calcic chloride yield white insoluble calcium oxalate and ammonium chloride. On strongly igniting the oxalate of lime decomposes thus—$CaC_2O_4 = CaO + CO_2 + CO$. Calcium oxalate yields caustic lime, carbonic oxide, and carbonic acid gases. The lime readily absorbs moisture to form a hydrate, thus—$CaO + H_2O = Ca(HO)_2$. On evaporating the filtrate from the lime with strong nitric acid, the somewhat large amount of $AmCl$ necessarily present for ensuring the separation of the lime and magnesia is decomposed into ammonium nitrate, and the latter as the evaporation proceeds is volatilized as water and laughing gas N_2O. The operation of precipitating the magnesia with phosphoric acid is the converse of that theoretically considered on p. 139. It is necessary to separate manganese and nickel, otherwise both the lime and magnesia precipitated are respectively liable to be contaminated with the oxides or phosphates of these metals. The introduction of bromine into the foregoing analysis is dangerous, because on evaporating down the filtrate from the lime with nitric acid the ammonium bromide is decomposed into a mixture of bromine and hydrobromic acid, which attacks the glass of the beaker, throwing silica and the bases in the glass into solution, and consequently making the result of the MgO estimation seriously high.

If bromine could be safely employed the precipitation of the whole of the manganese with the iron could be readily ensured, rendering the sulphide precipitation unnecessary.

DETERMINATION OF CO_2.

(Time occupied, about 2 hours.)

Weight taken.—In the case of oxides, 5 grammes should be employed for the estimation. When a raw carbonate is under examination 0·5 gramme of the finely-divided ore is weighed out into a dry 8-oz. wide-mouthed flask.

Remaining operations.—The flask is attached to the apparatus sketched in Fig. 7, in the manner described in the process for the estimation of carbon in steel by moist combustion. A current of air having been aspirated through the apparatus, the weighed absorption tubes are attached, and, whilst continuously maintaining a gentle flow of air, 50 cc. of dilute sulphuric acid, 1 in 3, are gradually admitted from the stoppered funnel. For a few minutes the action should be continued in the cold, but afterwards a gentle heat is applied to the sand-bath till no further evolution of CO_2 takes place. Every trace of CO_2 is then swept forward to the absorption tubes by the aspiration of at least a litre of air.

weight in the potash bulbs and chloride of calcium tube is then determined in the manner described for the estimation of carbon in steel by combustion, described on p. 37.

Precaution.—It is absolutely essential to avoid any back pressure from the flask into the purifying tube containing the potash pumice.

Example.

Analysis of uncalcined Derby ore (Staveley).

Weight taken 0·5 gramme.

Weight of absorption tubes before evolution.

$$KHO = 32\cdot6934$$
$$CaCl_2 = 58\cdot1754$$

$$\overline{90\cdot8688}$$

Weight of absorption tubes after evolution.

$$KHO = 32\cdot8202$$
$$CaCl_2 = 58\cdot2002$$

$$\overline{91\cdot0204}$$
$$90\cdot8688$$

$$\overline{\cdot1516 \text{ gramme } CO_2}$$

$$\frac{\cdot1516 \times 100}{0\cdot5} = 30\cdot32\%\ CO_2$$

or briefly, $15\cdot16 \times 2 = 30\cdot32\%\ CO_2$ as before.

DETERMINATION OF COMBINED WATER AND ORGANIC CARBON.

These are determined by strongly combusting in oxygen 1 gramme of the very finely-divided ore contained in a porcelain boat, placed in a combustion tube contain-

ing the usual column of recently-ignited CuO scales in
the apparatus sketched in Fig. 7. The potash pumice
tube is, however, replaced by a bulb containing strong
sulphuric acid, and between the combustion tube and the
chromic acid bulb is also placed a weighed bulb containing strong H_2SO_4.[1] The first-named bulb serves to dry
the oxygen; the second, to absorb the water formed.
The apparatus having been connected up, a current of
air is aspirated through to remove any condensed moisture in the tube. The three absorption tubes are then
carefully weighed with the usual precautions, replaced,
and the combustion is made exactly as described on p.
29 et seq., for the estimation of carbon in steel. The
final aspiration must, however, be continued until every
trace of moisture has been carried forward into the
H_2SO_4 bulb. The increase in the sulphuric acid bulb represents the total combined water, which is due not only
to inorganic hydrate, but also to that existing in any
organic matter present in the ore.[2] The organic water in
pure hematites and magnetites is very small. In black-
band ores the water obtained will be largely of organic
origin. The increase in the potash and chloride of calcium
tubes represents the inorganic CO_2 (driven off by heat
from its combination with the oxides in the ore), augmented by the carbon of the organic matter (burnt by
the oxygen). The weight of CO_2 obtained by evolution
in the manner described in the last article is deducted
from the total weight, and the remainder multiplied by
27·27 gives the weight of organic carbon.

[1] The limb of this bulb must be inserted direct into the india-
rubber bung of the combustion tube.
[2] See footnote to "organic carbon."

Example.

Analysis of a sample of Northamptonshire brown hematite.
Weight taken 1 gramme.
Increase in H_2SO_4 bulb $0.1167 = 11.67°/_o$ of total combined H_2O.
Increase in KHO and $CaCl_2$ bulbs $= 0.6264$ ⎫
Less weight of CO_2 obtained by evolution $= 0.5956$ ⎬ gramme.

$\overline{.0308}$ organic CO_2.

$.0308 \times 27.27 = 0.84°/_o$ organic carbon.[1]

DETERMINATION OF COPPER.

Dissolve 12 grammes of the ore in a mixture of 30 cc. of aqua regia and 30 cc. strong HCl, evaporate to dryness, take up in about 50 cc. of HCl, evaporate to 10 cc. and obtain 100 cc. of clear solution, corresponding to 10 grammes of ore, by fractional filtration. The liquid is transferred to a 30-oz. registered flask, neutralized with ammonia, reduced with sulphurous acid, and the copper is precipitated in a volume of 300 cc. by means of sodium thiosulphate. The precipitate is filtered off, and the copper determined exactly in the manner described on p. 213 *et seq.*

DETERMINATION OF NICKEL.

Obtain 10 grammes of the ore in 100 cc. clear HCl solution in the manner just described for copper. The

---

[1] The percentage of organic carbon multiplied by 60 and divided by 40 gives the approximate percentage of organic matter, the difference between the "carbon" and "matter" being organic water, which may be deducted from the total water to obtain the water of hydration in the ore.

liquid is transferred to a 30-oz. registered flask, and the nickel separated from the iron by the method described under steel, the nickel being determined cyanometrically.

DETERMINATION OF Cr_2O_3.

Some ores of iron, such as those from the Tasmanian mines, contain about 3% of Cr_2O_3. The latter may be estimated as phosphate by the process described for steels containing aluminium on p. 178. The precipitate contains 60·95% of Cr_2O_3.

DETERMINATION OF TITANIC ACID.

Six grammes of the ore are dissolved in a 20-oz. beaker in about 60 cc. HCl, 10 cc. of a 10% solution of ammonium phosphate are added, the liquid is evaporated to complete dryness, and strongly heated in the centre of the plate. The dry mass is taken up in HCl, the insoluble residue filtered off, washed, dried and ignited. The residue is fused with 10 times its weight of sodium carbonate, and the mass thoroughly disintegrated by boiling out with water. Before filtering evaporate to a small bulk. Collect the sodium titanate on a small pulp filter and ignite, after washing, at a low red heat. Dissolve in the least possible quantity of hydrochloric acid, dilute slightly, add dilute ammonia until nearly neutral, then 6 grammes of sodium thiosulphate and lastly 20 cc. of acetic acid. Boil for 20 minutes, filter, wash, ignite strongly and weigh as TiO_2 containing 60% of titanium.

DETERMINATION OF THE ALKALIES.

Potash, K_2O, and soda, Na_2O, when present in ores of iron, seem to be almost entirely found in the residue insoluble in HCl, probably in the form of the insoluble silicates orthoclase $(K_2Al_2Si_6O_{16})$ and albite $(Na_2Al_2 Si_6O_{16})$. The residue is therefore examined for alkalies by the method described for their estimation in fire-clay (p. 374).

ANALYSIS OF THE INSOLUBLE RESIDUE.

One gramme of the ignited residue is thoroughly fused with 10 grammes of a mixture of K_2CO_3 and Na_2CO_3; the fusion is extracted, and the SiO_2, Al_2O_3, CaO, MgO, and FeO present are estimated as described for fire-clay on pp. 371-4. The last-named oxide when present, as is usual, in minute quantity, is estimated colorimetrically.

ANALYSIS OF MANGANESE ORES.

Determination of CaO and MgO.—As a rule, the methods given for the estimation of the various constituents of iron ores are also available for manganese ores. In determining lime and magnesia, however, it is advisable to originally weigh out 1·44 grammes, and after precipitating the MnS in the manner described on p. 338, to make up the solution and precipitate to 301 cc., filter off 250 cc. of clear liquid, corresponding to 1 gramme of ore, and so avoid the troublesome washing of the some-

what bulky precipitate. The lime and magnesia are then
determined in the fractional filtrate by the processes
given for iron ores.

DETERMINATION OF TOTAL MANGANESE.

Gravimetric method.—The manganese may be estimated by the gravimetric acetate process, but the results
are liable to be high, owing to the final precipitate of
Mn_3O_4 containing oxide of zinc or sulphate of barium,
which are not infrequent constituents of manganiferous
ores.

Volumetric Process.

(Time occupied, about 2 hours.)

Weight taken.—Weight out into a 20-oz. covered
beaker from ·25 to 0·5 gramme of the finely-pulverized
ore, dried at 100° C. In the case of rich ores, in which
the weight first named is employed, 0·5 gramme of
Swedish bar-iron is also weighed out.

Remaining operations.—These are carried out respectively by the processes described for the assay of ferro-
manganese on p. 269 and spiegel on p. 267 by Pattinson's
method. The bismuthate process can be applied after
evaporating with strong sulphuric acid to remove the
hydrochloric, and then diluting freely with nitric acid
1·20.

DETERMINATION OF MnO_2 (BUNSEN) (AND MnO BY DIFFERENCE).

(Time occupied, about 1 hour.)

Re-agents required.

Standard solution of sodium thiosulphate.—Prepared by dissolving 27·091 grammes of hypo in a litre of water in the manner described on p. 211.

10% solution of KI.—Dissolving 10 grammes of pure potassic iodide crystals in 100 cc. of water.

The Process.

Weight taken.—Weigh out into a clean, dry 6-oz. flask exactly 0·25 gramme of the finely-pulverized dry ore.

Apparatus required.—The flask is then fitted with an india-rubber stopper[1] carrying a stopper funnel and exit bend, and is attached to the absorption cylinder sketched in Fig. 12.[2] The cylinder is charged with 70 cc. of the 10% solution of pure potassic iodide in distilled water, and is attached to an aspirator.

Dissolving.—Add from the stoppered funnel 20 cc. of strong HCl (proved to be devoid of free chlorine). Place the flask on the edge of the hot plate, and gently heat till

---

[1] This must be freed from surface by well boiling with dilute sodic hydrate solution, and afterwards in several changes of water.

[2] The exit tube from the flask should touch the inlet tube to the cylinder, the two being joined with a short piece of sound india-rubber tubing so as to avoid any absorption of Cl by the material last named.

Theoretical Considerations.[1]

The manganese dioxide in the ore evolves free chlorine from the *HCl*, thus—

$$MnO_2 + 4\ HCl = 2\ Cl + MnCl_2 + 2\ H_2O$$

Seventy-one parts by weight of chlorine correspond to 55 parts of metallic manganese existing as peroxide. The evolved chlorine liberates iodine from the solution of potassic iodide (the iodine remaining dissolved in the excess of the latter present), thus—

$$2\ KI + 2\ Cl = 2\ KCl + 2\ I$$

Therefore, 254 parts by weight of iodine are equivalent to 55 parts of manganese existing as dioxide.[1] The results obtained are liable to be low in the presence of organic matter and of ferrous oxide (see p. 319), owing to the conversion of some of the liberated chlorine into *HCl* by the action of such readily oxidized substances.

DETERMINATION OF MnO_2, BY PATTINSON'S METHOD.

(Time occupied, about 1 hour.)

Cut off by means of a small, sharp saw-file a half-inch test tube 1 in. from the bottom, and carefully fuse the cut edge in the blow-pipe flame.

Weight taken.—Weigh out into the short test tube 0·25 gramme of the dry ore previously reduced to an impalpable flour in the agate mortar; also weigh out

[1] See theoretical notes on p. 219.

consists essentially of a mixture of Cr_2O_3, MgO,
$._2O_3$, FeO,[1] together with smaller percentages of CaO
ad SiO_2.

Determination of Cr_2O_3.

Chromic oxide is easily determined by fusing 1
gramme of the ore with 6 grammes of sodium peroxide.
The subsequent treatment is exactly that described
under the determination of chromium in ferro-chrome.
The bichromate used in the latter case is too strong,
however, and a decinormal solution is much more suitable. This is prepared by dissolving 4·905 grammes of
the crystals in water, and making up to 1000 cc., when
exactly 50 cc. should be required to titrate 0·2806
grammes of Swedish bar iron dissolved in dilute sulphuric acid.

1 cc. decinormal bichromate represents 0·00254
gramme Cr_2O_3.

Determination of SiO_2.

Fuse 1 gramme of the ore with sodium peroxide as
above, and extract the cooled melt with water. Remove
the nickel crucible, and transfer the liquid from the
beaker to a large porcelain dish. Acidify with sufficient
hydrochloric acid to effect complete solution, and evaporate to complete dryness, baking only slightly. Re-
dissolve in acid, dilute and filter off the silica. After
ignition the residue may be purified, as already described,

[1] In reporting the analysis the iron is usually calculated to FeO,
but occasionally notable quantities of the iron present may exist in
the form of Fe_2O_3.

A A

by fusion with acid potassium sulphate, or the amount of pure silica determined by treatment with hydrofluoric acid.

Determination of MgO, Al_2O_3, and FeO.

Fuse 1 gramme of the ore with sodium peroxide, and extract with water as before. Boil well and allow to settle. Decant the yellow supernatant liquid through an asbestos filter and wash the insoluble oxides repeatedly with water by decantation, passing the washings through the same filter.

The residue.—This contains all the iron, and practically all the magnesia, along with oxide of nickel from the crucible. Boil the asbestos filter with hydrochloric acid, and pour the acid liquid through a small pulp filter, so as to remove the asbestos fibres, the filtrate being caught in the beaker containing the main residue. More acid is added, if necessary, to effect complete solution, and the iron is separated from the magn ... (lime and nickel) by two precipitations with am ... ferric oxide is re-dissolved, the solution r ... ... educed, and the iron determined by ... ... sium bichromate. The lime and ... in the customary manner in the ... the nickel. If the ignited ... ny trace of this element, ... and re-precipitated.

... ellow filtrate containing the ... ... silica, and perhaps also a trace of sively ... ... eated to boiling, and a current of carbon open-hearth ... sed through the hot solution for an hour.

The precipitated basic carbonate of aluminium is filtered off, washed well, re-dissolved in hydrochloric acid, and the aluminium determined as phosphate.

$$\text{Weight of } AlPO_4 \times 0\cdot418 = Al_2O_3.$$

ANALYSIS OF WOLFRAM.

This mineral consists essentially of ferrous tungstate, containing an appreciable percentage of MnO, and in smaller quantities, silica; occasionally about 1% of lime is also present. It is seldom necessary to do more than estimate the WO_3, as the percentage of this constituent determines the value of the mineral for the production of ferro-tungsten and tungsten metal.

Assay for WO_3.

(Time occupied, about $\frac{3}{4}$ day.)

Weight taken, and fusion.—Weigh out into a covered 3-in. platinum dish $0\cdot6$ gramme of the floured mineral, and fuse it over the gas blow-pipe for five minutes with a mixture of 3 grammes each of pure anhydrous sodic and potassic carbonates. *Potassic nitrate must not be employed.*

Extracting the fusion.—Place the dish and cover when cool in a 20-oz. beaker containing 200 cc. of nearly boiling water. When all soluble matter has been taken up the cover and dish are washed and removed.

Fractional filtration.—Transfer the liquid and residue without loss to a 300 cc. flask, make up to the mark, mix well, note the temperature, and filter off through a dry double paper 250 cc. corresponding to 0·5 gramme of ore.[1]

Precipitating the WO_3.—Transfer the solution without loss to a 20-oz. beaker, and neutralize the liquid with dilute nitric acid, free from nitrous acid. The acid is added little by little down the lip of the beaker till the last addition produces no further evolution of CO_2, showing the excess of alkaline carbonates to be completely decomposed and the nitric acid slightly in excess. The liquid must next be made neutral or *faintly* alkaline by the very cautious addition of a moderately strong solution of sodic carbonate. The exact point is carefully determined[2] by placing on a white tile some small drops of a fairly strong aqueous solution of methyl orange indicator. As long as the liquid is acid the orange tint of the indicator is changed to a much richer, almost purple colour, when a small drop of the solution from the beaker is mixed with it, but the reaction is not affected by carbonic acid, so that when the free nitric acid has all been neutralized by the sodium carbonate, a drop of the liquid no longer changes the colour of the orange spots. The tungstic acid is next precipitated by bringing the solution almost to boiling, and adding, drop by drop, with constant and vigorous stirring with the glass rod, 3 cc. of a saturated solution of mercurous nitrate crystals in hot water. The tungsten is totally precipitated as mercurous tungstate Hg_2WO_4 mixed with basic mercurous nitrate: the rod is well washed, and the contents of the covered beaker are boiled for a few minutes, and are

---

[1] At this stage alumina, if present, may be separated by the process described on p. 178.

[2] See note after *Theoretical Considerations*, p. 358.

then allowed to digest on the corner of the plate till the precipitate has flocked out and the liquid is clear.

Filtering.—The somewhat bulky precipitate is collected on a 125 mm. pure paper contained in a 3-in funnel. The precipitate is very thoroughly washed with nearly boiling water, but it must not be too vigorously disturbed, or some may pass through into the filtrate.

First ignition.—The precipitate is dried, ignited, and weighed when cold in a tared platinum dish. The ignition should at first be gentle, so as not to volatilize the mercury salts too violently, and so cause a mechanical loss of WO_3. The residue obtained is $(x \, WO_3 + y \, SiO_2)$.

Removal of SiO_2 with HF and final ignition.—The residue is treated with about 2 cc. of pure aqueous hydrofluoric acid, and the latter is evaporated off in the draught cupboard. When the mass is dry the dish is again ignited, cooled and weighed; the increase over the original weight of the dish is WO_3, containing $79\cdot3\%$ of tungsten metal.

Example.

Weight of wolfram taken, 0·6 gramme.
Weight of dish + WO_3 = 43·6920
Weight of dish = 43·3116

·3804 gramme WO_3.

$$\frac{\cdot3804 \times 100}{0\cdot5} = 76\cdot08\% \; WO_3, \text{ or}$$

$$\frac{76\cdot08 \times 79\cdot3}{100} = 60\cdot33\% \; \text{Tungsten.}$$

Theoretical Considerations.

The fusion with alkaline carbonates converts the tungstic and silicic acids into soluble alkaline tungstates

Analysis of Scheelite.

Scheelite is essentially a tungstate of calcium with impurities in the form of silica (variable) and small quantities of iron and molybdenum. The steel chemist is occasionally called upon to make a determination of the tungsten in the mineral.

This can be done by opening out with the mixed carbonates of sodium and potassium, or with sodium carbonate containing a small quantity of peroxide. The subsequent treatment does not differ from the method described under the analysis of wolfram.

Scheelite can also be opened out easily by prolonged digestion with a large excess of strong hydrochloric acid. The finely ground ore is mixed with 80 cc. of strong hydrochloric acid for each gramme taken, and the mixture warmed but not boiled. By shaking or stirring at frequent intervals the mineral is decomposed, leaving only a siliceous residue. The liquid is then evaporated to a paste, and the latter treated with a mixture of one part of strong hydrochloric acid with four parts of water. The tungstic oxide and silica are filtered off, and the filtrate assayed for iron and calcium by the customary methods.

The Analysis of Tantalite.

Tantalite is essentially a tantalate of iron (ferrous), but it almost invariably contains more or less niobate of the same base, together with oxides of manganese, tin, and tungsten. The mineral is with difficulty opened out, all the ordinary acids and mixtures of them being without appreciable effect. Sodium peroxide decomposes it at a red heat, but in so doing does not provide a melt suitable to the application of the somewhat tedious method usually adopted for the determination of the most important constituent. Acid potassium sulphate is the reagent generally used for opening out tantalite, columbite, fergusonite, etc., but the authors have found it practically impossible to effect complete decomposition by the use of three times the weight of ore taken, the amount usually specified.

Opening out the mineral.—One gramme of tantalite, reduced by assiduous grinding in the agate mortar to an impalpable powder, is mixed in a capacious platinum crucible provided with a lid with from eight to ten times its weight of pure finely powdered acid potassium sulphate, by means of a glass rod. After brushing adhering particles of the mixture from the end of the rod into the crucible, the latter is heated over the bunsen flame. The temperature is cautiously raised until there is no longer any vigorous frothing, and then the crucible is placed over the blow-pipe flame, and the highest possible temperature maintained for about twenty minutes, until, on cautiously removing the lid, the red hot molten mass appears to be thoroughly homogeneous, and entirely devoid of tiny dark floating particles of undecomposed material.

Extracting the melt.—After cooling, the crucible and lid are placed in a beaker, and water more than sufficient to cover them is added. The beaker is placed on the hot plate, and the obstinately adhering mass detached from the crucible by frequent application of a glass rod. When this somewhat tedious operation has come to a successful issue, the crucible and lid are carefully lifted out, cleansed by means of the policeman and copious application of wash-water, and the contents of the beaker boiled for a few minutes. The boiling is attended with bumping.

Filtration.—Remove from the plate and allow to settle; hold the beaker well above the head, and inspect carefully the creamy white heavy residue at the bottom. If dark-coloured particles or streaks (unfused tantalite) are discernible, the fusion has not effected complete decomposition, and the assay must be rejected. If all is well, decant the supernatant liquid through a hardened filter paper and wash the residue several times, by decantation, with hot water, pouring the washings through the same paper, but retaining the bulk of the insoluble residue in the beaker.

The filtrate (A), which is set aside, contains most of the iron, manganese, etc., and may be opalescent on account of the presence of small quantities of hydrated Ta_2O_5, which have passed through the pores of the hardened filter paper. The residue contains tantalum (and niobium) as hydrated oxides, with silica, tungstic, and stannic oxides, and small amounts of iron and manganese sulphates not extracted by the water.

The residue.—The filter paper is opened out, and all adhering particles washed into the beaker containing the bulk of the residue by means of a fine stream of water. The paper is then placed in a small beaker with 10 to 15 cc. of yellow ammonium sulphide, and after digestion short of boiling for a few minutes, the ammonium sulphide extract is poured into the beaker containing the main residue, and the filter paper washed. A black stain on the paper indicates the presence of a trace of iron,

now existing as sulphide, and the originally creamy white
residue of tantalic (and niobic) oxides will also be blackened by the formation of the same compound. The digestion with ammonium sulphide is continued for five or ten
minutes in order to dissolve out completely the oxides of
tin and tungsten. The liquid is again filtered, this time
through pulp, the residue washed with water containing
ammonium sulphide, and the filtrate (B) set aside.

The new residue.—The whole filter, with its precipitate, is transferred to a beaker, and heated with 20 cc.
of concentrated hydrochloric acid until the residue is
perfectly white; an equal bulk of water is then added
and the liquid filtered. The filtrate is added to the
original one (A) and the residue, after thorough washing with hot water, dried, strongly ignited along with
the small amount recovered from filtrate (A) *q. v.*, and
weighed. The amount of silica in the ignited residue is
then determined by the usual treatment with hydrofluoric acid, and deducted. The remainder is a mixture
of pure Ta_2O_5 and Nb_2O_5, and is reported as such.

Filtrate (B).—This contains the tin and tungsten,
and may be conveniently dealt with, whilst the now
bulky filtrate (A) is allowed to concentrate on the plate,
as follows. Hydrochloric acid is added to strong acidity,
and the mixture, with its precipitated sulphur, and
SnS_2, boiled down rapidly to about 5 cc., about 20 cc. of
water are added, the mixture boiled and allowed to settle.
The sulphur and tungstic oxide are filtered off, washed
with water slightly acidulated with hydrochloric acid,
dried and ignited thoroughly to burn off the sulphur.
The WO_3 is weighed and reported as such.

The filtrate from the tungsten contains the tin in the
stannic condition; it is heated to boiling point, and a

stream of washed sulphuretted hydrogen gas passed through to saturation. After digestion for a few minutes, the stannic sulphide is filtered off, washed with water containing sulphuretted hydrogen and a small quantity of ammonium nitrate, dried and ignited strongly in the muffle. After ignition the residue is moistened with a few drops of strong nitric acid, the excess of this carefully removed on the plate, and the dry residue again strongly ignited, cooled, weighed, and reported as stannic oxide, SnO_2.

Filtrate (A).—This contains the iron (by this time nearly all converted into the ferric state), manganese, and perhaps traces of calcium and magnesium, together with free hydrochloric and sulphuric acids, the latter resulting from the decomposition of the potassium bisulphate used in opening out the mineral.

The small amount of tantalic oxide which it also contains, and which has now become granular by the prolonged boiling, is filtered off through a small but very compact pulp filter, and the latter well washed and ignited along with the main residue of this constituent. To the filtrate is added the solution obtained by dissolving the minute quantity of iron sulphide remaining as a black stain on the hardened filter paper in a few drops of hot dilute nitric acid, and after adding a few cc. of concentrated nitric acid to ensure the complete oxidation of the iron, an acetate separation of this metal from the manganese is performed exactly as described in the estimation of nickel on p. 190. The precipitated basic ferric acetate is filtered off, thoroughly washed, and either ignited strongly to ferric oxide and weighed, or dissolved from the filter in hot dilute hydrochloric acid, the solution neutralized with dilute ammonia, reduced with SO_2,

the excess of the latter expelled by boiling, and the iron
determined by titration with potassium bichromate in
the manner already fully described. The filtrate from
the iron is cooled, brominized, and the manganese precipitated in the usual manner, and strongly ignited to
Mn_3O_4. The results are calculated to FeO and MnO
respectively.

The filtrate from the manganese is examined for
calcium and magnesium by the usual methods. As a rule,
they are absent entirely, or if present, exist only as
traces.

The tantalic oxide residue.—The determination of
niobic oxide in the mixture of it with tantalic oxide is
unnecessary for the purposes of the steel-works chemist,
and can only be made by a tedious, and, at best, an approximately accurate process. This depends upon the
sparing solubility of the double fluoride of tantalum and
potassium, and the comparatively ready solubility of the
corresponding niobium compound.

The mixture of oxides, before being ignited,[1] is dissolved in fuming hydrofluoric acid, and a boiling solution of hydrogen potassium fluoride added. (Needless to
say, the operation must be conducted in platinum vessels.)
The tantalum gradually precipitates as K_2TaF_7, and is
separated by concentration from the niobium, in fractions,
as well as may be. The tantalum compound is soluble in
about 200 parts of water, and the niobium analogue in 12.

The double fluorides, after separation, are decomposed
with sulphuric acid, the solutions evaporated to very low
bulk, and after dissolving out the K_2SO_4 with water, the
residues are strongly ignited to oxides again, with the
addition of ammonium carbonate to facilitate the change.

[1] Ignited Ta_2O_5 and Nb_2O_5 are insoluble in HF.

SECTION III. REFRACTORY MATERIALS.

ANALYSIS OF GANISTER, SILICA BRICKS AND SANDS.

The above materials consist almost entirely of silica, but contain in addition small percentages of alumina, ferric oxide, and lime. These impurities when present in small quantities, so far from being injurious, are valuable, from the fact that their presence causes the materials when used for furnace purposes to bind well without splintering or crumbling whilst being raised to the intense heat they are required to withstand. Of course, an excessive quantity of bases is fatal, causing the lining to fuse at steel-melting heat. Chemical analysis, however, does not completely decide the quality of ganister either in the raw state or in its manufactured form of silica bricks, inasmuch as materials practically identical in chemical composition may possess distinctly different physical properties.

Determination of Water and Organic Matter.

Weigh out about 2 grammes of the finely-divided material (previously passed through a sieve 20 meshes to the inch) into a tared platinum crucible, the cover of which is also weighed and left in the balance-case.

material is strongly ignited in the muffle for about twenty minutes. The crucible after becoming quite cold in the desiccator is covered and re-weighed; the loss represents moisture and organic matter; the weight multiplied by 100 and divided by the weight of material taken = percentage.

Example.

Analysis of Deepcar silica brick.

Weight of crucible and cover = 34·4934
Weight of crucible, etc. + material = 36·5067
$$\text{Weight of brick taken} = \overline{2·0133}$$

Weight of crucible, etc., after ignition = 36·5030

36·5067 − 36·5030 = 0·0037 gramme = loss.

$$\frac{·0037 \times 100}{2·0133} = 0·18°/_o \text{ loss on ignition.}$$

Determination of SiO_2, Al_2O_3, Fe_2O_3, and CaO.

(Time occupied, about $1\frac{1}{2}$ days.)

Weight taken.—Weigh out into a deep 3-in. platinum dish 1 gramme of the finely-divided substance.

Fusing.—Intimately mix the material with 5 grammes each of sodic and potassic carbonates and half a gramme of KNO_3, and thoroughly fuse the contents in a covered dish over a gas blow-pipe for at least five minutes.

Extracting.—When cool, the dish and cover are placed in a 6-in. porcelain dish supported over a boiling water bath; the fusion is extracted with the smallest possible quantity of water, and the dish and cover are thoroughly washed and removed.

Double evaporation of HCl.—The porcelain dish is covered, and down the spout are poured 50 cc. of *HCl*, previously heated in two portions in the covered platinum dish in which the fusion took place. When the evolution of CO_2 has ceased, the cover is rinsed and removed, and the contents of the dish are evaporated to complete dryness on the bath. When nearly dry, the mass is broken up with a glass rod, the dry powdery chlorides are then drenched with 25 cc. of *HCl*, are again evaporated to dryness, the dish being finally carefully heated over a Bunsen flame.

Estimating the SiO_2.—When cold, the perfectly dry mass is heated in the covered dish with about 20 cc. of *HCl*, and then with 100 cc. of water, till everything but the insoluble silica has passed into solution. The residue is collected on a 125 mm. pure paper, is washed first with hot dilute *HCl* and cold water alternately, and then very thoroughly with nearly boiling water.

The filtrate and washings are received into a clean 20-oz. beaker, and are preserved for the determination of the bases. The precipitate is dried, ignited, and weighed in a tared, covered crucible in the usual manner, and the weight multiplied by $100 = \% \ SiO_2$.

Separating the oxide of iron and alumina from the lime.—The filtrate from the SiO_2 is brought to boiling, and little by little dilute ammonia is added down the lip of the covered beaker till in faint excess; the liquid is boiled for a few minutes, removed from the plate, and the precipitate after settling somewhat is collected on a 90 mm. pure paper, thoroughly washed with hot water (the filtrate and washings being preserved in a clean 20-oz.

basket), dried, ignited at low redness and weighed as $x Fe_2O_3 + y Al_2O_3$.

Estimating the Fe_2O_3.—The mixed precipitate is transferred without loss to a 30-cc. flask, the crucible being twice rinsed out with 10 cc. of boiling HCl, which is poured into the flask and quietly boiled down to low bulk, till the whole of the Fe_2O_3 and most of the Al_2O_3 have dissolved.[1] The acid liquid is then neutralised with very dilute ammonia, 1 in 10, reduced with 10 cc. of H_2SO_4 solution (be careful to boil off every trace of SO_2), and the iron is titrated in the usual manner[2] with a specially diluted standard solution of $K_2Cr_2O_7$, made by carefully measuring 100 cc. of the solution specified on p. 222 into a half-litre flask, diluting to the mark and well mixing. Each cc. required equals $0 \cdot 1 \%$ Fe. The number of cc. used multiplied by $0 \cdot 14286 = \%$ Fe_2O_3.

Calculating the Al_2O_3.—The percentage of Fe_2O_3 subtracted from the weight of the mixed precipitate multiplied by $100 = \%$ Al_2O_3.

Estimating the lime.—The ammoniacal filtrate from the oxide of iron and the alumina is evaporated down to about 100 cc., made slightly alkaline with ammonia, and the lime is precipitated by boiling the solution after adding 10 cc. of a saturated solution of ammonium oxalate. After digesting for some time the oxalate of calcium is allowed to settle, is collected on a 90 mm. pure paper, and is washed, dried, ignited, weighed, and estimated as oxide or sulphate in exact accordance with the instructions given on p. 339.

[1] If the oxides have been heated too strongly in the muffle, it will be found impossible to dissolve them again.

[2] The addition of a few cc. of dilute H_2SO_4 must not be forgotten.

Examples of results obtained in the foregoing analysis.

Weight of SiO_2 obtained $= 0\cdot9617$ gramme $= 96\cdot17°/_o$ SiO_2.

Weight of $(x\ Fe_2O_3 + y\ Al_2O_3) = 0\cdot0209$ gramme.

Cc. of $K_2Cr_2O_7$ used for iron $= 7\cdot5$, and $7\cdot5 \times \cdot14286 = 1\cdot07°/_o$ Fe_2O_3. $2\cdot09 - 1\cdot07 = 1\cdot02°/_o$ Al_2O_3.

Weight of $CaO = 0\cdot0096$ gramme $= 0\cdot96°/_o$ CaO.

Precaution.

As sodic and potassic carbonates are seldom perfectly pure, it is very advisable to make a blank analysis on the same weight of mixed carbonates and nitre as that used for the fusion, and to estimate the SiO_2 and Al_2O_3 contained therein.   The results are of course deducted from the respective constituents. If this precaution is neglected, the appreciable percentage of these substances sometimes present may cause the apparent percentage obtained to be distinctly high.

Theoretical Considerations.

On fusing, the ganister, etc. is decomposed by the alkaline carbonates into the silicates of soda and potash thus—

$$3\ SiO_2 + 4\ Na_2CO_3 = Na_8Si_3O_{10} + 4\ CO_2$$

Silica and sodium carbonate yield sodium trisilicate and carbon dioxide—

$$SiO_2 + K_2CO_3 = K_2SiO_3 + CO_2$$

Silica and potassium carbonate yield potassium metasilicate and carbon dioxide.

The alumina is converted partly into alkaline aluminate, partly into oxide, the lime and oxide of iron remain

B B

as such. On treating the extraction from the fusion with HCl the alkaline silicates are decomposed, forming chlorides and partially soluble silicic acid, the latter during the double evaporation to dryness is dehydrated and converted into insoluble SiO_2, whilst the lime, oxide of iron, and alumina form soluble chlorides. A single evaporation has not been found to render the whole of the silica soluble, hence the mass is taken to dryness twice, and is finally ignited gently over the Bunsen flame. On taking up with HCl and water, the chlorides of aluminium, iron, calcium, and the alkalies pass into solution as chlorides. The lime is separated from the oxide of iron and alumina by taking advantage of the fact that its hydrate is not precipitated by ammonia. When great accuracy is desired, the oxide of iron and alumina may be precipitated twice, and the filtrate from the lime be examined for magnesia by the processes described for the analysis of iron ores.

Determination of the Alkalies. (*See Fire-clays.*)

ANALYSIS OF FIRE-CLAYS AND BRICKS.

Fire-clays consist essentially of hydrated silicate of alumina containing greater or lesser percentages of the oxides of iron, calcium, magnesium, potassium, and sodium. The bases, particularly the two last named, if present in large quantities, are fatal to the refractory quality of the clay and bricks made therefrom. The steel chemist's horror, titanic acid, may also be present in small amount. The plastic properties of fire-clays depend upon the presence of a considerable percentage of combined water.

Determination of Hygroscopic Water.

The moisture present is estimated by the process given for iron ores on p. 316. The clay thus dried at 100° C. is finely pulverized, passed through a sieve of 90 meshes to the inch, and bottled for the remainder of the analysis, which will of course have reference to the dried material.

Determination of Combined Water and Organic Carbon.

The plastic water and organic carbon are most accurately determined by the method given for iron ores on p. 344. In clays free from FeO, however, their amount may be determined with sufficient exactness for practical purposes by igniting about 2 grammes of the clay. The details of the estimation are identical with those given for ganister on p. 365. When dealing with burnt fire-bricks, it is merely necessary to ignite the material and calculate and report the percentage of loss as total water and organic matter.

Determination of CaO and MgO.

Proceed on 1 gramme of the material as for ganister till the double precipitate of Al_2O_3 and Fe_2O_3 is obtained.

This is collected on a 125 mm. paper, is allowed to drain, re-dissolved in *HCl*, the solution being received into the beaker in which the precipitation took place. The paper is washed and put aside till required for the second filtration. The yellow liquid is evaporated to low bulk, diluted to 200 cc., and re-precipitated with ammonia. The filtrate, which contains a small quantity of lime and magnesia, carried down by the alumina is added to the first filtrate containing the main quantity. The combined filtrates are evaporated to 200 cc., and the two constituents are then determined by the process described for iron ores on p. 339.

Determination of SiO_2 and Fe_2O_3.

SiO_2.—The SiO_2 in fire-clay, etc., is estimated on 1 gramme of the dry material by exactly the same process as that described for ganister: the final residue may contain a little TiO_2.

Fe_2O_3.—The filtrate from the silica is evaporated to low bulk, neutralized, reduced, and the percentage of iron is determined by titration as in the analysis of ganister.

The number of cc. of bichromate required multiplied by $0·14286 = \% \ Fe_2O_3$.

Determination of Al_2O_3.

The alumina is very carefully determined working on $0·25$ gramme of clay or brick (a larger weight gives a very unwieldy precipitate), by the process described for its estimation in ganister, but it should be twice precipi-

tated to free it from lime and magnesia. The weight of
the mixed precipitate multiplied by 400, minus the percentage of oxide of iron (as calculated from the titration
made in the last article), equals % Al_2O_3.

A small percentage of TiO_2 may possibly be present in
the double precipitate, and is registered as alumina, unless separated and determined as described under iron
ores on p. 346.

Determination of FeO.

The iron in fire-clays and bricks is usually reported as
Fe_2O_3: it may, however, exist as FeO, in which form it is
more injurious to the refractory qualities of the material
owing to the comparative fusibility of ferrous silicate.
The proportion of ferrous oxide may be approximately
estimated by the following process, due to Avery, Wil-
bur, and Whittlesey.

The Process.

One gramme of the material is reduced to impalpable
powder in the agate mortar, and very intimately mixed
with 1·5 grammes of finely-divided calcium fluoride
(fluorspar), free from iron. The mixture is placed in a
covered platinum dish, 20 cc. of strong HCl (devoid of
free chlorine) are added. The mass is mixed with a
platinum wire, and the dish is placed on the corner of
the hot plate and digested for about an hour at a temperature slightly under 100° C. in an atmosphere of CO_2,
in the apparatus sketched in Fig. 16, p. 328, for the
determination of FeO in insoluble iron ores. The fire-

clay crucible is merely placed over the dish on the iron plate. The solution is rinsed from the dish into a 20-oz. beaker containing 50 cc. of recently-boiled distilled water by means of a jet of the same liquid, and the ferrous iron is determined by titration, with the dilute standard bichromate solution specified for ganister on p. 368. The number of cc. required multiplied by $0.12857 = \%\ FeO$.

The percentage of Fe_2O_3 is obtained thus—

[cc. of $K_2Cr_2O_7$ required for total iron (in filtrate from SiO_2)]—(cc. required for FeO titration) $\times 0.14286$ = $\%\ Fe_2O_3$.

DETERMINATION OF THE ALKALIES.

Method I. (Lawrence Smith, modified.)

(Time occupied, about 2 days.)

Weight taken.—Weigh out 1·44 grammes of the substance *reduced to an impalpable powder* into a platinum dish, and intimately mix it with 1 gramme of pure ammonium chloride and 9 grammes of pure calcium carbonate (both re-agents must of course be quite free from potassium and sodium salts).

Dry fusion.—The covered dish is heated for about 1 hour in the muffle at a fair red heat, say 700° C.

Extracting the fusion.—When cold, the dry mass is detached and transferred without loss from the platinum to a 6-in. porcelain dish, heated on the water-bath with 250 cc. of water, the insoluble residue being broken up and afterwards occasionally pulverized with a small Wedgwood ware pestle during at least an hour.

Fractional filtration.—The pestle is rinsed, and the solution and residue are transferred without loss to a 302 cc. graduated flask, and when cold are diluted to the mark, thoroughly mixed, and 250 cc., corresponding to 1·2 grammes of material, are filtered off through a dry double filter into a graduated flask.

Removing the lime.—The 250 cc. of solution are transferred to an *old* 20-oz. beaker, boiled down to 200 cc., made alkaline with ammonia, and, a few cc. at a time, a saturated solution of pure ammonium oxalate is added till no further precipitation takes place. The beaker should be removed from the plate, and the oxalate allowed to settle between each addition, and about 5 cc. excess should be used. The liquid is boiled and afterwards quietly digested till the lime has precipitated and the liquid is almost clear. The solution and precipitate are transferred to a 301 cc. flask, diluted to the mark, thoroughly mixed, and 250 cc. of liquid, corresponding to 1 gramme of material, are filtered off with the usual precautions.

Separating traces of MgO and CaO.—The 250 cc. of filtrate are boiled down and evaporated to about 40 cc., made strongly alkaline with 10 cc. of 880 ammonia. add not more than three drops of a 10% solution ammonium phosphate, which must be quite free from and sodium salts. The liquid is allowed to some hours, being occasionally briskly Any ammonium magnesium phosphate, a little oxalate of lime, which usually pro the evaporation of the filtr so, is filtered with ammonia water, the filtrate and eived into an old clean 20-oz. beaker. The alkaline liquid is boiled down till almost free from ammonia, made faintly acid with *HCl*, and 5 cc. of the standard solution of *FeCl₃* specified on p. 132 are added. The liquid is brought to boiling, and little by little dilute ammonia is poured down the lip of the covered beaker till in slight excess. The contents of the vessel are then quietly digested till the phosphate of iron has flocked out and the liquid is crystal clear. The precipitate is filtered off and washed with hot water, the filtrate and washings being received into a clean old 20-oz. beaker.

Removing ammonium salts.—Add to the filtrate from the phosphate of iron 30 cc. of strong nitric acid, and quietly boil the liquid down to 5 cc., then, with as little wash-water as possible, transfer the solution from the beaker to a tared 3-in. *porcelain* dish.

Weighing the alkalies as chlorides.—Quietly evaporate the liquid in the porcelain dish to very low bulk on a pipe-stem triangle placed on the hot plate; add 10 cc. of strong *HCl* and evaporate to dryness; cool the dish, add 5 cc. of *HCl*, again evaporate to dryness, and *gently* ignite over a Bunsen flame. When the dish has become quite cold in the desiccator, re-weigh it; the increase over the original weight of the dish $= (x\,KCl + y\,NaCl)$.

Estimating the chlorine.—Make a standard solution of nitrate of silver by dissolving 2·897 grammes of the pure dry salt in 500 cc. of water. Each cc. is equivalent to 1 milligramme of chlorine. (The solution may be standardized by means of a solution of pure dry *NaCl*, of which salt 0·0826 gramme dissolved in a little water should require exactly 50 cc. of the silver solution when titrated in the manner about to be described.)

The alkaline chlorides are dissolved by gently boiling with 10 or 15 cc. of water, the dish is well rinsed out, the solution and washings being received in a 4-in. deep porcelain dish. Add to the liquid a few drops of a strong solution of yellow normal potassic chromate (K_2CrO_4),[1] and then from a 50 cc. burette slowly run in the silver solution, constantly stirring the liquid meanwhile till the last two drops of nitrate produce a permanent reddish tinge. Each cc. of standard solution used $= 0.001$ gramme *Cl.*

Calculating the alkaline oxides.—The percentage of the mixed oxides ($x K_2O + y Na_2O$)—and for practical purposes it is unnecessary to separate them—is calculated thus : (Weight of chlorides − weight of chlorine) + (weight of chlorine × 0.2256) = weight of ($x K_2O + y Na_2O$), and weight of mixed oxides multiplied by 100 = the percentage of alkaline oxides.

Example of Analysis.

Weight of clay taken 1·44 (= 1) grammes.
Weight of dish + mixed chlorides = 43·6298
Weight of dish = 43·6112

Weight of (x KCl + y NaCl) =   ·0186

Volume of silver solution required 9·8 cc. = 0·0098 gramme *Cl.*
Then (·0186 − ·0098) + (.0098 × ·2256) = ·0088 + ·0022 = 1·10°/$_o$ of alkaline oxides.

Theoretical Considerations.

On heating, the *AmCl* of the fusion mixture converts a portion of the $CaCO_3$ into chloride thus :

$$2\ AmCl + CaCO_3 = CaCl_2 + CO_2 + 2\ NH_3 + H_2O$$

[1] This indicator is rendered more sensitive by adding a few drops of nitrate of silver solution, shaking well, and filtering off the clear solution from the precipitate of chromate of silver.

The surplus carbonate of lime is converted into oxide with evolution of CO_2. The calcic chloride and oxide thus formed together attack the insoluble alkaline silicates, forming by a complex reaction silicate of lime and soluble potassic and sodic chlorides.[1] On extracting the fusion with water the calcium silicate, silica, alumina, and oxide of iron remain insoluble, whilst the alkaline chlorides, calcic chloride, together with some calcic oxide, and possibly a little magnesia, pass into solution. The bulk of the MgO, however, even if originally soluble, seems to be carried down with the carbonate of lime precipitated during the extraction owing to the action of atmospheric CO_2 on the calcic hydrate in solution. In the filtrate from the extraction the lime compounds are removed by precipitation as calcium oxalate, CaC_2O_4. The magnesia is precipitated as phosphate $AmMgPO_4$. The iron added is precipitated as hydrate on the addition of ammonia, and carries down with it the excess of P_2O_5 as $FePO_4$. The removal of $AmCl$, etc., from the final solution by evaporating with HNO_3 has been explained on p. 341. The double evaporation with strong HCl is necessary to expel the nitric acid from the alkaline nitrates, and convert them into chlorides. The reaction between the chlorides and the silver nitrate may be exemplified thus :

$$KCl + AgNO_3 = AgCl + KNO_3$$

As soon as the whole of the chlorine has been reacted upon, the next addition of silver solution throws down from the yellow chromate of potash indicator a reddish precipitate of chromate of silver, thus :

$$K_2CrO_4 + 2\ AgNO_3 = Ag_2CrO_4 + 2\ KNO_3$$

[1] The chlorides are volatile at about 800° C.

In calculating the results, the factor given substitutes 1 atom of oxygen for the 2 atoms of chlorine, combined with the alkali metal, thus, diagramatically:

$$2\,KCl + 2\,NaCl + 2\,O = K_2O + Na_2O + 4\,Cl$$

or $\quad K_1 \quad\quad Na_2 \quad\quad O_1 \quad$ and $\quad\quad Cl_4$

$$\frac{Cl_2 = 70\cdot74}{O_1 = 15\cdot96} \text{ and } \frac{15\cdot9}{70\cdot74} = 0\cdot2256 = \text{factor,}$$

It is very necessary that the analysis be conducted in old, well-used beakers; glass (which contains about 10% of alkaline oxides) is palpably soluble when new, but the error from old beakers is small.

Method II.—Hydrofluoric Acid Method.

Treat 1·44 grammes of the finely-divided material in a platinum dish with 5 cc. of strong sulphuric acid and up to 50 cc. of the purest aqueous hydrofluoric acid. The digestion is continued with frequent stirring by means of a stout platinum wire until no gritty particles of undecomposed material can be felt, whereupon the solution is evaporated until nearly all the sulphuric acid has been volatilized. Digest the residue with hydrochloric acid until complete solution is effected and then dilute freely. (A small insoluble residue may be collected and again treated with sulphuric and hydrofluoric acids.) Now add dilute ammonia until faintly alkaline, boil for a minute, transfer to a 300 cc. flask, cool, dilute to the mark, and filter off 250 cc., representing 1 gramme of material. The filtrate is heated to boiling, and a strong solution of barium chloride added in drops until no further precipitate is obtained, the amount of sulphuric acid being thus precipitated. The excess of barium thus introduced together with the lime and magnesia of the original material are precipitated in the same solution by the addition of ammonium carbonate and ammonium phosphate. After allowing to stand for half an hour, make up to 300 cc. and again filter off 250 cc., representing 1 gramme of the material.

The filtrate should contain now only the alkalies, volatile ammonium salts and ammonium phosphate. From this point to the end of the determination the operations are identical with those described already in the Lawrence Smith method, commencing with the removal of the phosphoric acid.

ANALYSIS OF BAUXITE.

This mineral consists essentially of a double hydrate of aluminium and iron, containing about 50% Al_2O_3, 25% Fe_2O_3, 20% H_2O, together with small percentages of silica, titanic acid, etc. It is sometimes used in the form of bricks as an isolating course in basic open-hearth furnaces.

Determination of Hygroscopic Water.

The hygroscopic moisture is determined as for iron ores on p. 316. The remainder of the analysis is made on the mineral thus obtained dried at 100° C.

Determination of Water of Constitution.

The combined water may be determined by simple ignition in the manner described on p. 365, when any little organic matter present will render the result obtained slightly high. It may be more accurately estimated by the process described for iron ores on p. 343.

Determination of SiO_2.

One gramme of the finely-divided mineral is fused with 3 grammes each of pure sodic and potassic carbonates, the fusion is extracted in porcelain, and evaporated twice to dryness on the water-bath with strong HCl. The dry mass is taken up in HCl and water, the insoluble silica being filtered off, thoroughly washed, dried, ignited, and weighed in the usual manner. It will probably contain a little TiO_2.[1] The details of the above operations will be sufficiently obvious on reference to the articles on the analysis of ganister and fireclay.

Preserving the filtrate.—The filtrate and washings from the SiO_2 are received into a 250 cc. graduated flask; the liquid is cooled, made up to the mark, well mixed, and portions are employed for the estimation of the Al_2O_3 and Fe_2O_3.

Determination of Ferric Oxide.

Measure off 125 cc. of the filtrate from the silica, corresponding to 0·5 gramme of bauxite, into a 20-oz. flask. The liquid is then neutralized, reduced, acidified, titrated, and the percentage of Fe_2O_3 calculated as though dealing with an iron ore.

[1] The SiO_2 may, if desired, be purified by fusion with $HKSO_4$ (see p. 261).

Determination of Alumina.

50 cc. of the filtrate from the silica, corresponding to
0·2 gramme of bauxite, are measured into a 20-oz.
beaker, diluted to 200 cc., brought to boiling, and the
oxide of iron and alumina are precipitated by pouring
down the lip of the covered beaker a faint excess of
dilute ammonia. The precipitate after digesting is
filtered off on a 125 mm. pure paper, slightly washed, re-
dissolved in HCl, re-precipitated with ammonia, and is
filtered off, thoroughly washed with hot water, dried,
ignited, and weighed as ($x Al_2O_3 + y\ Fe_2O_3$). The percentage of Al_2O_3 is calculated by difference in the manner described on p. 368, of course using the percentage
of Fe_2O_3 as determined in the last article. The result
will probably be a little high, small quantities of
$K_2O \cdot TiO_2$ being estimated as alumina.

ANALYSIS OF MAGNESIAN LIME BRICKS.

The operation of crushing these bricks must be performed as expeditiously as possible, so as to quickly get
the pulverized material into a closely-stoppered bottle,
as it is very liable to absorb moisture and CO_2 from the
air.

Determination of SiO_2.

Dissolve 1 gramme of the pulverized brick in 20 cc.
of HCl, evaporate to dryness, take up in HCl, filter off
the insoluble SiO_2, then wash with HCl and water,
and dry, ignite, and weigh in the usual manner. The

weight obtained multiplied by $100 = \% \ SiO_2$. The residue may contain small quantities of basic oxides, and where scientific accuracy is required, a considerable quantity of it may be analyzed as if a sample of ganister, the magnesia being of course determined.

Determination of Alumina and Oxide of Iron.

Dissolve 2 grammes of the powdered brick in 30 cc. of HCl, dilute the solution to 200 cc., bring to boiling, and precipitate the oxide of iron and alumina with a faint excess of ammonia. Filter off the precipitate, wash it slightly, re-dissolve in HCl, and re-precipitate as before. Thoroughly wash the precipitated oxides with boiling water, dry, ignite[1] and weigh as $(x \ Fe_2O_3 + y \ Al_2O_3)$. The residue, however, may contain traces of Mn_3O_4 and P_2O_5. It is boiled with HCl, and when all the iron has passed into solution the liquid is neutralized, reduced, and the iron is titrated in the usual manner, with the bichromate solution specified on p. 368 for ganister. The result obtained is, however, divided by two, the respective percentages of oxide of iron and alumina are then calculated as usual.

Determination of Lime and Magnesia.

0·5 gramme of material is dissolved in HCl and evaporated to dryness; the mass is taken up in 5 cc. of HCl, diluted to 200 cc., and the oxide of iron and alumina are precipitated with dilute ammonia. They are filtered off and slightly washed, the filtrate and washings

[1] See footnote on p. 368.

being preserved. The precipitate from the ammonia is re-dissolved in HCl, the solutions and washing being received into the beaker in which the precipitation took place. The liquid is evaporated to 5 cc., and diluted, precipitated with a faint excess of ammonia as before. The precipitate is filtered off, and the resulting filtrate, probably containing a little lime and magnesia, is added to that containing the main quantities. The solution is evaporated to 200 cc., and the lime is precipitated with 20 cc. of a saturated solution of ammonium oxalate, and estimated in the manner described for iron ores on p. 339.

$MgO.$—The filtrate from the calcium oxalate is acidified with HCl, evaporated down to about 100 cc., and 25 cc. of a 10% solution of ammonium phosphate are added, then, constantly shaking the liquid round, add dilute ammonia till in distinct excess. The total volume is then made up with strong ammonia to 200 cc. After standing a few hours with an occasional brisk shaking, the phosphate is filtered off, washed with water strongly alkaline with ammonia, and is dried, ignited, and weighed as $Mg_2P_2O_7$ in the usual manner, 4 milligrammes being added to the weight of the precipitate as a correction for solubility. The corrected weight of pyrophosphate multiplied by $72 \cdot 2 = \%$ MgO.

ANALYSIS OF DOLOMITE.

Typical dolomite consists of a double carbonate of lime and magnesia containing about 48% CO_2, 30% MgO, 20% CaO, and as impurities, small percentages of FeO, MnO, Al_2O_3, and SiO_2. Small quantities of SO_3, FeS_2, P_2O_5, and TiO_2 may also be present in this mineral, and consequently the compounds resulting from their ignition may be found in the magnesian lime bricks made from it. An exhaustive analysis, however, is seldom necessary for practical steel works purposes. The analytical procedure given below is of course applicable to ordinary limestone ($CaCO_3$ + impurities) and magnesite ($MgCO_3$ + impurities).

The methods for estimating in limestones SiO_2, FeO, Al_2O_3, CaO,[1] MgO,[2] do not differ in their details from those given in the previous article.

CO_2.—Carbon dioxide is estimated by the process described for carbonated iron ores on p. 342.

Determination of MnO.

Dissolve 12 grammes of the pulverized stone in dilute HCl in a large covered beaker, and evaporate to low bulk. Transfer the solution and insoluble residue to a 600 cc. graduated flask; when cold, make up to the mark, thoroughly mix, and by fractional filtration obtain 500 cc. of liquid containing the MnO in 10 grammes of dolomite. Transfer the liquid to a 30-oz. registered flask, add 4 cc. of bromine, shake the liquid till it is nearly all dissolved, and then add cautiously 50 cc. of strong ammonia. The solution is shaken round and then digested, nearly at boiling, till clear. The precipitate is filtered off, washed, dissolved in HCl, the solution and washings being neutralized with ammonia and the iron precipitated with ammonium acetate. The ferric acetate is filtered off; the manganese in the filtrate is precipitated

[1] Weight of $CaO \times 1.7846 = CaCO_3$
[2] Per cent. $MgO \times 2.125 = \% \ MgCO_3$

c c

with bromine and ammonia, and estimated in the usual manner. The weight of Mn_3O_4 obtained $\times 0.93 =$ the weight of MnO: this $\times 10 = \%$ MnO.

Determination of P_2O_5 and Sulphur.

P_2O_5.—Dissolve 10 grammes of the pulverized mineral in a 20-oz. covered beaker in 50 cc. of HCl. Evaporate to low bulk, and dilute to 200 cc. Bring the liquid to boiling, and precipitate the Fe_2O_3, Al_2O_3, and P_2O_5 with a faint excess of ammonia. Filter off the precipitate, wash it, and re-dissolve in HCl; evaporate the solution and washings to low bulk, add excess of dilute ammonia, just take up the resulting precipitate in strong nitric acid, boil for a few minutes, remove the beaker from the plate, and add excess of nitric acid solution of ammonium molybdate specified on p. 139. The resulting yellow precipitate is filtered off and dealt with in one or other of the methods specified in connection with the determination of phosphorus in steel.

S.—Sulphur is estimated working on 6 grammes of the stone as in the case of an iron ore; the remarks made on p. 335 concerning the insoluble residue apply also to the present case.

Determination of Alkaline Oxides.

The alkalies in raw dolomite in its burnt form as bricks may be determined by working on 10 or 5 grammes of the material with 1 gramme of ammonium chloride the process described for fire-clay of course calculated on 10 may be.

SECTION IV. FUELS.

COAL.

Coal is a fossil fuel resulting from the accumulation of vegetable matter during past geological ages. The duration of the action of mechanical pressure of super-imposed strata and internal chemical change, determine the character of the coal, which ranges from incompact, peaty brown coal, through the ordinary black pit coal to compact, vitreous anthracite, the last-named being the oldest formation. Chemically, coal consists mainly of carbon, together with varying quantities of hydrogen, oxygen, a little nitrogen, and the inorganic constituents found in its ash. The most noticeable chemical change marking the inconceivably slow passage from peat to anthracite is a diminution of oxygen, accompanied by a consequent increase of carbon and heating power.

PROXIMATE ANALYSIS OF COAL.

The industrial analysis of coal usually includes the following items:

Moisture.

Coke (= fixed carbon + ash).

Volatile matter (= weight of original dry coal — coke).

Sulphur.

Ash.

Determination of Sulphur (Eschka, modified).

(Time occupied, about ¾ day.)

Weight taken.—Weigh out 1·2 grammes of the coal in a very fine state of division into a 2½-in. flat platinum dish, and very intimately mix it with about 1·25 grammes of calcined magnesia and 0·6 gramme of anhydrous sodium carbonate. The mixture is tapped down and covered with a layer of about half a gramme of magnesia.

Blank estimation.—A blank determination of the sulphur in the weight of re-agents used must be made, and the $BaSO_4$ obtained is deducted from that resulting from the analysis of the coal.

Dry fusion.—Place the uncovered dish in the muffle at a moderate red heat for about an hour till the coal has burned off and no black particles of coke remain.

Extracting.—When cold, the dish is placed in a 20-oz. beaker containing 80 cc. of boiling water. When the mass has disintegrated the dish is rinsed with hot water and removed. The contents of the covered beaker are digested at incipient boiling for about half-an-hour.

Fractional filtration.—The solution and residue are carefully transferred without loss to a 120 cc. graduated flask, and when cold are made up very slightly over the mark, thoroughly mixed, and 100 cc. of clear solution, containing the sulphur in 1 gramme of coal, are filtered off through a dry double filter.

Precipitating the sulphur.—The 100 cc. of liquid are washed out into a 20-oz. covered beaker, and 10 cc. of bromine water and afterwards about 5 cc. of *HCl* are added. The liquid is brought to boiling, and 10 cc. of

10% solution of $BaCl_2$ are poured down the lip of the beaker. The boiling is continued for about 15 minutes, when the $BaSO_4$ should be granular, and not so liable to pass through the filter-paper as when precipitated cold. It is allowed to settle somewhat, is collected on a 90 mm. pure paper, washed, dried, ignited, and weighed with the precautions given on p. 109 *et seq.* The corrected weight obtained multiplied by $13\cdot7 = \%\ S$.

Theoretical Considerations.

The sulphur in coal is known to exist in at least two forms, namely, as SO_3 in the metallic sulphates constituting several units per cent. of the inorganic ash, and in brassy scales and particles of iron pyrites FeS_2.

In the foregoing analysis, both forms of sulphur are converted mainly into the soluble sulphates of magnesium and sodium; small quantities of the sulphides of those metals may also be formed. The latter are converted into sulphates by the oxidizing action of the bromine water added to the extract from the fusion.

Determination of Ash.

2 grammes of the powdered coal are placed in a tared platinum crucible, the weighed cover being left in the balance-case. The organic constituents of the coal are burnt off in the muffle very cautiously at first, till the ash is free from dark specks of coke. Its colour may be nearly white, red, or grey. The crucible is allowed to go quite cold in the desiccator, and is then covered and re-

weighed: the increase in weight multiplied by 100 and $\div 2 = \%$ ash.

Precaution.—The initial heating of the coal must be very gentle till the mineral has coked, otherwise the violent evolution of gas may carry away some of the ash.

ANALYSIS OF COAL ASH.

When an analysis of the ash of coal is required several grammes must be prepared and weighed out as required, from a well-stoppered bottle. The various constituents will be seen on reference to the analysis given on p. 456. The silica, oxide of iron, alumina, magnesia, and alkalies are determined as if the substance under examination were a fire-clay. The SO_3 is determined on half a gramme of ash by the process specified on p. 335 for the analysis of the insoluble residue from iron ores.

Determination of P_2O_5.

One gramme of the ash is fused with 3 grammes each of a mixture of sodic and potassic carbonates free from phosphorus: the fusion is extracted in HCl, the solution made slightly alkaline with dilute ammonia, and the oxide of iron and alumina are filtered off and slightly washed. The precipitate, which contains the whole of the P_2O_5, is re-dissolved either in strong hydrochloric acid or in 1·20 nitric acid, and the solution treated in accordance with the instructions specified for the determination of phosphorus in steel.

ELEMENTARY ANALYSIS OF COAL.

The determination of the percentage of carbon and hydrogen in coal is seldom required in steel works practice. The analysis is made by the process described for the determination of combined water and organic carbon in iron ores on p. 343. Exactly 0·2 gramme of the coal is weighed out into a porcelain boat for the analysis. The increase of weight in the sulphuric acid bulb multiplied by 55·65 = % H. The increase in the potash and chloride of calcium tubes × 136·35 = % C when precisely 0·2 gramme of coal is burnt: water containing 11·13% H and CO_2, 27·27% C.

ANALYSIS OF COKE AND CHARCOAL.

The processes just described for coal are also applicable to coke and charcoal.[1]

ANALYSIS OF PRODUCER GASES.

Gaseous fuel as employed for open-hearth furnaces seldom contains more than 40% by volume of combustible gases, the remainder being chiefly nitrogen, together with a few units per cent. of CO_2 and possibly traces of oxygen. The gases useful for fuel are hydrogen, carbonic

---

[1] In estimating the moisture in charcoal the latter may require a prolonged heating at a temperature considerably over 100°. It should then be weighed quickly, as it is capable in a damp atmosphere of absorbing a considerable weight of moisture.

oxide CO, and marsh gas or light carburetted hydrogen CH_4. A small amount of olefiant gas or heavy carburetted hydrogen C_2H_4 may also be present. The determination of oxygen and C_2H_4 is hardly necessary for practical purposes: the amount of the former is so minute and the separate determination of the inconsiderable percentage of the latter usually present so complicates the analysis as to render it inadvisable. Its elements, moreover, will be reported as CH_4 and CO, so making an inappreciable difference in any calculation of the calorific intensity of the gas made on the result of the analysis.

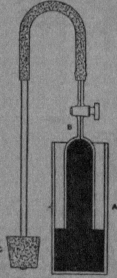

The Process.

(Time occupied, about 1 hour.)

Sampling.—This operation is carried out in the simple apparatus sketched in Fig. 17. A is a glass cylinder 5 in. long by 2 in. diameter. It is about one-third filled with mercury. In it

FIG. 17.

is placed the laboratory vessel B, also (by suction) filled with mercury right up to the end of the capillary tube above the tap, the latter being then closed. c is a cork slightly carbonized outside, fitting the sampling aperture in the gas main and carrying a glass tube and piece of thick-walled india-rubber tubing. The cork is inserted

in the sampling hole, and in close producers a flush of gas
is put on by widely opening the steam jets. When the
gas is freely issuing from the end of the india-rubber
tubing the latter is slipped over the capillary tube of the
laboratory vessel; the tap is opened, the gas drawn in
till the vessel is about half full, when the tap is closed,
and the india-rubber tubing detached.

Analyzing the Gas.

(Method 1.)

The volumetric analysis of the gas is conveniently
made in the apparatus designed for this purpose by Mr.
J. E. Stead, which is essentially that sketched in Fig. 18.
It is placed in a large square tray to prevent the loss of
mercury accidentally spilled.

Measuring off a definite volume.—Over the capillary
tube of the laboratory vessel containing the gas is slipped
a piece of thick-walled india-rubber tubing, which is then
filled with mercury.

The laboratory vessel and its capillary attachments up
to B are filled with *KHO* solution (1 in 3), drawn up from
the cylinder by previously filling the endiometer tube
with mercury, and then lowering the reservoir M. The
tap B is then quickly closed.

The tap A is opened; the reservoir of mercury M is
raised by pulling down the weight W till mercury drips
from the end of the capillary tube at C. The tap is then
closed. The india-rubber tubing of the gas vessel having
been firmly slipped over C, the reservoir M is lowered,
the tap A and that of the gas vessel are opened, and

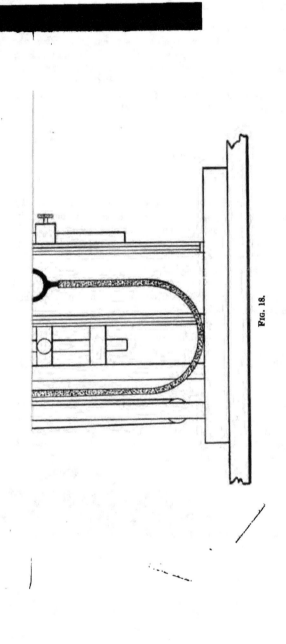

FIG. 18.

about 80 volumes of gas are drawn into the graduated eudiometer tube ᴇ. Both taps are then closed and the gas vessel detached. The reservoir ᴍ is next carefully adjusted till the levels of the mercury menisca in the tubes ᴇ and ᴘ are exactly coincident when sighted across the top of the adjusting level ʟ. Carefully note the number of volumes of gas in the eudiometer (first reading).

First absorption.—Raise the reservoir ᴍ and open the tap ʙ till the gas has passed into ᴠ, and mercury drips into the vessel; then close the tap. Whilst the potash is absorbing the CO_2 open the tap ᴀ, till mercury drips from c, thus sweeping out the gas in the capillary between ᴇ and ᴀ; then close ᴀ. In five minutes ᴍ is lowered, the tap ʙ opened, and the gas is transferred back to ᴇ, *taking great care not to let the KHO solution get past* ʙ. The levels having been carefully adjusted, the reading is again noted (second reading).

First explosion.—Introduce from a glass gas-holder containing pure oxygen (prepared from $KClO_3$ and well washed through caustic soda) about 30 volumes of the gas, being very careful to allow the oxygen to sweep out all the air in the india-rubber tubing from the gas-holder before attaching it to c. ᴀ is closed, the columns are levelled, and the volume noted (third reading). From the terminals of a sufficiently powerful Ruhmkorff coil worked by a storage cell, pass a spark through the platinum wires fused in at the top of the tube ᴇ.[1] After

---

[1] If the spark will not pass some *KHO* solution has probably passed into the tube, and the current is passing round the glass instead of across the spark terminals. In such a case return the gas into ᴠ and wash out ᴇ with dilute *HCl*, and then two or three time with distilled water. Return the gas to ᴇ when the spark will pass

the explosion temporarily set the levels, wait till the heat produced has radiated, and the reading is constant (fourth reading).

Second absorption.—Pass the gas as before into v for five minutes, return to E, level and read off (fifth reading).

Second explosion.—Next introduce from a gas-holder, with the same precaution as in the case of oxygen, about 50 volumes of pure hydrogen (prepared from HCl and re-distilled zinc free from carbon); level and read off (sixth reading). Again explode, cool, and note the volume (seventh reading).

Calculating the volumes.—

Let difference between 1st and 2nd reading = a = Contraction after 1st absorption.
  ,, ,, ,, 2nd and 3rd ,, = b = Volume of added oxygen.
  ,, ,, ,, 3rd and 4th ,, = c = Contraction after 1st explosion.
  ,, ,, ,, 4th and 5th ,, = d = Contraction after 2nd absorption.
  ,, ,, ,, Let the 5th ,, = e = Volume after 2nd absorption.
Let difference between 6th and 7th ,, = f = Contraction after 2nd explosion.

Then—

$$\text{Volume of } CO_2 = a$$
$$\text{,,}\quad\text{,,}\quad CO = \tfrac{1}{3}\,(4\,d + c + f) - b$$
$$\text{,,}\quad\text{,,}\quad H = c + \tfrac{1}{3}\,f - b$$
$$\text{,,}\quad\text{,,}\quad CH_4 = b - \tfrac{1}{3}\,(d + e + f)$$
$$\text{,,}\quad\text{,,}\quad N = e - \tfrac{1}{3}\,f$$

Example.

Analysis of gas entering the open-hearth furnace, Sheffield University. Producer not working satisfactorily.

1st Reading	87·5 vols.				
2nd ,,	81·0 ,,	diff.	6·5 vols.	= a	
3rd ,,	127·0 ,,	,,	46·0 ,,	= b	
4th ,,	95·0 ,,	,,	32·0 ,,	= c	
5th ,,	73·0	,,	22·0 ,,	= d	
6th ,,	150·5 ,,		78·0 ,,	= e	
7th ,,	80·0 ,,	diff.	70·5 ,,	= f	

Then:—

$$CO_2 = \qquad\qquad\qquad\qquad 6\cdot5 \text{ vols.}$$

$$CO = \frac{88\cdot0 + 32\cdot0 + 70\cdot5}{3} - 46 = 63\cdot5 - 46 = 17\cdot5 \text{ ,,}$$

$$H = 32 + 23\cdot5 - 46 \qquad = 55\cdot5 - 46 = 9\cdot5 \text{ ,,}$$

$$CH_4 = 46 - \frac{22 + 32 + 70\cdot5}{3} \qquad = 46 \ -41\cdot5 = 4\cdot5 \text{ ,,}$$

$$N = 73 - \frac{70\cdot5}{3} \qquad\qquad = 73 \ -23\cdot5 = 49\cdot5 \text{ ,,}$$

$$\overline{\qquad 87\cdot5 \qquad}$$

Then to convert volume into percentage.

$$\frac{6\cdot5 \times 100}{87\cdot5} = 7\cdot4 \ \%/_\circ \text{ by vol. of } CO_2$$

$$\frac{17\cdot5 \times 100}{87\cdot5} = 20\cdot0 \text{ ,,} \qquad \text{,,} \qquad CO$$

$$\frac{9\cdot5 \times 100}{87\cdot5} = 10\cdot9 \text{ ,,} \qquad \text{,,} \qquad H$$

$$\frac{4\cdot5 \times 100}{87\cdot5} = 5\cdot1 \text{ ,,} \qquad \text{,,} \qquad CH_4$$

$$\frac{49\cdot5 \times 100}{87\cdot5} = 56\cdot6 \text{ ,,} \qquad \text{,,} \qquad N$$

cal Considerations.

The reactions involved in the above operations are as follow:

The CO_2 present is absorbed in the caustic potash with formation of K_2CO_3.

On exploding the remaining gas with excess of oxygen the nitrogen remains unaltered, but the hydrogen, carbonic oxide, and marsh gas are converted into gaseous carbon dioxide and liquid water, thus:

$$\underset{\text{2 vols.}}{2\,H} + \underset{\text{1 vol.}}{O} = \underset{\text{0 vol. (practically)}}{H_2O}$$

$$\underset{\text{2 vols.}}{CO} + \underset{\text{1 vol.}}{O} = \underset{\text{2 vols.}}{CO_2}$$

$$\underset{\text{2 vols.}}{CH_4} + \underset{\text{4 vols.}}{4\,O} = \underset{\text{2 vols.}}{CO_2} + \underset{\text{0 vol.}}{2\,H_2O}$$

The total CO_2 formed is absorbed by the second treatment with KHO.

In the second explosion the surplus oxygen is converted into water, leaving the nitrogen and some surplus hydrogen. The contraction after the first explosion = (the volume of hydrogen $+\frac{1}{2}$ its volume of oxygen) + (oxygen equivalent to $\frac{1}{2}$ the volume of CO) + (oxygen equivalent to twice the volume of CH_4). The contraction after the second absorption = (volume of CO) + (volume of CH_4). The contraction after the second explosion = (volume of surplus oxygen) + (twice its volume of hydrogen).

The various volumes measured do not require correcting for variations in temperature, pressure, or humidity, because during an analysis the thermometer and barometer do not sensibly alter, and the gas as it comes from the producer and throughout the analysis may be regarded as having a constant tension, viz. that due to uniform saturation with aqueous vapour.

(If it is desired to use the volumetric analysis of the gas for calculating its theoretical calorific intensity, proceed in accordance with the instructions and examples given in the Appendix on p. 449.

Rapid analytical Valuation of Producer Gas.

If rapidly obtained results sufficiently near the truth to form a guide for practical working are desired, the estimation of the CH_4 may be omitted, its elements reported as CO and H, and the nitrogen by difference.

In this case the process is considerably simplified, becoming as follows:

(1) Measure off a definite bulk (80 vols.) of the gas = 1st reading
(2) Absorb the CO_2 in the potash. Vol. afterwards = 2nd „
(3) Add about 30 vols. of oxygen. Vol. afterwards = 3rd „
(4) Explode the gases. Vol. afterwards (when cold) = 4th „
(5) Absorb the CO_2 formed in potash. Vol. afterwards = 5th „

Let (a) = Difference between 1st and 2nd reading.
„ (b) = Difference between 3rd and 4th reading.
„ (c) = Difference between 4th and 5th reading.

Then—

$$CO_2 = a$$
$$CO = c$$
$$H = \tfrac{2}{3}\left(b - \tfrac{1}{2}c\right)$$

Precautions.—The taps of the gas apparatus should be slightly smeared with vaseline, and great care should be taken not to let those coming into contact with the caustic potash set in the sockets; otherwise the apparatus may be broken in attempts to loosen them. When not in frequent use the taps should be removed, and be replaced for the time being by corks to keep dust out of the capillaries.

Notes.—An experience extending over many years has led the authors to the conclusion that the analysis of producer gas as obtained in the Stead apparatus cannot be regarded as absolutely accurate. The sum of the per-

measured at atmospheric pressure by bringing the meniscus in the pressure tube (Fig. 19, P) level with that in

Fig. 19.

the burette. The apparatus must be handled by the wooden portions only, and the confining liquid, if water, must be first saturated with the gas to be analyzed.

D D

ig. 19, w w') which preserves the contained re-agent
om atmospheric action. The explosion pipette (Fig. 21)
charged with mercury.

Analyzing the Gas.

Absorption of carbon di-oxide.—The re-agent in the
tassium hydrate pipette is caused to rise to a mark

ip
o-
is
ig
or
ed
c-

then agitated, and, after two
withdrawn into the burette
tube and opening the tap.
re-agent, following the gas,
capillary, or has dripped thro
conditions of working. A co
is allowed for the draining
burette, and the reading is
previously mentioned being
the readings before and after
of carbon-di-oxide in the ori

Absorption of oxygen.—
with alkaline pyrogallate i
mechanical working are ess
first absorption. The differe
and after this absorption giv
sent in the volume originally

Absorption of carbon-mono
as recorded above. If two
should be agitated with the
the fresher one for three mi

the capillary) closed with a screw clip. The mixture is then fired by sparking with a Rhumkorf coil, returned to the burette, and after cooling measured. The carbon-di-oxide formed during the explosion is then measured by absorption in the potassium hydrate pipette.

The volume of carbon-di-oxide found after explosion measures the volume of methane originally present in the sample. The volume of hydrogen is two-thirds of the difference between the contraction found after explosion and twice the volume of methane as determined above. The volume of nitrogen is found by difference. An absorption of the surplus oxygen in the gas residue will serve to check the result.

Apart from slight experimental errors the one most likely to arise is due to the incomplete absorption of carbon-monoxide. Any volume of this gas not absorbed by the cuprous chloride re-agent goes forward in the analysis, and is ultimately registered as methane. Whether the absorption has been complete or not can be determined as follows: let the total contraction due to the explosion and the subsequent absorption of carbon-di-oxide formed $= C$; the volume of oxygen actually used in the explosion (*i.e.*, the volume added minus the volume found with the nitrogen residue) $= O$;

Then the methane originally present $= O - \frac{1}{2} C$.
and the hydrogen „ „ $= \frac{4}{3} C - 2O$.

If these estimations so made agree fairly well with the previous ones, then the absorption of carbon-monoxide has been satisfactory. Very small amounts of hydrocarbons other than methane are always present, and the varying products formed by their explosion with oxygen preclude absolute concordance of results.

SECTION V. SUNDRIES.

ANALYSIS OF SLAGS.

In order to avoid unnecessary repetition of analytical details already fully described in connection with iron ores and refractory materials, the authors propose with reference to slags to give only brief, skeleton instructions for their analysis. Cinders of five typical constitutions will be dealt with, which may be divided into two classes—

1. Slags insoluble in *HCl*, and which therefore require fusion with alkaline carbonates to render their bases soluble.

2. Slags practically soluble in strong *HCl*.

The first class includes—

(a) Blast furnace slags, which consist of a neutral double silicate of lime and alumina.

(b) Finery slag, consisting essentially of ferrous silicate.

(c) Slag from the acid Bessemer process, consisting of a double silicate of the protoxides of manganese and iron.

The second class comprises—

(a) Slag from the basic process, consisting chiefly of basic phosphate of lime.

(b) Tap cinder from the puddling furnace, consisting mainly of a highly basic silicate of ferrous and ferric oxides.

Analysis of Blast Furnace Slag.

SiO_2.—Fuse 0·5 gramme of the finely-divided slag with a mixture of 2 grammes each of Na_2CO_3 and K_2CO_3, and 0·5 gramme of KNO_3 in a platinum dish. Extract in a porcelain dish with water, evaporate twice to dryness with HCl on the water-bath, take up in HCl and water, filter off, and estimate the SiO_2, preserving the filtrate and washings.

Al_2O_3 and Fe_2O_3.—The oxide of iron and alumina are precipitated in the filtrate from the SiO_2 in a bulk of 200 cc. with a faint excess of ammonia. The precipitate is filtered off (the filtrate being preserved), re-dissolved in HCl, and re-precipitated with ammonia. The precipitate is collected, washed, dried, ignited, and weighed as $(xAl_2O_3 + y\ Fe_2O_3)$, the second filtrate being added to that from the first precipitation.

CaO and MgO.—The double filtrate is evaporated down, and in it the lime and magnesia are estimated as in an iron ore containing a considerable percentage of manganese.

FeO.—Fuse 3 grammes of the slag with 12 grammes each of K_2CO_3 and Na_2CO_3. The fusion is extracted with HCl, the solution evaporated down till the oxides of iron and manganese have totally dissolved, and is then boiled with the addition of 1 cc. of strong HNO_3. The liquid having been made up to a definite volume, $\frac{5}{6}$ths, corresponding to 2·5 grammes of slag, are filtered off. The solution is neutralized with ammonia, the iron precipitated with ammonium acetate, filtered off (the filtrate and washing being preserved), re-dissolved in HCl, neutralized, reduced, and titrated with the standard bichromate solu-

FeO.—In the acid filtrate (and washings) from the silica the iron is precipitated with ammonia, filtered off, redissolved in *HCl*, neutralized, reduced, and titrated as in the case of an iron ore. The number of cc.s required × 1·2857 = % *FeO*.

MnO, P₂O₅, S.—The manganous oxide, phosphoric acid, and sulphur are estimated in the manner described for the analysis of blast-furnace slag.

CaO, MgO.—1·2 grammes of the slag are fused with 10 grammes of fusion mixture, extracted, evaporated, and the silica is separated by filtration in the manner described for *SiO₂*. From the filtrate the oxide of iron and alumina are twice precipitated with ammonia, and in the evaporated double filtrate the lime and magnesia are determined as usual, the manganese being separated as sulphide in the manner described on p. 338, and the *CaO* and *MgO* results being calculated to percentage on 1 gramme.

Al₂O₃.—The precipitate of oxide of iron and alumina from the last filtration is re-dissolved in *HCl*, neutralized, reduced, and the alumina determined as phosphate as in the case of an iron ore, the result being of course calculated on 1 gramme.

Acid Bessemer Slag.

SiO₂.—Fuse 0·5 gramme of the finely-divided slag with 3 grammes each of *K₂CO₃* and *Na₂CO₃*. The fusion is extracted in *HCl*, the silica is rendered insoluble by evaporation to dryness, and is determined as usual.

MnO.—The filtrate (and washings) from the *SiO₂* is saturated with bromine, and the manganese precipitated with excess of ammonia. The precipitate is filtered off,

Analysis of Tap Cinder.

The constituents of this slag are determined as if the material under examination were an iron ore. If necessary, the ferrous oxide and silica may be determined from a fusion with acid potassium sulphate.

Analysis of Basic Slag.

SiO_2.—1 gramme of the finely-divided slag is dissolved in aqua regia and evaporated to dryness. The dry mass is re-dissolved in a little HCl and water; the insoluble silica is filtered off, and estimated as usual.

P_2O_5.—The filtrate and washings from the silica are evaporated to low bulk, excess of ammonia is added, the resulting precipitate is *just* re-dissolved in strong HNO_3. The liquid is boiled, and 100 cc. of the nitric acid solution of ammonium molybdate are added. The liquid is then digested nearly at boiling till clear. The yellow precipitate is filtered off, washed with 2% HNO_3 till free from iron, etc., and is re-dissolved in ammonia;[1] some ammonium chloride is also added, and the P_2O_5 is then precipitated in the strongly ammoniacal solution by means of magnesia mixture, and is estimated in the usual manner.

CaO and MgO.—The lime and magnesia are determined in a solution of 0·6 gramme of the slag, from which the SiO_2 has been separated by filtration after evaporation to dryness with aqua regia. The P_2O_5, Fe_2O_3, and Al_2O_3 are

---

[1] A measured fraction of this may then, as an alternative method, be conveniently carried forward to lead molybdate.

separated as usual by double precipitation with ammonia, the manganese is removed as sulphide by fractional filtration from the double filtrate from the Fe_2O_3, etc. (see p. 338). In the $\frac{5}{6}$ fraction, corresponding to 0·5 gramme of slag, the CaO and MgO are determined as usual by precipitation as oxalate and double phosphate respectively.

Al_2O_3.—The alumina is determined as phosphate from a HCl solution of 1·2 grammes of slag by the process described for iron ores. The final precipitate may be slightly contaminated with Cr_2O_3.

FeO and Fe_2O_3.—The oxides of iron are determined as in the case of an iron ore, working, however, upon 2·5 grammes of slag, the results obtained being of course divided by five.

MnO.—For the determination of the MnO 2½ grammes of slag are dissolved in HCl, evaporated to low bulk, and the HCl is expelled by evaporation with sulphuric acid, the manganese being estimated as before by the bismuthate process.

$Sulphur$.—The sulphur is determined exactly as in the case of steel by the aqua regia process. That existing as calcium sulphide may be determined by the volumetric lead acetate process described on p. 117 et seq.

CrO_3.—Basic open-hearth slags often contain one or two-tenths % of CrO_3 derived from the chromite bricks used as an isolating course. To estimate it, 4 grammes of the slag are dissolved in HCl; the solution is boiled with 10 cc. of sulphurous acid, and then with 2 cc. of strong nitric acid. The solution is .... and the oxides of iron, aluminium, chromium, ... thrown down by digesting with a .... The precipitate is filtered off, ...

in hot dilute sulphuric acid, 1 in 4, and the chromium
present is determined by one of the volumetric methods
already described.

TECHNICAL ANALYSIS OF BOILER WATER.

Solutions required.

$\frac{N}{10}$ (*Decinormal*) *HCl.*—Make a mixture of strong *HCl*
solution and distilled water, placed in a tall cylinder, and
adjusted till the hydrometer indicates its sp. gr. to be
1·10; the solution will then contain about 20% of true
HCl. Counterpoise a beaker on the coarse balance and
weigh out 181 grammes of the 20% acid; transfer without loss to a litre flask, dilute to the mark with distilled
water, and thoroughly mix. Ignite in a platinum dish at
a moderate heat about 15 grammes of specially selected
pure anhydrous Na_2CO_3. Cool in the desiccator, and
weight off into a 250 cc. graduated flask exactly 13·25
grammes of the carbonate. Dissolve in warm distilled
water, and when cold dilute to the mark and thoroughly
mix. Measure off 50 cc. into a 10-oz. flask, add about
half a cc. of a strong solution of methyl orange, and from
a burette run in the normal *HCl* solution, finally drop by
drop, till the methyl orange changes to a much deeper
tint, showing the alkali to be just neutralized. Thus—

$$Na_2CO_3 + 2\ HCl = 2\ NaCl + CO_2 + H_2O.$$
$$106 \qquad 73$$
$$= 53 \qquad 36\text{·}5$$

If the *HCl* solution is exactly normal just 50 cc. will
be required, but probably such will not be the case, and

it must be adjusted for weakness by the addition of 1·10 acid, or for strength by the addition of distilled water, in accordance with the principles explained on p. 89 in connection with the bichromate solution, till of exact normal strength.

Decinormal NaHO solution.—Weigh off in a platinum dish about 23 grammes of pure caustic soda from sodium metal. Transfer to a convenient porcelain dish, and dissolve in about 400 cc. of distilled water. When cold, transfer to a 500 cc. flask, dilute to the mark, and thoroughly mix. Measure off 50 cc. into a porcelain dish, and add a few drops of a solution of phenol-phthalein in dilute alcohol, then run in the normal *HCl* solution till the last drop from the burette just discharges the pink colour. If the sodic hydrate is normal just 50 cc. of acid will be required. The soda solution will, however, probably be too strong, and the number of cc. of distilled water necessary to bring it to normal strength are calculated, added, and the liquid is again checked with *HCl* to ensure its exact strength. Thus—

$$NaHO + HCl = NaCl + H_2O$$
$$40 \qquad 36·5$$

The alkaline liquid should be preserved in a green glass bottle provided with a well-fitting india-rubber stopper, and it is covered with a layer of pure light petroleum about $\frac{1}{8}$ in. thick, to prevent the absorption of CO_2 from the air. When required the solution is withdrawn from the bottom of the bottle by means of a pipette.

The solutions thus made are of normal strength. For the determination of the hardness of boiler water, it is convenient to use solutions of one-tenth the strength, so

that 100 cc. of each of the above stock solutions should
be diluted to 1000 cc. to furnish decinormal solutions.
There will also be required a solution of Decinormal
Sodium Carbonate. This is at once prepared from the
pure solid after ignition by dissolving 5·3 grammes in
water and making the liquid up to one litre with distilled
water.

Sampling.

For a technical analysis about one gallon of the water
to be examined should be collected under average conditions in a clean, dry, stoppered Winchester quart. Suspended matter should not be separated, but before withdrawing the portions of the sample required for the
various determinations the bottle should be thoroughly
shaken.

Determinations of Temporary Hardness.

(Hehner, modified.)

Measure off 100 cc. of the sample into a clean conical
flask, add one drop only of a strong solution of methyl
orange from a dropping bottle, and deliver the standard
$\frac{N}{10}$ acid until the neutral point is obtained, or until distinct
acidity is reached. The determination of the exact point
depends largely upon the colour sense of the operator,
but this difficulty may be entirely obviated by titrating
100 cc. of pure distilled water containing one drop of
methyl orange to the same colour (orange or pink), as
in the actual determination. The amount of acid thus

used in the blank determination on the indicator is subtracted from the total amount used on the sample.   Th
hardness of water is expressed in parts of calcium carbo
ate per 100,000, and each cc. of decinormal acid is equi
alent to 0·005 gramme $CaCO_3$ so that the number of c
of acid used (less the blank) when multiplied by th
factor, and then by 1,000 gives the number of "degre
of hardness."   Otherwise stated, 1 cc. of decinormal ac
represents 5° of hardness.

The above determination yields the temporary har
ness of the water.

Determination of Permanent Hardness.

To 200 cc. of the sample add 25 cc. of the $\dfrac{N}{1}$ sodiu

hydrate solution and the same volume of sodium ca
bonate solution. Boil the mixture in a porcelain bas
until the volume is reduced to about 150 cc., and the
transfer to a flask marked at 200 cc. After cooling, mal
up to the mark and filter off through a dry paper, rejectin
the first 20 or 30 cc. of filtrate before collecting 100 c
This is then titrated exactly as described for the tot

hardness, and the difference between the amount of

acid used and 25 cc. corr   alka
neutralized in precipita   ness.
This difference multipl
hardness expressed as m
ate per 100,000.

Theoretical Considerations.

The hardness of water is due to the presence of dissolved salts of calcium and magnesium. Of these, the bicarbonates are precipitated by boiling and constitute what is known as the temporary hardness.

$$Ca(HCO_3)_2 = CaCO_3 + H_2O + CO_2.$$

The soluble sulphates (and chlorides) are not thus precipitated by simple boiling, and the softening of the water must be brought about in other ways. By titrating a sample of the water with dilute acid it is evident that the carbonates only will be acted upon so that the temporary hardness alone is registered. When the water is boiled with an excess of alkali, the soluble sulphates are converted to insoluble carbonates (and hydrates) and these are precipitated along with the temporary hardness. The titration of the excess of alkali used evidently measures the permanent hardness. In Hehner's original process, sodium carbonate alone was used, and it was then necessary whenever magnesium salts were present not only to boil but to evaporate to dryness and heat the residue in order to convert the magnesium carbonate into more insoluble oxide. By adopting the modification described above, due to Pfeifer and Wartha, the magnesium is precipitated as hydrate along with the calcium as carbonate, after a comparatively short boiling and much time is saved.

A large excess of alkali is used because the insolubility of calcium carbonate in solutions containing an excess of sodium carbonate and correspondingly of magnesium hydrate in solutions containing an excess of sodium

E E

hydrate is greater than in water alone, or in water made only feebly alkaline by a slight excess of the precipitants.

Occasionally a water is submitted which contains sodium carbonate, and which possesses therefore no permanent hardness because this is decomposed by an alkaline carbonate. The temporary hardness of such a water will be indicated as more than it really is, and similarly the amount of alkali added in a determination of the permanent hardness would be found by titration to be greater than was actually introduced. This latter difference, deducted from the observed temporary hardness, gives the correct temporary hardness.

Determination of Total Solids.

Clean, gently ignite, cool and weigh a large platinum dish, and in it evaporate to dryness on the water-bath a carefully measured litre of the sample, introduced about 50 cc. at a time as the water evaporates. The litre-flask is well rinsed out with as little distilled water as possible, the washings are added to the dish, and the whole is taken to complete dryness, being finally heated for five minutes in the air-bath at 110°. The dish is allowed to go quite cold in the desiccator, and is quickly re-weighed. The increase = grammes of total solids in 1 litre of water: this multiplied by 70 = total solids in grains per gallon.

Determination of Fixed Solids.

Place the dish on a pipe-stem triangle supported on a tripod, and by means of a small Bunsen burner gently ignite the contents of the dish till the volatile organic matter (together possibly with nitrous fumes resulting from the decomposition of nitrates) has burnt off. When the dish is cold, in order to re-carbonate any lime or magnesia from which the CO_2 has been driven off, saturate the residue with a few drops of a 10% solution of pure ammonium carbonate. Gently dry the contents of the dish, and finally again ignite at a temperature just sufficient to volatilize the ammonium salts: cool and re-weigh dish. The increase over the original weight or the loss from the second weighing gives the fixed solids in grammes per litre.

Calculation of Volatile Solids.

The total solids—the fixed solids = the volatile solids in grammes per litre.

Analysis of the Fixed Residue.

CO_2.—Transfer about one-third of the residue from the platinum dish into the flask of the apparatus sketched in Fig. 4, and determine the CO_2 in the manner described for iron ores on p. 342.[1]

SO_3.—The residue remaining in the dish, the weight of which must be carefully noted, is dissolved by heating with a little moderately dilute HCl, and the solution is transferred, being, if necessary, filtered, without loss into a graduated 100 cc. flask, and when cold is diluted to

---

[1] The weighing is best made by re-weighing the platinum dish after transferring approximately the portion specified to the flask; the loss = the weight taken.

the mark, and thoroughly mixed. It is then divided int
two equal portions of 50 cc. each. In one the SO_3 i
determined as $BaSO_4$ in the usual manner by boiling wit
an excess of $BaCl_2$.

CaO and MgO.—In the other 50 cc. of solution th
lime and magnesia are precipitated respectively as oxa
late and double phosphate in the manner described fo
iron ores. Any iron present may be determined in th
usual manner in the ammonia precipitate by titratio
with the dilute solution of $K_2Cr_2O_7$ specified on p. 368.

Example.

Analysis of a sample of somewhat hard river water.
Volume taken for analysis 1000 cc.

Weight of dish + total solids = 55·6239
Weight of dish = 55·4190

·2049 gramme per litre.
70

Total solids 14·3530 grains per gallon.

Weight of dish + fixed solids = 55·4087
Weight of dish = 55·4190

·1897 gramme per litre.
70

13·2790 grains per gallon.

Total solids = 14·3430
Fixed solids = 13·2790

Volatile solids = 1·064 grains per gallon.

Analysis of Fixed Solids.

CO_2— Weight of dish + fixed solids = 55·6687
After taking portion for CO_2, = 55·

Weight of CO_2 obtained 0·0073 gramme.

Then if 0·0655 yield 0·0073

$$0.1897 \quad,, \quad x$$

$$x = \frac{·1897 \times ·0073}{·0655} = 0·0211$$

$$70$$

$$\overline{}$$

1·4770 grains of CO_2 per gallon.

SO_3.—Weight taken $= \dfrac{·1897 - ·0655}{2} = 0·1242$ gramme.

Weight of $BaSO_4$ obtained $= 0·1267$ gramme.

Then $\dfrac{·1267 \times 34·35}{100} = 0·0435$ gramme SO_3.

Then $\dfrac{·1897 \times ·0435}{·1242} = ·0665$

$$70$$

$$\overline{}$$

4·6550 grains SO_3 per gallon.

CaO.—Weight taken 0·1242.

Weight of CaO obtained $= 0·0436$ gramme.

$$\dfrac{·1897 \times ·0436}{·1242} = ·0666$$

$$70$$

$$\overline{}$$

4·6620 grains CaO per gallon.

MgO.—Weight taken 0·1242 gramme.

Weight of $Mg_2P_2O_7$ obtained 0·0103 gramme.

$$\dfrac{0·0103 \times 27·93}{100} = ·0029 \text{ gramme } MgO.$$

Then $\dfrac{·1897 \times ·0029}{·1242} = ·0044$

$$70$$

$$\overline{}$$

·3080 grain MgO per gallon.

Results $- \left.\begin{array}{l} SO_3 - 4·655 \\ CO_2 - 1·477 \\ CaO - 4·662 \\ MgO - 0·308 \end{array}\right\}$ grains per gallon.

Which within the limits of error calculate out to

$$
\left.
\begin{array}{l}
CaSO_4 - 7\cdot913 \\
CaCO_3 - 2\cdot506 \\
MgCO_3 - 0\cdot647 \\
\hline
11\cdot066
\end{array}
\right\} \text{ grains per gallon.}
$$

Thus out of about 13 grains of fixed solids per gallon of water 11 grains consisted of a mixture of sulphate of lime and the carbonates of lime and magnesia; all compounds certain to deposit crust or scale on the plates of the boiler in which such water is used.

Determination of Chlorine.

Chlorides in moderate quantities are not objectionable in boiler water. Their determination is therefore seldom necessary. If required they are easily estimated and reported in terms of $NaCl$ by the process described for the alkalies in fire-clays on p. 376. In the present case, however, the standard solution of nitrate of silver is made by dissolving $1\cdot711$ grammes of the pure dry neutral salt in 500 cc. of distilled water.

Then working in a small porcelain dish on 50 cc. of the sample of water to be tested, each cc. used corresponds to 1 grain Cl per gallon of water. The grains of chlorine multiplied by $1\cdot6479$ equal grains of $NaCl$ per gallon.

ANALYSIS OF BRASS.

Determination of Tin.

Weigh off 3 gra   the brass drillings, transfer to a 20-oz. beaker   tric acid $1\cdot20$,

Heat gently until the alloy is decomposed and then evaporate quickly to very low bulk. Add 10 cc. nitric acid of the same strength and again evaporate. Dilute with water up to 50 cc., boil, allow to settle, and filter off the oxide of tin. Wash with water containing a few drops of nitric acid, dry, ignite in a porcelain crucible and weigh the SnO_2.

$$SnO_2 \times 0.787 = Tin.$$

The residue thus obtained may without sensible error be treated as pure stannic oxide in the case of brass, which contains usually a small amount of tin. If more than 2% of this metal is found, however, a further examination of it must be made in the manner described under the analysis of bronze.

Determination of Lead.

The filtrate and washings from the stannic oxide, collected in a 20-oz. beaker, are treated with about 10 cc. of strong sulphuric acid and the mixture is evaporated until it evolves copious fumes of sulphur trioxide. After allowing to cool somewhat, dilute up to about 50 cc. with water and warm until the anhydrous copper sulphate passes into solution leaving a small but heavy fine residue of lead sulphate. Proceed to filter into a 300 cc. flask, and during the process, disturb the residue as little as possible. Wash it by decantation with water containing one part of sulphuric acid in every six, using small quantities at a time and as small a total amount as possible. Reserve the filtrate for the copper and zinc determinations. The filter paper, containing only a few milligrams of the lead sulphate, is removed from the funnel and placed in a clean beaker with 10 cc. of ammonium acetate and the solution boiled. The hot liquid is strained off through a very small filter and caught in the 20-oz. beaker, containing the greater part of the lead sulphate, which dissolves almost at once in the ammonium acetate. Another 5 to 10 cc. of hot ammonium acetate are used for washing the two filters once more and the combined liquids heated to boiling. To the hot solution add one or two grammes of ammonium chloride, 5 cc. of acetic acid, and an excess of clear neutral ammonium molybdate solution. Heat to boiling, filter, wash, etc. The lead is precipitated as molybdate and weighed.

$$PbMoO_4 \times 0.564 = \text{Lead.}$$

Determination of Copper.

The filtrate in the 300 cc. flask is cooled, diluted to the mark, mixed well, and two separate 50 cc. removed by a pipette for the copper determination by the follow-in methods.

(1) Make the solution just ammoniacal, and then acid again with acetic acid. Add several grammes of potassium iodide crystals and $\frac{N}{10}$ sodium thiosulphate solution (24·8 gr $\ldots$ $\ldots$ crystals per litre) as previously descri $\ldots$

1 cc. $\frac{N}{10}$ $\ldots$ phate $\ldots$ $\ldots$ $\ldots$

(2) To $\ldots$ represen $\ldots$

brass, add 20 cc. of a saturated solution of sulphurous acid, and about 2 grammes of ammonium thiocyanate dissolved in 10 cc. of water. Boil and allow the white precipitate of cuprous thiocyanate to settle.

The clear supernatant liquid is poured through a hardened filter paper and the precipitate washed several times by decantation with water containing a small quantity of sulphurous acid. The filter paper is opened out over a cover glass and the small quantity of precipitate on it washed into a weighed porcelain dish with a fine jet of water. The main bulk is then rinsed from the beaker into the dish and the liquid evaporated to dryness on the water bath and weighed. The precipitate is hygroscopic.

$$Cu_2(SCN)_2 \times 52 \cdot 1 = \text{Copper \% on 1 gramme.}$$

The result obtained by this gravimetric process should confirm that obtained by the volumetric method. As a further check, the cuprous thiocyanate may be assayed for copper very rapidly as follows. Decompose it with 1·20 nitric acid very carefully to prevent loss by the violent action which sets in. Boil well to expel hydrocyanic acid, etc., and treat the pale blue cupric nitrate which remains, exactly as previously described, by the iodometric-thiosulphate process.

Determination of Zinc.

The remainder of the filtrate from the lead determination, representing 1·8 grammes of the brass, is emptied from the 300 cc. flask into a 20-oz. beaker, 50 cc. of a saturated solution of sulphurous acid added, and then about

4 grammes of ammonium thiocyanate dissolved in 20 cc. of water. After boiling for a short time, the liquid and precipitate are transferred to a 500 cc. flask, and after dilution to the mark, 250 cc. of filtrate are collected.

This contains the zinc with traces of arsenic and iron. Boil well till SO_2 is expelled completely and pass sulphuretted hydrogen gas through the liquid to saturation. Any small precipitate of arsenic sulphide (or antimony sulphide) is filtered out and washed. The filtrate is again well boiled to expel sulphuretted hydrogen, several cc. of nitric acid added, and the liquid made strongly alkaline with ammonia. After digesting for some time the precipitated ferric hydrate is filtered out, washed well, ignited and weighed as Fe_2O_3. The ammoniacal filtrate containing now the zinc only from 1·5 grammes of the brass is made up to a suitable volume, and one-third or one-half of the total used for the zinc determination. Make the solution freely acid with hydrochloric acid, then alkaline again with ammonia, and finally, by using diluted acid, very feebly acid again, as indicated by a spot test on litmus paper. (In this way, a considerable amount of ammonium chloride has been generated in the solution, and no harm is done by adding more in the form of the pure solid.) The faintly acid liquid is heated nearly to boiling, and a solution of ammonium phosphate added with stirring. The amount of this re-agent added should be between ten and twenty times the amount of zinc present. The solution is stirred continuously until the flocculent precipitate of zinc phosphate suddenly and strikingly changes to a heavy crystalline precipitate of zinc ammonium phosphate. On removing the stirring rod from the now alkaline solution, the double phosphate at once settles to the bottom of the beaker. The precipitate is filtered off, the beaker being cleansed from adhering particles by using the filtered mother liquor with the policeman, washed well, and ignited along with the paper. The ignition should be conducted at the mouth of the muffle to destroy the filter, and finally at a low red heat until the residue is white. It consists of zinc pyrophosphate, $Zn_2P_2O_{\gamma s}$ and contains $42\cdot55\%$ of zinc.

Note.

Except for very exact purposes, the preliminary operations involved in the separation of arsenic and iron from the solution can be omitted, as these occur only in very small amounts in brass. In such a case, after boiling off the excess of SO_2 in the filtrate from the cuprous thiocyanate, generate or add ammonium chloride, and adjust the solution to faint acidity before adding the ammonium phosphate.

Minor Constituents.

Provision has been made in the foregoing account of the analysis of brass for the determination of small amounts of lead, tin, and iron. The first two of these, if desired, can be more exactly determined by using a much larger weight of material, say 10 grammes, operating in exactly the same way. The iron is more quickly determined on 10 grammes of the material by dissolving in $1\cdot20$ nitric acid, filtering from stannic oxide, diluting largely, adding a large quantity of ammonium chloride, and finally making alkaline with ammonia. After digestion, the

precipitated ferric hydrate containing some copper and
zinc is filtered out, washed, redissolved in hydrochloric
acid and re-precipitated as pure ferric hydrate by means
of ammonia.

Sulphur is determined exactly as in steel by the gravimetric process.

Arsenic, if present, may be determined as follows:

To 5 grammes of the drillings, contained in a 20-oz.
beaker, add about 0·1 gramme of bar iron and 50 cc. of
1·20 nitric acid. Evaporate to low bulk and dilute up to
250 cc. Now add, a little at a time with stirring, solid
sodium bicarbonate until the free acid is neutralized and
a permanent precipitate of a dirty green colour is obtained. In this way most of the copper remains in solution, but some is incorporated with the precipitate containing the iron and the whole of the arsenic (and
antimony). When the precipitate has settled completely,
decant the clear liquid through a small asbestos filter and
wash the precipitate by decantation repeatedly.

The asbestos filter is then placed bodily in a beaker
with 20 cc. of strong hydrochloric acid, stirred well, and
the acid strained off into the beaker containing the main
precipitate. The solution is then filtered from insoluble
matter through asbestos and washed with strong acid. The
filtrate, without dilution, is treated with a slight excess
of stannous chloride solution to reduce the iron, and
saturated in the cold with sulphuretted hydrogen. In
such a strongly acid solution, the arsenic is completely
precipitated as sulphide without serious contamination
with tin, copper (and antimony). The arsenic sulphide
is filtered through asbestos, washed well with strong
hydrochloric acid saturated with sulphuretted hydrogen,
and finally with water. The asbestos filter is then boiled

with a large volume of distilled water and the arsenic
determined exactly as described under the analysis of
steel for this element.

Analysis of Bronze.

The analysis of this alloy does not differ much from
that of brass, except in respect of the fact already mentioned, viz., the stannic oxide residue is impure. The
impurities consist of small quantities of copper, lead
and iron, together with all the phosphorus from such
alloys as phosphor bronze.

After filtering off and washing the impure stannic
oxide from one gramme of the alloy, dry, and ignite in
a porcelain crucible. Mix with a large excess (twelve
times its weight) of powdered thiosulphate of sodium,
adjust the lid and heat, gently at first, over a bunsen
flame. When the water of crystallisation has been expelled, increase the heat until the crucible is red hot,
and the flame of burning sulphur appears. When cold
boil out well with water and filter off the sulphides of
lead, copper, and iron, retaining the filtrate. (The
residue, after washing, is dissolved in nitric acid, the
liquid filtered from sulphur, and the solution added to
the main filtrate from the original stannic oxide precipitate.) The aqueous extract of the fusion, containing the
tin, is made slightly acid with hydrochloric acid, whereupon the tin is precipitated almost completely as yellow
stannic sulphide. The precipitation is completed by
passing sulphuretted hydrogen for a short time and
digesting. The precipitated stannic sulphide (with sulphur) is filtered off and washed well. It is then dried

and ignited in a weighed and covered porcelain crucible. After ignition it is moistened with the strongest nitric acid, the excess cautiously removed, and the residue again strongly ignited. The treatment with nitric acid is repeated so as to fully convert the sulphide to oxide, in which form it is finally weighed. The difference between its weight and that of the original precipitate gives the amount of impurities associated with the latter.

For practical purposes, the determination of tin as thus described may be considerably shortened. After fusing with thiosulphate and extracting with water, the sulphides of lead, copper, and iron are filtered off, washed, dried, ignited, and weighed. The weight so obtained is then deducted from that of the original residue.

Phosphor-Bronze.

The analysis of this material differs from that of ordinary bronze in respect of the fact that an examination of the insoluble residue from an opening out with nitric acid must be made for phosphoric acid, which is present to the extent of the whole of the phosphorus in the alloy. This rarely exceeds two per cent.

The ignited residue of stannic oxide is mixed in the porcelain crucible with six times its weight of powdered potassium cyanide, and the mixture well fused at a good red heat. After cooling, the mass is boiled out with water, and the metallic tin filtered off. The filtrate is then acidified with hydrochloric acid, the liberated hydrocyanic acid expelled by boiling, and the phosphorus determined in the acid solution of potassium phosphate by any suitable method. The solution is especially suitable for precipitation as ammonium magnesium arsenate.

Analysis of White Metal Alloys.

The essential constituents of these alloys are lead, antimony, and tin. Small amounts of copper, and traces of bismuth, arsenic, iron and zinc are usually present.

Determination of Lead, Copper, Zinc, and Iron.

Weigh off one gramme of the alloy into a small beaker, add aqua regia a little at a time until decomposition is complete, and then from 5 to 10 grammes of tartaric acid dissolved in water. (The quantity of tartaric acid is conditioned by the amount of antimony present, the maximum amount specified being sufficient for alloys, such as type metal, containing up to 30 per cent.) Add a strong solution of pure sodium hydrate until alkaline, and then pour the whole liquid into a 40-oz. beaker containing about 25 grammes of pure sodium hydrate dissolved in about half a litre of water. Heat the solution to boiling, and pass sulphuretted hydrogen through it until the precipitated sulphides of lead, copper, etc., flock out. It is unnecessary and undesirable to pass the gas to complete saturation of the solution. Allow to settle in a warm place, decant the supernatant liquid through a filter, and wash well by decantation with a dilute solution of sodium sulphide made by saturating pure caustic soda solution with sulphuretted hydrogen. Put the filter back into the beaker containing the main bulk of the precipitate, and digest all with 20 cc. of nitric acid. Filter off from separated sulphur and disintegrated filter paper and wash well. The filtrate, collected in a 20-oz. beaker, is then evaporated to low bulk, and any small quantity of stannic oxide filtered out.

As a general rule, no such filtration is required, and the liquid is treated with sulphuric acid, evaporated to fumes, and the lead sulphate determined as such or converted to molybdate, as already described. The filtrate from the lead sulphate is treated exactly as described under the analysis of brass for the determination of the copper. After removing copper, only traces of iron and zinc remain. These may be precipitated together with sodium carbonate, ignited to oxides, and the iron determined in the residue volumetrically or colorimetrically.

Small quantities of bismuth, found occasionally in some anti-friction metals, have not been allowed for in the foregoing account. For the determination of this element the following method may be applied after removing the lead sulphate. Add ammonia till alkaline, then ammonium carbonate solution, boil and filter. Determine the copper in the filtrate by the iodide-thiosulphate method. The residue contains the bismuth with traces of iron. The detection and approximate determination of the bismuth can be made by dissolving in hydrochloric acid, precipitating the bismuth with sulphuretted hydrogen, dissolving in nitric acid, concentrating and adding potassium iodide. The yellow colour thus obtained is then matched by the addition of a measured amount of a standard solution of bismuth nitrate.

Determination of Antimony and Tin.

The alkaline filtrate from the sulphides of lead, copper, etc., contains the antimony and tin, and can be used for their determination. Time is perhaps saved, however, if a separate amount of the metal, 1·2 gramme, is opened out as before, precipitated with sulphuretted hydrogen, the liquid made up to 600 cc. with sodium sulphide, and 500 cc. filtered off through a dry paper. Transfer the solution to a 30-oz. registered flask, and add, a little at a time with shaking, hydrochloric acid until the solution is acid. Complete the precipitation of the sulphides by passing sulphuretted hydrogen to saturation, and allow to digest for a short time to allow the precipitate to settle. Decant the clear liquid through a filter paper, and wash the precipitate by decantation with sulphuretted hydrogen water several times. Remove the filter paper, and dissolve from it the traces of precipitate in hot hydrochloric acid and a crystal of potassium chlorate. Strain off the strongly acid solution into the flask containing the bulk of the sulphides, and wash the paper with more acid, adding the washings to the main precipitate. Potassium chlorate, about eight grammes, is added, and the liquid heated till the sulphides pass completely into solution, and then vigorously boiled down to about 10 cc. Dilute with 250 cc. of a hot saturated solution of oxalic acid, and whilst boiling pass sulphuretted hydrogen through the liquid for half-an-hour, when the sulphide of antimony is completed precipitated free from tin. Filter, wash well and dry. Retain (filtrate and washings for the determination of tin. dried filter paper with its precipitate of antimor

phide and free sulphur is then washed several tim[...]
small quantities of carbon bisulphide to dissolve [...]
sulphur, and again dried. It is then placed bodil[...]
large weighed porcelain crucible, provided with a [...]
covered with strong nitric acid. The excess of the l[...]
after the vigorous action has ceased, is then ca[...]
removed by evaporation, and the residue finally i[...]
at low redness. The sulphide is thus converted into [...]
weighed as tetroxide.

$$Sb_2O_4 \times \cdot 884 = \text{Antimony}.$$

The determination of the tin in the filtrate from [...]
antimony sulphide is, in the case of anti-friction [...]
containing large amounts of this metal, convenie[...]
carried out on a fractional part only. To the sol[...]
add 50 cc. of hydrochloric acid (or a large excess) [...]
then add solid permanganate, a little at a time, until [...]
oxalic acid is all decomposed (care must be take[...]
prevent loss by effervescence). The complete decom[...]
sition is indicated by the formation of a persistent [...]
cipitate of manganese dioxide. Clear the solution [...]
adding a few cc. of a solution of ferrous sulphate, [...]
then reprecipitate the tin by passing sulphuretted hydr[...]
gen gas through the hot solution. Collect the sulphi[...]
and convert to oxide in a weighed porcelain crucible[...]
previously described.

APPENDIX.

DETERMINATION OF THE SPECIFIC GRAVITY OF IRON OR
STEEL.

THE metal of which it is desired to find the specific
gravity should be in the form of a turned and polished
bar about 2 in. long by 0·3 in diameter, which will
weigh about 20 grammes, and is of convenient size to
introduce into an ordinary 50 cc. specific gravity bottle.
The latter is filled with pure distilled water at a temperature of 15° C., which should also be the temperature
inside the balance-case.

The Method.

First.—The bar of steel, after lying in the balance-
case for some little time, is accurately weighed.

Second.—The bottle having been filled with the water,
the stopper is inserted, and the whole is carefully wiped
with a clean soft linen handkerchief, and is accurately
weighed.

Third.—The stopper is then removed, the bar of steel
cautiously introduced, taking care that no air-bubbles
adhere to the metal; the stopper is replaced and the
bottle wiped as before. The weight of the bottle, wat-

and steel is then determined; the result is calculated as follows:

Let s = the specific gravity @ 15° C.
„ x = the weight of the metal in air.
„ y = „ „ (bottle full of water) + (the weight of the steel in air).
„ z = „ „ bottle, water, and metal.

$$\text{Then } s = \frac{x}{y - z}$$

Example.

Weight of steel bar in air   = 19·7754 grammes ($= x$)
„   bottle + water   = 71·8480 „
„   bottle + water + steel = 89·1663 „   ($= z$)
    Then 19·7754 + 71·8480 = 91·6234 „   ($= y$)
   − (bottle + water + steel = 89·1663 „

Weight of water displaced = 2·5181

$$\frac{19\cdot7754}{2\cdot5181} = 7\cdot8514 = \text{specific gravity @ 15°.}$$

DETERMINATION OF THE CARBIDES EXISTING IN STEEL.

(J. O. Arnold and A. A. Read.)

To estimate the carbide of Fe_3C or double carbides of the iron with manganese, chromium, etc., weighed polished bars of the steel 3 in. long by $\frac{3}{4}$ in. diameter are galvanically decomposed (by a modification of the method proposed by Binks and Weyl for the estimation of carbon in iron) in pure dilute HCl, specific gravity 1·02, in the apparatus sketched in Fig. 22. The 40-oz. beaker A containing the dilute acid is provided with a porous cell and platinum plate, the latter being attached to the screw terminal B, which is connected with a zinc pole of a pair of pint Daniel cells, well charged in the shelf with $CuSO_4$ crystals. The bar is suspended at the pole C, 2 in. being immersed in the acid, which is attached to the copper terminal of the cells; D is a well-fitting cardboard disc to prevent any copper salt (dissolved from the binding screw by the acid fumes) running down the bar. The circuit having been completed a stream of ferrous chloride

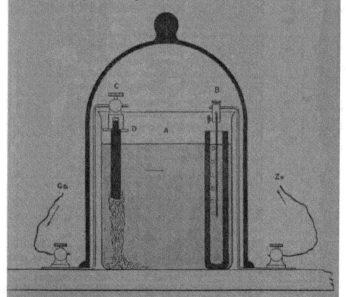

Fig. 22.

(together in special steels with the chlorides of manganese, nickel, etc.) falls through the liquid, and hydrogen briskly evolved at the platinum plate. In from six to twelve hours the bar is removed, and if it contains any considerable quantity of carbon it will be unaltered in shape, but dark in colour (where it was immersed in the acid), with an insoluble residue of the stable carbides present. The latter are scraped off with a clean blunt penknife, and are collected without loss on a small hardened filter-paper, the bar being finally well cleaned with a policeman. The residual metal is then wiped, dried, and re-weighed, the loss indicating the weight taken for analysis. The carbide residue is well washed with water containing a very little sulphurous acid, then with absolute alcohol, and finally with pure ether. It is then as far as possible transferred from the spread-out filter-paper to a weighed porcelain boat, first by means of a penknife, and then with a fine jet of ether. (The filter-paper to which a very small quantity of carbide adheres is burnt, the residual oxide weighed, and the iron in it calculated to carbide in accordance with the analysis of the main quantity.) The porcelain boat containing the carbide and ether is placed over strong sulphuric acid in a desiccator, till in about half-an-hour the ether has evaporated. The carbide is then dried *in vacuo* at $100°$ C. for two hours. This operation is simply carried out by boring two holes, about $1\frac{1}{2}$ in. diameter, and exactly opposite each other, through the sides and near the bottom of a deep water-bath. Through these holes, made water-tight by good india-rubber bungs, is passed a glass tube about $\frac{3}{4}$ in. diameter inside, and attached at one end to a Sprengel pump, being closed at the other by means of an india-rubber bung carrying a tap and capillary tube. The boat containing the carbide having been inserted so as to lie in the middle of the bath, the tube is closed and the pump worked till a vacuum is obtained. The bath is then charged with water so as to well cover the tube, and is brought to boiling by means of a Bunsen burner. After about two hours, during which the action of the pump is maintained, the lamp is removed, and the hot water taken out and replaced by cold. When the tube is cool air is very cautiously admitted through the capillary tube; the boat is taken out, cooled in the desiccator, and re-weighed, the increase giving the weight of carbide. The amount of carbon present is determined by strongly igniting the boat in a porcelain tube containing a column of copper oxide scales, the CO_2 being determined as in an estimation of carbon by combustion in steel. The residual oxide of iron is gently dissolved out of the boat in a flask containing strong nearly boiling HCl, is neutralized with ammonia, reduced with sulphurous acid, acidified with sulphuric acid, and the amount of iron present is determined by very careful titration with a standard bichromate solution of suitable strength. (Before titrating great care must be taken to boil off every trace of SO_2.)

In the case of double carbides the solution of the residue is divided into two parts, the iron being determined in one portion, and the other elements in the second portion by the ordinary methods.

The carbon in the carbide obtained may equal from 70 to 96% of the total carbon in the steel. The loss is due to the formation of liquid and gaseous hydrocarbons at the anode, a slight evolution of gas being almost invariably observed from the bar. Whether the loss is due to a very partial decomposition of the normal carbide, or to the existence of a readily decomposed sub-carbide, is not yet certain, but the evidence extant favours the latter view (see *Journal of the Chem. Soc.*, August, 1894).

The carbide obtained from steels in an ordinary condition is a dark gray powder; that isolated from well-annealed steels exists in the form of bright silvery plates; both varieties, however, correspond to the formula Fe_3C.

Example.

Determination of Fe_3C in a well-annealed crucible cast chisel steel containing 0·96%, of carbon. (Determined from the mean of two very closely agreeing combustions.)

$$
\begin{aligned}
\text{Weight of bar before immersion} &= 47\cdot9828 \\
\text{,, \quad ,, after \quad ,,} &= 41\cdot5670 \\
\hline
\text{Loss} = \text{Weight taken} &= 6\cdot4158
\end{aligned}
$$

Carbide all attached to the bar, and when dry presented the appearance of a somewhat coarse powder made up of minute silvery plates.

$$
\begin{aligned}
\text{Weight of boat} + \text{carbide} &= 12\cdot4380 \\
\text{Weight of boat} &= 11\cdot5549 \\
\hline
\text{Weight of carbide obtained} = &\quad \cdot8837
\end{aligned}
$$

Weight of CO_2 obtained on combustion $= 0\cdot2126$
$= 0\cdot05797$ gramme carbon

Weight of iron found in residue by titration $= 0\cdot316$ gramme Fe.
$Fe_2O_3 + $ filter ash $= 0\cdot0120$
ash $= 0\cdot0007$

$0\cdot0113$ gramme $Fe_2O_3 = 0\cdot0079$ gramme Fe.

Then $\dfrac{\cdot0079 \times 6\cdot67}{93\cdot33} = 0\cdot00056$ gramme carbon on filter.

$$
\begin{array}{lll}
 & \text{Found.} & \text{Theory.} \\
\text{Total } Fe = 0\cdot8160 + 0\cdot0079 = 0\cdot8239 = 93\cdot37\% \; Fe & 93\cdot33 \\
\text{,, } \quad C = 0\cdot05797 + 0\cdot00056 = 0\cdot05853 = 6\cdot63\% \; C & 6\cdot67 \\
\hline
& \cdot88243
\end{array}
$$

Total residue $= 0\cdot8942$ (= residue in boat + residue on filter).
Iron and Carbon $= 0\cdot8824$

$\cdot0118$ gramme impurity.

Analysis of Total Residue.

Carbide of Iron $Fe_3C = 98\cdot69$
Impurities (SiO_2, H_2O, etc.) = $1\cdot22$

Total carbon in steel taken $= \dfrac{6\cdot4158 \times \cdot96}{100} = 0\cdot0606$ gramme.

Total carbon $= 0\cdot00060$
Carbon in carbide $= 0\cdot05853$

$0\cdot00207$ gramme lost.

Then $\dfrac{0\cdot05853 \times 100}{0\cdot0606} = 96\cdot58\%$ of total carbon obtained as Fe_3C.
Therefore loss of total carbon as hydrocarbons and from errors of analysis $= 3\cdot42\%$.

The foregoing example is an exceptionally satisfactory determination. The micro-section of the steel when examined at 600 diameters revealed the fact that the carbide had very beautifully crystallized out in innumerable definite and well-formed plates.

DETERMINATION OF THE EVAPORATIVE POWER OF COAL.

(Method I. The Lewis Thompson Calorimeter.)

The evaporative power of coal may be approximately determined in the laboratory by means of the apparatus shown in section in Fig. 23. This calorimeter consists of a capacious glass cylinder marked to contain when about two-thirds full of water at 60° F., 29010 grains; a copper tube or furnace fitting into a recess in a perforated stand, over the spring clips of which fits the combustion chamber, the latter consisting of a copper cylinder perforated round the edge of the open bottom end, and having a long pipe provided with a stop-cock at the closed top end. There is also a suitable thermometer for reading off the temperatures to $\frac{1}{5}$ of a degree F. With the apparatus is also supplied a second broad shallow furnace tube for burning coke or anthracite coal. The mixture used for burning the fuel is composed of 3 parts by weight of pure $KClO_3$, and 1 part by weight of pure KNO_3, both salts being very finely divided, intimately mixed, and dried at 100° C. before using. Of this mixture ordinary coal requires 300 grains, but coke and anthracite coal require 360 grains to completely burn 30 s of the very finely-divided fuel dried at 100° C.

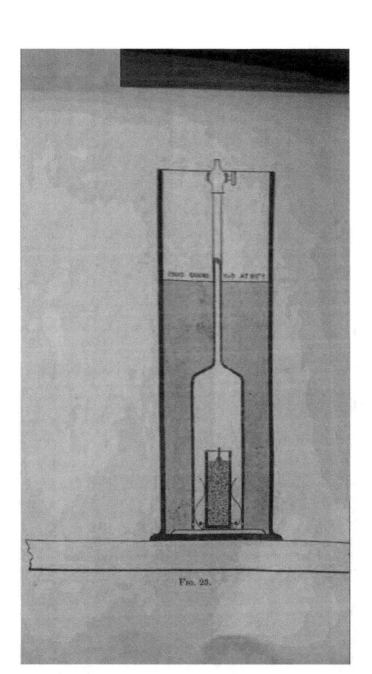

FIG. 23.

The Process.

The 30 grains of dry coal and the 300 grains of dry combustion mixture are very intimately incorporated by means of a clean palate knife on a sheet of stout glazed paper. The mass is transferred without loss to the copper furnace tube. After gently tapping the mixture down, a little hole about half-an-inch deep is made in it with a pointed wire, and into the cavity is inserted a little piece of rolled-up fuse (made by soaking strands of cotton wick in a solution of KNO_3,[1] and allowing them to dry spontaneously) about one inch long, the mixture being packed round the fuse so that it (the fuse) projects about half-an-inch above the surface. The furnace tube is placed in the recess of the base-piece, the fuse is carefully ignited with a taper, and the combustion chamber, the tap of which must be shut, is *quickly* forced over the springs, and the whole is lowered into the glass cylinder previously accurately filled to the mark with water, the temperature of which was accurately noted. As soon as the fuse fires the combustible mixture, the elements of the coal are burnt to water and carbon dioxide by the oxygen contained in the chlorate and nitrate of potash. The steam formed is condensed, but the CO_2 and excess of oxygen violently bubble through the water, which absorbs their heat. The gases leave the water in the form of copious white fumes, due to the presence of finely-divided alkaline salts in a peculiar physical condition in which they escape being dissolved by the water. As soon as the combustion is over, the stop-cock is opened to allow the water to rise into the

[1] Lead nitrate is perhaps better still.

combustion chamber so as to take up the heat from the
furnace tube. The thermometer is then put back into
the cylinder, and the copper portion of the apparatus is
bodily raised and lowered in the water two or three
times so as to render the temperature of the mass even
throughout; the reading of the thermometer is then
noted.

Example.

30 grains of a sample of coal suitable for making
ordinary producer gas were intimately mixed with 225
grains of $KClO_3$ and 75 grains of KNO_3, and burnt as
just described.

Temperature of water after combustion 70°·6

,,   ,,   before   ,,   58°·4
                                    ——————
                        Difference 12·2
                        + 10%   1·22
                                    ——————
One pound of coal evaporates 13·42 lbs. water.
                                    ══════

That is to say, 1 lb. of coal converts 13·4 lbs. of
water at a temperature of 212° F. into steam.

The 10% added to the actual reading is a correction
for the heat absorbed by the apparatus, which is set to
this standard amount by the maker of the instrument.

Theoretical Considerations.

The capacity of the water cylinder is set in terms of
the weight of fuel used and the latent heat of steam:
thus, the latent heat of steam in British units is 967,
and $967 \times 30 = 29,010$. In other words, each grain of

fuel burnt has ready 967 grains of water to absorb the heat it has produced. In the example given, 1 part by weight of fuel has heated 967 parts by weight of water 13·4° F., which is equivalent to converting 13·4 lbs. of water at 212° into steam at 212°.

(Method II. Mahler's modification of Berthelot's Bomb Calorimeter.)

Description of the Apparatus.

This consists essentially of (1) The bomb (B, Fig. 24) made of high quality mild steel lined internally with enamel and plated externally with nickel. The walls are 8 mm. thick, and the cubic capacity is approximately 650 cc. The closing of the bomb is effected by a screw stopper with a fine thread, and pressing on a leaden washer. The stopper carries a pointed screw top to shut off the oxygen supply, and it is traversed by an insulated platinum electrode, the latter being continued to the point at which ignition of the fuel is made by the platinum rod E. A similar rod fixed to the stopper carries the capsule c in which the fuel is placed. The ignition is effected by connecting the electrodes by means of a short length of very fine iron wire, F, which is readily brought to incandescence on passing the current from the bichromate battery, P. (2) The calorimeter, D, which is made of brass. (3) An isolating envelope, A, which consists of a hollow casing filled with water, and covered externally with felting. (4) A nickel-plated agitator, s, with the necessary supporting and adjustment fittings. (5) An oxygen cylinder with fittings,

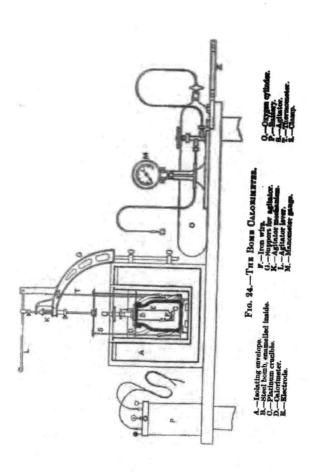

FIG. 24.—THE BOMB CALORIMETER.

A.—Isolating envelope.
B.—Steel bomb, enamelled inside.
C.—Platinum crucible.
D.—Calorimeter.
E.—Electrode.

F.—Iron wire.
G.—Supports for agitator.
K.—Agitator medallion.
L.—Agitator lever.
M.—Manometer gauge.

O.—Oxygen cylinder.
P.—Battery.
R.—Agitator.
T.—Thermometer.
S.—Clamp.

and a pressure gauge attachment. (6) Three thermometers reading to 0·01° C. for use at varying atmospheric temperatures.

The Process.

Weigh one gramme of the fuel into the capsule, adjust the fine iron wire, place the stopper in position and screw up tightly, using the spanner and clamp. Attach to the manometer tube, and after screwing down the manometer valve connect with the oxygen cylinder. Open the pin-valve in the stopper an exact half turn, then open the oxygen supply and control the admission by means of the manometer valve until a pressure of 25 atmospheres is attained. Close the valves in the following order: (1) manometer valve; (2) oxygen cylinder; and (3) pin valve in stopper. Detach the bomb and place it in the calorimeter containing 2,200 cc. of water, and then adjust the agitator and thermometer. Agitate the water, noting the temperature at intervals of a minute. (This is continued for several minutes if the water is initially at a lower temperature than the room in order to determine the rate of increase.) Connect one electrode from the battery to the raised platinum electrode, and touch the shell or stopper with the other in order to explode. Note the temperature at one minute intervals until a maximum is reached, and then for a further equal period in order to determine the rate of decrease. The agitation is regularly maintained throughout. After the experiment remove the bomb from the water and cautiously open the pin-valve, so as to allow the gases to escape before opening the bomb.

Example.—One gramme of " Clowne cobbles."

Times.		Temperatures
Min.	Sec.	
0	0	20·28° C.
1	0	20·28
2	0	20·28
2	30	20·28 [1]
3	0	22·10
4	0	23·00
5	0	23·07
6	0	23·06
7	30	23·05

[1] Coal fired at this point.

The rise in temperature is $23·07 - 20·28 = 2·79$. To this must be added the correction of $23·07 - 23·05 = 0·02$ for cooling during a period of two minutes from the time of reaching the maximum temperature. Total rise $= 2°·81$. Water in calorimeter $= 2200$ grammes. Water equivalent of colorimeter $= 481$.

Calorific power $= (2200 + 481) \times 2·81 = 7533·6$ calories.

Evaporative power $= 7533·6 \div 537 = 14·03$.

For more exact purposes it is necessary to introduce further very small corrections. The small amount of nitric acid formed by the combustion is determined by rinsing out the bomb after the experiment, and making a titration of the acid solution. The iron wire is weighed before adjustment, and its heat of combustion allowed for. The calorific power is then given by the expression

$$d \ (W + W') - (0·23 \ n + 1·6 \ f)$$

where

$d =$ the corrected rise in temperature in degrees C.

W = weight of water in calorimeter in grammes.
W' = water equivalent of calorimeter in grammes.
n = weight of nitric acid formed in grammes.
f = weight of iron wire used in grammes.

The constants 0·23 and 1·6 are respectively the heat of formation of one gramme of dilute nitric acid, and the heat of combustion of 1 gramme of iron.

The water equivalent of the calorimeter is determined by burning a definite weight of some pure substance such as naphthalene, whose heat of combustion is known, using different weights of water in the calorimeter.

THEORETICAL CALCULATION OF THE CALORIFIC POWER AND INTENSITY OF PRODUCER GAS FROM ITS VOLUMETRIC ANALYSIS.

Convert the percentage composition by volume into percentage composition by weight. Example—

Let the percentage composition of a gas by volume be

$$\left.\begin{array}{ll} H \text{ Hydrogen} & 15 \\ CO \text{ Carbonic oxide} & 17 \\ CH_4 \text{ Marsh gas} & 7 \\ CO_2 \text{ Carbonic acid} & 6 \\ N \text{ Nitrogen} & 55 \end{array}\right\} \% \text{ by volume.}$$

First find the weight in grammes of each constituent in 100 cc. of the gas at 0° and 760 mm. pressure.

Data.

cc.
1000 H = 0·0896 grammes.
$$\left.\begin{array}{lll} \text{,,} & CO & =(\;·0896 \times 14)=1·2544 \\ \text{,,} & CH_4 & =(\;·0896 \times \;8)=0·7168 \\ \text{,,} & CO_2 & =(\;·0896 \times 22)=1·9712 \\ \text{,,} & N & =(\;·0896 \times 14)=1·2544 \end{array}\right\} \text{ Grammes @ 0° C. and 760 mm. barometer pressure.}$$

Then—

$$15 \text{ cc. } H = \frac{\overset{\text{cc.}}{15 \times \cdot 0898}}{\underset{1000}{\text{cc.}}} = 0 \cdot 0013440 \text{ grammes } H.$$

$$17 \text{ cc. } CO = \frac{17 \times 1 \cdot 2544}{1000} = 0 \cdot 0213248 \quad \text{,,} \quad CO.$$

$$7 \text{ cc. } CH_4 = \frac{7 \times 0 \cdot 7168}{1000} = 0 \cdot 0050176 \quad \text{,,} \quad CH_4.$$

$$6 \text{ cc. } O_2 = \frac{6 \times 1 \cdot 9712}{1000} = 0 \cdot 0118272 \quad \text{,,} \quad CO_2.$$

$$55 \text{ cc. } N = \frac{55 \times 1 \cdot 2544}{1000} = 0 \cdot 0689920 \quad \text{,,} \quad N.$$

100 cc. of gas @ 0° C. and 760 mm. = 0·1085056 grammes.

Then—

grammes %	% by weight.
$\dfrac{0 \cdot 001344 \times 100}{\underset{0 \cdot 1085056}{\text{grammes}}} =$	1·24 H.
$\dfrac{2 \cdot 13248}{0 \cdot 1085056} =$	19·65 CO.
$\dfrac{0 \cdot 50176}{0 \cdot 1085056} =$	4·62 CH_4.
$\dfrac{1 \cdot 18272}{0 \cdot 1085056} =$	10·90 CO_2.
$\dfrac{6 \cdot 89920}{0 \cdot 1085056} =$	63·58 N.
	100·00

The calculation is then made as in the case of the
following example of coal, only in the present instance
the volume of nitrogen in the gas must be included with
that introduced from the air. The following additional
data will also be required.

Calorific Powers.	Metric Units.	British Units.
CO	2403	4325
CH_4	13063	23513

Example of the Theoretical Determination of the Calorific Power and the Calorific Intensity of a Compound Fuel.

PROBLEM.

Assuming an initial temperature of $0°$ C., and ignoring sulphur and nitrogen,[1] calculate (in gramme units) the total heat and (in degrees Centigrade) the sensible temperature resulting from the combustion in air of 1 gramme of Welsh anthracite coal having the following percentage composition:

Carbon	91·44
Hydrogen	3·46
Oxygen	2·58
Nitrogen	0·24
Sulphur	0·76
Ash	1·52
	100·00

NECESSARY DATA.

Atomic Weights.	Reactions.	Specific Heats.	
$H = 1$	$2H + O = H_2O$	Water	$H_2O = 1·000$
$C = 12$	2 16 18	Steam	$H_2O = 0·480$
$O = 16$	$C + 2O = CO_2$	Nitrogen	$N = 0·244$
	12 32 44	Carbon dioxide ..	$CO_2 = 0·217$
		Ash	$= 0·200$

	Calorific Powers		Latent Heat of Steam.
Carbon = 8080 units	⎫	⎧ Grammes of water raised through	537 grammes
	⎬ = ⎨ 1° C. by the heat of the combustion	Centigrade
Hydrogen = 34460 „	⎭	⎩ in oxygen of 1 gram. of the element.	units.

Composition of Air by Weight

Nitrogen	77	⎫ Per cent
Oxygen	23	⎭

METHOD OF CALCULATION.

Step 1.

Determine the Calorific Power.

Step 2.

Calculate the weights of carbon dioxide, nitrogen, steam and ash resulting from the combustion of 1 gramme of the coal; multiply these weights by the respective specific heats and add the results. The number thus obtained represents the heat units necessary to raise the products of combustion through 1°.

---

[1] The exact reactions of these elements during the combustion are not known, but in any case their influence upon the results would be very small.

THEORETICAL CONSIDERATIONS.

A consideration of the following facts will assist to render the above operations clear :

The temperature of a mass equals the number of sensible heat units in it divided by the product of its weight multiplied by its specific heat.

Thus if the 8287 sensible units present in the products of combustion could be absorbed (without giving up the 183 latent units also present) into 1 gramme of a body of specific heat 1, the temperature would be $\frac{8287}{1 \times 1} = 8287°$.

But the actual weight of mixed matter yielded by the perfect combustion of the gramme of coal is 12·6837 grammes ; and through this mass (the mean specific heat of which will be $\frac{3·0771}{12·6837} = 0·2426$) has to be distributed 8287 units of heat. Hence

the temperature or calorific intensity $= \frac{8287}{(12·6837 \times 0·2426)} = \frac{8287}{3·0771} = 2693°$ as before.

NOTE.

Theoretical temperatures thus calculated give only the comparative values of fuels, and are considerably in excess of the temperatures obtained in practice. This is due mainly to the fact that the calculations are based upon three erroneous premises, viz. :

1st.—It is assumed that the combustion of the fuel is perfect, whereas a variable portion escapes as finely-divided carbon (smoke), hydrocarbons, and carbonic oxide CO.

2nd.—It is assumed that only sufficient air enters a furnace to just effect the combustion, whereas in practice that entering the fire is in excess of the quantity required theoretically, and the variable surplus of air absorbs an amount of heat dependent upon its weight.

3rd.—It is assumed that the specific heat of the products of combustion is the same as at the ordinary temperature, whereas it is known that their capacity for heat increases with the temperature, but to what extent cannot be ascertained at furnace heats.

EXPRESSION OF RESULTS IN BRITISH UNITS.

To make the foregoing calculations in British units (lbs. of water raised 1° F.) and degrees Fahrenheit, the following data are substituted to obtain the Calorific Power and Intensity of 1 lb. of the coal :

CALORIFIC POWERS.

Hydrogen .. .. 62032 } units— lbs. of water raised 1° F. by the combustion
Carbon .. .. .. 14544 } in oxygen of 1 lb. of each element.

Latent Heat of steam 967 units + diff. in Specific Heat from 32° to 212° = 967 + [(1 ·· ·466) × 180] = 967 + 94 units = 1061 units. This number multiplied by total $H_2 O = L$.

TABLES OF TYPICAL ANALYSES.

TABLE I.—METALS.

Material	Combined Carbon	Graphitic	Silicon	Manganese	Sulphur	Phosphorus	Tungsten	Chromium	Aluminium	Molybdenum	Vanadium	Titanium	Tantalum	Iron
Swedish Lancashire hearth-iron		—					—	—	—	—	—	—	—	
Crucible bar iron and sheet steel		—					—	—	—	—	—	—	—	
Best English wrought iron		—					—	—	—	—	—	—	—	
Best crucible steel (1½% nickel?)		—					—	—	—	—	—	—	—	
(A) percent		—					—	—		—	—	—	—	
Crucible cementation tool steel (percent quality)		—					—	—	—	—	—	—	—	
Hardening steel		—					—	—	—	—	—	—	—	
Swedish Bessemer spring steel		—					—	—	—	—	—	—	—	
Open-hearth boiler-plate steel		—					—	—	—	—	—	—	—	
English Bessemer spring steel		—					—	—	—	—	—	—	—	
Best steel castings (35 percent)		—					—	—	—	—	—	—	—	
(A) percent		—					—	—	—	—	—	—	—	
Swedish white-iron							—	—	—	—	—	—	—	
Swedish Bessemer mottled-iron							—	—	—	—	—	—	—	
Pig iron for local process							—	—	—	—	—	—	—	
Ordinary foundry pig-iron							—	—	—	—	—	—	—	
Pig-iron		—					—	—	—	—	—	—	—	
Ferro-manganese		—					—	—	—	—	—	—	—	
Ferro-silicon		—					—	—	—	—	—	—	—	
Ferro-chrome		—					—	63·40	—	—	—	—	—	
Ferro-aluminium		—					—	—	9·80	—	—	—	—	
High-speed tool steel		—					51·90	3·33	—	—	—	—	—	
High-speed alloy		—					11·16	10·57	—	—	—	—	—	
Molybdenum powder		—					50·55	—	—	80·61	—	—	—	
Ferro-vanadium		—					—	—	—	—	47·14	—	—	
Ferro-titanium		—					—	—	6·74	—	—	30·70	—	
Ferro-tantalum		—					—	—	—	—	—	—	71·93	

TABLE II.—ORES.

Material	Fe₂O₃	FeO	MnO₂	MnO	Al₂O₃	Cr₂O₃	WO₃	CaO	MgO	SiO₂	TiO₂	CO₂	P₂O₅	S	Combined Water	Organic Matter	Ta₂O₅	SnO₂
Red Hematite	74·23	—	—	—	6·61	—	—	1·02	0·01	8·62	—	0·79	0·02	0·02	8·43	—	—	—
Brown Hematite	64·63	—	0·28	—	3·92	—	—	0·90	0·25	13·50	—	2·30	2·16	0·05	11·63	—	—	—
Magnetite¹	59·19	25·82	Trace	—	1·90	—	—	1·60	2·31	3·23	—	3·02	Trace	Trace	0·21	Trace	—	—
Clay ironstone	—	36·30	—	0·94	4·60	—	—	8·86	1·06	7·95	—	31·20	0·80	0·23	2·83	4·10	—	—
Impure Bauxite (Belfast)	29·74	0·78	—	1·67	41·30	—	—	1·70	0·23	14·05	0·30	—	0·02	0·01	13·85	—	—	—
Chrome iron ore	—	15·68	—	Trace	14·96	42·20	—	0·98	15·10	7·03	—	—	0·07	0·13	2·71	0·32	—	—
Manganiferous iron ore²	48·57	—	39·47	3·46	3·12	—	—	2·00	1·06	10·90	—	1·55	0·05	0·04	6·20	—	—	—
Wolfram	—	19·29	—	4·36	0·26	—	71·20	0·39	—	2·76	—	—	—	—	—	—	—	—
Tantalite	—	12·46	—	5·49	—	—	0·13	—	—	1·63	—	—	—	—	—	—	79·31	1·81

¹ Personally sampled by J. O. Arnold in the workings of the celebrated Dannemora mine, Sweden.
² ZnO 2·90, BaO 0·64.

TABLE III.—REFRACTORY MATERIALS. (Dry.)

	SiO_2.	Al_2O_3.	Fe_2O_3.	CaO.	MgO.
ington)	50·93	32·72	2·06	Trace	0·97
year)	64·03	29·48	3·60	0·21	0·99
... ...	96·20	1·17	1·06	0·98	Trace
... ...	96·32	1·26	0·86	Trace	Trace
... ...	1·86	0·84	1·30	58·65	36·70

TABLE IV.—FUELS. (Dried at 100° C.)

Volatile matter.	Ash.	Sulphur.	Carbon.	Hydrogen.	O

TABLE V.—SLAGS.

Material.	SiO₂.	CaO.	MgO.	Al₂O₃.	Fe₂O₃.	FeO.	MnO.	P₂O₅.	S.	Alkalies.
Blast furnace slag ...	36·50	43·50	1·03	14·64	—	0·95	2·35	0·02	0·82	1·27
Cherry slag (ferrous silicate)	53·53	1·19	0·50	5·57	—	34·94	2·71	2·30	0·10	—
Acid Bessemer slag ...	47·80	1·35	0·56	3·98	—	15·30	31·60	Trace	Trace	—
Basic Bessemer slag ...	11·64	51·90	6·37	0·92	1·80	7·30	4·83	14·60	0·17	—
Tap cinder	14·90	3·16	0·27	2·96	13·30	55·69	1·25	5·60	1·98	—

TABLE VI.—TECHNICAL ANALYSES OF BOILER WATERS.

Class of water.	Solids in grains per gallon.			Hardness by soap test in degrees.†			Analyses of fixed solids in grains per gallon.			
	Total.	Volatile.	Fixed.	Total.	Tem-porary.	Per-manent.	CO₂.	SO₃.	CaO.	MgO.
Very bad	53·78	5·42	48·36	38·5	2·0	34·5	0·98	25·92	19·30	0.35
Good	5·63	0·73	4·90	3·0	2·5	0·5	0·98	0·02	1·37	Trace

† Each degree is equivalent in hardness to one grain of CaCO₃ per gallon.

ATOMIC WEIGHTS OF THE MORE IMPORTANT ELEMENTS.

(Stated to the nearest first decimal.)

Element.	Symbol.	Atomic weight.	Element.	Symbol.	Atomic weight.
Aluminium ...	*Al*	27·3	Mercury ...	*Hg*	199·8
Antimony ...	*Sb*	122·0	Molybdenum	*Mo*	95·8
Arsenic... ...	*As*	74·9	Niobium ...	*Nb*	94·0
Barium	*Ba*	136·8	Nickel	*Ni*	58·6
Bismuth ...	*Bi*	210·0	Nitrogen ...	*N*	14·0
Boron	*B*	11·0	Oxygen... ...	*O*	16·0
Bromine ...	*Br*	79·6	Palladium ...	*Pd*	106·2
Cadmium ...	*Cd*	111·6	Phosphorus ...	*P*	31·0
Calcium ...	*Ca*	39·9	Platinum ...	*Pt*	196·7
Carbon	*C*	12·0	Potassium ...	*K*	39·0
Chlorine ...	*Cl*	35·4	Rhodium ...	*Rh*	104·1
Chromium ...	*Cr*	52·2	Selenium ...	*Se*	79·0
Cobalt	*Co*	58·6	Silver	*Ag*	107·7
Copper	*Cu*	63·1	Silicon	*Si*	28·0
Fluorine ...	*F*	19·1	Sodium	*Na*	23·0
Gold	*Au*	196·2	Strontium ...	*Sr*	87·2
Hydrogen ...	*H*	1·0	Sulphur ...	*S*	32·0
Iodine	*I*	126·5	Tantalum ...	*Ta*	183·0
Iridium... ...	*Ir*	192·7	Tin	*Su*	117·8
Iron	*Fe*	55·9	Titanium ...	*Ti*	48·0
Lead	*Pb*	206·4	Tungsten ...	*W*	183·5
Lithium ...	*Li*	7·0	Uranium ...	*U*	240·0
Magnesium ...	*Mg*	23·9	Vanadium ...	*V*	51·2
Manganese ...	*Mn*	54·8	Zinc	*Zn*	64·9

TABLE OF THE PERCENTAGES OF ELEMENTS OR COMPOUNDS IN THE PRECIPITATES.

Formula of Precipitate.	Element or Compound required.	Percentage in Precipitate.
$AlPO_4$	Al	22·18
$AlPO_4$	Al_2O_3	53·00
$BaSO_4$	S	13·75
$BaSO_4$	SO_3	34·35
$CaSO_4$	CaO	41·20
CO_2	C	27·27
Cr_2O_3	Cr	68·48
$Cr_7P_4O_{19}$	Cr	42·48
$Cr_6P_?O_{?}$	Cr_2O_3	60·95
$Cu_2(SCN)_2$	Cu	52·1
Fe_2O_3	Fe	70·00
$Mg_2As_2O_7$	As	48·30
$Mg_2As_2O_7$	As_2O_5	74·20
$Mg_2P_2O_7$	MgO	36·04
$Mg_2P_2O_7$	P	27·93
$Mg_2P_2O_7$	P_2O_5	63·96
Mn_3O_4	Mn	72·05
Mn_3O_4	MnO	93·01
Molybdic yellow ppt.	P	1·65
Molybdic yellow ppt.	P_2O_5	3·75
NiO	Ni	78·56
$PbMoO_4$	Pb	56·40
$PbSO_4$	Pb	68·32
$PbMoO_4$	Mo	26·16
$PbMoO_4$	P	0·7
$PbMoO_4$	P_2O_5	1·61
$2PbO_3V_2O_5 \cdot PbO$	V	13·8
SiO_2	Si	46·67
TiO_2	Ti	60·00
V_2O_5	V	56·19
WO_3	W	79·31
SnO_2	Sn	78·7
$_2O_3$	Sb	88·40
$_2O_3$	Zn	42·55

TABLE OF FACTORS.

Weight of Fe multiplied by $1.2857 = FeO$

,,	Fe	,,	1.4288	$= Fe_2O_3$
,,	Cr	,,	1.4600	$= Cr_2O_4$
,,	Mn	,,	1.2909	$= MnO$
,,	Mn	,,	1.5818	$= MnO_2$
,,	Mn_3O_4	,,	0.9300	$= MnO$
,,	CaO	,,	1.7846	$= CaCO_3$
,,	MgO	,,	2.2150	$= MgCO_3$

COMPARISON OF ENGLISH AND METRIC WEIGHTS AND MEASURES.

Weights.

1 gramme	=	15.432348 grain.
1 grain	=	0.064792 grammes.
1 oz. troy	=	31.103496 grammes or 480.0 grains.
1 oz. avoir.	=	28.349540 grammes or 437.5 grains.

Lineal Measure.

1 inch	=	25.39954 millimetres.
1 millimetre	=	0.03937079 inch.

Square Measure.

1 square inch	=	645.13669 square millimetres.
1 square mm.	=	0.001550059 square inch.

Cubic Measure.

1 cc.	=	0.0610270734 cubic inches.
1 cubic inch	=	16.386 cubic centimetres.
1 cc.	=	0.0352754 fluid ounce.
1000 cc.	=	1.76077 pints or 0.2200967 gallon.
1 gallon	=	4543.458 cc.

To convert grammes per litre into grains per gallon multiply by 70.

Conversion of Thermometer Scales.

To convert degrees Centigrade into degrees Fahrenheit

$$\frac{°C. \times 9}{5} + 32 = °F.$$

To convert degrees Fahrenheit into degrees Centigrade

$$\frac{(°F. - 32) \times 5}{9} = °C.$$

Determination of Nitrogen in Steel.

The authors are indebted to Mr. A. Grabe for the following description of the method employed by him for the determination of nitrogen in steel.

Dissolve 15 grammes of potassium hydrate (or 10 grammes of sodium hydrate) in about 300 cc. of water, contained in a flask of about 700 cc. capacity. The flask is fitted with a double-bored stopper, in which are inserted a tap funnel and an exit tube for carrying the vapours into a Liebig's condenser. Add a little powdered graphite previously treated with strong hydrochloric acid, and boil until a sample of the distillate gives no colour with Nessler's re-agent. (The graphite prevents violent bumping.) During this preliminary boiling, 1 gramme of the sample drillings is dissolved in 20 cc. of hydrochloric acid (equal parts strong acid and water). The ferrous chloride solution is cautiously added to the hot alkaline liquid in the flask through the tap funnel, and the distillation is continued until all the ammonia is driven over. The distillate is conveniently collected in 200 cc. graduated stoppered glass cylinders. After adding 2 cc. of the Nessler re-agent, a suitable volume of standard solution containing 0·0381 gramme ammonium chloride per litre (1 cc. = 0·00001 gramme nitrogen) is poured into a similar cylinder and treated with 2 cc. of the re-agent. The two solutions are diluted so as to show the same depth of colour and the percentage of nitrogen calculated from the volumes.

A blank determination is conducted as follows. 15 grammes of potash or 10 grammes of soda are dissolved in 300 cc. of water, and after adding graphite, the solution is boiled until all ammonia is expelled and half the liquid has passed over. To this solution is added the residue of ferrous hydrate from a previous determination, which is consequently free from ammonia and nitrate. The distillation is continued until the distillate shows no colour with Nessler's re-agent, which is generally the case when about 50 cc. have passed over. In this distillate the nitrogen is determined as before. This nitrogen is due to the nitrite contained in the alkali, graphite, and 300 cc. of water. 20 cc. of the acid used are then added and the distillation continued. The ammonia obtained is due to ammonia and nitrite in the acid. The contents of the flask are then boiled nearly to dryness, and the last distillate tested with Nessler. If colour is obtained, this is an indication of nitrates in the alkali or acid used.

If the blank test shows any considerable amount of nitrogen, the alkali must be purified by Langley's method as follows. 300 grammes of the alkali are dissolved in 500 cc. water, and the solution poured into a flask in which are laid strips of zinc plate, on which copper has been precipitated by immersing them for 10 minutes in a warm solution of copper sulphate.

INDEX

CHISWICK PRESS: PRINTED BY CHARLES WHITTINGHAM AND CO.
TOOKS COURT, CHANCERY LANE, LONDON.

A LIST OF BOOKS PUBLISHED BY

WHITTAKER & CO.

2 White Hart Street, Paternoster Square, London, E.C.

*A complete catalogue giving full details of the following books
will be sent post free on application.*

		s.	*d.*
ADAMS, H. Practical Trigonometry, for the use of Engineers . . . . *net*		2	6
ALEXANDER, J. Model Engine Construction . *net*		5	0
ALLSOP, F. C. Practical Electric Light Fitting . .		5	0
ARNOLD, J. O., and IBBOTSON, F. Steel Works Analysis *net*		10	6
ASHWORTH, J. R. Magnetism and Electricity . .		2	6
,, Heat, Light and Sound . . *net*		2	0
ATKINS, E. A. Practical Sheet and Plate Metal Work *net*		6	0
BAMFORD, H. Moving Loads on Railway Underbridges *net*		4	6
BARR, J. R. Direct Current Electrical Engineering *net*		10	0
BARTER, S. Manual Instruction—Woodwork . .		6	0
,, Manual Instruction—Drawing . . .		3	6
BEAUMONT, R. Colour in Woven Design . . .		21	0

2 White Hart Street, Paternoster Square, E.C.

		£	d.
Burns, D., and Kerr, G. L. Modern Practice of Coal Mining. 10 parts . . . . . . each *net*		2	0
Chambers, G. F. Astronomy, for General Readers *net*		1	0
Cooke, C. J. B. British Locomotives		7	6
Coppock, J. B. Volumetric Analysis		2	0
Cullver, J. Tables for Measuring and Manuring Land		2	6
Davis, W. E. Quantities and Quantity Taking . *net*		3	6
Denning, D. Art and Craft of Cabinet Making . .		5	0
Elliott, A. G. Gas and Petroleum Engines . .		2	6
Elsden, J. V. Principles of Chemical Geology . *net*		5	0
Engineer Draughtsmen's Work. Hints to Beginners in Drawing Offices		1	6
Explosives Industry, Rise and Progress of the British *net*		15	0
Farrow, F. R. Specifications for Building Works *net*		3	6
,, Stresses and Strains, their Calculation, etc. . . . . . *net*		5	0
Findlay, Sir G. Working and Management of an English Railway		7	6
Fletcher, B. F. and H. P. Carpentry and Joinery *net*		5	0
,, ,, Architectural Hygiene, or Sanitary Science as applied to Buildings *net*		5	0
Foden, J. Mechanical Tables		1	6
Gay, A., and Yeaman, C. H. Central Station Electricity Supply . . . . *net*		10	6
Gray, J. Electrical Influence Machines. (Wimshurst Machines) . . . . *net*		5	0
Greenwell, A., and Elsden, J. V. Roads, their Construction and Maintenance . . . . *net*		5	0

			s.	*d.*
HORNER, J. G.	Principles of Fitting . . . *net*		5	0
,,	Helical Gears		5	0
,,	English and American Lathes . .		6	0
,,	Principles of Pattern Making . .		3	6
,,	Metal Turning		3	6
,,	Practical Ironfounding . . .		3	6
JUKES-BROWNE, A. J.	Geology		2	6
KAPP, G.	Transformers for Single and Multiphase Currents . . . . *net*		10	6
KENNEDY, R.	Steam Turbines, their Design and Construction			
KERR and BURNS.	Coal Mining. 10 parts . each *net*		2	0
KINGSLEY, R. G.	Roses and Rose Growing . . *net*		6	0
LANDOLT, H.	Optical Activity and Chemical Composition		4	6
LELAND, C. G.	Drawing and Designing . . .		2	0
,,	Woodcarving		5	0
,,	Leather Work		5	0
,,	Metal Work		5	0
,,	Practical Education		6	0
LODGE, Sir O.	Lightning Conductors and Lightning Guards		15	0
LOPPE and BOUQUET.	Alternate Currents in Practice .		6	0
MAGINNIS, A. J.	The Atlantic Ferry, its Ships, Men and Working . . . . *net*		2	6
MASSEE, G.	The Plant World, its Past, Present and Future		2	6
MAXIM, Sir H.	Artificial and Natural Flight . *net*		5	0
MAYCOCK, W. PERREN.	First Book of Electricity and Magnetism		2	6

s. d.

POOLE, J. Practical Telephone Handbook and Guide to the Telephonic Exchange . . . . *net* 6 0

PUNGA, F. Single-Phase Commutator Motors . *net* 4 6

RIDER, J. H. Electric Traction . . . . *net* 10 6

ROBERTS, C. W. Practical Advice to Marine Engineers *net* 3 0

„ Drawing and Designing for Marine Engineers 6 0

RUDORF, G. Periodic Classification and the Problem of Chemical Evolution 4 6

RUSSELL, S. A. Electric Light Cables 10 6

SALOMONS, Sir D. Management of Accumulators . *net* 6 0

„ Electric Light Installations—Apparatus 7 6

SERRAILLIER, L. Railway Technical Vocabulary: French, English and American . . . . . *net* 7 6

STEVENS, T., and HOBART, H. M. Steam Turbine Engineering . . . . . . *net* 21 0

STILL, A. Alternating Currents of Electricity and the Theory of Transformers 5 0

„ Polyphase Currents . . . . *net* 6 0

SUTCLIFFE, G. L. Sanitary Fittings and Plumbing *net* 5 0

SUTCLIFFE, G. W. Steam Power and Mill Work . . 10 6

TAYLOR, J. T. Optics of Photography and Photographic Lenses . . . . *net* 3 6

THOMSON, M. Apothecaries' Hall Manual . . *net* 2 0

THURSTON, A. P. Elementary Aeronautics . . .

TREADWELL, J. Storage Battery . . . . *net* 7 6

TURNER, H. W., and HOBART, H. M. Insulation of Electric Machines . . . . . *net* 10 6

2 White Hart Street, Paternoster Square, E.C.

WHITTAKER & CO., 2 White Hart St., Paternoster Sq., London, E.C.